Jeremy Bowen was born in Cardiff in 1960. He attended University College London and Johns Hopkins University in Italy and the USA before joining the BBC as a news trainee in 1984. He became a foreign correspondent in 1987, covering major conflicts in the Middle East, El Salvador, Afghanistan, Bosnia, Croatia, Chechnya, Somalia, Rwanda and Kosovo. From 1995 to 2000 he was the BBC's Middle East Correspondent, winning awards from television festivals in New York and Monte Carlo as well as a Best Breaking News report from the Royal Television Society on the assassination of Yitzhak Rabin. After two years presenting *Breakfast*, BBC1's morning news programme, as well as major history documentaries, he now has a roving brief as a Special Correspondent. He lives in London.

Further praise for *Six Days*:

'[Bowen] reveals a compelling yarn behind the myths . . . Perhaps *Six Days* can help us both remember and heal'

Independent

'Jeremy Bowen is a war reporter for whom contentment begins when bullets fly . . . Bowen knows the Middle East. For five years he was the BBC's main correspondent there . . . That kind of experience has taught him that simple judgments of right and wrong, good and evil, are never possible . . . Bowen tells the story of the war with an hour-by hour account of each of the six days. What comes across is a sense of tragic inevitability'

Scotland on Sunday

'Unflinching . . . Bowen's straightforward style is backed up by meticulous research . . . lending both balance and authority to his conclusions'

Catholic Times

SIX
DAYS

HOW THE 1967 WAR SHAPED
THE MIDDLE EAST

JEREMY BOWEN

POCKET
BOOKS

LONDON • SYDNEY • NEW YORK • TORONTO

First published in Great Britain by Simon & Schuster UK Ltd, 2003
This edition first published by Pocket Books, 2004
An imprint of Simon & Schuster UK Ltd
A Viacom company

1 3 5 7 9 10 8 6 4 2

Simon & Schuster UK Ltd
Africa House
64–78 Kingsway
London WC2B 6AH

Simon & Schuster Australia
Sydney

www.simonsays.co.uk

PICTURE CREDITS
1, 8, 12,13, 14, 19, 26: Magnum Photos
2, 4, 6, 7, 9, 10, 15, 16, 17, 20, 24, 25, 27, 28: Hulton Getty
3: Popperfoto; 5, 13, 22, 29: Camera Press
11, 18: Don McCullin/Contact/NB Pictures
21: Gilles Caron/Contact/NB Pictures

A CIP catalogue for this book is available
from the British Library.

ISBN: 0-7434-4969-X

Typeset by M Rules
Printed and bound in Great Britain by
Cox & Wyman Ltd, Reading, Berks

For Julia, Mattie and
Jack – and my parents.

Contents

'Euphoria after victory is dangerous.
But what's even worse is arrogance.
You stop thinking and learning.'

Uri Gil, fighter pilot, Israeli

'I want peace – but how can I teach my children to
extend their hands to others when I carry so
much pain in my memory?'

Fayek Abdul Mezied, archivist, Palestinian

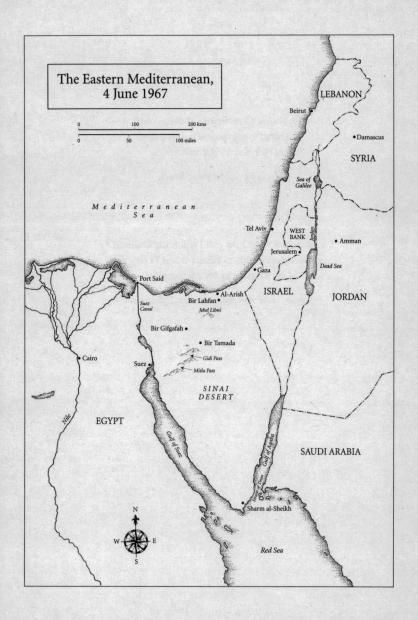

The Eastern Mediterranean,
4 June 1967

0   100   200 kms

0   50   100 miles

LEBANON

Beirut

•Damascus

SYRIA

Sea of
Galilee

*Mediterranean
Sea*

Tel Aviv

WEST
BANK

•Amman

Jerusalem

Gaza

Dead Sea

Port Said

Bir Lahfan   Al-Arish

ISRAEL

JORDAN

*Suez
Canal*

Jebel Libni

Bir Gifgafah   •

•Bir Tamada

•Cairo

Suez

Gidi Pass

Mitla Pass

*SINAI
DESERT*

EGYPT

Gulf of Suez

SAUDI ARABIA

Gulf of Aqaba

Nile

N

W   E

S

Sharm al-Sheikh

Red Sea

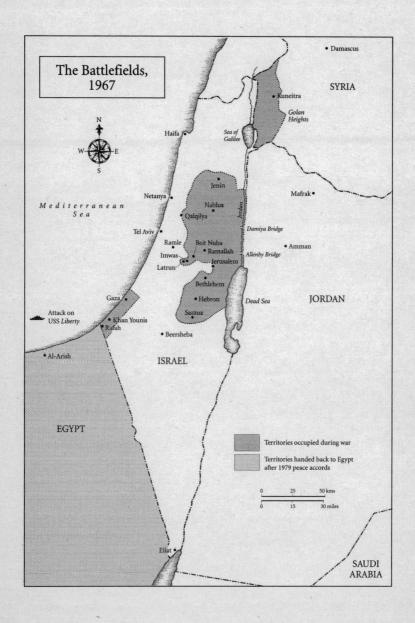

The Battlefields, 1967

- Damascus
SYRIA
- Kuneitra
Golan Heights

N
W—E
S

Haifa *Sea of Galilee*

Mediterranean Sea

Netanya
Jenin
Nablus
Qalqilya
Jordan
Damiya Bridge
Mafrak

Tel Aviv
Ramle
Beit Nuba
Ramallah
Allenby Bridge
Amman
Imwas
Jerusalem
Latrun
Bethlehem
Hebron
Dead Sea
JORDAN
Samua

Gaza
Attack on
USS *Liberty*
Khan Younis
Rafah
Beersheba

Al-Arish
ISRAEL

EGYPT

Territories occupied during war

Territories handed back to Egypt
after 1979 peace accords

| 0 | 25 | 50 kms |
| 0 | 15 | 30 miles |

Eilat

SAUDI
ARABIA

Introduction

Roads into war zones feel the same wherever you go. It is something to do with the way that tanks churn up tarmac and verges and flatten parked cars and buildings. When it is wet, mud gets everywhere. If it is dry, you breathe and eat dust. Normal civilian traffic is stripped away by war, and roads turn into something more alien and primitive. Weeds grow where people walked and talked and did their shopping. And there are always jumpy, armed men. The road into Jenin in 2002 had all of that. The Israeli soldiers on the checkpoint were aggressive and hostile. When I got out of my car to talk to one of them he pointed his gun and threatened to shoot me. I did not think he was joking. Lines of cars belonging to Palestinians were kept for hours in a queue that did not move. Armed Israelis who lived inside the West Bank on Jewish settlements raced by, unchecked.

In the end my press pass from the Israeli government worked and the soldiers let me cross into Jenin. They had just been into the town themselves, on a raid to destroy the house of a man they had assassinated the previous night. A refugee camp stands in the heart of Jenin. Or used to. Now there is a great wide space instead. Children in school uniforms were trudging across it. It used to be a poor, densely populated district. The Israelis flattened it with armoured bulldozers after they entered Jenin on 3 April 2002 in the biggest and most ambitious military operation, until then, against the Palestinian uprising. They were after Palestinian militants who they believed had been behind the deaths of more than seventy civilians in Israel in the previous month or so.

The biggest Palestinian attack in a bloody and frightening few weeks was on 27 March 2002. Two hundred and fifty guests were sitting down to their Passover dinner at the Park hotel in Netanya, a seaside town north of Tel Aviv. A man came in wearing a long-haired wig and a big black overcoat. He seemed to be going from table to table looking for his place. His name was Abdel-Basset Odeh and his last act was to detonate the bomb that he had strapped to his body. The explosion blasted back off the walls and ceiling. It killed 29 people and injured 140. Most of them were elderly, many were couples, some had come to Israel after their families were slaughtered by the Nazis in the Holocaust. The attack caused terrible shock and outrage in Israel, because it killed so many innocent people and because it desecrated one of the most important Jewish nights of the year. Passover is a religious festival, commemorating the exodus of Jews from Egypt in the days of Pharaoh, but it is also a night when families, even if they are not religious, try to be together, like Christians do at Christmas. The bomber came from the Palestinian town of Tulkarem, which is around ten miles east of Netanya, not too far from Jenin.

After the Netanya bomb it was clear that the Israeli government would carry out its threat to mount big punitive operations in the West Bank, parts of which had been administered by Palestinians since 1995. In the end they reoccupied it completely. When the Israeli army entered Jenin, Palestinian fighters were ready. They put up a hard fight. After they killed thirteen Israeli soldiers in an ambush on 9 April, the armoured bulldozers went to work. The Israelis said it was a military necessity, and that minimum force was used.

Unwisely and inaccurately, the Palestinian leader Yasser Arafat claimed there had been a massacre. An investigation by the widely respected American group Human Rights Watch found no evidence for the allegation. But they also found that Israeli soldiers had carried out serious violations of international humanitarian law, which if proved in court would be war crimes. According to Human Rights Watch, at least fifty-two Palestinians were killed. Twenty-seven or so were armed men who fought the Israelis. At least twenty-two were civilians, including children, the elderly and the physically disabled. One 37-year-old man, who was paralysed, was killed when the Israelis bulldozed his home on top of him. Human Rights Watch found that Kamal Tawalbi, the father of fourteen children, was kept with his fourteen-year-old son in the line of fire as human shields during a three-hour gun battle. Israeli soldiers used Tawalbi and his son's shoulders as rests for their rifles while they fired.

The conflict between Jews and Arabs started when the first Zionist settlements were established in Palestine more than a century ago. But it took on its current shape after the Middle East war of 1967, when Israel captured large swathes of Arab land, much of which it still holds. The Israeli government that prosecuted the war in 1967 said that it had no territorial ambitions, that it was fighting for security, not land. But since then hundreds of thousands of Israelis have been settled on the land that Israel's forces seized. The occupation that started in 1967 has become the driving force behind the violence that Israelis and Palestinians are inflicting on each other. I wrote this book because during the years I lived in Jerusalem as the BBC's Middle East Correspondent I found that the best way to understand the conflict now is to understand 1967.

The dangers the war was creating were spotted very early on by President Lyndon Baines Johnson, one of the staunchest friends of Israel ever to occupy the White House. On the third day of the war, as Israel completed its capture of Jerusalem and the West Bank, he warned that by the time the Americans had finished with all the 'festering problems', they were going to 'wish the war had not happened'. The war's legacy has now been festering for more than thirty-five years. Four days after the war ended, Johnson's Secretary of State, Dean Rusk, warned that if Israel held on to the West Bank, Palestinians would spend the rest of the twentieth century trying to get it back. At the beginning of the twenty-first, nothing has changed.

The Six-Day War swept up a generation of Israelis and Arabs

whose children still cannot live peacefully in the world the war created. Israelis deserve peaceful, safe lives. Palestinians who were dispossessed and exiled if they became refugees, humiliated and abused if they stayed, deserve justice. Israel's overwhelming victory turned into a curse. It has never been able to digest the land swallowed in 1967. It has poured money into colonising the Occupied Territories, defying international law and splitting its own people. Thirty-six years after the end of six days of fighting with Jordan, Egypt and Syria, after thousands more deaths and the failure of six years of negotiations, Israelis and Palestinians are fighting again over the future of the West Bank and Gaza. It is still a low-intensity war. But if another full-blown Middle East war breaks out, its roots will lie in those six days in 1967. The Middle East will have no peace until Israelis and Palestinians, as equal partners, settle the future of the land that was captured in 1967 and unwind the consequences of the war.

Pre-War

Israelis

Mount Zion is a grand name for a small hill. It dominates the south-west corner of the walls of the Old City of Jerusalem. Christians venerate Mount Zion because they believe it was the place where Jesus and his disciples ate their last supper. Running east from Mount Zion outside the city walls is the Himnon Valley, a narrow, rocky canyon where Canaanites once carried out human sacrifices to their god, Moloch. So many funeral pyres burned in the valley that the sky was turned black with their smoke.

On 28 May 1948 smoke was rising over Jerusalem again. A young Jewish commander, Yitzhak Rabin, one of Israel's top soldiers, stood on Mount Zion, looking down at houses and synagogues on fire inside the Old City. The Jewish quarter was burning and there was nothing he could do about it. His men had tried. The nearest entrance to the city, the turreted Zion Gate, was blackened and blasted by explosions and pitted with bullet holes. Twenty-six-year-old Rabin was the commander of the Har'el Brigade of the Palmach, the strike force of the Haganah, the Jewish army. It was two weeks since Britain had pulled out its last troops and given up the mandate under which it had controlled Palestine since the First World War. Jewish leaders immediately declared Israel independent. The new state was recognised and admitted to the United Nations by world leaders who believed that the Jewish people deserved a state after the horrors of the Holocaust. Arab armies invaded to try to kill off the new state. A civil war in one of Britain's colonial territories between its native Arabs and Jewish settlers blew up into the first all-out Middle East war of modern times.

Below Mount Zion, inside the walls, was a 'shattering scene' that stayed with Rabin for the rest of his life. The Jewish quarter was surrendering. A procession led by two rabbis was walking towards what Rabin knew were the positions of the Jordanian Arab Legion. The young Jewish state was losing its last toehold inside the walls of the holy city. Nine days before, on the 19th, men from the Palmach captured Mount Zion and held it against a fierce Jordanian counter-attack. Some of them were 'so bone-tired' that even though they expected a counter-attack at any moment they kept dozing off.

Failing to capture the Old City, which contains places holy to Jews, Muslims and Christians, was the biggest Israeli defeat of the 1948 war. One of Rabin's senior officers was a 23-year-old Jew from Jerusalem called Uzi Narkiss. He had led the counter-attack through Zion Gate that reached the Jewish quarter. But his unit was exhausted, under strength and without reinforcements, and Jordanian troops drove them out. Like Rabin, the failure haunted him for years. On the eve of war in 1967, Uzi Narkiss was a general, still suffering 'from guilt that Jerusalem was divided, that no Jew remained in the Old City . . . for one night I held the gate to the city in my hands – but it was torn out of them'. He had one war aim – to go back.

Palestinians

In July 1948 tens of thousands of exhausted Palestinian civilians were forced out of their homes and into territory controlled by the Jordanian army on the foothills of the West Bank. An Israeli intelligence officer called Shmarya Guttman watched them go: 'A multitude of inhabitants walked after one another. Women walked burdened with packages and sacks on their heads. Mothers dragged children after them . . . warning shots were heard . . . occasionally, you encountered a piercing look from one of the youngsters . . . and the look said: "We have not yet surrendered. We shall return to fight you."' They had been expelled by the Israeli army from the towns of Ramle and Lydda, on the orders of Rabin. During the assault on the towns the Israelis killed around 250 people, including dozens of unarmed Palestinian detainees who were being held in the church and the mosque. Yeruham Cohen, an Israeli intelligence officer, reported: 'The inhabitants of the town became panic-stricken. They feared that . . . the Israeli troops would take revenge on them. It was a horrible, ear-splitting scene. Women wailed at the top of their voices and old men said prayers, as if they saw their own deaths before their eyes.' All but around 1000 of Lydda and Ramle's population of 50–70,000 was expelled in the next few days. Some of them were robbed of their valuables along the way. On the long and hot walk to the Jordanian lines, many refugees were killed by dehydration and exhaustion. 'Nobody will ever know how many children died,' wrote Glubb Pasha, the British commander of the Arab Legion. Ramle and Lydda, which was renamed Lod, are now medium-sized Israeli towns. Rabin was not proud of what he did, but regarded it as necessary: 'We could not leave Lod's hostile and armed populace in our rear.'

Palestinians use the Arabic word *nakba*, which means catastrophe, to describe 1948. A society that had grown up over more than a thousand years was destroyed and scattered across the Middle East. Palestinians fled for the reasons that civilians do in all wars, to save their lives and protect their children and also because, in some places, Israel practised what is now called ethnic cleansing. In Deir Yassin, a village on the outskirts of Jerusalem, Jewish extremists carried out the most notorious massacre of the war. They boasted that they killed 250 people. Afterwards, it was enough for Jewish psychological warfare units to broadcast the village's name for traumatised Palestinian civilians to head for the border. The truth about Deir Yassin was bad enough, but the versions that went out on Palestinian radio stations made brutal slaughter sound even worse. Hazem Nusseibeh, a young man from one of Jerusalem's leading Palestinian families, sat at the microphone at the Voice of Palestine radio station and rebroadcast grisly details of murder, mutilation and rape. He concentrated on the rapes, hoping that it would strengthen Palestinian resistance, which was collapsing. It had the opposite effect. More Palestinians decided their only chance of survival was to get out. Nusseibeh realised he had made a mistake when group after group of refugees coming into Jerusalem's Old City through Jaffa Gate told him the thought of death was one thing but the prospect that their women would be dishonoured was even worse.

Between 600,000 and 760,000 Palestinians were refugees by the summer of 1949. A few had enough money left to relocate their families and start businesses somewhere else. Most of them were poor peasant farmers or labourers who became utterly destitute. The vast majority ended up in miserable camps in the surrounding Arab states. Their property was seized by the Jewish state. The Palestinians' old homes were either bulldozed or occupied by new immigrants to Israel. By the 1960s the refugees' resentment was one of the main engines of Palestinian nationalism. What Shmarya Guttman saw in the eyes of the refugees being expelled from Lydda came to pass. The Palestinian refugees' children, grandchildren and great-grandchildren became foot-soldiers in the Middle East's long war.

Egyptians

At the end of 1948, what was left of the Egyptian army that had entered Palestine to destroy the new Jewish state was besieged south-east of the port of Ashdod in what was known as the Faluja pocket. In a lightning campaign the Israelis broke a United Nations truce, seized the Negev desert, delivered a crushing blow to the Egyptian army and captured hundreds of square miles of territory along with Beersheba, the only real town in the desert. But the Egyptians left behind in the pocket were fighting back hard. A meeting was arranged between the two sets of commanders to discuss a truce. Among the Egyptian officers was a young major called Gamal Abdul Nasser. Yigal Allon, the Israeli commander of the southern front, and Yitzhak Rabin, his head of operations, led the Israelis. Both sides were courteous, complimenting the bravery of each other's soldiers. The Egyptians refused to surrender. They went back with their jeeps and white flags to their own lines, and the siege of the Faluja pocket continued. Four years later, in the aftermath of the humiliation of 1948, Nasser led a group of young officers who seized power in Egypt. He became president. After he defied Britain, France and Israel in the 1956 Suez crisis, Nasser was seen as the leader of the Arab world. Allon left the army and went into politics. In 1967 he was one of the leading hawks in the cabinet. Rabin continued his military career. In 1967 he was chief of staff, the Israeli army's most senior officer.

Jordanians

King Abdullah of Jordan had a grandson, a prince called Hussein. On 20 July 1951 Abdullah invited Hussein, who was sixteen, to go with him to Jerusalem. Hussein was delighted. He idolised his grandfather, who had just appointed him captain in the army to celebrate a fencing prize he had won at school. On Abdullah's orders he wore his new uniform for the trip. Abdullah was going to Jerusalem for a secret meeting with Jewish officials, with whom he had been quietly negotiating for thirty years. Between them, they made sure that the Palestinians had no chance of creating their own state. Even though his army fought Israel fiercely in 1948, especially in and around Jerusalem, many Arabs regarded Abdullah as a traitor for colluding with the Jews and not fighting harder. The king also wanted to pray at the Aqsa mosque, Jerusalem's great Islamic shrine. The British ambassador to Jordan, Sir Alec Kirkbride, a man some people said was as powerful in the land as the king, warned Abdullah not to go.

There had been talk that he might be assassinated. The king brushed the warning aside. He was a descendant of the prophet Mohammed. He was not going to be scared out of Jerusalem. Besides, he had important business.

Sir John Glubb, 'Glubb Pasha', the British officer who commanded Jordan's Arab Legion (for which Britain paid the bills and issued most of the orders), sent extra troops to line the streets and flood the 2000-year-old compound that encloses Jerusalem's two great Islamic shrines. The soldiers milled around the Aqsa mosque, the holiest place in the world for Muslims after Mecca and Medina and the great golden Dome of the Rock, the oldest, most striking building in the Islamic world. As he went into al-Aqsa, Abdullah told his guards to drop back. They were crowding him. A young man called Shukri Ashu stepped out from behind the door with a revolver. He shot the king behind his right ear. The bullet came out through his eye. He died instantly. The assassin kept on firing until he was cut down by Abdullah's bodyguards. One of his bullets ricocheted off a medal on Hussein's chest. In the confusion twenty more people were killed and hundreds wounded. Prince Hussein was hustled away and flown back to Amman. 'The next day,' he wrote, 'I carried a gun for the first time.'

War without end

Peace was possible just after 1948. The United Nations brokered armistice agreements between Israel and Jordan, Syria, Lebanon and Egypt, which were signed in the early part of 1949. Yitzhak Rabin took part in the negotiations in Rhodes. He was given a khaki tie to wear with his uniform, the first one he had owned. Despite lessons from his driver, he never mastered the art of tying it. He kept it permanently knotted, loosening it and pulling it over his head when it was time to take it off. At night he hung it up with his trousers. The UN hoped that the armistices would lead to proper peace agreements. Diplomatic contacts took place between Israel and all its neighbours.

It was a real opportunity. But both sides, blaming each other, squandered their chance.

With no peace agreements, they slid into a series of vicious border wars. In the first few years after 1948 the quality of the Israeli army deteriorated. David Ben-Gurion, Israel's prime minister, disbanded the Palmach, its highly effective but independent minded strike force. Early cross-border operations of the new Israel Defence Forces (IDF) were embarrassing fiascos until, from the early 1950s, Israel started to develop the strategic doctrines and forces that fitted its own unique challenges. The armistice lines after 1948 left Israel with long borders that, in places, were extremely vulnerable. The centre of the country was not much more than ten miles wide. There was another narrow 'neck' connecting Jerusalem with the rest of Israel and the south. It would not have taken much for Jordanian and Egyptian forces to link up to cut off Eilat.

Israel decided to ignore its lack of strategic depth by fighting on Arab territory with flexible, highly mobile armoured ground forces backed up by air power. Intelligence, surprise and aggression were vital. They would not wait passively in static defences for their enemies to attack. From around 1952 Israel started a long project to build a modern army, a plan that came together spectacularly in 1967. First, though, came another full-blown war. It was launched in 1956 after Israel made a secret alliance with Britain and France to attack Nasser's Egypt. Israeli tanks moved fast across the Sinai, showing what the rapidly evolving Israeli army could already do. Yet this was a work in progress. The most important air operations in the 1956 war were flown by the British and the French. But the diplomatic ground had not been prepared properly. Israel and the two declining imperial powers were treated as aggressors by the USA and the USSR, the two rising superpowers. Britain and France were humiliated and Israel had to give up the Egyptian territory it seized. In return, Egypt had to allow ships bound for Israel through the Straits of Tiran into the Gulf of Aqaba and on to the Israeli port of Eilat. Blue helmeted peacekeepers from the United Nations Emergency Force (UNEF) were deployed on the border, in the Gaza strip and at Sharm al Sheikh, an Egyptian village overlooking the Straits of Tiran.

After 1956 it suited Egypt and Israel to keep their border quiet. Both had a lot to do. The Israelis wanted to develop their economy, absorb more than a million immigrants and build the army. Nasser used his position as the Arab hero who vanquished the imperialists to lead a pan-Arab nationalist movement that his supporters fully expected would recreate Arab greatness. Nasser's followers had huge faith in Egypt's military power. The fact that its soldiers were roundly beaten in 1956 was quickly forgotten. The Soviet Union provided weapons and Nasser's propaganda machine trumpeted his army's prowess. Throughout the Arab world, listeners to Cairo Radio (which meant almost everyone) thought that Egypt could take on not just Israel, but the world.

But the truth was very different. The problems started at the top, with Field Marshal Abd al-Hakim Amer. Although he was a five star general with the post of commander-in-chief, his main qualification for the job was not his military achievements but the fact that he was the man Nasser trusted most. As a young officer he fought bravely in 1948. Soon, though, he became better known for his love of hashish and the good life, which remained a life-long interest, than for his martial prowess. His military knowledge did not progress after 1950, when as a major he attended Staff College. After that, he did nothing to master the art of preparing soldiers for the battlefield and leading them to victory on it. His real job, which he did very well, was to make sure that the army stayed loyal by stamping out plots and keeping the officers happy. Nasser wanted the Free Officers' coup, in which he deposed the king in 1952, to be Egypt's last military rebellion. Major Abd al-Hakim Amer was promoted to major-general overnight. His field marshal's baton was not far behind.

In 1967 Amer led the Egyptian army to disaster. The warning signs were there in 1956, when he lost his nerve badly, begging Nasser not to resist the British and French. During the fighting, Nasser found him paralysed with indecision in his headquarters, tears pouring down his face. After the war Amer offered his resignation, which Nasser,

12

presumably out of loyalty, refused to accept. He then allowed Amer to persuade him not to sack Sidqi Mahmoud, the air force commander. In 1956 he left his aircraft lined up at their bases to be destroyed on the ground by the British and French. In 1967 he did exactly the same thing for the Israelis.

Officers regarded Amer as decent, friendly and generous – especially generous. If they needed a favour, he would see that it was done. He made things happen. Smart flats in the best parts of Cairo were presented to trusted officers. Their families were looked after. When generals retired they were given well-paid jobs at the top of newly nationalised state enterprises. During the high point of pan-Arabism in the 1950s, when Egypt and Syria formed a brief union, Amer and his cronies illegally imported huge numbers of goods from Syria in military aircraft, which they sold off or presented to their wives and mistresses. Amer shouted down one of Nasser's entourage who had the temerity to tell him to stop treating Syria as his private ranch. By the early 1960s Nasser and Amer were rivals as much as they were friends. Amer did not have a fraction of Nasser's public presence and following. But Nasser never knew whether Amer would turn the army against him. In the early 1960s he made ineffectual attempts to reassert some control over the armed forces. But when Amer resisted him, he would not risk a showdown. After that, Nasser still needed Amer, for all the old reasons and they still had strange vestiges of friendship, but he did not trust him.

The Syrian syndrome

Syria had the worst army of all the Arab countries bordering Israel. The reason was that it was not designed to fight. Its speciality was politics. After independence from France in 1946, Syria had three years of shaky civilian government, followed by twenty years of equally shaky military government. Discontented young officers kicked out the politicians after the humiliation and defeat of 1948.

The last straw was a scandal about the army's cooking fat. It should have been a local staple called *samnah*, made from sour milk, as important to Arab warriors as apple pie was to American GIs. Instead it was discovered that the army fat was made from bone waste that gave off a terrible stink when it was cooked. But Syria's first coup was not aimed at protecting the stomachs of its soldiers. Instead, the president made the mistake of trying to blame an officer for the scandal instead of the supplier. The chief of staff, more outraged by civilian interference than by the food his men were eating, seized power. By lunchtime, the officer who had been blamed for ordering the inferior fat was free and the merchant who supplied it was behind bars. There were two more coups in 1949.

The military became the dominant force in the country. The Syrian officer class was highly politicised. Most of them were poor boys who had joined up because the military academy offered them a free education, regular hot meals and a way out of the poverty-stricken, almost feudal provinces. Unlike European aristocrats, Syrian landowners did not consider soldiering a respectable way to earn a living. It was their biggest mistake. Ambitious, nationalistic officers seized on a new political ideology called Ba'thism, which had been invented by a Syrian Christian from Damascus called Michel Aflaq. The word Ba'th means resurrection. Ba'thism's followers believed they would rebuild the Arab nation, without Western colonialists and feudal landlords. The best organised people in Syria were the Ba'thists inside the armed forces.

Training for a war with Israel came a very distant second. Army officers concentrated on the art of seizing and then keeping power. By 1966 every serving officer above the rank of brigadier had a political job. Almost half the leadership of the Syrian Ba'th party were officers. The British defence attaché in Damascus, Colonel D. A. Rowan-Hamilton, tried to compare the set-up to Britain. 'If the same conditions existed in the United Kingdom as existed in Syria, the Chief of the Imperial General Staff and Chief of Air Staff would have been not only MPs but members of the executive committee of the Labour Party. GOC Southern Command and the military secretary

14

would have been vociferous MPs. All four would have been subject to incessant interference and insubordination from a group of totally unqualified and irresponsible young officers, each with his own regimental following and each after a plum job.'

Syria was in no shape to fight an enemy as well organised and determined as Israel. Colonel Rowan-Hamilton sniffily concluded that the morale of the 'proletarian' officer corps was quite high. But they were not capable of conducting a mobile or protracted war. Officers who had been on liaison visits to Western countries had 'not taken the opportunity to advance their military knowledge nor absorb ideas new to them, but have treated the expedition as a free holiday'. The Syrian army had been reasonably well armed since the mid-1950s, mainly with second-hand weapons no longer needed by the Soviet army. Even though they were not the most modern weapons, learning how to use and maintain them was not easy. Some technicians were trained in the USSR. But the rank and file of the army had very little education. Rowan-Hamilton had something to say about that too: 'Knowing well the problems facing even a Western army in training the soldiery to use and maintain sophisticated arms and equipment, I shudder to think of the difficulties which Syria has to face . . .'

In the mid-1960s the border between Syria and Israel was the place where the conflict between the Arabs and the Jews was hottest. Israel was much stronger than Syria. Its aggressive behaviour along the border set the pace, and started the slide to war in 1967. As early as 1964, as a pattern emerged, the British Embassy in Damascus was commenting that 'while the Syrians were wrong in opening fire, the Israelis were plainly provocative in sending patrols into an area they knew was in dispute, and also that they were disproportionately severe in their retaliation'. An edge of hatred crept into this particular Arab–Israeli front that did not exist elsewhere. Colonel Israel Lior, who was the Israeli prime minister Levi Eshkol's military aide, identified what he called a 'Syrian syndrome' in the IDF. Suffering from it especially badly, Lior believed, were Yitzhak Rabin, who commanded the northern front in the 1950s and became chief of staff in 1964, and the general in charge of Northern Command, David Elazar. 'Service on this front, opposite the Syrian enemy, fuels feelings of exceptional hatred for the Syrian army and its people. There is no comparison, it seems to me, between the Israeli's attitude to the Jordanian or Egyptian army and his attitude to the Syrian army. We loved to hate them.' Rabin and Elazar, Lior noted, were 'very aggressive' in combat operations over the two biggest flashpoints – the control of water and possession of the demilitarised zones.

The feeling was mutual. Destroying Israel was the only strategic military objective of the Syrian armed forces. But, preoccupied as they were with internal politics, they spent very little time thinking about how they would do it. Colonel Rowan-Hamilton recorded a typical conversation with a Syrian officer about Israel: 'His eyes become glazed and his face flushes. When invited to explain how the Arabs intend to defeat Israel with the US Sixth Fleet pledged to its support if attacked, the officer will say: "I don't know, but we will throw them into the sea."' The Americans agreed with the British about the Syrian army. It was barely adequate for peacetime 'and would be totally inadequate in a war environment', with poor training, 'highly deficient' command and control procedures, extremely weak logistics, and 'especially lacking' in reserves of electronic and other technical equipment. The Syrian leadership knew how weak they had become. After an abortive coup on 8 September 1966, the army suffered yet another wave of dismissals and desertions. The leadership saw enemies everywhere. They thought the kings of Jordan and Saudi Arabia were plotting against them. They had no confidence that Egypt would intervene if it came to a fight with Israel. Most of all, they feared what the Israelis could do to them. In the autumn of 1966 the foreign minister, Dr Ibrahim Makhus, seemed to the British ambassador to be 'chastened . . . affected by the hopelessness of it all'.

But Israel saw danger lurking in Damascus. Syria had become a radical, politically aggressive state, which encouraged and sheltered the first Palestinian guerrillas. Its Soviet advisers helped it build impressive defences on the Golan Heights. Behind them Syrian artillery periodically shelled Israel's border settlements, often because of Israeli provocations. Casualties were low but it was politically awkward for the Israeli government.

Water and land

The night of 2 November 1964 was cold on the high ground near Israel's border with Syria. A group of Israeli soldiers sat shivering around their tanks. The next day they were expecting combat, the first that Israel's Armoured Corps had faced in six years. Captain Shamai Kaplan, their commander, brought out his accordion. 'Lads, let's sing a bit. It'll warm us up!' He started singing. At first, no one joined in. 'Men,' the sergeant called out, 'liven it up! Pretend you're having a picnic on the beach.' They started singing and their voices drifted out into the darkness.

They were there because of water. Since 1959 Israel had been building its national water carrier, a system that sent water from the Sea of Galilee in the north through pipes and canals to irrigate the Negev desert in the south. In 1964 it was ready. The Arabs' belated response was to sabotage it by diverting two of the three sources of the river Jordan that fed the Sea of Galilee. The men from 'S' Brigade of Israel's Armoured Corps were going to attack the Syrian earth moving machines and the tanks that were protecting them.

To get the Syrian guns firing, the next day the Israelis set up an incident. A patrol went down a dirt road, just over the border from a Syrian village called Nukheila. When, as expected, the Syrians opened fire from two old German Panzers that were dug into the hillside, the Israeli tanks were ready. They pounded the Syrian positions for an hour and a half. The Syrians fired back as hard as they could. Smoke, dust and the smell of gunpowder filled the air. Once the UN had managed to negotiate a ceasefire, Brigadier-General Israel Tàl, the newly appointed commander of the Armoured Corps, came to see how they had done.

'How many Syrian tanks were knocked out?'

'None, sir . . . One may have been slightly damaged,' replied a lieutenant-colonel.

'Did their tanks fire all the time?'

'We didn't silence a single tank, sir. The Syrians were still firing after we stopped.'

'How many shells did we fire?'

'Eighty-nine, sir.'

The attack was a failure. Kaplan, the accordion player, was blamed. Ten days later, after Tal had administered a general dressing-down to the Corps' senior officers, the Israelis manufactured another incident at the same place. Once again the tanks were ready. This time they destroyed the two Syrian Panzers. The Syrians shelled Israeli farming settlements and, in a major act of escalation, the IDF sent in the air force.

Using the Syrian border as a test bed Tal worked on the Armoured Corps until, by 1967, he had turned it into a ferociously efficient weapon. Tal was born in 1924 on a Jewish agricultural settlement in Palestine. As a teenager he designed a gun to kill moles and tried to build a submarine to explore a local waterhole. In the Second World War he joined the British army and fought in the Western Desert and Italy with the East Kents. He was demobilised as a sergeant and went home to pass his expertise on to the Haganah, the Jewish underground army.

Tal instilled professionalism and discipline into the Armoured Corps. Traditionally the Israeli army is relaxed about uniforms and saluting. Tal was a martinet, not just on uniform but everything else. He stopped bullying, which had included forcing soldiers to bury a cigarette with full military honours in the middle of the night, or to carry around the 'pocket wrench' of their tank, which weighed eleven pounds. He was accused of trying to turn his soldiers into robots. He answered that it was fine for paratroopers to ignore what seemed like military routine, as long as they were brave. But dealing with tanks was a technical business, which was why they needed rules for everything from the right way to zero a sight to making sure that the oil and fuel were checked. Tal improved the gunnery of Israeli tanks

18

to such an extent that they could hit targets eleven kilometres away. Sometimes he operated the guns himself. By 1965 the Arabs gave up trying to divert the rivers.

After Israel won the fight over water the action shifted to small parcels of land lying between the armistice line of July 1949 and the old Palestinian frontier. In the armistice the two sides agreed that they would be demilitarised with the issue of sovereignty postponed until a final peace treaty. In practice both sides occupied and cultivated demilitarised zones. Israel went about it more aggressively and efficiently than Syria, working tirelessly and successfully to alter the status quo in its favour. Many of the United Nations military observers who were based on the frontier believed that while the Syrians 'often lie to UN officers but subsequently admit their untruths, the Israelis, while professing to offer complete co-operation, lie even more of the time and do all they can to deceive UN officers'. A widely held belief among the military observers was that the Israelis would periodically 'fabricate' incidents. Israel evicted Syrian farmers from the zones it controlled and gave their land to Jewish settlements. Periodically the tension blew up into exchanges of fire. According to Matityahu Peled, who was one of Israel's senior generals in 1967, 'over 50 per cent of the border incidents [with Syria] before the Six-Day War were the result of our security policy of maximum settlement in the demilitarised areas'. (Peled went from being an especially hawkish general in 1967 to the leadership of a joint Arab–Jewish party that campaigned for peace.) By 1967 a British diplomat reviewing the two sides' claims to the land grumbled that 'no amount of pseudo-legality or case law can justify the fact that in what was basically an Arab populated area there is now not a single Arab living'. General Odd Bull, who commanded the United Nations Truce Supervision Organization (UNTSO) which did its best to make the armistice arrangements work, warned that Israel's activities deepened the mistrust on the border.

Only highly motivated people went to live in the Israeli border settlements. They were dangerous places. Families spent long periods in bomb shelters. Fathers could find themselves driving armoured tractors under fire to prove Israel's claim to small pieces of land with strange names like de Gaulle's nose, the beetroot lot, and the bean patch. The settlers believed that if the Syrians shelled a particular field, it was even more important to cultivate it. In their view, 'Making concessions to the Syrians does not further the cause of peace. We would only invite them to challenge our rights to the next tract.' These days the popular Israeli version is that the settlers of the mid-1960s were defenceless farmers. But they saw themselves as nation builders. Once when Levi Eshkol, who had succeeded David Ben-Gurion as prime minister, visited the settlements after they had been thoroughly shelled they gave him a statement saying, 'This is our home. Every bit of destruction is painful for us. But we settled here in order to confirm the sovereignty of Israel along these borders. We therefore accept all the risks and ask the Government that the work be allowed to continue.' For the Israelis, cultivating the demilitarised zones was about building the state, not agriculture. In April 1967 a local security official admitted that 'the cost of the kernel we reap is higher than if we had imported it from the United States, each wrapped separately in cotton and cellophane'.

According to Moshe Dayan, Israel's most famous soldier who became minister of defence on the eve of the Six-Day War, Israel provoked 'at least 80 per cent' of the border clashes. 'It went this way. We would send a tractor to plough somewhere where it wasn't possible to do anything, in the demilitarised area, and knew in advance that the Syrians would start to shoot. If they didn't shoot, we would tell the tractor to advance further, until in the end the Syrians would get annoyed and start to shoot. And then we would use artillery and later the air force also, and that's how it was.' Dayan said he provoked the Syrians, as did Rabin and his two predecessors as chiefs of staff, Chaim Laskov and Zvi Tsur. But 'the person who most enjoyed these games' was General David Elazar, who led the IDF's Northern Command from 1964 to 1969. Dayan believed it was all about a hunger for land: 'Along the Syrian border there were no farms and no refugee camps – there was only the Syrian army. The kibbutzim saw the good agricultural land . . . and they dreamed about it.'

Israel set the pace, but the Arabs did their best to keep up with the violence. On the last day of 1964, Yasser Arafat, the leader of a Palestinian faction called Fatah, entered the life of Israelis for the first time. A small team of Palestinians tried to sneak into Israel from south Lebanon, intending to attack a pumping station on Israel's national water carrier. Before they could reach the border fence they were arrested by the Lebanese secret police. The following night another team made it into Israel and planted a bomb which did not explode. Palestinian organisations celebrate New Year's Day 1965 as the start of the armed struggle. When Arafat seized control of the Palestine Liberation Organization after 1967, his people put round a story that he had led the first cross-border raid. In fact, until he too was arrested, Arafat was in Beirut, busily circulating exaggerated details of the raid in Fatah's Military Communiqué Number One, under the name of the so-called Asifah 'Storm' forces.

Arafat and his friend Khalil al-Wazir were known as 'the madmen' in Palestinian circles. (Wazir, who was also known as Abu Jihad, remained one of the few people close to Arafat who was not a yes-man until Israeli commandos riddled his body with 150 bullets in front of his wife and child in Tunis in 1988.) The 'madmen' believed they could do for their people what the Vietnamese and the Algerian national liberation movements had done for theirs. Other groups appeared. The Palestinian Liberation Front, under Ahmad Jibril, was followed by 'Vengeance Youth' and the Heroes of the Return, who came together as the Popular Front for the Liberation of Palestine.

According to Fatah's communiqués they were fighting a bruising guerrilla war, killing scores of Israelis and causing serious damage to the infrastructure of the Jewish state. In fact when it came to the military punch, they were never more than a nuisance. But politically and psychologically, they made an impact. For Palestinians, they kept the idea of resistance alive. For Israelis, they were terrorists bent on the destruction of the state and the expulsion of the Jews, who had to be resisted.

President Nasser had established the Palestine Liberation Organization in 1964 to control the activities of people like Arafat.

The last thing he wanted were guerrillas carrying out freelance operations against Israel. Nasser planned to create a noisy and relatively harmless organisation, which would satisfy the desire shared by all Arabs to do something about the Palestinian catastrophe but which could be contained and controlled. He installed Ahmed Shukairy as leader of the PLO. Shukairy was a charlatan, who specialised in bombastic speeches threatening Israel with a bloody and savage end. Nasser ignored Shukairy's windy rhetoric. He repeated many times that the Arabs were not strong enough to attack Israel. They should wait, building their strength until the time was right. He allowed the creation of a Palestine Liberation Army as part of the standing forces of Egypt and Syria, under firm political control.

But by 1966 Nasser's strategy of keeping the borders quiet started to fall apart. Syria had its ninth military coup in seventeen years. It was bloody. Several hundred people were killed. The mastermind behind the coup was General Salah Jadid, who installed Nureddin al Atassi as head of state. Jadid, like many officers, was an Alawi, an ethnic and religious minority that followed its own form of Islam. The easiest way for the Alawis to ingratiate themselves with Syria's Sunni Muslims, who were the majority, was to work even harder to heat up their border with Israel. It was a labour of love for radical Arab socialists.

The level of violence rose throughout the spring and summer of 1966. There were artillery exchanges, guerrilla raids, even a fight between Israeli patrol boats on the Sea of Galilee and Syrian shore batteries that ended up with an air battle. In Israel the government of Levi Eshkol came under more and more pressure to hit back. On 16 October the top Israeli military commanders talked about their plans for a major reprisal raid against Syria at a lunch for a visiting British air marshal. Rabin and Ezer Weizman, his number two, dropped heavy hints that they were planning a 'large-scale operation to occupy the Syrian border areas, including all the high ground . . . with maximum destruction of Syrian military personnel and equipment'.

But early in November Syria signed a mutual defence agreement with Egypt. For the Syrians, it was more than just an insurance policy.

Now they had a chance of getting the Egyptians, who had said many times that they were not ready to confront Israel, to march alongside them whether they liked it or not. Nasser hoped the pact would restrain the hotheads in Damascus. But all it did was encourage them. An Israeli intelligence officer commented that Nasser was 'the only Rabbi who can give the Syrians a kosher certificate of respectability as revolutionaries'. The Syrian junta did not trust the Egyptians enough to let them station troops in Syria. But they knew that Israel would be alarmed by an alliance between Egypt, its most powerful Arab neighbour, and Syria, its most hostile one. The new agreement made Israel think again about launching a major raid on Syria. They hit Jordan instead.

Raiding Samua

King Hussein started counting down to the next Middle Eastern war on Sunday 13 November 1966, the day that Israel raided the village of Samua on the West Bank. Life in Samua was never easy. For at least 2000 years peasant farmers had grazed sheep and goats and raised a few dusty crops on its bare, rocky ground. In the summer the heat blasts off the stones and the scrub. Though the winter is short, the wind and rain bite at the shepherds on the hills and flash floods can sweep away anyone foolish enough to walk along the deep wadis. Samua is on the edge of two deserts – the Judean to the east, and the Negev to the south. Since 1948 it was also on the border with Israel. Generations of Palestinians in Samua had worked out ways to deal with nature. Dealing with the Jewish state was much more complicated.

The people of Samua were early risers. The men went to pray in the mosque at dawn. The women started clattering around their kitchens even earlier. They had big families. Water had to be fetched and there was bread to bake. That morning in November 1966 seemed like any other. The first rain clouds of winter were building up over the high plateau that comes down from Mount Hebron. Then, at about six o'clock, they started to hear tanks firing. The sound came from the border, which was only five kilometres away. The villagers grabbed their children and went as quickly as they could to the fields and the limestone caves around the village. From hard experience, they knew about Israeli reprisals.

What they could hear were Israeli tanks destroying the Jordanian police post at Rujim El-Madfa, about a kilometre inside the border. A big force of Israeli tanks, supported by infantry mounted in armoured half-tracks had crossed the border and was heading towards them. Tank shells started whooshing over the top of the village. Ouragan ground-attack aircraft flew low over their heads. Higher up, supersonic Mirage fighters provided air cover, waiting for the arrival of the Royal Jordanian Air Force.

Major Asad Ghanma, commander of the 48th Infantry Battalion of the Jordanian army, knew that the Israelis were coming and that he had to fight them. His unit was the only one in the area at the time. The border with Israel was more than 600 kilometres long. The Jordanian army was spread thinly along it. It was bigger than it had been in 1948, but less efficient since King Hussein dismissed its British officers in 1956.

The major and his men drove fast out of their barracks and raced headlong down the road towards the Israelis. There had been rumours of a raid for a couple of weeks, since saboteurs had tried to blow up a block of flats on the Jewish side of Jerusalem and derailed an Israeli train. Nobody had died in those attacks. But the day before, on Saturday, a routine Israeli border patrol had driven over a mine. Three Israeli soldiers had been killed and six others injured. The Israelis believed terrorists from Samua had left the mine. Now they wanted revenge.

Their plan was to enter Samua, blow up a lot buildings, then pull back. General Rabin calculated that it ought to take about an hour and a half to deliver what he thought was a clear and uncompromising message: that the people of Samua, and all the other 700,000 Palestinians on the West Bank, should not harbour terrorists, and that King Hussein himself should do more to stop them crossing the border to kill Jews. It was the biggest Israeli military operation since 1956. Two raiding parties crossed the border. The bigger one headed for Samua, led by 8 Centurion tanks, followed by 400 paratroopers mounted in about 40 armoured, open-topped half-tracks. Ten more half-tracks followed with 60 combat engineers who were going to do the demolition. The second force was made up of 3 more Centurion tanks and 100 paratroops and engineers in 10 half-tracks. They had a separate mission, to blow up houses in two other smaller villages, Kirbet El-Markas and Kirbet Jimba. Five more Super Sherman tanks and eight field guns supported them from the Israeli side of the border. Behind them were powerful reserves, in case the raiding force ran into trouble. In the air the Ouragans were armed with rockets to attack Jordanian armour or artillery if it appeared.

The smaller force cleared civilians out of Kirbet El-Markas and Kirbet Jimba and set to work blowing up houses. Then three companies of Major Ghanma's men drove straight into an Israeli blocking position on the high ground to the north-west of Samua. Another two companies that tried to get in from the north-east were also intercepted by Israeli troops. But a platoon of Jordanians with two 106 mm recoilless guns entered Samua and attacked the Israelis. There was some fierce close-quarter fighting at the southern end of the village until Israel cleared the Jordanians out with tanks. The Israelis fought bravely, following their orders and adapting them efficiently as things changed. Individual Jordanians also fought bravely, but without a plan. Once they had been dealt with, Israeli paratroopers went from house to house to check the village was clear while the engineers laid the charges.

By 0945 the Israelis were back on their own side of the border. During the raid three Jordanian civilians and fifteen soldiers were killed. Fifty-four other Jordanian soldiers and civilians were wounded. The Jordanian army, a proud force that believed itself to be the best in the Arab world, had been humiliated. On the Israeli side the commander of the paratroop battalion was killed and ten others were wounded. Four hours later, when a missionary called Eric Bishop arrived, the 'dazed and frightened' people were drifting back. The bridge into the village was blocked by three smoking, burnt-out Jordanian army vehicles. Bishop followed the villagers down off the road and across the dry river bed. Unexploded shells and twisted scraps of metal were all over the roads. The village's only clinic had been reduced to a pile of rubble. So had the girls' school. The town bus was crumpled under stones from a blown up building. In all, 140 houses had gone. So had the post office and the coffee shop. Bishop saw a couple and their four children 'rolling rocks down from a mound where their home had been. Someone shouted that they should look out for unexploded shells but they paid no attention.'

King Hussein was aghast. He had been having secret meetings with the Israelis. On the morning of the raid on Samua, he received an unsolicited message from his Israeli contacts that they had no intention of attacking Jordan. In what the White House considered 'a quite extraordinary revelation' he told American ambassador Findley Burns and the head of the CIA's Amman station, Jack O'Connel, that for three years there had been secret correspondence and clandestine meetings with Abba Eban, Israel's foreign minister, and with Golda Meir, his predecessor. They had talked about peace and he had assured them he was doing everything he could to stop terrorist attacks from Jordan.

'I told them I could not absorb or tolerate a serious retaliatory raid. They accepted the logic of this and promised there would never be one.' Burns and O'Connel saw tears in the king's eyes as he told them that the attack was 'a complete betrayal of everything I had tried to do for the past three years in the interests of peace, stability and moderation at high personal political risk. Strangely, despite our secret agreements, understandings and assurances, I never fully trusted their intentions towards me or towards Jordan.' Bitterly, the king ended the conversation by saying 'this is what one gets for trying to be a moderate, or perhaps for being stupid'.

The ambassador had 'never seen him so grim or so obviously under pressure. It was apparent that he had to use the utmost in self control to keep his emotions from erupting openly.' He asked that Hussein's request to keep his contacts with Israel secret should be respected. The king's grandfather, after all, had been assassinated for doing exactly the same thing.

The king concluded that his throne was in serious danger and that Israel still wanted the West Bank, just as it had in its early years of independence. Hussein knew that many Israelis believed that Israel would not be secure until its eastern border ran down the river Jordan. He told the diplomats that he had always thought it was possible to live with Israel. But now the only option he had left was irrevocable hostility. Highly emotional, the king even talked about mounting his own attack on Israel, a threat the Americans, knowing the weakness of the Jordanian army, did not take seriously.

The morning after the raid he summoned all the ambassadors accredited to his court to his palace in Amman. He told them it was the latest instalment in Zionism's long history of aggression and expansionism. Samua, he said, could not be seen as a mere reprisal. It was 'the first battle' in Israel's campaign to swallow the West Bank. He told them that if they did not 'restrain the aggressor' by moral and if necessary physical force, the crisis would drag in all their countries too. Britain and America believed Hussein when he said that he was doing everything he could to stop infiltration. One of the alleged organisers of the attack on the Israeli border patrol had been arrested before the Israeli reprisal happened. The United States was so concerned about the raid that even after it supported a resolution in the UN Security Council condemning Israel's actions, National Security Advisor Walt Rostow still thought they had not reacted strongly enough. The US airlifted urgent military aid to Jordan, a move the White House decided was necessary to save King Hussein's throne. They feared that if they did not send aid Hussein would call in Egyptian troops or even Soviet advisers and equipment.

Hussein was very focused when it came to matters of his own survival. Not only had he witnessed his grandfather's assassination; since becoming king he had faced a series of plots and would-be assassins of his own. Now the latest threat, he believed, was coming from Israel, his increasingly mighty neighbour. Hussein had learnt from his grandfather that he would always have to do business with

Israel. In return, Israel had humiliated him. He was determined that he was going to survive, along with his regime.

Since 1948 Jordan had two distinct halves. The East Bank, mainly desert, was Hussein's power base. He could rely on the support of the leaders of its Bedouin tribes whose men were the backbone of his army. But since 1948 there had also been more than half a million Palestinian refugees. Another 700,000 Palestinians lived on the West Bank and in the Old City of Jerusalem. Educated Palestinian urbanites tended to look down on East Bankers as country bumpkins. Hussein put members of aristocratic Palestinian families in his cabinets. But the king and his close advisers, rightly, were deeply suspicious of the great mass of Palestinians. They were seen as a potential fifth column, ready to be seduced by the violent criticism of Hussein and the Hashemite dynasty that came from the regime of Gamal Abdul Nasser in Cairo. Anyone found listening to Nasser's radio station Saut al-Arab, the Voice of the Arabs, could be arrested.

Hussein did not think Israel planned to march on Amman and take him prisoner. Instead he feared that its actions would stir up trouble on the West Bank that would be exploited by ambitious army officers. If a coup established a radical, pro-Nasser regime in Jordan, Israel could use it as an excuse to step in. The CIA believed his analysis was realistic. Whichever way it went, the result would be that Hussein would lose his throne, and his dynasty, the Hashemites, would lose their last hold on power. Mecca, Medina and the rest of the Hejaz were lost to Ibn Saud after the First World War. In a coup in 1958 the Hashemite king of Iraq, Hussein's cousin and friend, was slaughtered along with most of his immediate family. Hussein Ibn Talal, ruler of Jordan, descendant of the prophet, did not want to be the last Hashemite king.

As Hussein feared, Palestinians on the West Bank seethed with anger after the raid. The people of Samua refused offers of emergency food, tents and blankets. Instead they demanded weapons. One of them asked a reporter from the *Los Angeles Times* when he reached the village: 'What do they expect us to fight with – with women? With children? Or with stones?' It felt like a return to the early 1950s, when Israel carried out a long series of brutal and almost wholly counter-productive raids on the West Bank. Two days after the raid, demonstrators took over the centre of Hebron, the big Palestinian town close to Samua. The governor sent the fire brigade to turn their hoses on the crowd, only for them to be sent back to their fire stations by the local police chief, who said they would make things worse. A policeman who brandished his revolver at demonstrators was beaten up. Slogans were chanted against King Hussein, against America for protecting Israel, and against Syria and Egypt for not sending planes to protect them. Demonstrations spread to East Jerusalem and Nablus. The king slapped martial law on all the Palestinian towns. He could feel his throne shaking under him.

The government was accused of covering up the number of casualties and the size of the defeat. Jordanians were proud of their dead, but officers felt humiliated and shamed. A senior security official told the Americans that air force officers were especially bitter because they had been forced to go into action with 'completely inadequate equipment' – the ageing, subsonic, British-built Hawker Hunters. They thought they had been handed a choice – stay on the ground or commit suicide in the air. During the raid four Jordanian Hawker Hunter aircraft engaged Israeli Mirages in dogfights. One of them was shot down, after a long, low-level dogfight in which the pilot impressed the Israelis with his skill. At his funeral, army officers criticised the king violently. Instead of protecting the border, he had 'squandered' money on his own pleasures and cared more about hanging on to his throne than about the defence of his country. It was impossible to live in peace with Israel. Some of the officers thought Jordan should move against Israel now, whatever the consequences. King Hussein was told about the fury of his officers. He believed that only traditional Bedouin loyalty was keeping the army on his side.

Hussein's troubles pleased his enemies in the radical Arab regimes in Egypt and Syria. No message of support came from Cairo. Damascus was relieved it had got off so lightly. The Israelis regarded the guerrilla groups as Syrian proxies. The British ambassador in

Damascus thought it was more complicated than that: 'Even if the Syrian government do control one or more of these bodies, I doubt whether their control is sufficiently close for there to be day-to-day coordination between terrorist operations and military action on the border.' Still, no one in Damascus would deny that they encouraged and supported Palestinian attacks – and Israel had chosen not to attack them. The army chief of staff General Suwaydani ordered the cultivation of what Syria said was Arab land in the demilitarised areas. Let the Israelis shoot at us, he said. We'll shoot back harder. Samua did not stop cross-border raids, although the Jordanians tried even harder to stop infiltration through the West Bank into Israel. The violence escalated. The Israeli army was itching for a fight and every Zionist bone in Prime Minister Eshkol's body opposed making any concessions to Syria whatsoever over the disputed demilitarised zones. Added to that was growing political pressure, especially from the border settlements, to take tough action. It all came to a head on 7 April 1967.

Leading the country to war

Israelis who lived at Kibbutz Gadot, very close to the Syrian border, were standing in their yard, watching the action on the hills above them. All afternoon the air force had been bombing Syrian positions. A big battle had been brewing for the best part of a week. Now it was on.

Two Israeli tractors started work at 0930. Within fifteen minutes tanks, howitzers and heavy machine guns were exchanging fire. The battle increased in intensity. Israeli aircraft dive-bombed Syrian positions with 250 and 500 kg bombs. The Syrians shelled Israeli border settlements heavily. Israeli jets retaliated with an attack on Sqoufiye, a civilian village, destroying around forty houses. UN observers believed Syrian casualties were much heavier than the five Damascus admitted.

At 1519 shells started to fall on Kibbutz Gadot. One landed near the children's house (children on kibbutzim lived communally, visiting their parents at set hours and sleeping separately in their own accommodation). Adults ran in to the building, grabbed the children and took them to the shelters. The children's shelter was equipped for a long siege. It had cots, a kitchen for making food and lots of toys. Suddenly, it was very crowded, because the adults who had brought the children in were stuck there too. They started singing to try to take the children's minds off the crash of the shells outside. In 40 minutes 300 shells landed within the kibbutz compound. One mother had to be physically restrained from running out into the open during the bombardment to find her child. When they emerged from the shelter, with all the children safe, they saw their homes in ruins. Offers of help came in from all over Israel, everything from cows for the dairy to a loan of labourers from the atomic reactor in Dimona to help them rebuild.

Israeli Mirages routed the Syrian MiG-21s. Two were chased most of the way to Damascus and were shot down over the suburbs. The Israelis roared low over the capital to rub the Syrians' noses in what they had done. Four other Syrian MiG-21s were shot down, three of them over Jordan. The British air attaché, who examined the wreckage, was struck by how close they were to each other. He concluded that 'either the Israeli aircraft had carried out an almost unbelievably skilful operation and shot down three aircraft almost simultaneously whilst still in formation or that the Syrian pilots had abandoned their aircraft, again while still in formation, rather than face up to the Israelis'. The absence of obvious bullet holes in the wreckage encouraged his view that the Syrians, who all ejected safely, had chosen discretion over valour. Privately, the Jordanians claimed the Syrians had admitted as much in hospital, complaining that they did not stand a chance against well-trained Israeli pilots with better ground control. Syrian military weakness was clearer than ever. At the height of the battle, Mezze Airfield, one of its main bases, was wide open to attack from the air. Its army garrison was standing to, with five tanks and five armoured personnel carriers. But its twenty-four MiG-17s were lined up on the tarmac and only four of its six 54 mm anti-aircraft guns were manned.

The next morning young Palestinians in Jerusalem showed 'a stunned awe at the Israeli competence and Arab helplessness in the face of it . . .' and they asked 'where were the Egyptians?' Cairo had done nothing for Jordan after it had been humiliated at Samua. Now Syria had been humiliated, a country with which Egypt had a mutual defence pact. This time, Nasser had no choice. Something would have to be done.

Israel basked in a mood of national self-congratulation. Film of the MiGs being shot down from the Mirages' gun cameras played in newsreels in the cinemas to appreciative audiences. The army heavily reinforced the northern border, moving in thirty-five tanks, mainly Centurions, and at least fifteen 105 mm guns. In a corridor in the Israeli Knesset, Moshe Dayan, the former chief of staff and now member of parliament, bumped into General Ezer Weizman, the former head of the air force and now number two in the IDF. 'Are you out of your minds?' he said to Weizman. 'You're leading the country to war!'

After the 7 April battle Syria and the guerrillas it sponsored tried even harder to provoke the Israelis, who obliged them by rising to every provocation. Wearily, the British ambassador in Damascus commented that 'the Syrians are clearly in the wrong in not preventing infiltration. On the other hand, Israeli reaction to what after all are relatively little more than pinpricks, has been quite out of proportion.' Rabin and Eshkol used interviews and broadcasts granted for Independence Day, which was coming up, to warn Damascus to expect more of the same and worse. The British government believed Israel's threats were 'the starting point of the chain of events that led to war'. The CIA picked up the threats and told President Johnson to expect a move against Syria. The Egyptians drew the same conclusions. Israel 'is contemplating an attack on Syria . . . preparing world opinion for it and asking for assistance'.

The toughest threat was reported by the news agency United Press International (UPI) on 12 May: 'A high Israeli source said today Israel would take limited military action designed to topple the Damascus army regime if Syrian terrorists continue sabotage raids inside Israel. Military observers said such an offensive would fall short of all-out war but would be mounted to deliver a telling blow against the Syrian government.'

In the West as well as the Arab world the immediate assumption was that the unnamed source was Rabin and that he was serious. In fact, it was Brigadier-General Aharon Yariv, the head of military intelligence, and the story was overwritten. Yariv mentioned 'an all-out invasion of Syria and conquest of Damascus' but only as the most extreme of a range of possibilities. But the damage had been done. Tension was so high that most people, and not just the Arabs, assumed something much bigger than usual was being planned against Syria. Israel's English-language newspaper, the *Jerusalem Post*, took the threats and warnings as an authoritative ultimatum. A year later, Abba Eban, the foreign minister – who had been one of the first to weigh in against Syrian-sponsored 'marauders' that month – commented caustically: 'There were some who thought these warnings may have been too frequent and too little coordinated . . . if there had been a little more silence the sum of human wisdom would have remained substantially undiminished.'

The message received outside Israel was that Damascus was in the sights of the IDF. For Nasser, it became an article of faith that 'the Israeli leaders had announced that they would undertake military operations against Syria to occupy Damascus and bring down the Syrian regime'. The Egyptians claimed to have seen an Israeli plan for a powerful force to occupy the heights overlooking the Sea of Galilee. Israel, they claimed, planned to withdraw only if peacekeepers from UNEF were brought in to replace them.

The Syrians also believed they were about to be invaded. President Atassi, the head of state, sent messages to Cairo asking for military support under the terms of their mutual defence pact. The Syrian leadership did not mind provoking Israel, but they did not want all-out war. They had been taught a hard lesson in the air battle of 7 April. Members of the regime, like the air force commander General Hafez al-Asad, knew all too well that those who seize power in coups tend to have their power taken away in counter-coups, especially if they lose a war. Well before the 7 April battle, Asad already seemed 'extremely nervous and appeared to dread the prospect of a major incident'. Yet icy reality did not cool down their rhetoric. Israel was 'caught in the pincers' of Egyptian, Syrian and Palestinian commandos. America could not protect 'the foster child state of bandits'. The Grand Mufti went to inspect front-line positions and declared that religious leaders were ready to join the army in battle because Israel was 'the enemy of Islam, Arabism and humanity'. Local rallies were held, where slogans were chanted and speeches made. It would, a newspaper editorial predicted, be 'the last blow' against Israel.

At this point, as the British foreign office had it, 'the Russians pricked the Egyptian donkey'. Moscow delivered a warning to Cairo that Israel was massing troops on the border with Syria and would attack within a week. On 13 May the President of the Egyptian parliament, Anwar El Sadat, was at Moscow international airport, being seen off by Vladimir Semyenov, the Soviet deputy foreign minister, and Nikolai Podgorny, chairman of the presidium of the Supreme Soviet. Sadat's plane was late. They spent the extra hour talking, mainly about Syria. 'They told me specifically that ten Israeli brigades had been concentrated on the Syrian border.' He passed the message to Nasser who had also received it from the Soviet Embassy and the KGB. By the evening, General Muhammad Fawzi, the Egyptian army's chief of staff, had received a similar message from Major-General Ahmad Suwaydani, his Syrian opposite number.

Exactly why the Soviets delivered the warning is not clear. The Soviets seem to have believed they were passing on accurate intelligence. Perhaps they were misled by the Syrian regime, Moscow's ideological soul mate in a way that Egypt could never be. The Soviets wanted to protect their clumsy protégés, who as well as provoking Israel had now provoked Syria's Sunni Muslim majority with a newspaper article that was taken to be anti-Islamic. Tens of thousands took to the streets to protest. The Atassi regime was becoming so unpopular that it needed a good way to unite the country. The spectre of an Israeli attack was perfect.

A 'medium-level' Soviet official told the CIA that the Soviet Union had stirred up the Arabs to try to make trouble for the United States. They hoped the US, already embattled in Vietnam, might become involved in another long war. Perhaps that seemed like a good enough reason among Soviet hawks – but there were limits to the mischief that the Kremlin was prepared to make. The consensus in the CIA, the State Department and the White House throughout the crisis was that the Soviets did not want war and did not encourage the Arabs to go to war either, nor did it promise to take military action if things started to go wrong. A KGB officer told a CIA informant: 'I think this is difficult for the Arabs to understand, but everybody in the outside world believes that it is not worth it to have a world war over the question of Palestine.'

The message from Moscow to Cairo worried the Eshkol government. Was there a leak? 'Limited' retaliation against Syria (an elastic concept – the Samua raid was 'limited') had been authorised by the cabinet on 7 May. Secret plans existed and had been discussed in the prime minister's office and in the IDF General Staff. The real problem with the Soviet message to Egypt was that even though it was plausible, it was inaccurate. Israel was contemplating a big raid into Syria. But it had not concentrated a huge force on the border – Damascus had alleged fifteen brigades, which was not far off Israel's fully mobilised strength.

In Washington the White House, just like the Arabs and the Russians, had concluded that Israel was planning something big. President Johnson's information was that 'the Soviet advice to the Syrians that the Israelis were planning an attack was not far off, although they seem to have exaggerated on the magnitude. The Israelis probably were planning an attack – but not an invasion.' Another official agreed. 'It is probable Soviet agents actually picked up intelligence reports of a planned Israeli raid into Syria. I would not be surprised if the reports were at least partly true. The Israelis have made such raids before: they have been under heavy provocation: and they maintain pretty good security (so we might well not know about a planned raid). Intelligence being what it is, the Soviet agents may have not known the scale of the raid and may have exaggerated its scope and purpose.'

Jerusalem

Divided Jerusalem was a backwater between 1948 and 1967. Barbed wire, mines and machine gun posts marked the place where two hostile worlds butted against each other. UN Security Council resolution 181 that had partitioned Mandatory Palestine in November 1947 had declared that Jerusalem would be a separate entity under international control. Israel and Jordan ignored it, the big powers did not try to enforce it. The single crossing point was the Mandelbaum Gate, Jerusalem's Checkpoint Charlie. Only foreigners with special permission could cross between the Arab world and the Jewish state. Occasionally, after long bureaucratic campaigns, divided Palestinian families were allowed through for reunions. The two sides sometimes shot covetous glances – and bullets – at each other, but in Jerusalem no one was killed trying to escape from one side to the other. Plenty of people would have been quite happy if the people on the other side vanished. But they wanted to be in their world, not their enemy's.

The walled Old City was on the Jordanian side. Israelis were not allowed to visit any of the Jewish holy places. The Jordanians also had the Mount of Olives, which overlooks the Old City from the east. On its slopes is the Garden of Gethsemane, where Christians believe Jesus sweated blood on his last night before he was arrested by the Romans. A little higher up is the Jews' most important cemetery. The Jordanians paved the road with some of its gravestones. In the 1960s well-off Jordanians would motor over from Amman to have lunch at the brand-new Intercontinental hotel that had been built on top of the Mount of Olives. For them, Jerusalem was a beautiful symbol rather than a capital or a place to live. It was an easy drive of twenty-five miles or so from Amman, across the river Jordan, up past Jericho and through the Judean desert. They could eat looking down across the holy city at the mysterious and sinister Israelis on the hills opposite.

Jordanian Jerusalem was a quiet place. It was traditional, religious and poor. Helped by entrepreneurial Palestinian refugees, King Hussein was turning his capital, Amman, into a modern city. But after

1948 Jerusalem had lost its traditional hinterland in the rich farming land between the mountains and the Mediterranean coast. Palestinians grumbled not just because they were hard-up, but because they felt neglected and at times oppressed by Amman. A generation later, after more than thirty years of Israeli occupation, some Palestinians looked back sentimentally on what now seemed to have been golden years. One lamented: 'We were masters in our own houses and of every inch of the good and holy earth of our Jerusalem. Yet we seem[ed] to be perpetual grumblers, unsatisfied and never content, always wanting more and better. We never appreciated the treasures in our possession.'

Israeli Jerusalem was even quieter. It was centred on the New City, the commercial centre around Jaffa Street and King George Vth Street that had been built up during the British Mandate. Also in West Jerusalem were the impoverished ultra-religious Jewish communities centred on Mea Shearim and a belt of leafy suburbs that had been the home of the Palestinian middle class, which had either fled or been forced out in 1948. Israel declared Jerusalem as its capital city, an action that the rest of the world did not recognise. It did not matter to the visionaries on the Israeli side that shepherds still grazed sheep near their parliament or that most of its members took every opportunity they could to get out of the city. What mattered were the actions that had been taken and the point that was being made. Just as the only appropriate land for the Jewish state was the one given to the Jewish people by God, its only appropriate capital was the city about which they had prayed during all the centuries of exile.

The fact remained though, that between 1948 and 1967 Jerusalem felt different, unfamiliar and a little uncomfortable to most Israelis. It was high in the mountains. It was cold, wet and miserable in winter – unlike the Mediterranean coast between Tel Aviv and Haifa where most Israelis lived. It was old, reeking of a history that belonged not just to Jews, but to others as well. For the Israeli writer Amos Oz who grew up in West Jerusalem in the 1940s and 1950s it was 'the sad capital city of an exultant state', wintry even in the summer and 'surrounded at night by the sound of foreign bells, foreign odours, distant views. A ring of hostile villages surrounded the city on three sides: Sha'afat, Wadi Jos, Issawia, Silwan, Azaria, Tsur Bacher, Bet Tsafafa. It seemed as if they had only to clench their hand and Jerusalem would be crushed within their fist. On a winter night you could sense the evil intent that flowed from them toward the city.'

In this half-city, Israel decided to hold a pageant and a military parade on 15 May 1967 to mark its nineteenth birthday. For a country that never had the chance to celebrate peace, Independence Day was always something special. It was a loud raspberry in the faces of the Arabs who had tried to strangle the Jewish state at birth and who, everybody knew, would try again if they were given the chance. Israelis in 1967 knew a lot about war. Many men under forty, even fifty, had done little else than fight. As teenagers they fought the British and the Palestinian Arabs. Thousands joined the British army in the Second World War. They had fought Arab regular armies in 1948 and 1956 and mounted raids in between. Well over a million immigrants had arrived since 1948, often after traumatic journeys from the ruins of Europe or from Arab countries, which kept the Jews' property though not the Jews themselves. The youngest survivors of Nazi concentration camps were still barely thirty.

The swinging sixties passed the Jewish state by. But for Independence Day 1967 there was going to be a special concert in the big stadium on the coast near Tel Aviv. Topping the bill were the Shadows, Nana Mouskouri and Pete Seeger. All over the country there were bandstands and dancing and fireworks. And in Jerusalem the army was putting on a parade.

The UN believed that holding a parade in Jerusalem would only heighten the tension between Israel and Jordan. General Bull, the commander of the UNTSO military observers, and the senior UN representative in Jerusalem, was ordered not to attend. Most foreign ambassadors politely rejected their invitations. The CIA was worried about it too. It warned President Johnson that the parade 'would be a clear violation of the armistice of 1949; a nasty incident in the divided city may result'.

Two parades

On 14 May, twenty-four hours after the Soviet warning, the officers at the Egyptian army's operations command centre were thinking about lunch when they were jolted by entirely unexpected news. The supreme commander, Field Marshal Abd al-Hakim Amer, was putting the army on full alert for war. When Lieutenant-General Anwar al-Qadi, the chief of operations, asked why, he was told the Syrian border with Israel was about to explode. Amer issued the bellicose 'battle order number one'. There were 'huge troop concentrations on the Syrian borders'. Egypt was taking a 'firm stand'. Al-Qadi was 'astonished and alarmed'. He told Amer that the Egyptian army was in no state to fight Israel. The field marshal told him not to worry. Fighting a war was not part of the plan, it was just a 'demonstration' in response to Israeli threats to Syria. On 15 May General Fawzi, the chief of staff, went to Syria. He could not find any Israeli troops. 'I did not find any concrete evidence to support the information received. On the contrary, aerial photographs taken by Syrian reconnaissance on 12 and 13 May showed no change in normal military positions.'

Lt. Gen. al-Qadi was right. In May 1967 Egypt was no match for Israel. Economic problems meant that the defence budget had been cut earlier in the year. Training, never a religion, was now an even lower priority. In 1967 more than half the Egyptian army, including some of its best troops, were stuck in Yemen, where Nasser had intervened in the civil war. Yemen had the same corrosive impact on Nasser's army that the Vietnam war had on the Americans. According to General Abdel Moneim Khalil, one of Egypt's best commanders, 'we incurred heavy losses in manpower, our military budget was drained, discipline and training suffered, weapons and equipment deteriorated, morale and fighting capability was seriously affected . . . It was a very bad way to prepare to fight the highly trained and well organised Israelis.'

By 1967 the Egyptian high command had been concentrating on Yemen for five years. It had not done any serious training or preparation for a war with Israel. At the end of 1966 the military planners realised how bad things had become, warning that no offensive operations against Israel should be contemplated while Egypt was still involved in Yemen. Chief of Staff Fawzi approved the report. But in May 1967 Amer ignored it. He assured Nasser that, if it came to it, the army could fight Israel.

Troops were marched ostentatiously through the centre of Cairo on their way to the Sinai desert and the border with Israel. The public show of strength confirmed the CIA in its view that it was a response to Israeli threats to Syria. 'Nasser is going all out to show that his mutual security pact with Syria is something which the Israelis should take very seriously . . . [He] must be hoping desperately that there will be no need for him to fight the Israelis. He probably feels, however, that his prestige in the Arab world would nose-dive if he stood idly by while Israel mauled Syria again.' The British, too, thought the movement of troops was 'defensive-deterrent in character and were designed to show solidarity with [the] Syrians in the face of Israeli threats of action'.

In Jerusalem Israel's top politicians and soldiers were on their way to the Independence Day parade. They met up at the King David, the smartest hotel in West Jerusalem. Its grand public rooms overlooking the Old City were packed. Rabin updated Eshkol about the Egyptian deployments. More troops had been on the move during the night. Israel would have to mobilise some reservists. 'We cannot leave the south without reinforcements,' Rabin warned. They were not too worried. Something similar had happened in 1960, when Egypt moved tanks into Sinai after trouble on the Syrian border. Israel deployed its own reinforcements and, honours even, the crisis blew over.

It was time to move. Eighteen thousand people were waiting for them in the stadium at Givat Ram in West Jerusalem. Two hundred thousand more were lining the streets. Some of them had been there since dawn. Eshkol, his wife Miriam and Rabin were driven slowly along the crowded streets to the stadium. They settled themselves in the reviewing stand to watch a modest march-past of 1600 troops.

Colonel Israel Lior, Eshkol's military aide-de-camp, thought it looked like a scout parade. Independence Day was usually an excuse to show off Israel's strength. The streets would shake with the weight of armour. In deference to the international disapproval Israel had kept the tanks out of Jerusalem. Outside the stadium demonstrators waved cardboard tanks in protest.

Telephones were installed under the seats of the Israeli top brass at the parade. The phone under the seat of General Yeshayahu Gavish rang, with the latest news about Egyptian troops moving into Sinai. As soon as he could, he left and drove to his headquarters in Beersheba.

UNEF

Two days after it gambled by mobilising troops, Egypt dug itself deeper into crisis. A courier was dispatched from Cairo to Gaza with news for General Indar Jit Rikhye, the commander of the United Nations Emergency Force. In just over a decade in Gaza, the officers of UNEF had made themselves quite comfortable. When they were not on patrol or in their observation posts there were sand dunes and Mediterranean beaches, squash and tennis, a decent mess and a comfortable bar. UNEF even had a golf course laid out on its airstrip near the Mediterranean. It was not a classic seaside links. They played off strips of doormat, which were carried by their Palestinian caddies. Nonetheless, on the afternoon of 16 May, Rikhye, who was a general in the Indian army, was looking forward to a few holes. It was hot, sweaty and overcast. He was hoping there might be some breeze coming off the sea on to the first tee when the telephone rang. It was Brigadier General Ibrahim Sharkaway, who was chief of staff of the Egyptian team that liaised with UNEF. A special courier was on his way. General Rikhye was to stand by for a meeting at short notice. Rikhye was proud of his force of 1400 lightly armed peacekeepers. Originally they had been deployed to monitor the withdrawal of British, French and Israeli troops from Egypt after the 1956 war.

After they left UNEF stayed on with a new role as a symbolic buffer force on the border. Egypt promised to keep its troops 500 metres behind the armistice line in Gaza and 2000 metres behind the old international border between Egypt and Palestine. UNEF operated in the space in between. Israel would not let it on its side.

Rikhye decided not to play golf. He should have done. It was his last chance on the Gaza links and the courier from Cairo did not arrive until ten in the evening. At Sharkaway's office, which was in a khaki-coloured building behind the whitewashed UNEF head-quarters, Rikhye realised something big was happening. The courier was a brigadier general called Eiz-El-Din Mokhtar. He handed Rikhye a letter.

COMMANDER UNEF (GAZA)
To your information, I gave my instructions to all U.A.R.
[Egyptian] armed forces to be ready for action against
Israel, the moment it might carry out any aggressive action
against any Arab country. Due to these instructions our
troops are already concentrated in Sinai on our eastern
border. For the sake of complete security of all UN troops
which install OP's [observation posts] along our borders, I
request that you issue your orders to withdraw all these
troops immediately. I have given my instructions to our
commander of the Eastern zone concerning this subject.
Inform back the fulfilment of this request.
     Yours,
   Farik Awal (M. Fawzi)
   Chief of Staff United Arab Republic.

Nasser and Amer first talked about getting rid of UNEF in 1964. In December 1966 Amer sent Nasser a coded message from Pakistan suggesting it again. They were being damaged by criticism from Hussein's radio stations accusing Egypt of sheltering behind UNEF's skirts, using it as an excuse not to take action to protect other Arab countries. Amer's suggestion was public enough to be picked up by

British diplomats in Jordan. Still, for Rikhye, when the blow came it was 'shattering . . . [war] would be inevitable.' He wanted to tell the two Egyptian brigadiers that they were heading for disaster. Instead, stiffly, he told them that he had to pass the message on to the secretary general of the United Nations, U Thant, before he could comment. Then, as common Arab courtesy demanded, they drank coffee together. Rikhye asked them if they realised what they could be getting into. 'Oh, yes sir!' Sharkaway replied. 'We have arrived at this decision after much deliberation and are prepared for anything. If there is war, we will meet in Tel Aviv.'

Rikhye went back to his headquarters to cable New York. Then he summoned his senior officers. It was well after midnight. 'General, what's the occasion?' one of them asked. 'Is there a war on?' Not yet, Rikhye answered, 'but there will be one soon'.

The Syrians were delighted by what was happening. The British ambassador in Damascus thought they were trying to make sure that Egypt would 'willy-nilly be dragged in' if Israel attacked. Dr Makhus, the foreign minister, who had been in Cairo, came home claiming that the slogan of the unity of progressive forces was now a reality. That was code for Syria's satisfaction that Egypt was now in the front line.

Charade

At first, the Israeli army was remarkably understanding about Egypt's actions. Its Syrian syndrome bristling, it was still focused on Damascus. On 17 May Shlomo Gazit, who was head of analysis in military intelligence, sat back at the dinner table in Tel Aviv after the plates had been cleared. Yes, he admitted to the American diplomats who were his hosts, the IDF had been taken by surprise. But it was 'an elaborate charade'. It would only get serious if Egypt closed the Straits of Tiran and thus cut off the Israeli port of Eilat. That would mean war. The Israeli press picked up the army line that Nasser was playing a psychological game, to reassure and impress the Syrians. The service attachés from all the major embassies in Israel went looking for the concentrations of troops that Egypt had said were threatening Syria. They could not find any.

Abba Eban, Israel's foreign minister, warned that whatever the original intentions were, 'an unwanted chain of events' was the real risk. Eban wanted to wait for London and Washington to work out a diplomatic strategy 'before taking any unilateral action'. But other high-ranking Israelis were not that patient. For them, diplomacy had already failed. The Americans half expected Israeli military action and did what they could to head it off. Johnson wrote to Eshkol on 17 May telling him 'in the strongest terms . . . to avoid action on your side which would add further to violence and tension in your area . . . I cannot accept responsibilities on behalf of the United States for situations which arise as the result of action on which we are not consulted.' A long-delayed aid package was authorised as a sweetener.

Propaganda

Long before most of his generation, Nasser recognised the power of the media. His radio stations trumpeted his actions across the Middle East. By far the most influential was Saut al-Arab, the Voice of the Arabs, which broadcast from Cairo to the rest of the Arab world via four Czechoslovak-made 150,000-watt transmitters. Whatever it turned its attention to could suddenly become disproportionately important. The British, for instance, were worried and irritated by a programme broadcast every night attacking its control of the Gulf. A correspondent for Reuters reassured Anthony Parsons, the British political agent in Bahrain, that it came from 'one scrofulous room with five chairs and a table in a seedy building in Cairo'. It did not matter. The fact that it was being broadcast by Voice of the Arabs made it powerful.

In a country that was often chaotic, where important army units were under strength and badly trained, Cairo Radio was well funded and meticulously organised. Like Nasser, they had drawn lessons from their experiences in 1956, when the RAF had bombed their transmitters. A manual with detailed instructions about what they should do in time of war was updated every year. Contingency plans were in place if the ultra modern radio and television centre on the Nile Corniche was bombed. Five separate teams of engineers and announcers were ready to back each other up to keep the broadcasts going. Cairo Radio was the arm of Nasser's regime that was most ready for war.

Ahmed Said, the main political commentator of Voice of the Arabs, had the most famous voice in the Arab world after Nasser himself and the legendary Egyptian diva Umm Kulthum. In the Gulf, radios were nicknamed 'Ahmed Said boxes'. By 1959 there were 850,000 radios in Egypt and half a million in Morocco. They were set up in cafés or in village squares. Dozens of people listened to each one. For the first time, Arab mass opinion was created.

The problem for the Arabs was that Ahmed Said and his colleagues were just too convincing. As war came closer in 1967, Said's broadcasts became even more jingoistic. His listeners believed an easy victory was coming. Said believed he was doing for the Arabs what the BBC did for occupied Europe during the Second World War: 'You're asking people to fight, not to dance. I had to keep the soldiers going. Many of them had radios. And we were also asking the Arab world to be with us . . . We believed the broadcasts were our most powerful weapon . . . many of our listeners were illiterate, so radio was the most important way to reach them.'

Arabs often explain the broadcasts as exercises in sloganeering and rhetoric, not intended to be taken literally. But in 1967 most Arab listeners, even those with enough education to know better, were swept up in the excitement. The great mass of Arabs, especially the dispossessed Palestinians in their refugee camps, believed everything that Ahmed Said and his colleagues said. When reality crashed into their lives, their faith in their leaders only made defeat even more traumatic.

The gamble

Nasser was gambling for high stakes. It was, the Americans concluded, 'a massive power play which, if successful, will be his biggest political victory since Suez, even if no shot is fired . . . if the Israelis do not retaliate, Nasser will have forced them to back down and will have won the first Arab victory over Israelis, and incidentally will have won another victory over US in Arab eyes . . . He is playing for keeps and we should make no mistake in this regard.'

The next day, Monday 22 May, Nasser doubled the stakes. Israel had not called his bluff when he mobilised the army and reinforced the Sinai. So Nasser went one stage further. He banned Israeli shipping from the Straits of Tiran, the entrance to the Gulf of Aqaba, effectively reimposing the blockade of the port of Eilat that had been lifted in 1956. Nasser chose an airbase in the Sinai desert as the place to announce the news. 'The Israeli flag shall not go through the Gulf of Aqaba,' Nasser said. 'Our sovereignty over the entrance to the Gulf cannot be disputed. If Israel wishes to threaten war, we tell her, you are welcome.'

The wire services circulated a photo of Nasser, looking as debonair as ever, surrounded by equally happy young flyers. Some of them were wearing their cockpit pressure suits. White teeth flashed across the grainy black and white still. The image Nasser desired was pumped around the world – the leader of the Arabs challenging the Jewish state, surrounded by highly trained young experts ready for action. Nasser looks excited, almost like a child intoxicated by the enormity of the line that he has just crossed.

Forty-two minutes after the report from Cairo, the White House dispatched a letter from Johnson to Nasser. Denying that the United States was unfriendly to Egypt, the letter tried half-heartedly to suggest that Washington understood some of Nasser's preoccupations. The most important part of the letter dangled the prospect of a visit by Vice President Hubert H. Humphrey, 'if we come through these days without hostilities'. Johnson did not want to waste space on pleasantries. He scratched out the words 'with greatest respect' from the sentence before he approved it.

The announcement of the blockade embarrassed U Thant, the UN secretary general. He was in the air, travelling to Cairo on a belated peace mission when the news came through. By the time his Pan American airliner had taxied to a halt at Cairo International airport, the official welcoming party was swamped by a big crowd that rushed on to the tarmac, chanting slogans welcoming U Thant and glorifying Nasser. The press corps broke out of their pen to join them. The fastidious General Rikhye saw Mahmoud Riad, the Egyptian foreign minister, fighting his way over to them 'through sweaty, heaving, arm-flinging bodies'.

On the evening of 24 May U Thant and General Rikhye had dinner with Nasser at his villa in the Cairo military cantonment. Nasser had lived there since the early 1950s, when he was a lieutenant-colonel plotting to seize power. It was still the same relatively modest house, with an extension added to one side to give him an office and formal reception rooms. The UN delegation was received in a room furnished with golden chairs and sofas in the style of Louis XIV that was very popular among Cairo's middle classes. Nasser deployed all of his considerable charm. Disarmingly, he explained he had to close the straits before the secretary general reached Cairo because he knew U Thant was coming to ask him to keep them open. Personally, he did not want war. Egypt just wanted to get back what it lost in 1956, when it was the victim of British, French and Israeli aggression. He did not believe American assurances that Israel would not attack Syria. The CIA were out to kill him, and anyway they were saying something very similar just before Israel attacked Egypt in 1956.

Nasser led them past walls full of family photographs to the dining room. While they were eating he conceded that there was 'some foolhardy bravado' in the lower ranks of the army. At the senior level they were realistic. Egypt had been defeated in 1956. It was not a long time ago. But the army, if necessary, would do its job. He offered U Thant the same promise he had made to the Soviets and the Americans. Egypt would not fire the first shot. But if they were attacked, they would defend themselves. Back at his suite at the Nile

Hilton, overlooking Egypt's great, broad river and the lights of the capital, U Thant sat down with his advisers. Unless there was a way round the blockade, war was inevitable.

General Yariv, head of Israeli military intelligence, telephoned Rabin in the small hours on the morning of 23 May to tell him that Nasser had reimposed the blockade of Eilat. Rabin felt sick with worry. The morning papers had the story. Any idea that Nasser's actions were a charade had disappeared. The popular newspaper *Maariv* compared Nasser to Hitler and said he had declared war. For *Yediot Aharonot*, the other mass-circulation daily, the 'decisive day' had come, and just as they had done at Munich in 1938 when Hitler threatened Czechoslovakia, 'the great powers are abandoning those who are considered weak and are encouraging those who are considered strong'.

Rabin and responsibility

The day after Nasser closed the straits, Eshkol and the cabinet ordered a full mobilisation of Israeli forces. Israel was on a direct line to war. Mobilisation was a well-rehearsed procedure. In 48 hours 250,000 men could be put into the field. When an Israeli soldier completes his compulsory military service, he is allocated to a reserve unit. They exist only on paper, until they are called up for their annual training or for war. Mobilisation started with phone calls to the commanders of the most important units. One of them, a lawyer in civilian life, reported for duty with his private secretary and driver and 'within ninety minutes was busy getting his brigade out of the card index and into the field'. The message passed down the line to officers who called NCOs, who called the soldiers. Cars or lorries went from door to door to pick them up. Other units were called up by code words that were broadcast on the radio. The Israeli writer Abba Kovner, who led the revolt of the Jews in the Vilna ghetto in Poland in the Second World War, watched it happen.

I was leaning on a newspaper stall at the time. The newspaper seller was in the very act of stretching out his hand towards the paper I wanted when suddenly the voice caught his attention. His eyes widened, he looked through me rather than at me, and said, as if in surprise, 'Oh, they've called me up too.' He rolled up his papers and went. The salesgirl came out of the shop opposite, stopped jerkily at the door, adjusted her blouse, a little nervously, snapped her handbag shut, and walked off. A group of men stood huddled round a transistor in the middle of a patch of lawn. Whenever one of them heard his code word read out by the announcer, he detached himself from the group and left . . . a unique silence descended upon the town.

In a couple of days, most Israeli men under fifty were in some sort of uniform. Some units had a turnout of more than 100 per cent. Over-age men arrived at their unit's mobilisation points and demanded to be allowed to fight. One persistent 63-year-old, a veteran of the British army, was told his unit would only take him back if he brought a jeep. The next day he turned up with one from Hertz.

Full mobilisation made war feel much closer because the exodus of men effectively closed the economy down, and Israel could not do without its economy for long. The newspapers had been praising Israeli civilians' 'refusal to panic'. But after Nasser closed the straits housewives went on the offensive. By the evening of the 23rd, most of the supermarkets were empty. One columnist condemned 'rapacious animals at the canned goods shelves in the supermarkets . . . vultures with their shopping bags sagging down to the floor'. Some traders cashed in by putting up prices. The government opened its warehouses and flooded the shops with food. There were another few days of furious shopping before sales started getting back to normal around the 26th.

The pressure was crushing Rabin. The man who was responsible for planning the campaign was close to panic. Against all the military evidence, he convinced himself that he was leading Israel to catastrophe.

Rabin spent hours in angry, edgy meetings with the cabinet and with the military elite. Some of them wanted war. Others could not believe that Israel had been unable to head the crisis off. Rabin smoked pack after pack of cigarettes and hardly slept. On 23 May, after another frantic day that started at 4 a.m., he turned to David Ben-Gurion, who had led the fight for independence in 1948. He drove to his house, hoping for some guidance or consolation. Instead Ben-Gurion yelled at him. 'You have brought this state to this most dangerous situation. You are to blame for this! We must not go to war. We are isolated!'

Rabin was stunned. The leader of the National Religious Party, interior minister Haim Shapira, had shouted in the cabinet meeting: 'How dare you go to war? How dare you? We must dig in!' But now it was Ben-Gurion speaking, the most respected man in Israel.

'What if he's right? What if he's right?' Rabin asked himself, again and again as he paced up and down outside his house.

When he got himself inside, exhausted, distraught and panicking, he had a nervous collapse. At about eight in the evening he phoned his deputy, General Ezer Weizman, the head of the General Staff division, and asked him to come round to his house immediately. He was sitting on the edge of a settee, looking 'broken and depressed' when Weizman arrived. Rabin said he had made mistakes, led Israel into an entanglement that would be 'the greatest and hardest war the state has ever experienced'. Then, Weizman says, Rabin asked him to take over as chief of staff. Weizman told Rabin to pull himself together. He wanted the job but could not accept it. (It was not in Rabin's gift.) He told Rabin that his resignation would make the politicians even more hesitant about going to war. It would also be worth a few divisions to Nasser, would be a heavy blow to the morale of his own troops and would finish him for the rest of his life.

Ten years later, Rabin put it down to 'a combination of tension, exhaustion and the enormous amounts of cigarette smoke I had inhaled in recent days (I had suffered severe nicotine poisoning on two previous occasions). But it was more than nicotine that brought me down. The heavy sense of guilt that had been dogging me of late became unbearably strong on 23 May. I could not forget Ben-Gurion's words – You bear the responsibility . . .'

Rabin never said what he was guilty about. Perhaps it was his own policy of encouraging aggressive behaviour on the Syrian border. Rabin was an introspective man who bottled up pressure. He did not talk to his wife Leah about what was haunting him. She wrote after his death that the prospect of thousands of casualties was 'a crushing burden' to him. Ruhama Hermon, who ran Rabin's office, believes he broke because 'he was alone. There was terrible procrastination among the politicians. But among the generals there was a sense of confidence and determination. Rabin had to walk between the two. When he came back from seeing Ben-Gurion it was as if an extra boulder had been placed on his back. Every day his shoulders seemed to sag lower. He was sending young men off to war and he didn't know how many would come back . . .'

If only Rabin had realised. The blockade was all window-dressing, like so much else in Nasser's Egypt in 1967. Brigadier Abdel Moneim Khalil had been dispatched to Sharm al Sheikh with 4000 paratroopers on 19 May. On the 22nd he was sent orders by Cairo to impose a blockade, which he thought were contradictory and unenforceable. Israeli merchant ships were to receive shots across the bows and stern to stop them. Powerful coastal artillery had been delivered to do the job. But that was as far as the blockade went. No mines were laid in the shipping lanes. Brigadier Khalil's orders were to let all naval vessels through, even Israeli ones. Merchant convoys with a naval escort were also to be left alone.

Ready to fight

Israel's generals thought war was unavoidable, were confident they would win and wanted to get on with it. At the end of May an Israeli paratroop commander told his men that they would be fighting the same Arabs they had come up against in 1956, 'with the same deep chasm between officers and soldiers, with the same inferior fighting spirit, with the same tendency to disintegrate the moment something goes awry in their planning . . . they will crumble as their brothers did ten and twenty years ago.'

In 1967 Israel had the best armed forces in the Middle East by a long way. American and British military intelligence reports show Israel's existence was not in danger at any point. Together the Arab forces had more weapons than the Israelis. But they were incapable of mounting an offensive. The only way that the Israeli army could have lost would have been to decide not to fight.

Fifteen years of hard work had turned the IDF into the speedy, mobile force that had been envisaged in the early 1950s. Infantry rode into battle. Most heavy weapons were self-propelled. Even the chain of command was streamlined. Unlike most Western armed forces in 1967, Israel's army, air force and navy were fully integrated under one headquarters, commanded by Chief of Staff Rabin. Israel and Egypt had around the same number of tanks, armoured personnel carriers, artillery and self-propelled guns. But if Jordan and Syria were added the Arabs had a two-to-one advantage. In the air Israel and Egypt had about the same number of fighters, but Egypt had four times as many bombers. All that, though, would be cancelled out 'by the superior training and fighting effectiveness of the Israelis' and by attacks from their air force. Israel had other advantages. It could get its troops into the field faster and more effectively than the Arab armies. Its full force of twenty-six brigades (including four armoured and four mechanised) could be mobilised within forty-eight hours. In the same period Egypt could deploy a maximum of ten brigades, Syria six and Jordan eight. In the longer term the Arabs could find another five brigades between them. But, by then, Israel's plan was that the war could be over.

Just before war broke out, the US Joint Chiefs of Staff judged 'that Israel will be militarily unchallengeable by any combination of Arab states at least during the next five years. As presently trained and equipped, the armed forces of Israel are greatly superior in effectiveness and firepower to those of their potential opponents, individually or collectively.' Another report compiled on the eve of war, from the US National Military Command Center, judged that Israel had 'the most effective fighting force in the Middle East. It is highly literate, has a relatively young senior officer corps, and is highly motivated and patriotic. A large proportion of its officers and NCOs have had battle experience. The Israeli army is considered capable of defeating the forces of any or all of its Arab neighbours and could offer effective delaying action against the ground forces of a major power.' The report also accurately predicted Israel's chosen strategy: 'Israel, numerically outnumbered in combat aircraft and lacking territory and bases to effect adequate dispersion, must rely upon a pre-emptive strike to gain air parity or air superiority. Israel can, in a surprise attack, cause sufficient losses among UAR [Egyptian] and Syrian aircraft and facilities to render them unable to take effective offensive measures.' Even if Israel used its air force in a purely defensive role, it 'can maintain air parity'.

The British estimates were very similar. Six weeks before the war started, the British cabinet's Joint Intelligence Committee compared the armed forces of Israel and its main Arab enemies, Egypt, Syria and Jordan. At every level, Israel was far ahead. The study concluded that it was 'inconceivable' that the Arabs would improve their efficiency and morale to a point where they could beat Israel. The British defence attaché in Tel Aviv, a professional soldier, believed that 'in command, training, equipment and services the Israel army is more prepared for war than ever before. Well trained, tough, self-reliant, the Israeli soldier has a strong fighting spirit and would willingly go to war in defence of his country.' Before he was assailed by panic, General Rabin felt his country was secure. Israel 'enjoys superiority over her enemies which seems to be assured for many years to come . . .' and he could 'see nothing which would upset Israel's superiority in the next three or four years.' The British intelligence services thought General Rabin's estimate was 'conservative'.

Israel's major strategic objective was a nuclear weapon. In 1967 the Americans had deep suspicions that Israel had already built a bomb. Israel had a contract to buy the MD-620 surface-to-surface missile from the French firm, Dassault. Nothing had been delivered by 1967, but the Americans assumed that the missiles were being acquired as a delivery system for nuclear warheads. Periodically the Israelis allowed American inspections of their nuclear reactor at Dimona in the Negev desert. At their last visit before the war, on 22 April 1967, Israel was producing enough plutonium to make one or two bombs a year. They found no evidence that bombs were being made there but were concerned that they could be being made somewhere else. What deepened their suspicions was Israel's refusal to tell them what had happened to 80–100 tons of uranium it had bought from Argentina in 1964. Israel, they believed, also had a nuclear chemical separation plant – a big step towards a weapons capability. In May 1967 the Americans concluded that, at the very least, Israel could build a bomb at short notice if it wanted to do so. Top US military and intelligence chiefs disagreed about the findings. Richard Helms, the Director of Central Intelligence, was definite that there were no nuclear weapons in the area. General Earle Wheeler, chairman of the Joint Chiefs of Staff, declared himself 'more sceptical'.

The Egyptians could not build a nuclear power station, let alone nuclear weapons. In the 1950s Egypt hired German scientists to produce an Arab super weapon. But, by 1967, the scientists had left and Egypt's much-hyped missiles –which did not work – were no more than useful props at military parades. Experts at the US National Military Command Center analysed Egyptian strength on the eve of war. They concluded that it would stay on the defensive. Its three-to-two superiority in tanks 'would be insufficient to launch a successful attack against the Israelis without air superiority'. Another problem was the quality of its soldiers. 'The Egyptian army is capable of stubborn resistance in a static defense, but has difficulty adjusting to the fluid, rapidly changing mobile warfare which would be required against the Israelis.' The Egyptians also had 'chronic' problems with logistics. 'The enlisted men are often illiterate and difficult to train as mechanics and repairmen . . .'

Eban

Israel's generals knew how strong the IDF was and how weak were its enemies. They were angry and frustrated when the politicians vetoed an immediate military strike. They were incandescent when the foreign minister, Abba Eban, was sent to Washington to see whether the Americans could find a way out short of war. The generals were left fuming and putting the finishing touches to war plans they believed they would soon be using.

Abba Eban was familiar to television viewers across the world. His colleagues sometimes found him irritating and self-important, especially when he was enjoying the 'glory of the television cameras'. Since 1948 he had been the public face of Israeli diplomacy as their first ambassador to the UN and then ambassador to Washington. He started life as Aubrey Solomon in Cape Town in 1915, but he grew up in Britain where, via a classical education in London and triple first in Classics and Oriental languages at Cambridge he became a tall, cultivated and plump man. Eban's Zionist credentials were as strong as his academic ones. When he was two, his mother translated the Balfour Declaration, which was Britain's promise to the Jews of a state in Palestine, into French and Russian. Eban became an active Zionist, but his first visit to Jerusalem in 1942 was as a major in the British army, the liaison between the Special Operations Executive and the Jewish Agency for Palestine.

Eban arrived in Washington on Thursday 25 May after stopping over in Paris and London. In Paris President Charles de Gaulle dismissed Eban's argument that Nasser had started hostilities by blockading the straits. He told him that Israel must not fire the first shot. In London Prime Minister Harold Wilson sat him in the Cabinet Room at Number 10, lit his pipe and was much more reassuring. Both countries continued arms deliveries to Israel. A couple of days earlier Britain had come up with an idea for solving the crisis. With the Americans they would organise an international naval force to open the Straits of Tiran. The mere threat of it, they hoped, might persuade Nasser to back down.

Eban did a lot of thinking on the seven-hour flight across the Atlantic. More than anything, he wanted to avoid a rerun of 1956, when Israel was branded as an aggressor and forced to give back what it had taken. If Israel was to fight, it had to be with American consent. At the airport the biggest crowd of reporters and TV cameramen that he had ever seen wanted to know whether he was asking American soldiers to risk their lives for Israel – a big issue at a time when the US had half a million soldiers in Vietnam. No, he told them, all he wanted was for Washington to respect Israel's right to defend itself.

The Israeli ambassador Avraham Harman drove in with Eban the Mayflower hotel in downtown Washington DC. In the car he gave him a personal, top-secret message from Eshkol. Eban read it and had 'one of the severest shocks' of his life. He said nothing. When they got to his suite, 'he paced up and down . . . read the cable again, flung it on a table, as he used to do with papers which utterly displeased him, and in a tone of command completely unnatural for him he snapped: "Read it."' The telegram said Egypt would attack within twenty-four hours. Eshkol ordered him not to contact Israel to discuss the message. It was too risky. Instead he was to ask President Johnson immediately for 'practical, repeat practical measures' to deal with the 'anticipated explosion'. Johnson must declare publicly that any attack on Israel would be considered an attack on the United States. Eban, at the airport, had just told the world's press that that was one thing he was not going to do.

While Eban was crossing the Atlantic the IDF's generals and Yigal Allon, their leading ally in the cabinet, put Eshkol under huge pressure. Allon was minister of labour, Rabin's old commander in the Palmach and a national hero ever since his exploits in the war of independence. The generals and Allon made up a formidable military lobby, straining at the leash, utterly confident that Israel would win. On 24 May General Hofi, the head of operations in the General Staff, summed up their mood. 'We have no problems on the ground. As for the Jordanians, what they do depends on how well we screw the Egyptians.' Tanks, artillery and troops were everywhere they were needed. Above them was the air force. Even Egypt's poison gas did not worry Hofi. According to British intelligence sources Egypt had already carried out around a dozen attacks in Yemen in 1967, using phosgene and mustard gas, killing some 800 people, including many women and children. Hofi dismissed the threat. The air force would knock them out – the flyers were 'our best gas mask'. The only worry was that the longer they left it, the bloodier it would be. They convinced Eshkol to cable Eban that Egyptian tanks were repositioning for attack. Rabin, who had gone back to work after his breakdown, rewrote it to make it sharper. It was going to be a 'total, repeat total struggle'.

Icily, Eban suggested Rabin was still suffering from 'nervousness' after his collapse. It was 'a hypochondriac cable . . . [lacking] wisdom, veracity and tactical understanding'. Eban judged correctly that Nasser wanted victory without war. He thought Rabin was pushing him to ask Johnson for promises that he could not deliver so Israel would not be blamed for going to war. As a diplomat, he wanted to persuade Johnson to offer support, not to embarrass him by putting the US on the spot. But the military men were getting impatient. They wanted action, not talk.

Israel had wind of an Egyptian plan, called Operation Lion, to thrust into the Negev desert to cut off Eilat, which would be bombed. It was a pet scheme of Field Marshal Amer's, which he had been pushing Nasser for since the start of the crisis. After a succession of false starts, vetoed by Nasser, the latest time for the attack was 27 May. As soon as Nasser knew what Amer wanted he cancelled it. He intended to heed warnings from Washington and Moscow about not shooting first. Lieutenant-General Amer Khammash, Jordan's chief of staff, was in Cairo just before Eban went to Washington. He concluded that the Egyptians had no meaningful offensive plans. They were 'playing a political game rather than preparing for war . . . and did not expect there would be a need to fight a war'.

Washington

As the US Marine helicopter took off from Andrews Air Force Base, President Lyndon Baines Johnson was uneasy. He was on his way back to the White House after spending the day at EXPO 67 in Montreal. President Johnson knew Abba Eban was in town wanting public support. Johnson was going to have to go carefully. The USA was not the unchallenged hyperpower that it became by the end of the century. The Vietnam war was eating away at his and the US military's view of their own power. In Moscow they had what seemed a threatening and dynamic enemy. Johnson's own instincts were deeply pro-Israel, but he wanted to know what exactly America's obligations were and how much danger Israel really faced. The last thing he needed was another war.

During the ten-minute flight to the South Lawn of the White House, he asked for a compilation of every statement every president had ever made on Israel. He knew that in 1957, as part of the package of measures that accompanied Israel's withdrawal from the Sinai desert after its last war with Egypt, President Eisenhower had promised to keep the Gulf of Aqaba open. Promises that public were not easy to bury. On top of that, there was a more general assurance that the US would never allow Israel's destruction. Johnson needed to know whether Israel's existence really was at risk.

Johnson had the nasty feeling that the US might have to deal with the crisis without any of its major allies – just like Vietnam, where only Australia was contributing troops. When they landed on the South Lawn, Walt Rostow went straight to his office in the basement. He was LBJ's closest adviser on foreign affairs. They spoke almost every hour of every working day. The president would buzz down or phone and Rostow would hurry up the stairs to the Oval Office. Waiting in Rostow's office for the president to return were Dean Rusk, the Secretary of State and Richard Helms, the Director of Central Intelligence, who was carrying the latest intelligence report. It analysed information from Mossad, Israel's secret intelligence service, that Israel was at a 'turning point'. Egypt and Syria, Mossad claimed, were ready to strike.

The CIA rejected the Israeli warning as not 'a serious estimate of the sort they would submit to their high officials. We think it is probably a gambit intended to influence the United States to do one or more of the following: A) provide more military supplies B) make more public commitments to Israel C) approve Israeli military initiatives D) put more pressure on Nasser.' Twenty minutes after the helicopter from Andrews had landed, Rostow passed the Mossad document and the CIA's assessment up to the Oval Office. He scrawled a note to Johnson. Israeli anxieties and the desire of Nasser and the USSR to pick up prestige made for an 'explosive' mix.

Before they went in to see the president, Helms said he stood by what his people said, even though it was very different to what Israel was saying. Rusk sighed. 'Well, I just want to tell you this . . . if it's a mistake, it's a beaut.' Upstairs, in the Oval Office, Johnson sat in his rocking chair at the head of a coffee table in front of the fireplace. The other men sat down on cream sofas on either side. The table had a sliding drawer, containing the most high-tech phone 1967 had to offer. Close to his desk were two tall glass-faced cabinets, housing news agency tickers. Next to them were three black and white televisions, one for each network, encased in polished cabinets.

The president was not convinced. Too many over-optimistic reports from Vietnam had made him cautious about intelligence. He asked Helms and General Earle Wheeler, chairman of the Joint Chiefs of Staff, who had joined them, to have the information 'scrubbed down'. In the course of that day, the CIA, the US Defense Intelligence Agency and the British all reassessed what was happening in the Sinai. They all concluded that the Egyptian deployments were defensive. Israel was not showing any signs of going on the offensive, but as more intelligence reports stressed in the next few days, it was capable of attacking with little or no warning if it wanted to do so. According to Defense Secretary Robert McNamara, 'The only difference between the British and us was how long it would take the Israelis to beat the Egyptians. I have forgotten whether we thought it could be done in seven days and they in ten, or vice versa.' The CIA version concluded that Israel would beat all its Arab neighbours in about a week. Richard Helms summed it up: 'If the Israelis attacked first, it was going to be a short war. If the Egyptians attacked first, it was going to be a longer war, but there wasn't any question about who was going to win it . . .'

The CIA also analysed Nasser's behaviour. Moscow was not telling him what to do. Senior Soviet officials insisted that Nasser had acted on his own when he closed the gulf. The CIA's conclusions, written on 26 May 1967 and not declassified until the end of 2000, still stand up. Nasser, it said, was responding to Israel's threats to Syria. It was 'highly unlikely' that he wanted war. He had not changed his view (shared by the CIA and his allies in Moscow) that the Arabs could not beat Israel. But Nasser was gambling that his army could resist an Israeli offensive, as long as he could get enough men and machines into the Sinai in time. Nasser was hoping for a big political victory to relieve the pressure at home. The Egyptian economy was in bad shape and relations with the US were disastrous. There could also have been a 'fatalistic conclusion that a showdown with Israel must come sooner or later, and might best be provoked before Israel acquired nuclear weapons'.

Nasser, the CIA judged, had won the first round. Israel faced 'dismaying choices'. It had failed to take 'the instant military counteraction which might have been most effective'. It would still win a war quickly, but with heavy losses. War was not attractive for Israel, but neither was doing nothing. Allowing the permanent closure of the Straits of Tiran was an 'economic and political setback from which no early recovery would be foreseeable'. The CIA warned that unless the US and other major powers reopened the straits, the Israelis would 'feel compelled' to go to war.

President Johnson went to bed knowing that Israel had a serious problem, but satisfied that its existence was not in danger. Just before he finished for the evening he wrote to Harold Wilson in London that 'we are not inclined to be as alarmed as they appear to be'. The biggest danger now to US interests was Israel taking matters into its own hands, a point he planned to get over to Eban, who wanted to see him the next day. 'We are also urging upon Eban the real danger of any pre-emptive action by the Israelis which would create an impossible situation in the Middle East as well as in the US.'

Eban and his team went for cocktails and dinner at the State Department, in Foggy Bottom, close to the River Potomac in north-west Washington. So many reporters and cameramen were waiting in the State Department lobby on C Street that Eban was hustled in to the building through the basement.

As Secretary of State Dean Rusk poured the drinks he warned Eban that the president would not be offering him a NATO-style guarantee. Eban wasn't surprised: 'I did not get the impression that the US had ever decided to enter a new and complicated defence alliance between cocktails and the first course of a dinner party.' But over the dinner table, on the roof of the State Department on a balmy midsummer night, the Israelis had their own warnings for Rusk. Nasser had 'declared war' when he blocked the straits. It was a time bomb and in Israel, the mood of the cabinet was 'apocalyptic'. The choice was to 'surrender or fight'.

Just after 1:30 p.m. the next day, President Johnson summoned his main diplomatic and military advisers. What was he going to tell Eban? He needed advice and wanted it fast. The Texan looked round the table. 'Along about sundown I have to bell this cat. I need to know what I am going to say.' President Johnson was reassured that Israel was in no danger it could not handle. But Johnson was America's shrewdest politician, who dominated Capitol Hill before he became John F. Kennedy's vice-president. He knew he had to give Eban something for the Israeli cabinet.

But deciding what took time. The Israelis had an anxious afternoon, waiting for the White House to call. Ephraim Evron, the number two at the Israeli Embassy, had known Johnson since he was a senator. He went to the White House to fix a time for Eban's appointment. In the Oval Office Johnson told him that he could not do anything without the approval of Congress, 'otherwise, I'm just a six foot four friend Texan'. With the help of Britain and other maritime nations, the straits could be opened, but Israel must not try any 'unilateral action that will cause her great damage'. Eban was still being stalked by news teams. To avoid them the plan was that the foreign minister and Ambassador Harman would go into the White House through the diplomats' entrance. But they turned up at the wrong gate, where the guard would not let them in. The Israeli foreign minister preserved his dignity as the guard phoned into the executive mansion that 'some guy out here by the name of Eban says he is supposed to see the President'.

The Israelis were finally ushered into the Oval Office at 7:15 p.m. Both sides were keyed up. Johnson wanted to finesse his way between his genuine commitment to Israel and his desire to keep the United States out of another shooting war. Eban had to take something home for the impatient generals. He opened by saying that there had never been a moment like this in Israeli history. Nasser was trying to strangle Israel, which would fight and win rather than surrender. An Arab attack was coming soon. What was the United States going to do? Would it honour its commitment to keep the straits open? What was happening with the plan for an international maritime force to open the straits?

Johnson told him not to worry. Israel was not in imminent danger. If the Arabs attacked, the Israelis 'would lick them'. You can tell the cabinet, the president said, that 'we will pursue vigorously any and all possible measures to keep the strait open'. But Israel must not initiate hostilities. Johnson then spoke with what the official White House note-taker said was 'emphasis and solemnity'. Israel would not be alone unless it decides to go it alone. He repeated the sentence to make sure they understood. Johnson and his aides hoped that the carefully composed formula would stop the Israelis from launching a pre-emptive strike. The president used all the skills he had acquired in a lifetime of political persuasion. He was pushing for Congressional support. 'What I can do, I do,' he told them. He handed over some of his notes. Copy them if you like, he said.

Then it was Eban's turn to speak slowly and precisely. What was the US doing to take action in the straits? Nasser would think twice about stopping a ship if he saw it had a British or American flag. Looking at Johnson he asked, 'I would not be wrong if I told the Prime Minister that your disposition is to make every possible effort to ensure that the Strait and the Gulf will remain open to free and innocent passage?' One word came from Johnson. 'Yes.' And don't worry about an Egyptian attack, he said again. An attack from Egypt was not imminent. If it came, 'you'll whip hell out of them'.

At dinner that evening in the executive mansion Johnson thought he had given the Israelis, if not exactly what they wanted, then at least enough to hold them back. He was exultant, crowing, 'They came loaded for bear, but so was I! I let them talk for the first hour and then I finished it up in the last fifteen minutes. Secretary McNamara said he just wanted to throw his cap into the air, and George Christian [the White House Press Secretary] said it was the best meeting of the kind he had ever sat in on.'

Eban left immediately for home. On the way back he stopped off at the Waldorf Towers hotel for two hours, where he met the US ambassador to the UN, Arthur Goldberg, who deliberately tried to damp down what the president had said. Don't forget, he said, that Johnson said he needed the support of Congress before he did anything. That meant that Eban should assume that the presidential commitment was conditional – and Washington would tolerate no surprises.

Eban and his team arrived back in Tel Aviv late on the evening of Saturday 27 May. They were driven straight to the prime minister's office in Tel Aviv where the cabinet had started what turned into an all-night session. The army was ready to attack the following morning. Rabin, who was there too, warned Moshe Raviv, Eban's political assistant, that not going to war was going to be 'very difficult'. Eban urged the ministers to respect the American request for more time to work on opening the straits. After a fierce debate, nine ministers voted for Eban's proposition. Nine voted for immediate war. Overnight, there was another message from President Johnson warning against pre-emptive action. The next morning, the 28th, the cabinet agreed to give the Americans another two weeks.

Frustration oozed out of Yigal Allon. Israel, he said reluctantly, was committed to playing the American game. But it would go to war if it found credible intelligence that Egypt was about to strike the

Israeli air force. The American ambassador Walworth Barbour, a reclusive, very tall, immensely fat man with chronic emphysema, was especially close to General Yariv, the head of military intelligence. He reported that, 'They feel they can finish Nasser off . . . they are prepared to wait a few weeks but are maintaining mobilisation at top level which cannot be done indefinitely without serious economic effects [on] Israel.' The fact that it was Eban who had caused the delay was particularly infuriating. His classical education, often orotund style and metropolitan ways played brilliantly in the West but had always got under the skin of more down-to-earth *sabras*, native-born Israelis, who had spent their early years milking cows and mounting guard rather than reading Homer. They thought he was just plain wrong. What was he doing wasting his time over promises the Americans may or may not keep in the Straits of Tiran when the real issue had become the Egyptian divisions in the Sinai? General Yariv was furious. As far as he and other generals were concerned, Eban had disobeyed his orders. Tiran was 'not important'. What mattered was the big picture. Nasser was uniting the entire Arab world against Israel. Eban should have taken the cable that Rabin had rewritten more seriously. A rumour was started by Eban's enemies that he would be replaced by Golda Meir.

Nasser's bandwagon

The Egyptian capital was calmer than it had been. In the papers the government ran campaigns to give one day's wages to the army and to give blood at the newly opened donor centres around Cairo. There was no rush of volunteers. The minister of culture arranged for intellectuals to tour the provinces to make speeches and declaim patriotic verse to inspire the masses. For the foreigners who were left, Cairo was bleak. The American Embassy, desperate for something positive, was comforted that critical voices in the press and radio, which had 'reached upper decibel range . . . now describe British as our accomplice in the plot so we no longer alone'.

For Nasser, 28 May was an excellent day. The world's press waited for him as he strode confidently into the floodlit, circular council chamber of the Presidential Palace. A British foreign correspondent, Sandy Gall of ITN, felt Nasser's charisma. 'Physically he was an impressive man, tall for an Egyptian, well built, handsome and with a film star quality that turned heads and made him the centre of attention. But his most noticeable feature was his smile. It came on like an electric light, the shiny white teeth flashing on and off.' Among Arabs, his prestige had never been higher.

It was a confident, assured performance, broadcast live on radio in Egypt and, through Voice of the Arabs, across the Arab world. The crisis over UNEF and the Straits of Tiran, Nasser told them, were just 'symptoms' of the constant threat to the Arab world posed by Israeli aggression against Palestine. What could be more natural than an Egyptian response? He threatened anyone who tried to 'touch the rights of Egyptian sovereignty' with 'unimaginable damage'. Nasser warmed to his theme. Israel had been deceived by its 'sham victory' in 1956. Coexistence was not possible because Israel had robbed the Palestinians and expelled them from their country. Palestinian rights must be restored and Eshkol would get what was coming to him for threatening 'to march on Damascus, occupy Syria and overthrow the Syrian Arab regime'. Winston Burdett of CBS News thought Nasser sounded like a 'sleepwalker speaking in an exalted trance of fatalism'. But a British diplomat who was listening reported that Nasser was 'riding high and working coolly and cleverly'.

American diplomats in Cairo listened with dismay, certain that a crisis was becoming a disaster. The US position in the Arab world, already weak, was about to be destroyed. Nasser, they believed, would not turn back, except perhaps if he was faced with the threat of clear and overwhelming force. Even then, he would turn a retreat in the face of American power into a major political victory. They accepted he did not want to fire the first shot. But he hoped a showdown with Israel would strengthen his position in the Arab world. They dismissed a theory put around by some Nasser-watchers in Washington, who detected hints that he would let oil pass through the straits to Israel, as long as it went quietly in neutral tankers.

After Nasser had finished, King Hussein's private secretary, Ziad Rifai, switched off the radio he kept on the desk of his office in Amman. What Nasser had said, and the way he said it, meant war was coming. The king, who had been listening in his quarters in the palace, felt the same. Hussein's first reaction to Nasser's blockade of Eilat was that it was 'incomprehensible and extremely dangerous'. But he decided that his only chance was to try to repair relations with Nasser. New light has been thrown on Hussein's reasons for taking his decision by recently declassified CIA documents. The CIA had a special relationship with Hussein. For many years it channelled secret subsidies to the king. The CIA station chief in Amman, Jack O'Connel, became Hussein's close confidant. He reported that the king and his generals were more convinced than ever that the West Bank was Israel's 'strategic target'. Jordan's generals were pressing very strongly for coordination of defensive plans with other Arab states. Failure to do it, they argued, meant that they would lose more soldiers and more territory. The CIA reported that 'the army's mood was determined, their argument was irrefutable and the King faced serious morale and loyalty problems if he did not respond to it'.

Hussein warned Washington that its unilateral support of Israel was endangering its 'traditional Arab friends', a reference to himself. He warned them that he might oppose the US to 'survive the Arab wrath'. Even so, his friendship with the US might have made him 'too vulnerable to survive'.

Hussein realised that even if Nasser's actions were a lousy way to prepare for a war, they had propelled him right back into the hearts and minds of Arabs everywhere, and nowhere more so than among Palestinians on the West Bank. For Hussein, it all came down to survival. He could feel the Arab political bandwagon that had started in Cairo rumbling threateningly towards him. If he did not jump on to it, he would be squashed. War was coming and he would not be able to stay out of it. He was just too close to the action.

An alliance with the viciously anti-Hashemite regime in Syria seemed out of the question. Jordan did not even have diplomatic relations with Damascus. The king withdrew his ambassador after a lorry filled with explosives blew up at Ramtha on the Jordanian side of the border with Syria on 21 May, killing twenty-one Jordanians. Syria accused the king's men of planting the bomb. Hussein's court became convinced that the radicals in Syria saw the king as the real enemy, not Israel. All that was left to him was a reconciliation with Nasser. Hussein's reading of Israel's intentions, and the pressure from his generals and the people on the streets, especially Palestinians, left him with no choice. If he stayed out, an 'eruption' would cause his regime to collapse, which 'would result in an Israeli occupation of probably the West Bank or even more than the West Bank'. If he fought, Egyptian air cover might delay Israel's advance into the West Bank long enough for the UN to intervene. In his official business he gave the impression that he had become 'a lonely man'.

Just after dawn on the morning of Tuesday 30 May, King Hussein left for Cairo. He strode from his car to the plane, scribbling his signature on papers appointing his younger brother Prince Mohamed as regent while he was away. He told them to expect him back for lunch. Hussein was tense, excited and in a hurry. He was wearing a khaki combat uniform with field marshal's insignia, and a big American Magnum automatic handgun in a canvas holster on his left hip. The king found flying calmed him so he took the controls of the Jordanian Caravelle. He flew it south across the desert, over Petra, Wadi Rum and the Red Sea towards Cairo.

Nasser was waiting at the airbase, as usual wearing an immaculate business suit, in high good humour and in the mood for banter. He looked at the king.

'I see you are armed and in uniform.'

'It means nothing,' said the king, 'we've been dressing this way for more than a week.'

'Since your visit is a secret,' Nasser replied, 'what would happen if we arrested you?'

Hussein, who had travelled with his prime minister and his top generals but without bodyguards, smiled. 'The possibility never crossed my mind.'

It was a little awkward. They got into a black Cadillac and swept off to the Koubbeh palace. Nasser and Hussein went into a small drawing room on the first floor and started to talk. Field Marshal Abd al-Hakim Amer joined them. He was in a bullish mood. He told Hussein that Egypt did not need anything from him. 'We just want you to sit and watch what we are going to do with them. We are going to destroy them.' The king thought Amer's performance was absurd. He tried to convince Amer and Nasser that Israel was too strong and that they were risking a disaster. Don't worry, they told him. We know what we're doing. Nasser and Hussein were fatalistic. Both of them said, apparently sincerely, that whether the battle was lost or won, they could not shy away from the fight. Arab dignity demanded nothing less. (The CIA commented that 'dignity has unquestionably become an overriding priority in the scale of Arab considerations'.) The king asked to see the pact Egypt had signed with Syria. 'I merely skimmed the text and said to Nasser: "Give me another copy. Put in Jordan instead of Syria and the matter will be settled."'

They relaxed. Nasser and Hussein agreed that he would take back with him the leader of the PLO, Ahmed Shukairy. He came in, the king recalled with distaste, 'bareheaded, tieless, in a long-sleeved shirt and khaki pants, looking particularly unkempt'. In fiery speeches he had been hurling abuse at Hussein, 'the Hashemite harlot' who threw Palestinians into his 'towers'. Now he was ingratiating, all smiles, telling Hussein he was the real leader of the Palestinians. Nasser turned to the king. 'Take Shukairy with you. If he gives you any trouble, throw him into one of your towers and rid me of the problem.'

At 3:30 p.m., Cairo Radio interrupted its programmes with a news flash announcing the pact. Jordanians and Palestinians in Hussein's kingdom were amazed and delighted. The king was mobbed as he drove back to his palace from the airport. The deliriously happy crowds were more convinced than ever that victory was certain. They hated the Israelis and believed Nasser's propaganda. Hussein, though, was not deluded by his new fans who were trying to lift up his Mercedes so they could carry it to the palace. Nasser had been the real winner. The deal he had made only granted the Hashemites a reprieve. The crowds loved him because Nasser had accepted him, not the other way around. 'I knew that war was inevitable. I knew that we were going to lose. I knew that we in Jordan were threatened, threatened by two things: we either followed the course we did, or alternatively the country would tear itself apart if we stayed out, and Israel would march into the West Bank and even beyond.'

After he came back from Cairo, Hussein toured his units in the West Bank with his cousin Prince Zaid Ben Shaker. They started with the armoured brigade that Ben Shaker commanded, which was just inside the West Bank. Ben Shaker gathered all the senior officers. The king spoke frankly. 'He told the officers, "I am convinced that we are not going to win this war. I hope we do not get involved in this war but if we do, all I ask you to do is your best, respect your traditions and remember that you are fighting for your country" . . . And he said that time and again in every formation in the West Bank. In the car when we were going from one place to another he'd say, "I hope to God that there won't be a war but I think there will be one." He feared the worst from the very beginning.'

Fear

Strict military censorship meant that Israel's generals kept to themselves their overwhelming confidence about the coming victory. Cut off from official reassurance, Israeli civilians were desperately worried. Bloodthirsty threats were pouring out of Arab radio stations and on to the pages of the Israeli papers. Only twenty-two years after the end of the Holocaust, it is not surprising that Arab propaganda hit home. The official army minder attached to the British journalist Winston Churchill Jr told him that he was ready to kill his wife and baby daughter rather than let them fall into the hands of the Arabs. The crisis was especially frightening to Jews in the Diaspora, who looked at the map and saw tiny Israel surrounded by big, threatening neighbours. It all sounded appalling in Europe and the US, and helped strengthen already strong Western sympathies for Israel, which looked like a friendly democracy surrounded by a baying, murderous mob.

Translated, the Arab broadcasts are blood-curdling. No wonder many Israelis were scared stiff. Ahmed Said on Voice of the Arabs told his audience in a typical broadcast: 'We have nothing for Israel except war – comprehensive war . . . marching against its gangs, destroying and putting an end to the whole Zionist existence . . . our aim is to destroy the myth which says that Israel is here to stay . . . every one of the 100 million Arabs has been living for the past nineteen years on one hope – to live to die on the day Israel is liquidated. There is no life, no peace or hope for the gangs of Zionism to remain in the occupied land.' Faced with what seemed to be horribly clear threats from their biggest neighbour, Israelis pulled together.

A doom-laden mood overtook Israel in May 1967. Black jokes about imminent annihilation circulated – 'will the last one out at the airport turn off the lights – let's meet after the war . . . where? In a phone booth . . .' According to a kibbutznik on the border with Syria, 'Suddenly everyone was talking about Munich, about the Holocaust, about the Jewish people being left to its fate. A new Holocaust did not seem as real a possibility to us as it did to the people of Europe; for us it was a concrete picture of an enemy victory, and we decided that, come what might, we would prevent it.' The youngest Holocaust survivors were still in their twenties, but they were not given any special treatment in a society that valued military strength above all else. Native-born Israelis were brought up in the 1950s and '60s to reject what they assumed was the weakness and passivity of Jews who did not fight when the Nazis came.

The government made secret preparations for heavy casualties. Thousands of coffins were ordered. Rabbis consecrated parks as emergency cemeteries. During May, more and more men were called up into the army. Children delivered the mail, newspapers and milk, dug trenches and, when they finally got to school, practised air raid drills. The Civil Defence Corps, fully mobilised by 26 May, pasted up instructions in the streets, stockpiled medical supplies and made sure the shelters were clean and in good order. Civilians were drafted into essential services if they were not in the army. The working week was extended from forty-seven hours to a maximum of seventy-one. Vehicles were called up into national service as well. Yellow labels printed with the words 'mobilised equipment' were stuck on to their windscreens. Bread lorries, buses and their drivers were sent to the front to transport troops. Hitch-hiking became the most common form of transport. The insurance companies rallied around, extending driver's policies to cover hitch-hikers. In Tel Aviv, volunteer taxis ran along discontinued bus routes. In Haifa, second-hand car dealers offered vehicles and drivers. Some people started up shuttle services to and from military bases. Women with cars adopted shops and acted as their van drivers, picking up supplies from warehouses. By the Thursday before the war, 1 June, so few able-bodied men were left out of uniform that a visitor from the US thought Tel Aviv was like a 'sunny, sparsely populated colony for the infirm. Even the taxi driver wore a leather glove concealing an artificial hand . . .'

In Israel tens of thousands of pints of blood were donated. In Arab Jerusalem it was more casual. Towards the end of May a local journalist heard an appeal for donations on the radio. When he went to give blood at the Red Crescent centre in the Old City it was empty. The staff were not sure why he was there. 'Had there been an injury in the family? At which hospital was the patient? Forty-five minutes passed before Nabil could yield his patriotic pint.'

In Israeli factories clerks offered to work on the shop floors. People did unpaid overtime. Women took on jobs left empty by husbands and sons who were in the army. Taxpayers settled bills they had been trying to forget about, or even paid their taxes in advance. Other people just sent money to the government. Police officers who were not in the army gave back 10 per cent of their monthly pay. Foreigners who were studying at religious schools in Israel asked for military training. Religious Jews, who did not have to do army service and were often involved in furious rows with Israel's secular establishment, declared their own ceasefire for the duration, cancelling demonstrations against driving on the Sabbath in Jerusalem and against autopsies in Haifa. The rabbis told soldiers the obligations of the Sabbath were suspended.

Eshkol

On the morning of Sunday 28 May Israel's prime minister Levi Eshkol was exhausted. But there was no chance to rest. The next item on his agenda was a live radio broadcast to the nation. The people wanted reassurance and leadership. Eshkol tried to say all the right things, praising the strength of the army and the spirit of the country. But he fluffed his lines. The prime minister was reading from a script that had been written in a hurry. On his copy words had been changed around, crossed out and added on. Some of it was just military jargon. And he had not bothered to rehearse. When the red light went on he stumbled and stammered his way through the most damaging few minutes of his political life. It was a disaster. The irony was that Eshkol was correct. The IDF was in good shape. In Washington that day, both morning and afternoon White House intelligence situation reports stressed that 'nothing had changed to alter the findings of the 26 May special report of the Watch Committee. There is no information which would indicate that Egypt intends to attack. At the same time, the Israelis could attack with little or no warning if they decided to.'

Eshkol's wife Miriam was listening to the broadcast. She ordered her driver to take her straight to the studios. Her husband was angry, 'his advisers all running around like mice'. The broadcast was bad enough. For Eshkol, it was about to get much worse. At eight in the evening he was supposed to see the IDF high command. He was late. The generals had been listening to the radio and were very unhappy about what they had heard. As they waited the tension mounted. Brig. Gen. Ariel Sharon was angry about politicians who seemed to have run out of ideas. 'We felt as if the burden was on our shoulders.'

Sharon had been a famous soldier since the 1950s when he created Unit 101, an irregular unit that used brutal tactics, often killing civilians, in reprisal raids into Gaza and the West Bank. Now he was commanding a division that was poised to storm into the Sinai desert. When Eshkol arrived they were waiting in a conference room just off the main war room. Under harsh new strip lights that had just been put in, the generals' faces looked pale and grim. The air was clogged with cigarette smoke and the atmosphere was hostile and emotional. Nobody offered Eshkol any refreshments.

The generals gave him a roasting. They were furious, desperate for action, humiliated by the wait and utterly confident of the IDF's ability to win. Aharon Yariv, the head of military intelligence, started with a 'tongue-lashing'. Then the others lined up to condemn Eshkol. Sharon said, 'Our own actions have cancelled out the IDF's power to deter. We have removed our own principal weapon – fear of us.' Israel Tal demanded 'a clear war . . . The government's decision is not clear enough. We are entitled to clear instructions.' Uzi Narkiss mocked the Egyptians: 'They are soap bubbles – a pin will burst them . . . I don't know your views on the army. We here are all twenty years and more in the army and I want to tell you, this is a fantastic army. There is no need for concern.' Avraham Yoffe, called out of retirement to command a division, told the prime minister that he was stopping the army doing the job for which it was created. He and Brig. Gen. Matityahu Peled, the quartermaster-general, who told Eshkol he was insulting the IDF by not sending them to war, used aggressive, highly pejorative language comparing the government to leaders of Jewish communities in the Diaspora who were forced to beg like slaves.

Eshkol tried to get a grip on what was happening. 'We need to take a deep breath . . . We need patience. I don't accept that the fact that the Egyptian army is sitting in Sinai means that we have to go to war . . . Will we live forever by the sword?' He tried to tell what he had done for the army. 'You needed more equipment? Fine. You wanted 100 planes? You got them. You also got tanks. You got everything so that we could beat the Egyptian army. You didn't get it so that one day you could come and say: now we can destroy the Egyptian army – so let's do it.'

73

Eshkol wanted to crack the whip of civilian control over the generals. But the meeting was turning into a feeding frenzy. The atmosphere was 'extremely hard, almost unbearable'. The men staring at Eshkol, with the exception of Yoffe, were in their late thirties and early forties. Eshkol was old, and looked it, and liked speaking Yiddish and Russian, the languages of his youth, as much as Hebrew. Most of the generals had been born in Israel. They had fought in all Israel's wars. Eshkol was in the way. In their minds he embodied the weakness of the Diaspora. It was desperately unfair, because he had arrived in Palestine as a young man and had spent his life building the Jewish state. But he looked weak, and in the generals' world weakness was worthy only of contempt. Threats were to be faced and enemies dispatched. Brigadier-General Elad Peled, who was one of the four divisional commanders, was at the meeting. 'The mental generation gap was very important. We were the cowboys, frontier people. We looked at the older generation as people who were not free, they were not liberated . . . The minister of education asked me, "what if you're wrong? You're playing with the existence of the state." I told him I am one hundred per cent confident about the result of the war.' Yitzhak Rabin said they should discuss a declaration of war. Eshkol refused. Yigal Allon suggested a breather. Eshkol got up and walked out, furious, stunned by what had happened. He interpreted it as 'practically open mutiny'.

Yeshayahu Gavish insisted they were doing their duty by dishing out hard truths to the civilians: 'My purely military position was that we could not afford to let Egypt start the war. We had to push the government hard. It wasn't comfortable, but it wasn't a putsch. At no time did we discuss taking over. But as officers we had to tell the government what we thought – and if we hadn't, it would have been disastrous . . . and we were sabras and very confident. The ministers were all immigrants, and very hesitant.' After Eshkol left, Rabin stayed on with the generals. Waiting around for the war to start was telling on the soldiers' nerves before Eshkol's broadcast. Now they believed they had a serious morale problem.

It seemed as if all of Israel had been listening to Eshkol's broadcast and his stumbling, incoherent delivery reinforced all the worst fears about him. In the desert south of Beersheba a group of soldiers lay under a camouflaged Centurion tank around a transistor. According to one of them, Amos Elon, they were intensely frustrated. After Eshkol finished speaking, an officer said their real problem was not Nasser, but Eshkol's generation of Eastern European pioneers, who had dominated political life in Jewish Palestine and then in Israel since the 1920s. Letters criticising Eshkol's performance poured into his office. One, signed 'a loyal citizen', suggested he ask a radio announcer to read his speeches for him in future. Mrs Miriam Smolansk wrote about 'the imminent disaster . . . our state and people are being lost. Don't shed the blood of thousands or maybe all of us with your speeches which lack any spirit or power. Please hand over the command to someone who can inspire the people with power and strength.' Moshe Dayan's daughter, Yael, heard Eshkol's speech on a car radio as she drove through the desert towards the headquarters of General Ariel Sharon where she was attached as a military journalist. She was embarrassed by Eshkol's performance. 'Slow, uncertain, non-committal, uninspiring, it gave the listeners anything but an answer, even a provisional one, even the courage to continue the wait . . .' Most Israelis thought her father would provide the courage they needed.

Dayan

'Overnight,' according to Moshe Dayan's close ally Shimon Peres, 'the leadership of the nation became a problem of supreme concern.' He was already orchestrating a vicious political campaign to oust Eshkol as defence minister and possibly even prime minister on the grounds that his failure to take Israel to war was putting the state in danger. The press tore into Eshkol. Editorials demanded that Moshe Dayan be drafted into the cabinet as defence minister. Dayan was the one-eyed general whose black eye-patch and swashbuckling reputation had made him, as far as the outside world and much of the Israeli public were concerned, the archetypal Israeli fighting man. Dayan noted with some relish that Eshkol's broadcast had been 'catastrophic. Public doubt and derision gave way to an overwhelming sense of deep concern.' The Israeli people wanted to have a strong military man at the top. Eshkol did not fit the bill. Dayan did. In the eyes of the Israeli public, Dayan was everything Eshkol was not. He was a winner – a war hero, flamboyant, macho, and charismatic. He had two hobbies – women and archaeology. He could be a good friend, but only to people who were not in his way. Dayan had a reputation as a great strategist, which was not entirely deserved. Israel would have won the 1967 war without him.

Moshe Dayan was fifty-two. He was the first child to be born in Degania, the first Israeli kibbutz. His parents were immigrants from Russia. Life was hard. In 1921 they moved to a new agricultural settlement called Nahalal, where the main threats to life were malaria, trachoma and the local Palestinian Arabs. As a teenager Dayan joined the Haganah, the underground Jewish militia. It co-operated with the British army during the 'Arab revolt', a guerrilla insurgency against the Jewish settlers and Britain.

As the sun was setting one evening in the spring of 1938, a British officer called Orde Wingate joined them. Wingate 'walked in with a heavy revolver at his side, carrying a small Bible in his hand'. He was a deeply religious Christian, who believed it was his duty to God and the British Empire to teach the Jews how to fight Arabs. He ended a lecture about guerrilla tactics and night fighting with the suggestion that they go off to set up a real ambush. Dayan and the other young Jewish fighters had a new hero. He taught them how to fight and to move at night, how to use the terrain and about the devastating power of speed and surprise. Before an operation, Wingate would inspire himself by reading passages in the Bible that related to the chosen battle ground. After a hard night's fighting, they would return for breakfast. As the young Jewish soldiers made omelettes and tomato salad, Wingate would sit in the corner of the cook house stark naked, reading his Bible again and 'munching raw onions as if they were the most luscious pears'. Wingate was transferred back to Britain in 1939 because he was seen as out of control and too close to the Zionists. In 1944 Wingate became a hero in his own country, when he was killed leading the Chindits against the Japanese in Burma.

Dayan learnt Wingate's lessons well. He lost his eye fighting with the Australians against the Vichy French in Lebanon in 1941. A rifle bullet hit a pair of field glasses he was using, splintering a lens and its metal casing, which embedded themselves in his eye socket. David Ben-Gurion, who had established the tradition of holding the defence portfolio as well as the office of prime minister, made him IDF Chief of Staff in 1953. Dayan stated his essential philosophy at the funeral of Roy Rothberg, who was killed at a kibbutz near Gaza in 1956. Over his grave he said, 'It is the fate of our generation that our life requires that we be always prepared and armed, strong and determined, for if the sword be struck from our grasp, we shall die.' For Dayan, force was not just the best option for Israel, it was their only chance.

In May 1967 Dayan wanted a job. The army gave him a jeep and a driver. He wore a uniform without his general's badges and moved through the units that were lined up in the Negev desert, discussing battle plans with the commanders and glad-handing the troops. Eshkol's military aide, Israel Lior, was immediately suspicious. 'It was clear to me that he was playing politics. It was also clear to me that he would exploit the opportunity of touring IDF units to get headlines and to try to return to national leadership.'

The high command of the army openly joined the campaign for Dayan to replace Eshkol as minister of defence. The pressure behind him became irresistible. Eshkol's preferred candidate was Yigal Allon. But nothing could stop the Dayan steamroller. Ministers and MPs wanted him. Women, dubbed by Eshkol 'the Merry Wives of Windsor', were demonstrating for Dayan every day outside the headquarters of Mapai, the ruling party in Tel Aviv. The party functionaries inside could hear them chanting.

Eshkol fought for his job. On the evening of 30 May he addressed his parliamentary faction with what his aide Colonel Lior called 'a thundering voice, the roar of a wounded lion'. It did not work. Eshkol hung on for another day. He offered Dayan the job of deputy premier.

Dayan refused. He wanted the ministry of defence or a command in the army. So Eshkol decided to make Yigal Allon defence minister. He told the cabinet on the 31st that Dayan would take over Southern Command from Brigadier-General Gavish.

Nobody had told Gavish. He was a popular commander, a handsome man of forty-two who walked with a limp because of a serious leg wound he had picked up in the 1948 war. He had no idea that Dayan was after his job. Before dawn on 1 June Rabin summoned him to GHQ in Tel Aviv. Neither Brigadier-General Ezer Weizman, the head of operations, or Brigadier-General Haim Bar Lev, newly appointed as deputy chief of staff, would look him in the eye. Gavish went in to see Rabin, saluted and sat down. They had been colleagues since the days of the Palmach in the 1940s. Rabin said he was sorry. Dayan wanted the Southern Command. Gavish, staggered, managed to say that Dayan was ten times the soldier that he was so if he wanted the job he ought to have it. But when Rabin asked him to stay on as Dayan's deputy, he snapped. It was impossible. He wouldn't do it.

The generals outside asked him what had happened. You know what happened, Gavish snarled, and walked out. Bar Lev followed him out and flew back to Beersheba with him by helicopter. He tried to sympathise. Dayan, he said, didn't care who he stepped on. He told Gavish it would be a 'catastrophe' if he did not stay on as Dayan's deputy. Gavish had been working on the plans for a campaign in the Sinai for at least three years. Dayan was coming out of retirement. He knew nothing. Gavish still refused. He rang his wife and told her to expect him for dinner.

Gavish made one last tour of his front. He met his divisional commanders, Sharon, Tal and Yoffe and, without telling them what was happening, approved their final plans for the assault. But Eshkol's plan to save himself by sacrificing Gavish was not working. The National Religious Party ministers in his coalition government wanted Dayan as defence minister, not Allon. Eshkol was forced to change his decision.

Miriam Eshkol was on the road from Jerusalem to Tel Aviv in her husband's official car. The phone rang. It was Eshkol. 'He said,

"Come quickly to Tel Aviv," so I thought he must have had a heart attack or something . . . When we came to the office in Tel Aviv he said, "Look, don't be angry and don't worry. I'll have to give up the ministry of defence to Moshe Dayan and I'll manage and work with him." Then he said, "You go and find Dayan. We can't find him." I knew exactly where he was. He was with a girlfriend . . .' Losing the ministry of defence on the eve of the war was a political and personal blow from which Eshkol never recovered. His widow believes it finished him. He died two years later.

As well as Dayan, Eshkol brought in two ministers from the right to form a government of national unity. One of them was Menachem Begin, regarded by the British as a terrorist. In 1946 he ordered the bomb attack on the British headquarters in the King David hotel in Jerusalem that killed more than ninety people. The British police chief in Haifa at the time described Begin as a ruthless thug who made Al Capone look a novice. In the first meeting of the new cabinet Begin looked very much at home: 'He acted quite naturally, as if he had sat at that table for many years.'

General Gavish was relieved he had his job back. But he was staggered that politics had come before the security of the state. 'It wasn't just a personal insult, it was more than that. There were 1000 tanks facing us in the Sinai. How could they have considered removing the commander on the eve of war?'

Eshkol also felt a massive sense of injustice. He had taken his responsibilities as defence minister very seriously. Brigadier-General Weizman, who had yelled at Eshkol with the rest of them for delaying the war, even tearing his badges of rank off his shoulder and throwing them down on a table in disgust, later recalled, perhaps guiltily, that in the years before the war he 'delighted us repeatedly with his alertness, his sensitivity and his wide interest in logistic problems'. Just before the war started, the director general of the defence ministry sent him a note. 'The IDF has never been so well equipped. I have just seen the Quartermaster's branch, and there were practically no problems. The air force has almost no problems. All he asked for was six engines.' But Dayan's appointment boosted morale in the army and on the home front immeasurably at a time when it was flagging. Even Colonel Lior, Eshkol's loyal military assistant, detected a new sense of purpose in the cabinet room once Dayan was on board.

Arab dreams and nightmares

Many Arabs spent the last week of peace dreaming about the celebrations they would have when the war was won. In such a febrile atmosphere there was no room for anyone who suggested that victory was not certain. Abdullah Schliefer, an American Jew who had converted to Islam, was working as a journalist in Jordanian Jerusalem. He was horrified by the complacency of Palestinians who listened, entranced, to Voice of the Arabs. 'Arab confidence hung in the air like some horrible omen ... No one did anything but stand around, congratulate each other, and praise Gamal Abdul Nasser. Somehow this one man, by sheer weight of his audacity, was going to overwhelm the enemy in an amazing manner that could in no way affect the life-style or the activities of people most intimately involved in the struggle ...' When he wrote an editorial on popular resistance to an Israeli invasion in his local English-language newspaper, he was accused of being defeatist and his piece was spiked.

King Hussein kept his doubts inside his own tight circle. Adnan Abu Odeh, a major in Jordanian intelligence, tried to raise the alarm. Since the Samua raid he had been convinced that a war was coming and that the Israelis would snap up the West Bank. He was too junior to know that King Hussein felt the same way. Odeh was so certain that in January 1967 he moved his wife and four children out of his home town of Nablus on the West Bank to the other side of the Jordan. On the last weekend before the war he wrote a paper warning that Jordan was facing a disaster and that the West Bank would be lost. He went into the office of the director of intelligence, saluted, and presented his report. The director was sitting with two men, a relative of his and a government minister. As Abu Odeh stood there, the director leafed through his report. As he read it he kept up a sarcastic running commentary about its contents. He handed it to the minister, who added a few jibes of his own about wrong-headed people who doubted that victory was certain. He threw the report back across the desk at Abu Odeh. Furious and humiliated, he left the room and put his report through the shredder.

In Beirut the cafés and restaurants were as full as ever. The summer had started and the best beaches were packed. In the late 1960s the rich parts of the Lebanese capital were a cosmopolitan oasis, dedicated to making money and finding pleasure (not always in that order). The seismic shock of the June crisis helped, eight years later, to destroy the old Lebanon, to push it into civil war and years of slaughter and isolation. But in 1967 Beirut was still the Middle East's great crossroads. Passing through it was Robert Anderson, an American oil man, veteran of the Eisenhower administration and now on his way as President Johnson's unofficial envoy to a highly secret meeting with Nasser. In Beirut he realised how much support Nasser had. As well as Lebanese, Anderson saw Saudi Arabians, Kuwaitis and Iraqis, the kind of people a wealthy American businessman and diplomat would expect to meet. All of them applauded what Nasser had done. 'I am impressed,' Anderson reported, 'more because of the quality of the people who made these assertions than the fact they were made.' They were 'generally moderate with a tendency to oppose Nasser'. The middle classes, the people Americans assumed were their natural allies, believed in what Nasser was doing as much as the uneducated masses. Anderson's friends told him that closing the Gulf of Aqaba was just and that United States policy was yet again being dictated by Israel and its friends. Arabs wanted someone to redress the balance. In the last week before war broke out in 1967, Nasser seemed to be their saviour.

Anderson travelled on to Cairo and on 31 May saw Nasser, who was relaxed and expansive, dressed in 'sport clothes'. He seemed confident that he was getting the right intelligence and that Egypt's army was strong enough to deal with anything that was thrown at it. He repeated his familiar line – that he had mobilised his troops because Israel was on the verge of attacking Syria. Johnson had invited

Vice-President Zakkaria Mohieddin to Washington. Nasser wanted him to travel as early as 4 or 5 June. He knew war was getting closer. Getting Mohieddin to Washington to start a public dialogue with the United States was, he sensed, his last chance to head off an Israeli attack.

Anderson's trip was so secret that he had to travel to Lisbon to have his report encrypted and sent to Washington. By then it was 2 June. Nasser was realising that his gamble was going wrong. Dayan, his old enemy, was installed at the ministry of defence. Israel was on the brink and it was not blinking. The question now was whether Mohieddin could get to Washington before Israel attacked. If it was possible, Egypt had a chance of avoiding war and extracting some lasting political gains from the crisis. Nasser needed to buy time and his commanders had to brace themselves for war.

He summoned Field Marshal Amer and his senior generals. The war he told them, will start in two to three days, on Sunday 4 June or Monday 5. His calculation was based on the progress of the Iraqi forces that were already heading across the desert into Jordan. The Iraqis had plans to send a big force of at least three infantry brigades and a reinforced armoured division. It would take them two to three days to deploy. The Israelis, he understood perfectly well, had the same information. They could not allow such a fundamental change in the balance of forces on their eastern border. They were, therefore, certain to attack.

The army chief of staff General Fawzi, General Sidqi Mahmoud, the head of the air force and General Ismail Labib, commander of air defence listened as Nasser squashed any lingering hopes they might have had of seizing the initiative with a first strike. Even a limited attack was out of the question. President Johnson had told him not to strike the first blow. So had the Soviet ambassador. Egypt would do as it was told. It was now, he told them, all about absorbing the Israeli offensive, rolling with the punch and then hitting back. Sidqi protested that the air force was designed for attack, not to wait for Israel's warplanes to come calling. Since British and French aircraft had destroyed Egyptian air power in the 1956 war, Egyptian military intelligence had predicted that Israel would aim to open the next war with a devastating blow to the air force. Sidqi had put in a multi-million-pound request to build hardened shelters for his war planes, but the money had been cut from the budget. Surely, he argued, Egypt should mount its own pre-emptive attack.

Nasser was not used to being challenged so forcefully. He treated Sidqi like an impertinent schoolboy. Who gives the orders here, he asked. Is it the politicians or is it the military? Field Marshal Amer chipped in with his own question. Did Sidqi want to hit Israel first and then see the United States lining up with Israel to deliver its reply? Sidqi, chastened and humiliated, muttered that of course he would never dream of giving the president orders and he would be horrified if the United States came in on Israel's side. Very well, Nasser continued, tell me how great the losses would be if we have to take the first blow? Sidqi, not wanting to make matters any worse for himself by sounding defeatist, answered that the air force would probably lose 20 per cent of its strength if Israel mounted a surprise attack. Fine, Nasser told the meeting. That means we will have 80 per cent left for our fightback.

The same evening Mahmoud Riad, the Egyptian foreign minister, was still trying to see if there was a way for Egypt permanently to change the rules of the game in the Straits of Tiran and in Sinai without getting involved in a disastrous war with Israel. To prepare the ground for the vice-president's visit to Washington, he spoke to Charles Yost, the American special envoy attached to the Cairo Embassy, whom he had known for years. Riad told him that Egypt did not intend to start any war. But then, according to Yost, the Egyptian held forth for an hour and a half with 'intense and uncharacteristic bitterness' about Israel and the way, as he saw it, that America automatically backed it. There seemed to be one law for Israel and one law for the Arabs. Riad made an offer. The straits would stay closed to Israeli ships, because the long-standing state of war with Israel gave Egypt 'belligerent rights'. Even so, everything except oil would be allowed through on foreign vessels. Israel's problems with restrictions on the use of its port at Eilat were 'not economic but purely psychological'.

83

Riad was almost right about Eilat. Although Israel had Mediterranean ports, it would have suffered significant economic damage if it could no longer import Iranian oil through Eilat. But that was less important than a fundamental psychological and strategic point. Israel had never, in the previous nineteen years, allowed an Arab state to change the status quo in its favour through political or military action. The accepted Zionist wisdom was that if Israel took one backward step, its power to deter its enemies would start to crumble. Its guiding principle was to push constantly, with great stamina, to change the status quo in its favour. The strategy had worked very well. Small facts created on the ground in the teeth of Arab resistance or international criticism fast became big new realities. Now Egypt was trying fundamentally to reverse the trend by using Israel's own methods to change the status quo. Riad should have realised that Israel could never allow that to stand.

That evening in the White House Ephraim Evron, President Johnson's closest Israeli contact, warned that the political and psychological pressures for war were increasing in Israel. Evron had a suggestion. Forget the international armada. Israel would send a ship into the straits to test the blockade. Egypt would open fire, Israel would go to war and America would be off the hook. All the US had to do was to keep the Soviets quiet and agree that it would be self-defence. Walt Rostow liked Evron's idea. The State Department had discussed something very similar with the British more than a week earlier. The idea of Israel taking the risk was attractive, though as he told the president, it could turn into 'a terrible bloodbath'.

The last weekend

The political and psychological pressures of which Evron spoke in Washington were just as clear to Meir Amit, the head of Mossad. The virtual shutdown in the economy concerned him most. On 31 May, with a passport in a false name, Amit boarded a plane to Washington

DC to see his close friend Richard Helms, the Director of Central Intelligence.

The plan for a naval task force – known to its planners as the 'Red Sea Regatta' – was going nowhere fast. Politically and diplomatically it was the only idea that the Americans and the British had to head off a war. But the admirals and the politicians hated the idea. The Pentagon doubted it had the firepower to fight another war. The US Joint Chiefs of Staff warned that if they somehow cobbled together a naval task force, probably from American and British forces that were already east of Suez, 'the capability of these forces to prevail, if attacked by major Egyptian forces, is doubtful'. As far as they were concerned, as a military plan, it stank.

The Israelis had wind of the fact that the naval operation was a non-starter. On 2 June, the last Friday before war broke out, Israel's generals put the definitive case for war to the cabinet defence committee. Yariv, for military intelligence, told them not to worry about the Americans. Washington 'knows we must act' because it had no intention of breaking the blockade of Eilat itself. Picking up the signal sent by Rostow through Evron, he said the US would be relieved and as long as Israel moved fast it 'will not stand in our way'. Rabin added that 'a military-political noose is tightening around us and I don't believe anyone else is going to loosen it'.

Once again they told the politicians that they would beat the Egyptians, and the longer they had to wait to start the harder it would be. Brigadier-General Gavish, now back in place as head of Southern Command, urged immediate action because 'the most reliable information that couldn't be more reliable' was telling them that the Egyptian army was still no match for the IDF. Some of their soldiers had been given no food or water for forty-eight hours. Soldiers were arriving in their galabiyas because no one had uniforms for them.

Other generals, more temperately, repeated some of the words they had used during their showdown with Eshkol. Sharon warned that 'hesitation and delay' was eroding Israel's best deterrent, 'the Arab fear of us'. Peled, the head of the logistics branch, said, 'We know that the Egyptian army is not yet ready for war . . . they are relying on the hesitancy of the Israeli government. They did it out of confidence that that we would not dare to attack them . . . Nasser brought an unprepared army to the border and he is deriving all the benefits. The one thing working in his favour is that the Israeli government is not prepared to attack him. What has the army done to deserve these doubts about our capabilities? What more does an army have to do than to win every battle in order to gain the confidence of its government?'

The same day Moshe Dayan presented his war plan to Eshkol, Eban, Allon, Rabin and Ya'acov Herzog, the head of the prime minister's office. He wanted to smash the Egyptian army in Sinai – but without taking Gaza or going to the Suez canal. Allon, whose long-held dislike of Dayan was even deeper now that his rival had captured the ministry of defence, had his own ideas. It included going to Suez, and expelling hundreds of thousands of refugees across the canal. Dayan dismissed it as 'barbaric and inhuman'.

In Washington Meir Amit was with his friend Helms in the director's office at the CIA. Helms confirmed that the idea of opening the straits with a naval task force was sinking fast. Then Amit saw Secretary of Defense Robert McNamara. 'He was very impressive, wearing no tie or jacket. Mr Secretary, I said, I understand your position. Now listen to ours . . . I'm going to recommend a war.

'McNamara asked only two questions. How long? I said it would take a week. How many casualties? I said less than the war of independence, which was 6000. McNamara said I read you loud and clear.

'I asked a question. Should I stay a day or two, linger around? He said you have to go home, your place is there now.'

The Americans had given a clear signal. They had been told that Israel would be going to war and had made no attempt to stop it happening. Amit travelled back to Israel on an aircraft full of gas-masks and military equipment. Ambassador Harman, who had accused him of being 'trigger-happy' and wanted to urge moderation and delay, went with him. They landed in Tel Aviv on the evening of

Saturday 3 June. A car took them straight to Eshkol's apartment in Jerusalem, where he and his key ministers were waiting.

It was getting on for midnight by the time they arrived. Harman and Amit spoke. Amit said a war was necessary and that the Americans 'wouldn't sit Shiva about it' (in other words, go into mourning). It was his understanding that America would not intervene. Harman wanted Israel to wait another week or so. Dayan disagreed. 'If we wait for seven to nine days, there will be thousands dead. It's not logical to wait. We'll start it. Let's strike first and then look after the political side.'

Everyone who was there had no doubt that the decision had been taken. Israel was going to war. Eshkol invited Amit to present his case to the cabinet meeting the following morning. Every minister voted for war, except for two left-wingers, who abstained. Afterwards, Amit and Dayan went to the defence ministry in Tel Aviv to discuss what would happen on Monday. Amit advised Dayan that it would be 'smoother' if Israel first provoked Egypt into a response before launching the main offensive. Don't bother, Dayan said. 'We'll start.'

In Jordanian Jerusalem the strident Arab nationalism and the belief that Israel was about to be crushed spilled over into general anti-Western feeling. Six men went to the director of the British School of Archaeology in East Jerusalem to advise him that it would be 'better for his security' to leave. By the 4th, he had found urgent business abroad. A Canadian couple who were staying at the Intercontinental hotel on the Mount of Olives made the mistake of complaining about the service. The police were called and they were arrested for questioning. For Britain's consul-general in Jerusalem, 'the atmosphere vividly recalls Syria just before Suez'.

Late in the afternoon of 4 June, the last day before war, Rabin called in Narkiss and Elazar, Israel's commanders in the centre and north. Narkiss noticed immediately that Gavish of Southern Command was missing. As soon as he 'saw the face of Rabin, I knew that this was it. He was clearly exhilarated.' The meeting lasted only thirty minutes. Narkiss was jealous of the two other regional commanders.

Gavish was going to 'paddle his toes' in the Suez canal. Elazar 'would plant his feet' on the Syrian Heights. But Rabin kept telling Narkiss that action against Jordan would have to wait. Narkiss was desperate to capture Jordanian Jerusalem, was convinced he could do it and dreaded the possibility of missing out. Rabin was insistent. The southern front took priority. Later, after some final briefings with senior officers whom he could not tell that war was coming the next morning, Narkiss's driver came in to ask if he was going home. 'I thought that if I behaved differently tonight than on other nights, the secret would be out. "Home," I said.'

It was another warm Mediterranean evening. Generals Rabin and Hod chatted to their neighbours, strolled in their gardens and played with their children. They lived near each other in Tsalha, a small, green suburb of Tel Aviv that was favoured by senior officers. Rabin and Hod tried to seem normal, even nonchalant. Their minds were teeming with the detail of what was about to happen. As part of the deception plan, they decided to show themselves at their homes. Hod's logic was simple: 'If the chief of staff and the head of the air force are here, that means tomorrow is another quiet day.'

On that last weekend before the war the Israelis did everything they could to suggest that they were not about to go to war. The deception campaign was comprehensive and highly successful. It even extended to Winston Churchill, the grandson of Britain's wartime leader who was in Israel as a journalist. On Saturday he was invited to lunch at Moshe Dayan's house, which was also in Tsalha. He paid off his taxi, walked into the garden and almost tripped over what he assumed was the gardener who was working on an Egyptian mummy. It was Dayan. 'He gave a terrific show on my behalf to show he was relaxed. Winston, he said, let's drink wine from Tiberias . . . When I said the war was going to be all about air power, he said things are often grey, not black and white. It's most unlikely that either side could achieve total air superiority.' Churchill was convinced. The next day, he flew back to London. Dayan also helped convince the British ambassador, Michael Hadow, that the Israelis were going to give diplomacy a chance to work. Thousands of soldiers were given weekend leave, to pack the beaches in Tel Aviv. Hadow was taken in. He cabled London that there seemed to have been 'an extensive stand-down' for the armed forces. He concluded his report of 4 June: 'I propose to discontinue these SITREPS unless there is anything of significance to report.' During the night, the soldiers returned to their units.

At the British port of Felixstowe, as soon as it was dark, the Israeli cargo ship *Miryam* slipped silently away to sea. In its hold were cases of machine guns and 105 mm tank shells. Armoured vehicles were lashed to its deck. Journalists who had got wind of what was happening were banned from the quayside. In the docks, United States military police guarded an arms dump. The *Miryam*'s cargo was the latest of many consignments of arms that had been sent secretly to Israel from British and American reserves since the crisis started. Israeli transport planes had been running a 'shuttle service' in and out of RAF Waddington in Lincolnshire, a high-security facility that was one of the biggest bases of Britain's fleet of strategic V-bombers. British prime minister Harold Wilson had written to Eshkol that he was glad to help, but 'the utmost secrecy should be maintained'. The United States had held up a consignment of weapons to Jordan. But contracts with Israel were being honoured and expedited.

At Kibbutz Nachshon they spent Sunday night laying mines. The kibbutz was a border settlement close to the so-called Latrun salient, a segment of Jordanian-held territory that bulged into Israel. They did not know that the war was going to start in a matter of hours, but they sensed it was coming soon. 'The mining job was hard and serious, harder than our usual training routines. A vast, stubborn ground, untouched for years, filled with shoulder high thorns surrounded us along with complete darkness. We worked hard that night . . . swinging picks until dawn.' Dog-tired, just before first light they jumped out of their skins when one of them dropped his pickaxe on to a mine with a sharp clang of metal on metal.

Ran Pekker of the Israeli air force was summoned to a meeting of senior officers. His commander got up and wrote 0745 on the board. It was the time that the first air attacks would hit Egypt the next morning. There was not much else to say, except to stress again that secrecy and surprise now mattered more than ever. Pekker drove back to his squadron. He locked himself in the briefing room, going over the details again and again, and rehearsing what he would tell the pilots in the morning. He got home at midnight. His wife, Heruta, woke up. What's up? she asked. Don't worry, he told her, we'll talk in the morning. He set his alarm for 0330.

The pilots were not going to be told until the morning either, because secrecy was imperative and because their commanders wanted them to have a good night's sleep. There were some exceptions. One of them was Herzl Bodinger. He was the 24-year-old pilot of a French-built Vautour fighter-bomber. His mission, to attack a squadron of Tupolev-16 bombers at Beni Sweif airfield, was right at the end of the Vautour's range. So, with the three other pilots who would be making the raid with him, he had to move his aircraft the night before from Ramat David airfield in northern Israel to Tel Nof in the south. Every mile closer to Egypt counted. The four pilots' cover story was that they were instructors making some routine aircraft movements, in case anyone at Tel Nof asked awkward questions. They still did not know the exact date and time. But they were certain that, in a few hours, on Monday morning, they were going to put years of training into practice.

Israel mobilised a phantom unit around Eilat, generating radio traffic and fake vehicle movements in an area which just had its normal garrison. But it is hard to conceal everything an army needs to do before a battle. The Egyptians picked up signs that something big was about to happen. All of them were ignored. On Sunday evening, observers in Egyptian forward positions near the southern end of the Gaza Strip realised that they were watching the Israelis getting ready for an attack. But their warning sent at ten-thirty in the evening that Israel 'is expected to launch an attack on the land forces in Sinai at dawn on 5 June' was ignored. The air force's own intelligence service was in such chaos that a few days earlier Air Vice

Marshal Abdel-Hamid El-Dighidi, who commanded air operations in Sinai, sacked all his intelligence people after he decided they were spying on him. He had nothing and nobody to put in their place. One of Dighidi's men was meant to be on duty at the intelligence desk at his command post late on Sunday night. He had gone home early. King Hussein also had intelligence information that the war was about to start, with an air strike against Egypt. He sent an urgent message to Cairo. They replied that they knew about the attack and were ready for it. King Hussein put Jordan's tiny air force on full alert.

The Egyptian army was busy with something else. The next morning Field Marshal Abd al-Hakim Amer was going to fly to Sinai to meet his commanders with the air force chief, Sidqi Mahmoud. On Sunday night some of Egypt's senior commanders left their posts in the field to travel to Bir Tamada airfield in Sinai, so that they would be in good time to greet the field marshal in the morning.

By Sunday the Americans were accepting – and expecting – Israel to take action. President Johnson's mantra of Israel not being alone unless it goes alone was all but forgotten. Johnson was resigned to Israel going to war by the time he spoke to Harold Wilson on Friday 2 June. Walt Rostow, his National Security Advisor, wrote, 'It is now increasingly clear that the Israelis will wait only about a week to take on themselves the forcing of the blockade at the Gulf of Aqaba. They clearly envisage forcing Nasser to fire the first shot; they will respond on a limited basis in Sinai but be prepared to fight a war against all the Arab forces arrayed against them without external assistance . . .' Rostow ruled out the plan for an international regatta as 'unlikely to get operational support'. He had one major hope in the crisis – that Nasser would be 'cut down to size'. As long as that happened, only two extreme scenarios concerned him. The first was the destruction of Israel (which US intelligence reports had already ruled out as a military impossibility). The second was the creation of a bloc united by its hostility to the Jewish state, which would 'require us to maintain Israel as a kind of Hong Kong enclave in the region'.

The Soviet ambassador to the UN, Nikolai Fedorenko, was at Glen Cove, an estate on Long Island built in the style of a Scottish castle that had been bought at a bargain price by the USSR in 1948. For a time the Soviets had boarded their entire delegation to the UN there, to save money and to make it easier for the KGB to keep an eye on them. By 1967, though, it was a retreat for top diplomats and Fedorenko was its laird. He sat with his expert on arms control, Arkady Shevchenko, discussing the Middle East over a glass of cognac. They had just received a top-secret cable saying that Moscow had advised Nasser not to start a war. Shevchenko doubted Nasser would listen. 'My previous experiences with representatives of Arab nations taught me that our government followed the Arab line, not the reverse.' Both men thought a war was coming.

Levi Eshkol was having dinner with his wife Miriam, at a house near Tel Aviv operated by Mossad. He said to his wife, 'Tomorrow it will start. There will be widows, orphans, bereaved parents. And all this I will have to take on my conscience.' According to Mrs Eshkol, 'It haunted him. He didn't want war. He didn't like war. It was the last thing he wanted in his life. He just believed that if you wanted peace you had to prepare for it.'

In Amman, late in the day, the US ambassador Findley Burns collected his thoughts. War looked inescapable. Washington seemed to have run out of ideas. Perhaps the only solution was to return to some fundamental principles about the Middle East. The crisis over the Gulf of Aqaba was 'only symptomatic of the basic confrontation'. Everything went back to the Palestinian problem. Solve that and war would be prevented. Otherwise there was no chance. Burns told the State Department that the president should announce immediately, without telling anyone, except possibly the British, that 'the root of the crisis is the Palestinian problem'. Then the president should assemble a Middle East peace conference to settle the matter once and for all. 'Wars result in peace conferences, so better to have the conference as the first rather than the last step.' As for pre-existing commitments, like the promise to keep Eilat open for Israeli shipping that was made in 1957, simply speak privately to the Israelis and to the Arabs, to tell them that 'guarantees would not apply in the case of an aggressor in hostilities' until the peace conference had done its work.

Burns was right. Everything did come back to the Palestinian problem, which was about to get much worse.

DAY ONE

5 June 1967

Negev desert, Israel, 0100

Brigadier-General Ariel Sharon was shaving. When he had finished, he looked at himself in the mirror carefully, then put on after-shave lotion. Sharon caught the eye of Lieutenant Yael Dayan, the daughter of the new defence minister, who was sitting in his trailer. She was attached to Sharon's HQ as a military journalist. 'We're going to win the war,' he told her, radiating confidence. He seemed 'almost happy. The frustration had gone.' In the desert there was not much privacy. Dayan had just overheard his last phone call before the battle to Lily, Sharon's wife. He told her to 'be calm . . . kiss the children for me – don't worry'. An hour later, Sharon left his camp for a meeting with his brigade commanders. As they conferred, Yael Dayan felt confidence and professionalism in the air, 'and a touch of joy'. By 0400 Sharon's division was ready to go. He lay on the ground between his command half-tracks. He told them to wake him at 0630 and fell asleep.

Tel Aviv, 0330

Brigadier-General Mordechai Hod managed four hours' sleep. Now, he was not going to get any more. Well before dawn he was on the road to the Israeli air force command centre, deep below the ministry of defence in Tel Aviv. He prepared a message for his forces, to be circulated as they were going to war: 'Battle order of the officer commanding. Israeli Air Force. Urgent. To all units. Soldiers of the air force, the blustering and swashbuckling Egyptian army is moving against us to annihilate our people . . . Fly on, attack the enemy, pursue him to ruination, draw his fangs, scatter him in the wilderness, so that the people of Israel may live in peace in our land and the future generations be secured.'

Secrecy and surprise were everything. No last-minute leaks were going to be permitted. The day shift came in at six, the doors were locked behind them and they were told the war was about to start. The night team, who already knew what was coming, was not allowed home. Twelve years of planning had gone into the operation that Hod was convinced would win the war for Israel. It had even had its code word – Operation Moked, Hebrew for 'focus' – for more than twelve months.

Ran Pekker's alarm woke him at 0330. He shaved, put on a clean and ironed coverall and polished his black air force shoes. He kissed his sleeping children and turned round at the door of their bedroom for what, despite his confidence, he realised might be his last look at them. Then he headed for his squadron. Pekker arrived at his headquarters at 0345, woke the operations assistant who was there on a night shift and called his two deputies, who like him lived on the base. When they arrived he told them they had three and a half hours until the start of the war. They were to wake the pilots and get them in immediately. The same thing was happening at bases across Israel. Because most of the pilots had not been told what was happening, they were well rested. Everything was going according to plan.

Mafrak Airbase, Jordan, 0400

King Hussein's warnings had, at least, got through to his own air force. Ihsan Shurdom, a 25-year-old captain, and the other pilots at Mafrak took off at dawn, flying patrols over Amman and the Jordanian highlands that fall steeply down to the Dead Sea and the Jordan valley. As the sun came up, they could see the light filling the valley below them and glinting off the spires and domes of Jerusalem away to the west. Most of the pilots' families, Shurdom's included, lived on the base at Mafrak, which was ninety kilometres outside Amman on the road that leads to Damascus and Baghdad. Shurdom thought the Israelis would try to raid the base and he was worried about his family. But he told himself that Mafrak had good shelters and slit trenches against air raids. Anyway, he would not have attacked civilians and he expected the Israeli air force, which he respected, to observe the same standards.

Ihsan Shurdom was young and self-confident. He had been trained by the RAF in England. Back home there was more training in aerial dogfights by graduates of the RAF's Pilot Attack Instructors' School. Shurdom had read all the books about the RAF's Second World War fighter aces. Air combat, he believed, had not changed much since the Battle of Britain. The only difference was that they did it in jets, faster. His Hunter was armed with 30 mm cannon and it had no radar. Just like the Spitfire pilots, Shurdom had to rely on his own eyes. He had great confidence in his aircraft, even though it was ageing, subsonic and due for replacement by the more modern supersonic F-104 Starfighter. Six of them, with their American instructors, had been pulled out from Jordan only the day before. Never mind. The Hunters were not as fast as the F-104s, but they were reliable, powerful and highly manoeuvrable, especially at low speeds. The Jordanians were ready to fight, but there was no sign of the Israelis. After a fifty-minute patrol, they touched down again at Mafrak.

Jordan's air force was efficient, but tiny, with only 24 Hawker Hunters. Just before the war, American military experts analysed the

Syrian and Egyptian air strength. The Egyptian air force looked strong. It had 350 jet fighters. But it was in a poor state of readiness. Only 222 aircraft were assigned to the 18 operational fighter squadrons, of which only 2 MiG-21 and 3 MiG-17 squadrons were fully operational. The rest had only 30–50 per cent of their aircraft ready for combat. The Egyptian bomber fleet of 29 Tupolev-16s and 35 Ilyushin-28s was ready to go and was its strongest strategic weapon. Syria had 58 jet fighters and 4 Ilyushin-28 bombers. But of those only one squadron of MiG-17s was operational. The remaining fighter squadrons and the four bombers operated, the Americans said, at less than 50 per cent efficiency – in other words, for more than half the time, they were out of action. Both countries had a shortage of combat-trained pilots. Egypt had 700 pilots in total, but only 200 were considered ready to go into action. For Syria, it was 35 out of 115.

Ekron Airbase, Israel, 0430

Major Ran Pekker, commander of 102 squadron, made sure coffee was waiting for his pilots when they arrived in the briefing room. When they were seated, he turned the blackboard around. 0745, the time the war was going to start, was already chalked up. Next to the pilots' names were their targets and with whom they would be flying. He ran through the procedures. Radio silence was all important. If an aircraft had a mechanical problem, the pilot was to signal to the rest of the flight by dipping his wings, then without a word, he would turn for home. Even if the aircraft was going down, no Mayday messages were allowed. They would have to eject into the sea and wait for rescue. Pekker kept emphasising that it was not a drill. They were going to war.

Similar briefings were being given at airfields across Israel. Captain Avihu Bin-Nun was deputy commander at Tel Nof, leading a formation of Mysteres. He was talking to his men. The essentials – timing, radio silence – were all the same. Only the target details were different. Bin-Nun was solemn, convinced Israel's future rested on the shoulders of the air force. He was going to be one of the attack leaders. 'We trained, exercised and learned our targets by heart. Each formation had several targets, which it practised attacking in complete radio silence. We had reached a point where no words were necessary. We could have executed the plan with our eyes closed.'

No opening to a war had been better rehearsed than Operation Focus. The idea behind it was simple. If Israel could destroy the Arabs' air forces before the fighting had even started properly, it would win. The Israelis had first thought about a devastating air strike on Egyptian air force bases at the end of their war of independence in 1949. In those days the Israeli air force was still tiny, equipped with Dakotas and Spitfires, which had just replaced Messerschmidts, to the enormous relief of the first Israeli fighter pilots like Ezer Weizman, who thought the German fighters had 'an evil nature'. But in 1949 David Ben-Gurion thought the air force was not strong enough and, besides, the war against Egypt was as good as won. France and Britain proved the idea worked in 1956, when they destroyed most of the Egyptian air force when it was drawn up in neat lines at its bases. Weizman was frustrated and angry in 1956 that Britain and France had taken the lead in the air. When he became head of the air force in 1958, he made the pre-emptive strike the centre of the Israeli air strategy for the next war. He worked on the idea constantly, pushing the government to buy the right aircraft and demanding the best training. To relax he would fly a black Spitfire, which was kept for his personal use until he retired after the 1967 war.

By 1963, when the young and ambitious pilot Herzl Bodinger graduated from flying school, the idea was well-established. Every few months, Bodinger's routine training included simulated operations to bomb Arab airfields and to destroy parked aircraft by strafing. Every six months the entire air force rehearsed going to war. The pilots made models of their targets, based on intelligence reports, marking out the runways, main hangars and the positions of anti-aircraft batteries. The models were used to finalise and polish their tactics. Once the crisis started in May 1967, rehearsals stopped. Reservists were mobilised, the aircraft were fuelled and armed and put on stand-by for immediate action. But as the days went by, training resumed so the pilots could go through their missions yet again. They rehearsed by flying in attack configuration exactly the distance they would have to cover to get to their first targets. Herzl Bodinger, who was to attack Beni Sweif airfield in Egypt, would run up the same mileage by flying south from Ramat David airfield in northern Israel to the Egyptian border at Eilat, back north to the Lebanese border, turning round and going back to Beersheba before attacking a simulated airstrip in the Negev desert.

Bodinger, who had moved down to Tel Nof the night before, woke at 0430 on 5 June with the rest of the pilots. He phoned his wife to tell her that the war was starting in a few hours. He told her to take their baby from their married quarters at Ramat David to her parents in the Tel Aviv suburbs. 'She wasn't worried. She had been an officer in air force intelligence and she was as confident as we were that the plan would work.'

Hod and his commanders did not think of Focus as a gamble. For them it was audacious and sound. That morning, Israel had 197 operational combat planes. Only four were held back to defend Israeli airspace. One of the pilots who had to stay at home was Uri Gil. He had known for two weeks that he would be in an interceptor, waiting to see if there would be an Arab counter-attack. Gil told himself he was proud that his skills as an expert dogfighter had been recognised. But he was jealous when he saw his colleagues preparing for their missions. For a fortnight, he had been sitting in his jet, ready to be scrambled, while the pilots who were on bombing missions seemed just to be hanging out, playing ping-pong and waiting for their moment of glory.

Air Force Command Centre, Ministry of Defence, Tel Aviv, 0600

The next stage of the deception plan was put into action. Five flights of the Israeli air force's Fouga Magister trainers took off. It was meant to look like just another day. In the skies above Israel they used the radio channels and call signs normally allocated to the front-line strike aircraft to play tapes of radio conversations between fighter pilots and their controllers to make it sound like routine training. The plan was that they would be picked up, as the IAF's manoeuvres were every morning, by the powerful Jordanian radar station high above the Mediterranean in the mountains at Ajloun. They stayed in the air until 0745, H-Hour.

Israel–Gaza border, 0600

The soldiers of the reconnaissance unit of Israel's 7th Armoured Brigade had risen before dawn. Their jeeps, armoured cars and tanks were lined up along an avenue of eucalyptus trees on a road leading to the border with Gaza. The company commander, Ori Orr, knew that his men had spotted him coming back late the previous night from a briefing at regimental headquarters. He had already told them that his gut feeling was that war would start this morning. He knew they would be wondering whether it would. The morning was very quiet, no aircraft overhead and no shelling. Complete radio silence was already in force. The only walkie-talkie turned on in the whole company was in Orr's armoured command car, and it was set for listening only. Orr's senior NCO, Sergeant Bentzi Zur, was in the command car making some last checks. Everything was ready.

The headquarters of the Egyptian field army in Sinai was quiet too. Its commander, General Muhsin, and his deputy had gone to the conference with Field Marshal Amer at Bir Tamada airfield. Captain Salahadeen Salim, left behind with the other junior officers, was a little uneasy. He felt they should have done more by now. Salim's mind was racing. Why wasn't there more reconnaissance? Shouldn't they have established better co-ordination between the different units under Muhsin's command? Everybody at headquarters also knew that far too many of the forces that Egypt had poured into the Sinai were not fit for combat. Thousands of them were badly trained, barely equipped reservists. Some men who had done their military service in the artillery had been called up to serve in tanks. But all Salim could do was grumble discreetly to his contemporaries. In a deeply hierarchical army a 25-year-old captain, one of the most junior officers at field headquarters, was expected to be seen and not heard. General Muhsin had let it be known that they would have time to do everything that had to be done. He had assured them that they would be ready.

Egypt's position was even worse than Salim realised. Some of the units in the Sinai were 40 per cent under strength. Some armoured units had only half the number of tanks they were supposed to have. Overall, they were down 30 per cent in small arms and 24 per cent in artillery. One-third of the standing army, 70,000 men, was in Yemen. In the late 1960s the United States was so committed in Vietnam that it doubted it could fight a second conventional war elsewhere. Yet on 5 June 1967, Egypt found itself trying to do what the United States could not. Still, Egypt had deployed in the Sinai around 100,000 men, 950 tanks, 1100 armoured personnel carriers and over 1000 artillery pieces. The Egyptian force was made up of four infantry divisions, two armoured divisions and one mechanised infantry division, along with four independent brigades. Against them were 70,000 Israelis in eleven brigades, two of which were independent with the rest split between three divisional task forces. Four brigades were armoured, with up-to-date Centurion and Patton tanks. Two were mechanised, each with a battalion of Sherman tanks and two battalions of infantry who rode into battle on old American Second World War half-tracks. The two infantry brigades were transported in hundreds of requisitioned civilian buses, lorries and vans. Israel also had three brigades of paratroops, one of which was mechanised and reinforced by a battalion of Pattons.

Tel Nof Airbase, 0630

Captain Avihu Bin-Nun and his flight of Mysteres were ready. The timing of each take-off was a critical part of the plan. Bin-Nun and his men had been told that if their aircraft malfunctioned and risked disrupting the planned take-off times, they were to get off the runway immediately even if it meant crashing the plane. The IAF had five different kinds of combat aircraft, all supplied by France – Mirages, Super Mysteres, Mysteres, Ouragans and Vautours . It was not ideal, but in the 1950s and the early 1960s they had bought what they could when they could. The plan had been tailored to fit the planes' capabilities. All of the aircraft in the first wave had to be over their targets at 0745 sharp, Israel time. Take-off times had to take that into account. Depending where they started and where they were going, aircraft had anything from 10 or 15 to 45 minutes in the air before they reached their targets. So many aircraft would arrive over so many Egyptian airbases at the same moment that Egypt would be caught cold, like a boxer knocked out in the first minute of the first round. And it had been dinned into them – on no account were they to switch on their radios until the attack started.

On the way out to his Mirage Ran Pekker thought of his family. They were about to be woken to be evacuated from the base to hotels. Then, strapped in, he exploded with anger. There had been a foul-up. Something had not been ready. They would be taking off five minutes late, which meant that they would have to fly faster, using up some of their precious fuel.

Herzl Bodinger and his colleagues in their Vautours raced across the Sinai desert at less than one hundred feet. A fear that the plan might have been rumbled ate away at Bodinger. He was frustrated that he could not turn his radio on to have some reassuring chat with his colleagues – and delighted when Egyptian soldiers riding in a big convoy of armour looked up and waved enthusiastically at them as they streaked overhead. So far, it was working.

Air Force Command Centre, Ministry of Defence, Tel Aviv, 0730

General Ezer Weizman was in a state of high excitement. 'The suspense was incredible . . . The planes were on their way. At 7:40

they were to deliver the first blow at nine Egyptian airfields . . . I had been talking of this operation, explaining it, hatching it, dreaming of it, manufacturing it link by link, training men to carry it out. Now, in another quarter of an hour, we would know if it was only a dream, or whether it would come true.' In 1966 he had claimed in a lecture at Israel's command and staff college that the air force could destroy all the Arab air forces within six hours. Now he was going to be proved right or wrong.

The routes the aircraft would take had been plotted and adjusted over a period of years. Most of them had been tested by pilots who had been ordered to violate Egyptian airspace on 'training missions'. They were not told that their real purpose was to see how efficiently Egyptian air defences, especially radar, locked on to them. This constant probing uncovered gaps in Egypt's military radar system. There was another complication. Nearly a third of Israel's 197 war planes were Ouragans, which had a relatively short range. They could not go beyond the Suez canal. During the build-up to war the Israeli army's frustration increased every time they heard more Egyptian troops were crossing the canal to enter Sinai. In contrast, General Hod of the air force celebrated every time another Egyptian squadron moved into the Sinai airfields. It meant more short-range work for the Ouragans, releasing the Mirages and Mysteres for other missions.

Bin-Nun swung his Mystere out over the Mediterranean. He led a flight of four aircraft, flying as low as they could to avoid detection by Jordanian radar. They were so close to the water that their jet engines left a wake. Maintaining a steady altitude was vital. One dip meant disaster. Bin-Nun was worried about his Number 4, an inexperienced pilot, who seemed to be having trouble keeping his aircraft steady. But radio silence meant he could not say a word. He looked back again and saw Number 4 was not there. He assumed he had crashed into the sea, and pressed ahead with his mission.

Cairo was an hour ahead of Tel Aviv. The attack time of 0845, Egypt time, had been chosen very deliberately. In the short history of air combat, bombers usually went in at dawn or dusk, to hide in the rising or setting sun. The Israelis knew that the Egyptians flew dawn patrols every day. But by 0845, assuming the moment of maximum danger had passed, they were back at their bases to refuel and to have breakfast. Intelligence reports had told the Israelis that it was also the time when all the commanders of the Egyptian air force were on their way to work. They were on the road, in their staff cars, cut off from what was about to happen to their squadrons. Weather was also a factor. In June there are often low clouds at dusk over the Nile Delta. By a quarter to nine, they have usually burnt off.

In his Vautour Herzl Bodinger was starting to worry that this morning of all mornings, the weathermen had got it wrong. The four Vautours hit a canopy of low clouds as they flew along the Nile where feluccas, traditional sailing boats, were moving peacefully as on any other day. The moment Bodinger worried about most was when, just short of Beni Sweif airfield, he would have to pull up to around 6000 feet to start his bomb run. If there was thick cloud an accurate dive would be impossible. When the airfield came into view, Bodinger realised luck really was on their side. Beni Sweif had been built on dunes in the middle of irrigated farmland. All around the base mist was rising from the damp fields in the early morning sun. But nothing was coming up from the dry concrete runways. The way to Beni Sweif was open. It sat there in front of them, an open window in the mist, as the Egyptian sun rose higher in the sky.

Air Force Command Centre, Ministry of Defence, Tel Aviv, 0740

Weizman could hardly stand the suspense. 'The defence minister was there, as was the chief of staff and his deputy . . . Breathing was uneven, faces pale.' Though Mordechai Hod looked calm as he sat waiting, he too was affected by the crushing tension. He was drinking whole jugs of water, taking them in both hands and draining them dry. Weizman thought he was 'a kind of giant radiator'.

Bin-Nun and his flight were heading for the airfield at Fayed, west of the Suez canal. Intelligence had told them that it was the base for three combat squadrons – MiG-19 and -21 fighters and Sukhoi-7 bombers. 'Our plan of attack was to climb over the target, dive-bomb and then fire our 30 mm guns at the planes on the field.' Israel had deliberately kept everything as simple as possible. Except at the moment of attack, the aircraft operated in waves. They broke Egyptian radar cover simultaneously. To preserve the element of surprise they did not attack or try to jam Egyptian radar stations. Thanks to excellent, extremely comprehensive intelligence, the routes they followed were chosen to avoid concentrations of air defences or bases that could have raised the alarm. They used very simple methods of navigation – Weizman called it 'by clock and the good old compass'. They had good maps and accurate data about the terrain they flew over. Over the years, the IAF had flown hundreds of photo-reconnaissance missions to build up a picture of every airbase in Egypt, Syria and Jordan. Pilots had a target book, giving details of the layout, call sign and defences of every airfield. When the Jordanians searched downed Israeli pilots, they found the books in their coveralls. They showed exactly where to attack, where to crack the runways and where the air-defence network was weakest. From radio intercepts they built up voice-recognition files of the main commanders.

Fayed Airbase, Egypt, 0800

Tahsen Zaki commanded a wing of Sukhoi fighters, based at Fayed airbase, on the banks of the Suez canal. They were on full alert. War, they knew, was close and VIPs were coming that morning. At 0800 two aircraft had taken off from al Maza airbase, next to Cairo International airport. They contained a group led by Hussein al Shafei, a vice-president of Egypt and one of President Nasser's closest advisers. With him was Taher Yahya, the deputy prime minister of Iraq. The day before he had signed Iraq up to Egypt's defence agreement with Jordan; at the solemn ceremony in Cairo he said he was honoured to be in 'the beating heart of Arabism, participating in . . . the battle of the Arab nation's destiny'. He was about to get much closer to the battle than he could ever have expected. Shafei was taking Yahya to visit an Iraqi unit that had already installed itself in the Sinai. The son of the Iraqi president was one of its officers. As Shafei's aircraft approached Fayed, he looked out of the window and saw several grey warplanes flying close to them. Shafei, who had delivered his brother officers in the cavalry to Nasser's coup in 1952, was a man of some substance in Egypt. He assumed the planes were escorting him and his guest into Fayed. He pointed them out to Yahya and settled back in his seat.

Another party of Arab VIPs was in the air over Sinai. At 0730 Field Marshal Amer and Lieutenant-General Sidqi Mahmoud, the air force commander, had also left al Maza for their visit to Bir Tamada in the Sinai to meet the commanders of the troops who were lined up against Israel. In Tel Aviv the Israelis picked out the radar silhouette of the Egyptian commanders' Illyushin 14 over the Suez canal. The Israeli air force commander Mordechai Hod felt queasy. What if the Illyushin spotted the Israeli air armada and raised the alarm? He could not break radio silence to warn his pilots.

Tel Aviv, 0800

The daughters of Colonel Mordechai Bar On set off to walk to school. He had spent the night at GHQ in Tel Aviv, but he did not tell his family that war was starting. It was not just because of the orders to preserve security. Bar On was convinced by the pilots he had met that Egyptian bombers would not be able to take off, let alone threaten Israeli cities. 'I didn't think there was an existential danger. A pilot I spoke to at GHQ said I give you my word, not one Egyptian plane will get to Tel Aviv. I recall it vividly. You can't imagine how arrogant they were, but they were right.' In Israel sirens are usually heard only when the whole nation stops for a couple of minutes a year to remember the victims of the Holocaust and soldiers who have died in wars. When air-raid sirens sounded in Tel Aviv as Bar On's daughters were on their way to school, they stopped and stood to attention.

Cairo, 0845

Across Egypt the first wave of Israeli warplanes moved into attack. Like Bodinger, Bin-Nun had been worried about the morning mist as they roared low over the Nile Delta and the Suez canal. But just as the weathermen promised, it was clear over Fayed. As Bin-Nun approached the airfield, he pulled his Mystere into a climb. Israeli pilots were going to dive-bomb from an altitude of 6–9000 feet because it made them harder to shoot down and because the bombs had to be launched at an angle of 35 degrees if they were going to penetrate properly. He went to switch on his radio. It wasn't working. Never mind, he didn't need it. He entered a steep dive, letting his bombs go at 4000 feet. By now the attacking Israelis had been spotted and Egyptian interceptors waiting on the ground, their pilots strapped in, tried to scramble. 'As I dived and released my bombs, I saw four MiG-21s at the end of the runway lining up to take off. I pulled the bomb release, began firing and hit two of the four, which went up in flames.'

Radio silence ended when the first wave went in. In Tel Aviv, Hod could not believe what he was hearing. 'Everybody started to talk on the squadron channel among themselves, and I'm listening, I'm switching from one to another and I don't believe what I hear. Results!' The IAF recorded some of the cockpit radio traffic:

FLIGHT LEADER: Two MiGs at eleven o'clock below, two
  miles . . .
WING MAN: Permission to take the right one?
FLIGHT LEADER: Watch above, I'm going down . . . taking
  the left one . . . watch the rear . . . opening fire . . . hit . . .
  breaking left . . .
WING MAN: Taking the right one . . . got him . . .

At Bir Tamada airfield in the Sinai the Egyptian top brass on parade and away from their posts included the head of the advance command centre, General Murtagi, his chief of staff Major-General Ahmad Isma'il, and the commander of the field army General Salah Muhsin.

107

The guard of honour for the distinguished visitors was lining up when the first Israeli planes screamed in towards the airfield. Until they started to bomb, Murtagi thought they were Egyptian. Even when the first bombs exploded he assumed that it must be some sort of Egyptian betrayal, perhaps a coup. The last thing he thought of, as they dived for cover, was an Israeli attack. Then it became very clear where the fighters had come from – but where was the Egyptian air force? They waited in a trench while the Israelis went about their business. 'We were sure that our Egyptian fighters would soon appear in the sky and take matters in hand, but we waited for some time in vain . . .'

The abortive meeting with Amer at Bir Tamada meant that every Egyptian headquarters in the Sinai, from the field army down, was without its commanders. At General Salah Muhsin's field army HQ, Captain Salahadeen Salim heard jets screaming overhead, and then the sound of explosions. Soon reports were coming in that Israeli armour was moving forward in massive force. Salim and the others who were left at the headquarters tried to analyse what was happening and to rally their troops for defence. But even their own command post was not ready. It did not have proper dugouts or sandbags and was vulnerable to artillery or air attack. But for the time being at least the Israelis seemed to be leaving them alone. Salim had wanted desperately to trust his commanders. But in the first hour of the war he was cursing them. Muhsin was away from his post on what seemed to be a wild goose chase to meet the field marshal at a remote airbase, and the Israelis were attacking. It was crazy. Surely Amer and Muhsin should have worked out that a surprise attack was coming? The crisis had been going on for three weeks, after all.

Israel, 0800; Gaza, 0900

It was the day of the final examinations of the academic year in Gaza's schools. Kamel Sulaiman Shaheen, a 25-year-old teacher, was looking forward to the end of term. His classroom in Gaza City was full and the day's tests were starting when they heard the first shells falling.

Israeli aircraft were overhead as they evacuated the school. Shaheen's students were thirteen-year-old boys. He told them to run home as quickly as they could, then headed to his own home and family in Deir al Balah, about ten miles south. He took them to some agricultural land they owned, which was further away from places that could be targets and where they felt safer. They sheltered in a building close to the palm trees, and hoped for the best. On the roads they saw Egyptian and Palestinian soldiers leaving their posts and moving south to try to get to Egypt. Shaheen felt sorry for them. The Israelis seemed to have an unstoppable military machine, with big guns, helicopters and jets.

Ibrahim El Dakhakny, a 34-year-old major in Egyptian military intelligence, had been stationed in Gaza since 1965. His job was keep an eye on the movements of Israeli armed forces on the other side of the border and to liaise with Palestinians who were prepared to carry out guerrilla operations in Israel. Thanks to the blue-helmeted peacekeeping troops of UNEF, the border had been quiet for more than a decade. But nobody had ever formally stood down the Palestinian guerrillas, known by both sides as the *fedayeen* (the self-sacrificers). The major was a worried man. For two years he had been observing the Israelis, reading the intelligence reports from the special observation points he had established to spy over the border and listening to his radio. He was convinced that this was the right war for Israel and the wrong one for Egypt. The politicians in Cairo had given Israel the chance, for which it had been preparing since the last war ended in 1956, to finish off the Egyptian army once and for all. Like all Egyptian professional soldiers, he knew how the war in Yemen had drained the army beyond the point where it could fight Israel as well. Major El Dakhakny could not understand why Egypt's leaders were leading their country to war against an enemy which was sure to beat them. Maybe Nasser was hoping to turn defeat into a political victory, just as he had in 1956. He hoped so, because war would be bad. It would be very bad.

On 5 June he was woken by the sound of anti-aircraft fire. Close to where he lived in Gaza City was a battery manned by Palestinians who had enlisted in the Palestine Liberation Army. In Gaza the PLA amounted to a brigade, trained and equipped by Egypt. Their brigade was called Ein Galout, named after the battlefield where the Egyptians turned back the invading Mongol armies in the Middle Ages. A messenger came to tell El Dakhakny that anti-aircraft fire had brought down an Israeli Ouragan. A launch was on its way to pick up the pilot, who had ejected into the sea. A dripping wet Israeli called Mordechai Livon was brought in for interrogation. Livon told El Dakhakny that the Israeli air force was in the process of destroying Egypt's airfields and every aircraft on them. He was put into a car and sent to Cairo for more questioning.

Negev desert, Israel, 0815

Israeli Chief of Staff Yitzhak Rabin phoned Brig. Gen. Gavish in the Negev desert. 'The Knesset session is on,' he said, the prearranged code authorising him to launch the ground offensive into Sinai. Into his microphone, Gavish said 'Red Sheet', another code word which went out to his divisional commanders.

The plan was to hit the Egyptians with three main thrusts. Brigadier-General Israel Tal's division of two armoured brigades, a paratroop brigade reinforced by tanks and a couple of battalion-sized independent task forces was to take the northern route to the Suez canal, through Rafah at the border of Egypt and Gaza, via Al-Arish to Al-Qantarah on the canal. Tal's force of 300 tanks, 100 half-tracks and 50 guns included the 7th Armoured Brigade, Israel's elite tank formation.

Further south, Brigadier-General Ariel Sharon's division, made up of an armoured brigade, a paratroop brigade and an infantry brigade, was to attack a complex of defensive positions at Abu Ageilah, a strategic road junction, and then go west towards Mitla and Giddi, the two vital passes that run through the Sinai's otherwise impassable mountains. He had about 200 tanks, 100 half-tracks and about 100 guns. The third division was commanded by Brig. Gen.

Avraham Yoffe. It was made up mainly of reservists and had two armoured brigades with 200 tanks, 100 half-tracks and no guns. Yoffe's first job was to cross sand dunes that the Egyptians believed were impassable to guard the flanks of Sharon and Tal's divisions.

Waves of Israeli jet fighters roared over the heads of Ori Orr's reconnaissance unit at the gates of Gaza. He was going to attack Rafah by way of Khan Younis, a town in Gaza a few miles further east along the Mediterranean. The code word, Red Sheet, came over the walkie-talkie. It meant break radio silence and advance immediately into battle. Orr gave his men a last briefing: 'This is it. We've learned our objectives, we've practised them thoroughly. I'm relying on you. Everyone in their vehicles, we're off.' The men who were about to go into action were given a few minutes for some last postcards. There were simple messages like 'It's just starting. See you later,' or 'Don't do anything heroic. Get down into the shelters when there is an alarm. Look after the children,' or 'When you grow up you won't have to fight.' The Israeli troops, to a man, believed they were fighting for the survival of their families. One soldier with a sense of humour sent a postcard to Prime Minister Levi Eshkol.

Orr led his two squads out, positioning them between the battalion of Patton tanks and the battalion of Centurions. As they moved, Orr saw the unit's two clerks, Sara and Nira, 'left behind in the dust, gathering up the postcards. They wave goodbye through tears. A last memory from another world, from home.'

The battle for Rafah was going to be crucial. In his final briefing Tal told his officers: 'The one who wins this battle will harbour the spirit of the offensive. The one who loses will feel retreat in his soul . . . the fate of the State is bound up with what we now do . . . this battle must be fought, if necessary, to the death. There is no other course. Each man will charge forward to the very end, irrespective of the cost in casualties. There will be no halt and no retreat. There will only be the assault and the advance.'

Amman, 0850

King Hussein was at home with his family, waiting for his wife, Princess Muna, to join him for breakfast. She had been Toni Gardiner, the daughter of one of the officers in the British military mission to Jordan, when she caught his eye at a fancy dress party. He had been dressed as a pirate. Cheekily, she told him he looked scruffy. Now they had two sons. Before she appeared, though, the phone rang. It was the king's chief aide-de-camp, Colonel Jazy. 'Your Majesty, the Israeli offensive has begun in Egypt. It's just been announced by Radio Cairo.' The king called the military HQ, which told him a coded set of orders from Field Marshal Amer had come in. It claimed that three-quarters of the attacking Israeli planes had been destroyed and that the Egyptians were attacking in the Sinai. Amer was therefore ordering the commander-in-chief of the Jordanian front to attack. Hussein forgot about breakfast. He drove, fast, to army headquarters.

Ihsan Shurdom stood in a slit trench a short run from his Hawker Hunter fighter at Mafrak airbase. He was getting more and more frustrated. As soon as the news had come that the war had started, he had expected to take off again straight away. But they had waited and waited and they were still waiting. The reasons lay in Egypt's military HQ in Cairo – which was gripped by chaos and panic – and the chronic lack of trust in the Arab coalition, which made a nonsense of its own boasts about strength and unity. The Jordanian pilots were waiting for the Syrian and Iraqi air forces so they could mount a joint attack. King Hussein kept a record of what was going wrong. The first call to the Syrians was made at 0900. The outbreak of war has taken us by surprise, they said. Our pilots are on a training flight. 'They asked us to give them first a half-hour, then an hour, and so on until 1045 when they asked for yet another delay which we also granted. At eleven o'clock, we couldn't wait any longer.' When the king and the others at the headquarters saw radar screens showing waves of aircraft heading into Israel, they assumed they were Egyptians flying more missions. At that point they still had no idea that the Egyptians were lying to them. At Mafrak they had access to the same radar information. But Shurdom and his colleagues correctly deduced that the planes were Israelis, on their way back to their bases to refuel and rearm. 'When the balloon went up, we could see the Israeli aeroplanes on radar, coming back, and we said let's go and engage them. They're short on fuel. But they said no, because people thought that these were Egyptian aeroplanes bombing Israel . . . we could have damaged the Israelis, and stopped them launching so many sorties.'

Until the week before the war the Royal Jordanian Air Force had planned to raid Israeli airbases. It seemed like the best way to use its slim resources. But once King Hussein signed the agreement with Nasser, the Egyptians said their planes would do the ground attacks. Jordan's job was now air defence. The Jordanians swallowed their doubts and started to take the missiles off the Hunters. Then, they thought a little harder and kept the ground-attack missiles on six of them. Now the orders had changed again. They were to link up with the Syrians and the Iraqis to attack targets in Israel. The Jordanians were ready to go. But the Syrians and the Iraqis still had not turned up.

Herzl Bodinger and the three other Israeli Vautours each made two bombing runs on Beni Sweif. They put the runway out of action by hitting it a third of the way from either end, cutting it into three pieces. Their last bombs had delayed fuses so they would explode if they were moved by the men who would try to fix the runway. Then, with no bombs left, they each made three strafing passes. Only then did the Egyptian anti-aircraft batteries recover from the shock, elevate their guns and start firing. Each of the four Vautours knocked out a bomber with cannon fire. It was easy to hit the big Tupolev.

At Inshas base Ran Pekker released his bombs at 1500 feet. He pulled the stick all the way back and waited for his diving plane to respond. As it came up, he passed low over the main runway. Behind him there was a big explosion. When the three other Mirages in his flight had dropped their bombs, they started to attack the aircraft that were on the ground. 'I could see the MiGs shining below us, a short dive and a long press on the machine guns, the MiGs on the runway were ready to go, now they are in flames with their pilots in their cockpits.'

Pekker's 102 Squadron claimed twenty-three kills during the war, the highest score in the Israeli air force. Six were shot down by one man, Lieutenant Giora. Only one aircraft was lost, flown by the station commander, who was rescued by helicopter from Syria.

At Bir Tamada the Egyptian generals, in their trenches, realised that salvation was not coming from the sky. They embarked on a nasty drive overland back to their posts, while the Israelis hammered home their attacks. Murtagi's command post was only about three kilometres away. He swore to himself the whole way back, blaming Amer and Nasser for getting them into what looked like a serious mess. When he reached his headquarters, news was already coming in about the size of the Israeli raids. Over the next few hours the full picture emerged. The mess was much bigger than he could ever have imagined.

Some of the Egyptian pilots did manage to take off. Film taken by Israeli gun cameras shows that they were not well trained for aerial combat. Israeli aircraft shot them down with cannon fire at a range of 2–300 yards. It was not just that the Israelis were better trained. They knew exactly what the MiG-21 could and could not do. On 16 August 1966 an Iraqi pilot, Captain Munir Rufa, had defected to Israel, flying a MiG-21C, codenamed 'Fishbed' by NATO, at the time the Soviet Union's most modern fighter. It was one of Israeli intelligence's greatest coups. 'It never rains but it pours,' Hod commented cheerily at the time. 'We set up exercises. We gave the MiG-21 to each squadron for a week, to dog-fight and to learn all its tricks and capabilities.' Among the weaknesses they found was a small fuel tank under the pilot's seat which was used to start the engine. In dogfights, they tried to aim for it.

Egypt's entire air defence system had been effectively shut down in case it attacked Field Marshal Amer, General Sidqi and the other VIPs by mistake. The Egyptian anti-aircraft gunners had not been given the morning off – they were still at their posts – but they had been told to exercise great caution. Even if they had been ready to blast at everything that moved, it would not have made a great difference. The Israeli pilots came in low, at less than a hundred feet, below Egyptian radar cover and well below the lowest point at which its batteries of SAM-2 surface-to-air missiles could bring down an aircraft.

Tel Aviv

In Tel Aviv an ecstatic General Ezer Weizman phoned his wife, Re'uma. 'We've won the war,' he shouted. She said, 'Ezer, are you crazy? At ten o'clock in the morning? You've gone and finished the war?' With waves of Israeli planes coming in, Field Marshal Amer was still in the air. His pilot could not find a place to land. Every airfield in Sinai and Suez was under attack. Israel's air force commander, Mordechai Hod, thought about attacking Amer's aircraft, but decided there was no need. By now he had forgotten the anxiety that he had suffered earlier on when he feared Amer's pilot might spot his jets and raise the alarm. Hod and his assistants sat in their bunker in Tel Aviv, plotting the field marshal's progress, 'laughing and curious where he would land'.

In the end, Amer's pilot took him back to Cairo International airport. It was also being bombed by the time they got there, but its concrete runways and taxiways were too big to block. For ninety minutes Egypt's top soldier and the head of its air force were out of contact. The lost hour and a half was one of a series of thin excuses that were later used to explain the Egyptian air force's vulnerability that morning. Nasser's close associate Mohamed Heikal told his readers in *al-Ahram* newspaper that while they were in the air, 'many things had happened, making it impossible to act quickly and strike a strong counter-blow'. It is hard to see what they could have done had they been at their desks, in the face of such a well-planned onslaught. But it was yet another bonus for the Israelis on a morning when everything was going right for them.

Herzl Bodinger limped back to Ramat David, his home base. His Vautour had been hit by shrapnel as he pulled away from the smoking ruins of Beni Sweif airfield. On the way back he too was listening to the radio. Pilots would give their call sign and then report their results. It was already looking a great victory. After some rest, he was told to head back to attack Luxor airfield. Israel believed some Egyptian warplanes had been evacuated there. In contrast to his carefully plotted first mission, attacking an airfield so well known to him that he could draw its layout from memory, this raid would have to be improvised. All they had for navigation were tourist road maps. On the way to Luxor they would have to pass a base that was equipped with MiG-19 interceptors. To protect the Vautours, which would be flying at high altitude leaving clear vapour trails, the plan was that Israeli Mirages would destroy the interceptors' base. As they passed it, Bodinger could see plumes of smoke rising as the Mirages dropped their bombs. He was ordered to activate a new secret device that would jam Egyptian radar-guided weapons systems. To get at the switch Bodinger had to flip up a red plastic cover that was secured by wire. He found the engineers had used steel wire that he could not break. In desperation he tore off the plastic. The raid on Luxor was a success. They destroyed twelve state-of-the-art Tupolev-16 bombers.

On the way back from Luxor Herzl Bodinger's squadron leader radioed him to say that he could see fuel spraying from one of his engines. They decided he would climb as high as possible while he still had two engines, hoping he would sink slowly enough to be able to make it to Israel. His left engine flamed out and he sank to 25,000 feet. With only a few drops of fuel left, he landed on the short tarmac runway at Eilat, at Israel's southern tip. Locals around the airstrip rushed towards the Vautour. There was no ladder, so he climbed out on the back of the aircraft and jumped down into the crowd from the wing. Bodinger was carried off as a hero and given lunch. His hosts were desperate for news. Israelis knew the war had started, and had heard boasts from Cairo Radio that dozens of Israeli aircraft had been shot down. No details had come from the Israeli side. Bodinger told them he was on his second flight of the day and that Israel had won the war. The Egyptian reports were rubbish. It was two in the afternoon.

At Egypt's base at Bir Tamada, there was chaos. It was every man for himself. Ali Mohammed, a nineteen-year-old driver, had like the rest of the soldiers there been preparing for Amer's visit for days. A special bunker had even been constructed in case the great man needed to take shelter. It had not been needed, since Amer was not able to land. But it had received a direct hit from one of the Israeli bombs. Mohammed waited for orders about what to do next, but nobody issued any. More waves of Israeli bombers set about what was left of the base and its aircraft. He noticed that vehicles were being commandeered and driven away packed with men desperate to get out of the firing line. Mohammed took his own decision. He managed to get hold of a truck and drove it out, full of soldiers who were as anxious to get home as he was. The road back to the Suez canal was like a race track. Military vehicles were being driven at breakneck speed by panicking conscripts who wanted no part in the war. There were collisions, injuries and deaths. No one stopped. By the evening, Mohammed was safe.

The Egyptians had also been bothered by the heavier than usual morning haze, putting back some training flights an hour because of it. At 0845, as Vice-President Shafei's plane was coming in to land at Fayed airbase, the Sukhoi pilots boarded their aircraft for their delayed training flight. Then Zaki, the commander of the Sukhoi squadron, heard jet engines coming in fast. For a moment he was paralysed by surprise. All he could do was watch. Something was badly wrong. Two grey Israeli Super Mysteres started bombing the runway. Shafei's aircraft was still taxiing when the first Israeli bomb exploded. Then came another and then another. The VIPs tumbled out of the planes as soon as they could and took cover behind a small earth bank. The second plane in Shafei's group did not escape. It took a burst of cannon fire as it was coming into land. Its pilot managed to pull away from the battle. Eventually, he made a forced landing at a base near the Suez canal. Many of the people on board, mostly bodyguards and officials, were killed.

By now the main runway at Fayed was cratered and unusable. But the side runway was only blocked, by Shafei's plane, which was burning. Some of the Sukhoi pilots started up their aircraft to try to manoeuvre their way past it and take off. Zaki ran across, shouting and waving his arms to stop them leaving. Vice-President Shafei lay behind his small hummock and watched what was happening. 'It was an unforgettable sight. Our fighters were lined up in rows and the Israelis took them out with single bursts from their guns. They were an easy target.' The Israeli pilots flew so low that Shafei could see their faces. Zaki and ground crew and construction workers who had been working at the base tried to push some of the Sukhois out of sight, behind buildings or under the trees. 'There were explosions everywhere but we kept going and managed to save a few planes although some of the men doing the pushing were killed.' Zaki sent a pilot in a jeep to get Shafei and the Iraqi deputy prime minister out of the trench and into the base offices. After the jeep had careered to a halt outside the building and Shafei was dusting himself down inside, he was faced with a group of furious Egyptian pilots, who had watched their fighters being blown to pieces. Before the attack the air force had been full of the supposedly secret information that the previous Friday Nasser had ordered Sidqi Mahmoud to ride out an Israeli first strike. Now they were getting hammered. Look what you've done, they told him. Are you happy with this? Why didn't you let us strike first? Outside some of the anti-aircraft gunners had recovered themselves sufficiently to open up on the Israelis. Other soldiers were firing into the air with rifles and machine guns. Somehow, one of the Israeli aircraft was brought down. Tahsen Zaki, the squadron commander, went out to inspect the wreckage. The dead Israeli pilot was still strapped into his seat.

'He looked as if he was asleep. He was a handsome, elegant young man. I told the men to bury him immediately.' Zaki was hoping that the attack was limited. But when he went to his operations room, he found out just how much the Israeli first wave had destroyed – and more attacks were being reported all the time. He looked round his airfield. Burning aircraft were everywhere. The runways were destroyed. He thought about trying to get his few remaining fighters into the air from the road

118

outside the base, but that would mean demolishing a perimeter wall. At 1100 he had a call from Field Marshal Amer – the first time in his life he had ever spoken to the commander-in-chief. He gave him a damage report. All the MiG-21s were destroyed. Twelve Sukhois and three MiG-19s had been saved. Very well, Amer said, execute Operation Leopard, which was the plan to attack Israeli airbases. Zaki told Amer that he would try to clear the side runway. He would report back in two hours. Amer was so panic-stricken that he had forgotten about the chain of command. He was bypassing his subordinates and phoning desperately, on open lines, to try to make something happen. In the first few hours of the war, the Egyptian high command was already close to collapse.

Cairo, 0900

Mahmoud Riad, the foreign minister of Egypt, was sleeping late. He was woken by 'a shattering explosion'. He realised Israel must have started its attack. He left his house in a hurry for his office at the foreign ministry. Most of the foreign journalists were staying at the Nile Hilton, Cairo's most modern hotel. Trevor Armbrister of the *Saturday Evening Post* was having a lazy morning. He was woken by the rattling of the hotel's windows. He decided it was just the wind and called room service to order breakfast. The operator said, 'We cannot serve food, we are being bombed.' The lifts were not working so Armbrister rushed down the stairs. Winston Burdett, a veteran reporter who had been a correspondent for CBS News since 1943, heard a 'deep and laboured pounding'. He went to the balcony of his room to see what was happening. A few minutes later the first air-raid siren of the war wailed out across the city. There had been rehearsals for air raids before. But they had all been announced in advance. This one wasn't. It must, he realised, be the real thing. The traffic stopped outside the hotel, on the broad corniche that runs along the bank of the Nile. Burdett noticed the traffic lights went on flicking from green to red. Then, 'as silence fell on the streets, the smothered pounding of the ack-ack batteries grew more distinct.'

No one at the Soviet Embassy that morning was expecting war. They had gathered at the monthly meeting where they paid their subscriptions to the Communist Party. A deputy military attaché was the centre of attention, lecturing them on his theories about the coming war. It was going to be resolved in the next few days, and Israel would shoot first. He had just finished when a diplomat stormed into the room. 'Switch the radio on! It's war!' They heard the final phrase of the official announcement, that Egyptian troops 'have repelled Israel's treacherous aggression and are now advancing on all sections of the front'.

On the streets it felt as if every transistor radio in the city was on, with a crowd of people gathered around each one. They looked proud and anxious. At first, Cairo Radio just played military music. Listeners who had tuned into the Arabic service of Israel Radio heard the news first, at 0922, seventeen minutes after its Hebrew service had told the people of Israel. 'A spokesman for the Israel Defence Force has stated that fierce fighting started this morning between the Egyptian air force and tanks which were moving towards Israel, and the Israeli forces which rushed to repel them.' On Cairo Radio the military music faded out just before ten to ten. An announcer, sounding excited, made a brief statement. 'Citizens, here is important news: Israel has begun to attack Egypt. Our forces are confronting the enemy. We shall give you reports later on.'

In the Jewish quarters in Cairo and Alexandria, Jews were being rounded up by the authorities. Between 350 and 600 men between the ages of 18 and 55 were arrested, including the chief rabbis of both cities, out of a Jewish population of around 3000. In Libya, as soon as news of the war broke, mobs attacked the Jewish quarters of Tripoli and Benghazi. Many buildings were set on fire, including most of the synagogues. The army stepped in to restore order. Up to a thousand Jews were taken to an army camp where they were protected from the riots, which went on until the 8th. But others were still vulnerable – eighteen Jews were killed in the riots. By the end of July 2500 Jews had left for Italy. They were only allowed to take personal effects and £50. Everything else had to be left behind. In Tunis crowds attacked the

British and US Embassies, and then moved on to the Jewish quarter. Five synagogues and many shops were burnt down. It took police and firemen four hours to arrive. Tunisia's President Bourghiba, the most conciliatory Arab leader, went on television the same evening to condemn what had happened. He sent two cabinet ministers to apologise to the chief rabbi and to promise compensation. The next day police arrested 330 rioters. In July 113 of them were given sentences from two months to twenty years. In Aden British troops stepped in to protect the remnants of what had been a big Jewish community. There was still arson and after the war a Jew was beaten to death. More Jews left Aden, to Britain and Israel.

Sinai, 0900

Yahya Saad was a junior officer in an Egyptian reconnaissance unit near Kuntilla in the Sinai. One of the patrols they had sent into Israeli territory warned them of a large force of Sherman tanks heading straight towards them. It was the armoured brigade of Colonel Albert Mendler, which had been moving noisily up and down the southern border for several days, reinforced by camouflaged decoys, to convince the Egyptians that Israel was preparing to rerun the 1956 war by moving south to Sharm al Sheikh. Saad's unit fought doggedly, but they were outgunned. They tried to attack the Shermans with rocket-propelled grenades (RPGs).

'I lay down waiting for a tank. When it was in range I fired but the weapon did not work. The whole area was turning into hell. Another soldier's didn't work and a tank came at him shooting. He ran at the tank carrying the RPG. The tank squashed him . . . They fired machine guns and more soldiers fell . . . I tried the RPG again and it didn't work. I didn't know whether the weapons were bad, the ammunition was bad or the leadership was bad. Tanks were shooting at short range. We were expecting to die under the tracks like so many others . . . I was in total shock to see my group torn to pieces after we had fought so bravely. I looked around and saw squashed corpses and injured men I could not save.' The battle moved past Saad. He picked himself up and walked into the desert.

Gaza, 0900

Tal's division started its attack. The 7th Armoured Brigade went west over the border into Khan Younis. His other armoured brigade, the 60th, went south into the sand dunes to outflank Rafah's minefields, barbed wire, dug-in infantry and anti-tank guns. They got stuck in the soft sand. By nightfall, they still had not fired a shot. Between them, the paratroop brigade was supposed to attack the Egyptian and Palestinian forces who were holding Rafah. At first it also lost its way, along with the tanks it had in support.

Luckily for Tal, his 7th Armoured Brigade executed its mission, though it ran into much heavier fire than expected from a brigade of Egypt's 7th Infantry Division and a battalion of Palestinians, along with about 150 Second World War Stalin tanks – heavy but obsolete – and 90 artillery pieces. Much of the fighting was confused, out of the control of Tal or anyone else for that matter. Colonel Raphael Eitan, the commander of 202nd Paratroop Brigade, led his men through 'hand-to-hand fighting . . . We fought for our lives. I kept firing my Uzi, non-stop.' Ori Orr's Pattons, the 7th Armoured's reconnaissance unit, took the direct route, a frontal assault up the road into the suburbs of Khan Younis. Orr, following up the road with his half-tracks, saw 'Egyptian soldiers stand by the road in amazement, watching the line go past. One waves to our soldiers, who look cautiously back. Is this war? Suddenly, hell opens its mouth.' A radio operator picked up a voice lamenting in Arabic, 'They are on us. Two great columns of dust. What can we do? What can we do?' But most of the Egyptian and Palestinian soldiers were ready to fight. Heavy fire ripped into the Israelis. The Egyptian position was well prepared, with minefields and anti-tank obstacles that the Israelis had to manoeuvre around slowly. A sniper picked off one of Orr's tank commanders. They rode with their bodies exposed in their turrets. It was supposed to give them a better idea of the battlefield. It also made them easier to kill.

Shelling was coming from both sides of Orr's position. Another half-track was hit. All eight men inside were killed. Orr and his men and the tanks moved forward towards the Egyptian positions. After they had gone 150 metres, he realised they were in a minefield. His own half-track car hit a mine and turned over. He continued on foot, following the tanks, as 'turning back now would have caused many casualties'. Yarkoni, one of the men who had scribbled out a postcard as they moved off, jumped into a trench to start clearing it. A wounded Egyptian soldier shot him. 'This is the end,' he said to the men who carried him away, just before he died. Sergeant Bentzi Zur, the senior NCO in Orr's by now crippled command car, flagged down another jeep so he could go on fighting. When they stopped to help the crew of the knocked-out tank, the jeep had a direct hit and blew up. Zur and its other two occupants were killed.

The Israelis changed their plan, encircling Khan Younis before they entered it. Some of them, who had been hopelessly lost in the narrow alleys, noticed that the main attraction at the local cinema was the Beatles film, *Help*.

Ramadan Mohammed Iraqi drove one of the Egyptian army's communications trucks. On Sunday night he was warned that war could start in the morning by an officer from a reconnaissance unit who had crossed the border into Israel and seen the preparations. Since morning the two radio specialists who operated his truck had been complaining about the interference. Their sets seemed to be jammed. They were right. Throughout Sinai the chaos that was engulfing the Egyptian army was made worse by the successful jamming of their communications network. In the morning Ramadan and his two comrades felt optimistic about the war. But then stories started to circulate about the destruction of the Egyptian air force, which made them feel vulnerable. Initially their sector, near Rafah, was quiet. 'Then we were surprised to see the Israelis advancing and destroying our vehicles.' Ramadan left his truck to reconnoitre what he thought could be a way out. When he got back to his truck it was on fire. His two friends who worked the radios were lying in the sand, dead. 'Their air force was attacking us. It was every man for himself.'

UNEF troops found themselves in the firing line. Three Indian soldiers were killed south of Khan Younis when their column of white-painted vehicles was strafed by Israeli aircraft. At 1230, five more Indians were killed and more than a dozen wounded, by IDF artillery fire directed at their camp. From New York the UN secretary general sent a strong protest to the Eshkol government about the 'tragic and unnecessary loss of life'.

But the Israelis were making progress. Major El Dakhakny of Egyptian military intelligence was not surprised. He had realised some time before that it was impossible to defend a narrow, flat piece of land like the Gaza Strip from tanks and mechanised infantry, especially when it was backed up by artillery that was safely dug in well behind Israel's borders. He sent his *fedayeen* guerrillas into Israel, each with a target to attack. There was not much more he could do. Major Dakhakny radioed Cairo requesting permission to pull back with his men to Al-Arish. Not a chance, he was told. Tal's tanks had moved on from Khan Younis to Rafah. They put down accurate fire at long range and overwhelmed its defences. Israel had cut the Gaza Strip. Dakhakny knew the battle had been going badly, but the Israelis had moved much faster than he had imagined. He was told to try to escape by boat.

Qalqilya, West Bank, 0900

Seventeen-year-old Fayek Abdul Mezied was extremely excited. The Cairo radio station Voice of the Arabs had just announced the start of the war. The news raced around the town. Israeli aircraft were falling like flies. Victory seemed to be approaching fast, just as Ahmed Said and all the other commentators had predicted. Fayek was in the civil defence network. They were going to help the doctors at the four first aid centres that had been set up. Some of his friends, who had linked

124

up with Yasser Arafat's faction, Fatah, were being given weapons. They were old guns left over from 1948, but they were guns. Finally they were going to have a chance to fight the Israelis to restore the land and the dignity that had been lost.

The small town of Qalqilya made Israelis feel vulnerable. It was right on the Jordanian border, at the foot of the mountains that form the spine of the West Bank. From Qalqilya to the Mediterranean was around ten miles. Israel's strategic nightmare was a thrust from Qalqilya to the sea that would cut the state in two. Since 1948 there had been plenty of cross-border violence in and around the town. The bloodiest battle was in 1956, when Israel mounted a reprisal raid into Qalqilya to blow up the fortified police station. Seventy to ninety Jordanian legionnaires and eighteen Israeli paratroops were killed in the fighting. On 5 June Jordan had only two battalions from the Princess Alia Brigade to cover the border between Qalqilya and Tulkarem, another border town about fifteen miles away. But facing them were roughly the same number of troops. A thrust to split Israel might have been possible. But the Jordanians did not take their chance. Instead they sat tight, trading bursts of gunfire across the border and opening up with their artillery – two batteries of 25-pounders and two batteries of 155 mm 'Long Tom' long-range guns. The Israelis saw the big guns as a real threat. They sent warplanes after them as soon as they had finished off the Arab air forces.

As well as the Jordanian army around 200 men from the local detachment of the National Guard were dug in around Qalqilya. They were commanded by Tawfik Mahmud Afaneh, a 39-year-old who had fought the Israelis in 1948. The National Guard was made up of local men with light weapons. They were a sort of home guard, almost untrained locals with a scattering of old soldiers, who were supposed to help the army defend the frontier and to raise the alarm if Israel attacked. Like all the Palestinians along the border, after every Israeli incursion they demanded weapons from the Hashemites to defend themselves. The king always refused, because he thought Palestinians with guns would turn them either on him or on the Israelis, neither of which he wanted. The result was that on the

125

morning of 5 June, Tawfik Mahmud Afaneh's men dug in to fight Israeli tanks and heavy artillery with Bren and Sten guns, two British standbys from the Second World War. They had nothing heavier, not even mortars. They fought bravely against impossible odds. In two days in the front line, twenty-five of Tawfik's men were killed.

Memdour Nufel had always wanted to strike a few blows of his own. He was a young Palestinian man who had grown up during the border wars of the 1950s. As a small boy he sneaked across the border to put stones on the railway line, hoping he might derail a train. After 1965, like hundreds of other young Palestinians, he decided he wanted to be part of the armed struggle against Israel. Nufel linked up with two groups with the dramatic names of 'heroes of return' and 'youth of revenge'. In a society where young people were supposed to defer to their elders, a few eyebrows went up when he organised fourteen men of his father's age to spy on Israeli positions and military movements. He chose them because they knew well the ground on the Israeli side of the border. Some of it used to be theirs. They were experienced infiltrators, who usually earned a living smuggling or rustling cattle. Eighty per cent of Qalqilya's land had been lost to the Israelis in 1948. Nufel passed on their information to Palestinians in the Jordanian army, who told him they sent it to Cairo.

On the morning of 5 June, Nufel's middle-aged guerrillas came to his house to ask the young man what they should do. He told them they should take their weapons (Nufel had acquired an elderly Karl-Gustav machine gun) to fight alongside the Jordanian army. They all thought it was a bad idea. Once the war was over, the Jordanians would throw them into prison. It was a fair point. In June 1967 hundreds of Palestinian nationalists languished in King Hussein's prisons. The Hashemite regime saw them as greater threats to itself than they were to Israel. Various estimates put the number of captives from Yasser Arafat's faction, Fatah, at anything from 250 to 1000, or put another way up to eighty per cent of its strength. Abu Ali Iyad, the local Fatah leader, was on the Jordanians' wanted list. But Nufel persuaded them that this would be different. After checking on their families, who were heading out of town into caves and olive groves in the hills, Nufel's little band moved forward to the front line.

Tel Aviv, 1000

Israel wanted to keep its success quiet for the time being. The deception plan for the offensive was drawn up as carefully as the offensive itself. At the very start the priority was to deny that Israel had attacked. According to Meir Amit, the head of Mossad, '[General Moshe] Dayan did a very clever thing. He made a mask of fog about what we were doing at the moment that Egypt was announcing the enormous success of its army. Even my wife said to me, what's happening, they're killing us? For forty-eight hours Dayan kept it ambiguous. The whole world was listening to Egypt. It gave us another advantage.'

An official first version of how the war started was released, saying Egypt had fired the first shots: 'This morning Egypt has started an air–ground attack. Egyptian armoured forces advanced at dawn towards the Negev. Our own forces advanced to repel them. At the same time a large number of radar tracks of Egyptian jets were observed on the screen. The tracks were directed towards the Israeli shore line. A similar attempt was also executed in the Negev area. IDF air force aircraft took to the air against enemy aircraft. Air battles are still going on. The Prime Minister has called an urgent meeting with a number of ministers.'

But a journalist was already looking for the real story. An Israeli officer who had been in the desert stopped off at a friend's house in Jerusalem to wash off the dust before he went to Prime Minister Eshkol's office to brief the cabinet. The friend was Michael Elkins, who was the correspondent in Israel for CBS, Newsweek and the BBC. The officer was cheerful, serenading the Elkins household from the shower. Elkins, a New York Jew who had turned to journalism after he fought in the 1948 war, could not persuade his friend to tell him anything, but he guessed something big had happened. Elkins hurried over to the Knesset, the Israeli parliament, to see what he could find out. He went into the basement and started listening to the excited conversations going on among the politicians.

Jordanian Military Headquarters, Amman, 1130

General Odd Bull of the United Nations was put through to King Hussein. On the telephone from Jerusalem he passed on a message from Eshkol. Israel, it said, was engaged in operations against Egypt. If you don't intervene, Jordan will not be attacked. But for Hussein the message came far too late. His experience after the Samua raid, which came a day after he had received an unsolicited secret message from Israel telling him that Jordan would be left alone, had taught him not to trust Israeli assurances. He had made his decision days earlier. And, at that moment, with reports coming in from Cairo that the Israeli air force was being pulverised, it did not seem such a bad one. Hussein told Bull 'they started the battle. Now they are receiving our reply by air.'

Jerusalem

The Jordanians opened fire along the confrontation line. Its artillery fired into West Jerusalem, mainly, though not always and not accurately, at military positions. The UN observer force, that had maintained the armistice for a generation, tried unsuccessfully to arrange several ceasefires. Bullets narrowly missed Britain's senior diplomat in Jerusalem, the consul-general Hugh Pullar, and crashed into his offices. At 1130 he cabled: 'Very heavy automatic fire . . . Jerusalem totally engulfed in war. Guns and mortars . . .' Pullar had just returned from a meeting with a senior Jordanian official. He had asked him if the Arabs' basic intention was to eliminate Israel. In a 'distinctly chilly' way, the official said it was.

John Tleel, a Palestinian dentist, never liked Mondays. He had been at work at his dental surgery in the Christian quarter of the Old City since 6:30 a.m., as usual. Among the patients waiting for him was a schoolteacher, Miss Elisabeth Bawarshi, who was planning a trip to Lebanon. She needed a set of false teeth. At eleven o'clock when he had seen his other patients, he decided to walk across the Old City to pick up Miss Bawarshi's teeth.

'Are you mad?' his brother, who was also a dentist, asked him. 'Haven't you heard the war's started?'

Tleel told his brother not to worry, and set out. The streets, he thought, looked calm and peaceful. But then he realised the shops were closed and he was the only person around. Nobody was there. Garo the Armenian goldsmith, Suleiman the Muslim watch-maker, all the shopkeepers who normally kept their businesses open whatever was going on were all closed. The street leading to the church of the Holy Sepulchre, which is built on the quarry where Christians believe Jesus was crucified and buried, was empty too. Then he saw two men, talking loudly and carrying automatic rifles. They had come from the local police station, where, at the last minute, weapons were being handed out. It was still quiet, so he walked into the big open square just on the inside of Jaffa Gate. A few bystanders had gathered. Jordanian soldiers were trying to move them on. Tleel walked across the square, to check his post office box. It was empty.

Opposite the Jaffa Gate on much higher ground on the Israeli side of the city was the King David hotel. Tleel saw it perched there 'like a giant'. Suddenly, there were great bursts of gunfire. Bullets whizzed past Tleel's head. Terrified, he ran for his life, out of the square, through the narrow, empty streets of the Old City, sheltering sometimes from 'the whining gunfire' until he reached his home. Tleel and his brother were bachelors. They crowded, with some neighbours, into a small room which they thought was more protected than the others. They taped up the windows with sticking plaster, to stop them shattering if there was an explosion, and stretched a blanket across the window frames. The power went off. By candlelight they listened to their transistor radios. They went back and forth along the dials: 'Amman, Cairo, Israel, London, Voice of America. We even tried Athens and Cyprus.' They were hoping to find an honest account of what was happening. 'Soon we realised there were losers and winners and that the losing side was not broadcasting the truth. We argued all the time among ourselves about which side to believe, the Arab or the Israeli.'

Anwar Nusseibeh heard the news that the war had started on his car radio. He was a member of one of Jerusalem's most prominent Palestinian families. Nusseibeh moved in Jordan's royal circles. He had just finished a stint as King Hussein's ambassador in London. He had risen early, to drive to Amman from his home on the Jordanian side of Jerusalem. When he heard what had happened, he turned the car round to go home to his wife and children. Two days before the war, he sat with his brother Hazem, a former Jordanian foreign minister, having lunch on the balcony of their family home, which overlooked Israeli positions in West Jerusalem. They saw a big artillery piece was pointing straight at them. They were not unduly worried, because they assumed that Arab forces were as strong as the radio news claimed. Hazem remembers 'excitement, expectation, enthusiasm and hope. Fear was the last thing, if it existed at all . . . We were seeing Israeli helicopters throttling over our skies and watching them from the balcony and simply smiling.'

Back in Jerusalem, Anwar tried to ring Ahmed Shukairy, the leader of the PLO, who had been staying at the Ambassador hotel in the Sheikh Jarrah district. But Shukairy, who specialised in rabble-rousing, blood-curdling speeches about the destruction of Israel, had checked out. Now that the hour of which he had spoken endlessly had come, he was on his way to Damascus. Then Nusseibeh went to volunteer his services to the Jordanian governor of Jerusalem, Anwar al-Khatib, who was at the police headquarters. 'I went there and they were still talking about organising groups of resistance, issuing rifles, things like that. The day the war was on! Well, there wasn't much that one could do in that kind of situation. I told them that I was at home, you can telephone me. And I came back home.'

One crackpot scheme that was being discussed was a plan to arm the men of Isawiya, the nearest Palestinian village to the Israeli enclave on Mount Scopus, a high point on the escarpment to the east of Jerusalem that overlooked the Old City. With artillery support, untrained civilians would advance uphill and throw themselves on the Israeli defences. It would have been suicidal. Since 1948 Israel had been prohibited by the armistice from bringing in military supplies to its garrison on Mount Scopus. But over nineteen years they smuggled enough military contraband on the fortnightly resupply convoys to turn the enclave into a fortress. They even broke down jeeps armed with anti-tank guns into their constituent parts to get them in. Once when UN inspectors confiscated a suspicious-looking barrel Israel retaliated by confiscating the building in which the barrel was stored.

Jerusalem, 1130

Israel was keeping its success quiet because it did not want to do anything to encourage the Arabs and their friends to accept a ceasefire motion at the UN. But the BBC reporter Michael Elkins worked the story out for himself after a morning spent eavesdropping and asking questions in the basement of the Knesset. 'I heard enough bits and pieces to put it together. Then I went to Ben-Gurion in the basement of the Knesset and told him what I had. He said, yes, it was accurate. I asked him if he would record a message to the Jewish people because Eshkol was busy and wouldn't see me. The only thing he would say was, "Tell the Jewish people not to worry."'

As Elkins was compiling his report, the Jordanian authorities had finally overcome their reluctance to give weapons to Palestinians: 260 Enfield rifles, 20 Sten submachine guns and 20 Bren light machine guns were delivered to the resistance committee that had been set up by Bahjet Abu Gharbiyeh. The army gave out another 100 or so guns. A dozen Stens, still smothered in protective grease, turned up at the radio station. Some of the men had improvised positions in the radio station garden, while the women loaded bullets into magazines. Almost nobody had any military training. Men were taking up firing positions in front of windows that were closed and without tape to catch the pieces if the glass was shattered. Amman had sent them nothing to broadcast, so they played military music, recordings of bursts of machine gun fire and improvised interludes of nationalistic rhetoric. In Amman the Jordanian minister of information, Abd al-Hamid Sharaf, was having lunch with his wife. He was shifting between different stations on his radio. Suddenly he heard a shrieking, hysterical voice, calling for popular mobilisation and victory. It was Jerusalem. He phoned them, ordering them 'to calm down and be more reasonable'. Sharaf, who was in his twenties, venerated Nasser as the best hope of the Arab people. Nasser must be prepared for war, he told Leila, his Lebanese wife, or why would he let it happen?

In Israeli Jerusalem, Michael Elkins was filing his report. 'About three hours after the war started, I broadcast that the war was won. I knew of the air strike on the Egyptian airfields and planes. It was obvious that by fighting in the Sinai desert without air cover the Egyptians couldn't win.' Meir Amit, the head of Mossad, ignored Elkins's heroic efforts. The IDF spokesman denounced reports of Egyptian losses as 'premature, unclear and utterly unauthorised'. In Tel Aviv at midday, Amit briefed the US ambassador Walworth Barbour and Harry C. McPherson, President Johnson's envoy. McPherson was a little ragged around the edges. He had only arrived from Saigon at three that morning. Amit delivered a briefing which, like all the most effective disinformation, contained truth, lies and exaggeration, skilfully calibrated for its audience, whom he knew had its own intelligence sources. Amit told the Americans that Nasser had largely played his build-up by ear, until he had so much momentum he could not stop. Egypt had completed the encirclement of Israel, which had acted because the Arabs were about to launch an offensive. In the previous forty-eight hours the Egyptian 4th Armoured Division and the crack Shazli Brigade, which had 400 tanks between them, had been brought up to encircle and cut off Eilat, thus creating a land link with Jordan.

Amit said early that morning the Egyptians had shelled three Israeli settlements near the Gaza Strip. At the same moment, hostile Egyptian war planes entered Israeli airspace. No Egyptian troops had crossed the border. The day before, Amit told them, Israel had decided to 'punch all the buttons' if there was an attack. Amit then punched the cold war button that he knew was hard-wired into the Americans' minds. Nasser, he said, had started a process that could lead to heavy Soviet pressure on Turkey and Iran to side with the Arabs. It was a Middle East domino theory, which was language Americans in the 1960s understood well. Now, Amit suggested, Nasser might collapse, which would lead to more stability.

Amit had known for more than two hours before the briefing with the Americans that Israel had already won the air war. All the same, speaking with characteristic chutzpah that Barbour, who saw his role as maintaining and strengthening the US–Israel alliance, described as 'entire candour', he reproached his visitors. America's attempts, Amit complained, to restrain Israel had made the job its soldiers, sailors and airmen had to do much more difficult. As Israel had already demonstrated that morning, Amit's suggestion was nonsense. But the last thing he wanted was for the Americans to know how well Israel was doing. He requested political backing, money, weapons and for the Soviets to be kept out of the area.

During Amit's briefing the sirens went. When Harry McPherson 'asked the intelligence chief whether we should go to a shelter, he looked at his watch and said, "It won't be necessary."' The next day, when McPherson saw exhausted Israeli soldiers sleeping in the shade near the Gaza border, the Israeli colonel with him said they had earned their rest. 'They've been driving down here since Sunday afternoon. This place looked like Detroit Sunday night' – twelve hours, as McPherson realised, before the Egyptian 'attack'.

Governments without the USA's intelligence-gathering resources spent weeks trying to puzzle out what really happened. At the end of June a foreign military attaché still had to ask Brigadier General Hod, the commander of the air force, how they could have been so effective when they were responding to a sudden attack. Surely they needed at least six months to prepare such a crushing attack. Hod did not try too hard to keep the secret. He replied, 'Sir, you are right, but not quite. We have been preparing for it for eighteen and a half years.'

Washington DC, 0430

Washington was waking up. By 0430 Walt Rostow, the National Security Advisor, was preparing to rouse the president. The US government heard first about the outbreak of war from news agency reports. One of the overnight staff in the Situation Room at the White House saw them, picked up a phone and started dialling. He woke Rostow just before 0250. Groggily, Rostow told him to call back when the reports were confirmed. Five minutes later the phone rang again with the confirmation. Rostow was in the White House by 0320. He called Secretary of State Dean Rusk who had already gone into the State Department. Rusk suggested they waited an hour or so until they had more facts before they woke the president. Now at 0435, Rostow had a scrawled page of notes in front of him. He was put through to Johnson's bedroom. He told the president what they knew. Johnson asked very few questions and made no comment. At the end he thanked Rostow, who suddenly thought it seemed very ordinary, no different to all their other conversations. Then there was some confusion about the time difference with the Middle East. Was Cairo attacked at 0900 or 0800 local? For a while, the president's advisers tried to work out what time it was in Cairo and Tel Aviv.

By the time Rostow spoke again to Johnson, at 0615 Washington time, hard military intelligence was coming in from intercepts picked up by the National Security Agency. The Egyptian military in Cairo was receiving information that 'at least five' of its airfields in the Sinai and around the Suez canal were 'unserviceable'. The CIA recalled that 'Israel's war plans had put high priority on quick action against the Egyptian air force because of the threat to its own more vulnerable airfields and vital centres.'

Johnson, still in his bedroom, was being briefed on the phone by Rostow and his other top officials. Johnson ordered Rostow to bring in the elder statesmen of American foreign policy to offer their help. First of all McGeorge Bundy, who had been one of Kennedy's key advisers. Bundy took over Rostow's direct responsibility for coordinating Middle East policy. (Rostow was told to concentrate on

Vietnam, though in practice he remained deeply involved with the new war. Later on, the White House press secretary denied speculation that Rostow was taken out of the front seat because he was Jewish.) Also drafted were Dean Acheson, Secretary of State to President Harry Truman, and Clark Clifford, a lawyer who had been deeply involved with US foreign policy since the start of the Cold War. Bundy was made executive secretary of a Special Committee of the NSC. Rusk was the chairman. The idea was to recreate the Executive Committee, or 'ExCom', which handled the Cuban missile crisis in 1961. Just like the ExCom, they took their seats around the big table in the Situation Room, the crisis centre in the basement of the White House.

Cairo, 1030

A group of foreign correspondents hurried down to the TV centre, an impressive ultra-modern curved building, topped by a high-rise tower. It was just a few blocks down the Nile corniche from the Hilton hotel where they were staying. Crowds were mobbing it. 'Well, this is it, war with Israel,' someone said to Ron Chester of Canada's CBC. They pushed their way inside. Trevor Armbrister of the *Saturday Evening Post* saw Kamal Bakr, Egypt's public relations chief, who was 'pudgy [and] quietly unprofessional', pinning military communiqué No. 1 to a notice board. It read: 'Israel began its aggression this morning by raiding Cairo and now the governorates in the UAR [Egypt]. The UAR military crafts face the planes.' Communiqué No. 2 at 1020 reported Radio Tel Aviv had announced an Egyptian raid on the city. Ten minutes later the people grouped round the teleprinter for the Middle East News Agency ticker read that twenty-three Israeli planes had been shot down; 'pandemonium'.

'Twenty-three Israeli planes,' someone yelled, 'twenty-three Israeli planes shot down . . .' US diplomats reported 'effervescence and clapping in the streets' as the news started to spread. The radio went back to playing patriotic songs 'interspersed with calls for a return to

Palestine and a rendezvous in Tel Aviv'. No one seemed to know where the planes had been shot down. Outside, the sky was clear and empty. Just before eleven o'clock there were puffs of white smoke, which they took to be anti-aircraft fire.

A stream of lies was pouring out of the high command. They were passed on to the world through Cairo Radio and through Kamal Bakr at the press centre who kept pinning up the latest communiqués. At 1110 Bakr told them it was forty-two Israeli planes down, not twenty-three. Egypt, he announced proudly, had not lost one. At the press centre the military communiqués 'kept flowing in . . . each one couched in superlatives', with more whooping and cheering every time the latest went up on the notice board. Nothing suggested that the war was going badly for the Arabs. Eric Rouleau of *Le Monde* had plunged into the streets. 'We witnessed extraordinary outbursts of joy. In spite of the air-raid alarms, in spite of anti-aircraft fire, everybody was out in the streets and the crowd . . . shouted: "Nasser, Nasser, we are with you. Nasser, Nasser, finish with Israel." . . . Every time that the loudspeakers announced that an enemy aircraft had been shot down, people embraced, jumped for joy, applauded.' American cameramen trying to film the excited crowds were attacked. New peaks of emotion swept through the streets when an Israeli plane, hit by anti-aircraft fire, crashed into the city centre. Crowds gathered around it, chanting the name of Nasser. They believed he was humiliating the Israelis in the same way that he had humiliated the British and French in 1956.

The speaker of the Egyptian National Assembly, Anwar El Sadat, was in high good humour. He had heard on the radio that Israel had attacked. 'Well,' he thought as he shaved, 'they'll be taught a lesson they won't forget.' He took his time selecting an appropriate suit and tie, then drove himself to GHQ. He had 'unshakeable confidence' in an Egyptian victory. At the headquarters building he saw that the Soviet ambassador's car was there already, 'so I thought that he had called to congratulate us. "What's the news?" I asked. Some officers said we had shot down forty aircraft so far. "Splendid," I said.'

Mafrak Airbase, Jordan, 1150

The Jordanians gave up waiting for their unreliable allies. Sixteen RJAF Hawker Hunters took off on a mission to bomb Israeli bases including the one at Netanya, a town on the coast north of Tel Aviv. They came back half an hour later claiming they had destroyed four enemy planes on the ground, without loss. But they were the only aircraft they saw. The Israeli air force was still concentrating on the Egyptians. But the planners in Tel Aviv were about to switch their attention elsewhere. Hod gave the order to go to the next phase of Operation Focus, the attack on Syria and Jordan.

Damascus, 1200

In Damascus in the morning tension was high. Civil defence personnel were called to their posts after the news of the raids on Egypt came through. Ports and airports were closed. Students who turned up for their summer examinations were told they had been called off. They milled around in the streets, waiting for something to happen. They did not have to wait long. An hour or so later, Mirages started to bomb Damascus airport. Heavy anti-aircraft fire blasted back at them. The border between Syria and Israel was the least active front in the first four days of the war, but there were heavy artillery exchanges, instigated by Syria and answered by Israeli air strikes.

Israel's deception campaign continued. In the United States it was still very early in the morning. At 5 a.m. Gideon Rafael, Israel's ambassador to the UN, telephoned his American counterpart Arthur Goldberg to tell him that Egyptian forces had penetrated the Negev. Israeli foreign minister Eban told the US ambassador Walworth Barbour that Egyptian ground forces had started the fighting by shelling Israeli border villages. The Israelis were both lying for their country, as was Prime Minister Eshkol, who sent President Johnson a message about Egyptian aggression 'culminating in this morning's engagements and the bombardment . . . in Israeli territory'.

Cairo GHQ, 1200

Sidqi Mahmoud and Amer had arrived back from Cairo International airport, where they had finally been able to land. As soon as he reached his desk, Sidqi was swamped by reports of devastating Israeli attacks. Within minutes he telephoned Nasser to tell him what was happening. The full extent of the disaster was becoming clearer with every damage report that came into GHQ. Nasser started to feel that the battle was lost, before it had even properly started.

Anwar El Sadat went down to the basement of GHQ. He found Field Marshal Amer standing in the middle of his office 'looking around with wandering eyes. "Good morning," I said, but he didn't seem to hear me. I said "Good morning" again, but it took him about a minute to return my greeting.' Sadat's good mood disappeared. Something, he realised, had gone wrong. Other officers told him that the air force had been completely destroyed on the ground. Nasser came out of another room. Amer started talking, blaming the Americans. Nasser answered: 'I am not prepared to believe this, or to issue an official statement to the effect that the USA has attacked us, until you've produced at least one aircraft with a wing showing the US ensign.' Nasser left.

Around 11 o'clock Amer was visited by Abdul Latif Boghdady, who had commanded the air force in the wars of 1948 and 1956 and was now one of Nasser's vice-presidents. Boghdady did not want to get in the way. He said he would come back later if the field marshal was too busy to brief him. Amer, expansively, insisted Boghdady took a seat. Of course he had time. The commanders in the Sinai had everything under control. Why, Amer exclaimed, once we have the air battle out of the way, I'll have nothing to do! Boghdady noticed that Lieutenant-General Sidqi Mahmoud, his successor as air force commander, kept telephoning. He seemed, as far as the vice-president could tell, to be crying. Amer told him more than once to pull himself together.

'He kept asking him how many planes he had shot down so far. He'd answer with a figure which Abdul Hakim [Amer] would repeat loudly so we could hear it. Then he would say, so why are you upset then? Then Sidqi would call again, repeating that wave after wave of attacks were coming in on our airfields. Sidqi said there the Americans and the British must be helping the Israelis. They just did not have that many planes on their own. Abdul Hakim asked him to get proof of what he was saying.'

Field Marshal Amer clutched desperately at the suggestion that the big powers were involved. If it was going to be like Suez all over again, there might be a way out. He was losing himself in a world of panic and fantasy. No coherent orders were coming out of GHQ. The forces in the Sinai did not know if they were supposed to defend or attack, and sat in their positions while the Israelis picked them off.

The next phone call came from Nasser, who by now was back at his villa, from which he did not emerge for two days. When he asked how many planes had been lost, Amer would not give a straight answer. When Nasser insisted, he said forty-seven, of which thirty-five were usable at a pinch. All the rest could be repaired. It was another bare-faced lie. By lunchtime on 5 June, Egypt had lost all its heavy and light bombers and most of its fighters.

Mohamed Hassanein Heikal, the editor of *al-Ahram*, Cairo's leading newspaper, who was so close to Nasser he was considered his mouthpiece, claimed no one had the courage to tell the president the whole truth about what had happened. Heikal says while Nasser was at GHQ he was given the same exaggerated figures for downed Israeli planes as the public. He did not find out what was really happening until around four in the afternoon and it was not until the evening that the enormity of what had happened really came home to him. It seems clear, though, that Nasser knew long before that. General Hadidi says he knew 'within minutes'. Although GHQ in Cairo was Amer's domain, Nasser had his own people there, from the chief of staff General Fawzi, who was his appointee, down. Even if Amer had tried to keep the whole truth from him while he was visiting the headquarters building, Fawzi, a professional who took his responsibilities very seriously, would surely have told Nasser the truth.

Nasser had an eyewitness report at 2:00 p.m. Vice-President

Shafei, whose plane had landed at Fayed airbase moments before it was bombed, had driven straight from the Sinai desert to Nasser's house in Cairo. On the way he had passed three major airbases, all of which had been on fire. Shafei hammered on Nasser's front door. The president himself answered. Standing on the doorstep, Shafei told him everything that he had seen. Nasser told him to go to see Amer, and went back inside. Shafei went to GHQ, which was a 'total mess'. Amer gave an impression of 'total carelessness'. He seemed to be finding it hard to concentrate, not taking in everything that was being said to him.

At least Shafei was able to walk in on Amer. At the foreign ministry Mahmoud Riad had been trying to get through to Amer on the phone all morning. In the end he managed to speak to one of his aides. Riad suggested setting some sort of liaison between the foreign ministry and the military headquarters. His request was ignored by GHQ, where 'panic and confusion reigned supreme'. Riad had been trying to follow what was happening on the radio in his office. As foreign minister he knew as much about the war as the journalists in the press centre and the excited crowds on the streets. All he had, like them, were the communiqués from the military command claiming that more and more Israeli war planes were being shot down. But he wanted accurate information so he could work out a political strategy. In the end, Nasser telephoned and gave him the 'shock of his life' when he told him what had really happened.

Sinai, 1300

Command and control on the Israeli side of the lines was completely different. General Gavish, commander of Israel's armies in the Sinai, followed the action and directed it from a mobile headquarters unit based around a small command convoy. Where necessary, he would take a helicopter for a face-to-face meeting with his divisional commanders. Before the war, Gavish had tested his war plan against Egypt in big military exercises. One of them put a division of 10,000 men and 250 tanks into the field for three days, to check everything they could think of – mobilisation and deployment, war fighting, supplies of food, ammunition, and fuel. Scenarios for war against all Israel's main Arab enemies were constantly honed, sometimes on maps, sometimes in field exercises, sometimes with just a few command cars representing armoured formations. They had practised so much that now that his men were finally in the Sinai, one of his soldiers told Gavish that he felt he had been there before.

Gavish sat at a small table loaded with maps, surrounded by his staff and communications experts. Egypt's command and control very rapidly reduced itself to Field Marshal Amer's panicky phone calls. Gavish could be patched through not just to divisional commanders but to front-line units too. A reporter from the Israeli army newspaper followed him through the day. 'War noises leak out of the radios – assaulting tanks, crossing mine fields, a face-to-face fight while mopping up resistance, an exhausting journey of infantry walking in deep sand . . . the general asks to be out in touch with the commander on the southern axis: "Who is talking . . . where are you . . . were you in contact with the enemy? . . ." The general listens and says, "OK, don't get any closer to it, wait for them to come and then give it to them immediately."' Gavish was also in touch with Rabin, the chief of staff, in Tel Aviv, calling when necessary for air cover: 'The enemy is moving . . . if we can calm it down with some planes it will be very good for the Jews.'

In contrast to Gavish's tight and mobile team, Egypt had two sets of generals in Sinai. General Salah Muhsin was in charge of the army's well-established Eastern Command. It knew the territory and had made offensive and defensive plans. But just before the war Amer suddenly decided Muhsin was not good enough. Instead of relieving him, he invented a new Sinai headquarters, under General Murtagi, one of his favourites. Murtagi had no forces and no experience as a commander in Sinai. His exact relationship with Muhsin's Eastern Command was never clarified. Muhsin had all the fighting troops. Murtagi was told that he was setting up an advanced headquarters for the field marshal, who would take over when the battle started. Amer

141

always assumed that at the war's outbreak he would have a good forty-eight hours to shift himself and his cohorts to Sinai. The confusion created by the two parallel headquarters made a big contribution to the collapse of the Egyptian army as a fighting force. The two rival generals were reduced to competitive telephone calls to Amer, trying to sell him their ideas. Other Egyptian generals looked on with despair at the unfolding mess and at the spectacle of two of their colleagues fighting each other. After the war Murtagi tried to absolve himself of responsibility by admitting that his role and his command were unnecessary.

Another huge weakness was that just before the war Egypt's long-established plan for the defence of Sinai, codenamed 'Qaher', had been abandoned by Nasser. It envisaged pulling invading Israeli forces into a killing ground in central Sinai, between well-prepared defensive positions. Not all the positions were ready, but from a military point of view, it was a sensible scheme. Qaher sacrificed territory to draw the Israelis in, which Nasser, at the last minute, decided was not acceptable. He ordered a forward defence on the borders. It meant chaotic reorganisation and redeployment when the Egyptian army should have been digging in.

Egyptian military incompetence compounded the damage caused by Israel's efficiency. Somehow, six Tupolev bombers had been airborne when their base was raided and had escaped the attacks. Instead of looking for a friendly airfield – Sudan was suggested – they were ordered to land at Luxor. The message was intercepted. Not long afterwards a wave of Israeli warplanes, one of which was flown by Herzl Bodinger, destroyed them on the ground along with another eight Antonovs.

Elsewhere in the Middle East it was getting nasty for Westerners. In Libya the US Embassy in Benghazi was being attacked. Inside, as diplomats were burning papers, they sent out a message in such a hurry there was no time to encrypt it: 'Mob broke into Embassy. Staff locked in vault. Threw tear gas to hold the mob off.' Two hours later, a little calmer, they reported that British troops were on their way to make sure it was safe for them to come out of the vault. The message chattered off the teleprinter: 'Have completed destruction files and double checking make sure we have done job.' In Yemen, once news of the attacks broke, Yemeni and Egyptian military guards took up positions outside the US Embassy in Sanaa. Two Egyptian armoured cars deployed on the approach road to the Embassy. The radio broadcast nationalistic and military music and calls to arms. In Basra, in southern Iraq, a mob invaded the US representative's compound and buildings and smashed up the rooms until the authorities restored order.

At GHQ in Tel Aviv the General Staff was still worried about an Egyptian ground attack. Aharon Yariv, the head of military intelligence, told Rabin at 1300 that 'great attention should be given to the possibility that the Shazli force will try to cut the Negev'. Saad el Shazli was a 43-year-old major-general. Under his command were a tank battalion, an infantry battalion and two commando battalions, fifteen hundred men in all who had been causing the Israelis some anxiety. But while Yariv was briefing Rabin, Shazli himself was in a car, trying to rejoin his troops. He had travelled by helicopter to the ill-starred meeting with Field Marshal Amer at Fayed airbase. After the arrival of the Israelis broke up what Shazli remembers as 'a nice reunion', it took him until three in the afternoon to rejoin his men. He found they had only suffered two air strikes, with negligible casualties. No orders had come through from Cairo. He tried to raise Cairo on the radio. Nothing. Shazli moved his forces just over the border into Israel, where they hunkered down in an L-shaped defile, well sheltered from air attack. They stayed there until midday on 7 June. No orders came from Cairo. Shazli realised his men would be cut to pieces by air strikes if they went into the open desert. He decided not to try any ill-conceived initiatives of his own.

Mafrak Airbase, Jordan, 1230

Ihsan Shurdom was still waiting in his flying kit, in a trench near his aircraft, still on stand-by for action. He had not been sent on the

Netanya raid and he was still seething about not being allowed to scramble to attack the dots on the radar screens, which he was convinced – correctly – were Israelis returning to base low on fuel and ammunition. All the pilots had their transistor radios constantly tuned to the reports of the Arab triumph which, that morning, originated in Cairo and were then embroidered across the region. Suddenly, one of Shurdom's friends turned to him.

'He said we're losing this bloody war. I asked why. He said, "Because they're claiming they've shot down twice the number of Mirages Israel has."'

The field telephone in Ihsan Shurdom's trench rang. Scramble. Israeli planes were approaching. He was out of his trench and running. His Hawker Hunter was twenty yards away, ready to go. His first instinct, get airborne . . . much safer than sitting helplessly in a jet-powered aluminium coffin on the runway. Shurdom's Hunter was armed with twenty-four rockets for air strikes or for close support. But he had been scrambled for air defence, to intercept incoming Israeli jets. First priority, he thought, get rid of the rockets. As soon as he was in the air, he fired them into the ground. Then, he looked round and saw the Israeli jets approaching the airfield. He remembered the techniques he had learnt from the RAF. He knew about 'scissoring', where you aim to turn your enemy into your guns, how to use 'speed breaks'. He knew how to manoeuvre the Hunter using the flaps and how to use the sun to disappear. Most important of all, though, was to see the enemy first: then 'you gained the advantage, because you either went high or started manoeuvring . . . Air combat is decided within one minute.' Shurdom claims two kills, both Israeli Mysteres. One exploded over the airfield, one went down slightly to the north. Israel admits only one Mystere lost over Mafrak. Another, badly damaged, limped home. Later, another Jordanian pilot shot down two more.

Below them on the runway, the aircraft that had bombed Netanya were refuelling and rearming. A plan to disperse the planes to various airstrips in the desert had been made in peacetime. But in the excitement of the morning nobody had thought about implementing it. The maintenance crews had been listening to the radio reports. So many Israelis had apparently been shot down over Cairo it was hard to see how they could have planes left to attack them. When they saw the Israelis approaching, they assumed that they were friendly until they opened fire. Jordan had no hardened shelters for its aircraft. Most of the Jordanian Hawker Hunters were caught on the ground and destroyed. The squadron commander, Major Firass Ajlouni, who just an hour before had led the raid on Netanya, tried to follow Shurdom into the air. As he was trying to take off, his Hunter was hit by a burst of cannon fire and he was killed. The next pilot on the runway jumped from his aircraft and ran to the trench to take cover as the Israelis strafed and bombed the airfield. In a few minutes the Jordanians' only fighter base had been destroyed.

During Shurdom's second dogfight his aircraft was hit in the tail. He decided to check the trim of his aeroplane. It meant flying at a specified low speed. He told his wingman to '"Watch my tail. I want to do a slow-speed check." He asked me, "Aren't you afraid?" I said, "Of course I'm afraid."'

During the check he found that the Hunter had been damaged. He decided to land. From the cockpit he could see the base at Mafrak. It was on fire. He radioed in. 'Is the runway serviceable?' He spoke in English, which they always used for flying. A voice answered that it was. Shurdom did not recognise it and he suspected something. How could the runway be serviceable after a raid like that? Shurdom asked again for confirmation and when he got it, he asked the man for the name of his dog. Everyone at the Mafrak base knew Shurdom's dog. There was silence. Shurdom flew on, to Amman. He assumed the Israelis were trying to trick him.

Cairo, 1345; Jordanian Military Headquarters, 1245

Nasser was back at the office he maintained in his villa, where he conducted a lot of his business. He called King Hussein for the first time since the fighting started. He knew by then exactly what had happened to his air force, but he did not tell his new ally. Like Amer, there was no mention of what had really happened. 'Israel bombed our airbases. We answered by bombing theirs. We are launching a general offensive in the Negev.' Then he asked the king to seize as much land as quickly as he could, because he had heard the UN Security Council would be stopping the war that evening. King Hussein still had no idea about the damage that the Israeli air force and army was inflicting. After the war he never publicly criticised Nasser for deceiving him. A year later his private secretary confirmed to the Americans that they realised that Nasser had urged the king to commit his forces more deeply when he knew that his own air force had been destroyed – but only when it was too late.

The fighting in Jerusalem was escalating. After Egypt's appeals for help, the Jordanians dropped their well-established plan for war in Jerusalem. It was called Operation Tariq, a pincer attack to cut off the Jewish side of the city. The Jordanians calculated that their small army, of nine infantry brigades and two independent armoured brigades, the 40th and 60th, was not strong enough to defend the 630-kilometre-long armistice line with Israel. Operation Tariq was designed to give Jordan diplomatic leverage, by effectively holding Jewish West Jerusalem hostage in exchange for a ceasefire and the return of any other land that Israel would have seized. It was a realistic strategy. But Operation Tariq, which had been an integral part of Jordan's war plans since 1949, was dropped.

The message from Cairo was that an Egyptian division was advancing into the Negev desert to attack Beersheba. General Riad, the Egyptian who had been put in charge of the Jordanian army, did not know that the attack existed only in Amer's imagination. No one in Jordan had any idea what was really happening in the Sinai. Some Jordanian staff officers at GHQ in Amman argued bitterly with their Egyptian colleagues about ditching Operation Tariq. At one point the director of operations, General Atef Majali, made as if to storm out. But Riad, who had the support of the king, had the last word. The 60th Armoured Brigade was moved south to Hebron, while the 40th moved from the northern part of the West Bank to replace it near

Jericho. Cairo asked for a Syrian armoured brigade to move in behind the 40th. Written down on paper in front of Riad and the king, it looked like a good plan. Riad was recognised by the Jordanians, Egyptians and even the Israelis as one of Cairo's most competent commanders. The only problem for the Jordanians was that Amer's basic premise was founded on fantasy, and even if one of the ill-trained and barely operational Syrian divisions had been in a sufficient state of readiness to be moved to the West Bank, Damascus had no intention of helping Hussein out.

Amman, 1310

Just as Shurdom and two colleagues were landing at Amman another wave of Israeli warplanes was approaching the airport. The Israelis started rocketing and strafing. Hanan Najar, one of the Jordanian pilots, was hit in the hand. Shurdom grabbed the film from his Hunter's gun camera and ran for the slit trench to take cover. The raid went on for two and a half hours. By the end of it, the Royal Jordanian Air Force had no serviceable runways and had lost all its strike aircraft. Only two French-built Alouette helicopters were left. The royal palace was also attacked. According to Ziad Rifai, one of Hussein's closest advisers, the Israelis managed a direct hit on the king's office. 'The wall behind the desk and the King's chair was lacerated by the blast.'

Jerusalem, 1330

Since Israel's defeat at the gates of the Old City in 1948, General Uzi Narkiss had dreamt of another chance to conquer all Jerusalem. Pressing hard for permission to move against the Jordanians, he was 'in a constant state of excitement, as though knowing that his great moment was drawing near'. Narkiss and an ally tried to persuade General Ezer Weizman, the chief of operations, that 'this is a great

147

opportunity to do something terrific to the Jordanians. We mustn't miss it.' Throughout the morning Narkiss was refused permission to attack. It was not long, though, before the Jordanians offered him the opening that he needed. First, at 1245, Radio Amman declared, inaccurately, that Mount Scopus had been taken by the Jordanians. Then the Jordanians sent two companies into a badly planned attack on Government House, the headquarters of the UN in Jerusalem. For Narkiss, it was 'a gift from the skies'.

General Odd Bull of the UN saw it happening. It was 'one of the biggest surprises' of his life. Jordanian troops were coming into the wooded compound of Government House. It was the only big public building left behind by the British in Palestine, a mansion for its High Commissioners built of Jerusalem stone, on a ridge overlooking the Old City called Jabel Mukkaber, the hill of evil counsel. Under the terms of the armistice it was UN territory, demilitarised and off-limits to both sides. After a heated argument, unarmed UN officers, whose families were inside, persuaded the Jordanians not to occupy the building. But the Jordanians stayed in the woods around it.

The armistice also prohibited both Jordan and Israel from bringing tanks into Jerusalem. Israel kept a battalion of tanks just outside the municipal boundary. Secretly, a few were also kept inside Jerusalem, violating the armistice agreement. In charge was Aaron Kamera, a feisty veteran of 1948 who describes his role in the fight against the British occupation as 'terrorist.' When he heard sirens and shooting he made a unilateral decision to move all his tanks into Jerusalem. Kamera was the local driving instructor, so he was well known. As his tanks moved into Israeli Jerusalem, local people threw them cigarettes and cakes and cheered. The neighbourhood insurance man saw him, ran back into his office and wrote him a life insurance policy. Kamera took the tanks to the military headquarters in the centre of the New City, which was at the Russian Compound, a barracks built outside the city walls by the czars for Russian pilgrims. Kamera went looking for orders and was horrified to discover that a ceasefire had been declared. If he had brought his tanks into Jerusalem prematurely, he was in deep trouble. But like several other ceasefires that morning, it did not last long. Word came through of the Jordanian move against Government House. Kamera was told to get his tanks there as soon as possible.

Kibbutz Nachshon, 1400

A group of men sat in the observation post at Kibbutz Nachshon, across the border from the Jordanian garrison at Latrun. It was a hot, still afternoon. They could see explosions where Jordanian mortars were firing over the border. In the distance there was a heavy rumble, like summer thunder. It was the shelling in and around Jerusalem. They kept their transistor radio on for the news. Fighting was being reported on all fronts. Sometimes they moved the dial from Voice of Israel to Cairo Radio's Hebrew service, which kept up its bragging: 'Death will come to you in a black dress . . . at night . . .' They laughed nervously and made jokes. But they had no idea how the war was going for Israel. For all their bravado, they were deeply worried.

Damascus, 1415

Uri Gil, one of the handful of Israeli pilots who had missed out on the morning's raids because they were held back for air defence, finally got his chance. His team were ordered to take off for southern Syria, to intercept a flight of MiGs that had just taken off. When the Mirages were over the black, basalt landscape of the Syrian south, the Israeli flight controllers, who were following the MiGs on radar, fed them the latest information. Twenty miles and closing, then fifteen, then ten, then five. Gil and the other three pilots could not see anything. Then a warning came through their headsets – the MiGs were a mile and a half ahead. Something about what the controller was saying felt wrong to Gil. He broke to the right. Six hundred yards *behind* him was a Syrian MiG. He never really knew how it got there. He estimated it was two seconds from shooting him.

149

Gil practised aerial combat constantly. He considered himself an expert. But it was the first time he had done it for real. The two fighters twisted and turned around the sky, trying to get an advantage. Gil felt calm, even a little happy. Finally he was putting his skills to good use. At 10,000 feet the Israeli Mirage cut across the path of the MiG. For a second the two pilots could see each other. They were very close. Gil noticed the Syrian was wearing a brown leather helmet, before he cut his speed to get behind him. He did not feel anger or hatred as he killed its pilot. 'Calmly, I put the gun sight on him and fired a half second burst. I shot him in the cockpit. There was no parachute. I didn't feel anything about killing him. He was a target. So was I. If I hadn't broken to the right, he would have shot me. The hard decision was to break right, from the group. Breaking the formation is a big step.'

During the dogfight Gil had been silent. Now he could hear one of his three colleagues shouting over the radio. Later in the war, Meir Shahar, the pilot who had been shouting, was shot down by anti-aircraft fire over a Syrian base. His brother Jonathan was shot down on the same day over Egypt, but he was rescued.

On the first day of the war, Israel smashed the air forces of Egypt, Syria and Jordan and neutralised most of Iraq's. Nineteen Israeli aircraft were shot down. That was 10 per cent of its strength, a bigger proportion than it lost in the 1973 war. Nine Israeli pilots were killed. Avihu Bin-Nun's junior colleague, whom he thought had crashed into the sea in the first wave of attacks, survived. He had turned back because he was having problems with the fuel feed to his engine.

Tel Aviv, 1430

Ava Yotvat sat with her two daughters in the shelter under their apartment in Tel Aviv. Deep down, she felt it was going to be all right. She had been badly scared in the weeks before the war, for her daughters and for her husband who was an officer in the army. The

Arab propaganda was terrifying. Her parents had emigrated from Holland in 1927. The rest of their family was killed in Auschwitz. Like many Israeli women of her generation and background, from a family of Holocaust survivors who had grown up during a time of food rationing, she always had a full store cupboard upstairs in their flat. She never thought that the Arabs would be able to inflict another genocide on the Jewish people. Israel, she always felt, was the only place in the world that she could be really safe. A shell from one of the Jordanian Long Toms crashed into Frishman Street. Ava Yotvat sat between her two daughters, put her arms round their shoulders and said, right, now we'll sing. She started a chorus of 'Jerusalem of Gold', the hit song of the war for Israelis. All the neighbours joined in.

Israel's 55th Paratroop Brigade lay in the sun on the grass next to the runway at Tel Nof airfield. They were in full combat gear, waiting for the Nord-Atlas transport planes that were due to take them to war. They had trained for weeks for what they were going to do – a jump into a hostile landing zone at Al-Arish, the Egyptian town at the north-east corner of the Sinai desert, where it meets the Mediterranean sea. Everything was packed into 20 kg sacks for the jump. Israeli paratroopers had only ever jumped into combat once before, in 1956 when Ariel Sharon's men had landed at the Mitla Pass in Sinai. Veterans of the Mitla had the right to put a red background behind their parachute wings, to show that they had made a combat jump. The men at Tel Nof airfield were looking forward to getting the same honour. They had seen the jets taking off in the morning, and they had been told that the raids had gone well. The soldiers could hear shells from the Jordanian 155 mm 'Long Tom' artillery hitting Tel Aviv and Kfar Saba. The men who came from the two towns were worrying about their families.

They were keyed up. Then the field telephone rang. The advance into Al-Arish was going much faster than anyone had expected. They were not needed. The jump was cancelled. Instead, they were going to Jerusalem. A lot of the men were disappointed. Not only would they lose their chance to get the special combat wings, there wasn't even a proper war in Jerusalem. They were going to be no better than policemen. Arie Weiner thought it was even worse than that. Their rivals in the 202nd Paratroop Brigade were already in action in Sinai, so this was a double disappointment. Jacov Chaimowitz, a 21-year-old student, was one of the few who were not too bothered. He listened to them complain. 'I wasn't disappointed. We had some people who were always walking around with a knife in their mouths. They wanted the badge. But I didn't see myself as much of a fighter.'

Old municipal buses turned up to take the paratroopers to Jerusalem. They climbed aboard with what they could carry and their personal weapons. Their heavier gear was packed into the jump sacks and would have to follow on later. They had no maps of where they were going. Many of them had never even been to Jerusalem. They squashed into the cramped seats, grumbling. But the mind of Hanan Porat, a deeply religious young paratrooper in his early twenties, was racing about what they were about to do. He was convinced that his unit was, finally, doing God's work. They were going to complete the conquest of Jerusalem that had been left unfinished in 1948. Porat studied at the religious school in Jerusalem that followed the teachings of Rabbi Abraham Isaac Kook, one of the most influential Jewish figures of the twentieth century. He was the first rabbi to link orthodox Judaism with Zionism. It had not been easy. Most of the early Zionist pioneers were either atheists or indifferent about religion. Most orthodox Jews in the Holy Land were just as indifferent, or hostile, to Zionism. They believed that God, not East European immigrants, would establish a Jewish state. Rabbi Kook taught that working for the return of the Jewish people to Zion was God's will. That, Hanan Porat was convinced, was exactly what his unit of paratroopers, Battalion 66, was about to do in Jerusalem. On Independence Day, when the first warnings of Egypt's move into the Sinai were coming through, Porat's mentor Rabbi Zvi Yehudah Kook, the son of the school's founder, spoke passionately about how he had wept when the UN partitioned Palestine. He shouted, 'Where is our Schechem [Nablus]? Where is our Jericho? Where is our [river] Jordan?' Now Porat and his fellow students were in the army, about to fight to regain all the places that had been lost.

Porat had another, more personal reason to be happy. He had spent part of his childhood in a Jewish settlement called Kfar Etzion, about ten miles south of Jerusalem, near Bethlehem. In 1948 it fell to the Jordanians after a bloody siege. Many of its defenders were killed and, for Israelis, it had become a symbol of the sacrifices they had made to establish their state. After Jerusalem, Porat's dream was to return to his childhood home. Surely, if Israel captured the Old City of Jerusalem, Kfar Etzion would not be far behind?

Jerusalem, 1450

The UN's General Bull was about to leave Government House to find a Jordanian who would order the troops to withdraw when an Israeli burst in through the gate of the compound and heavy firing started. General Rabin at GHQ in Tel Aviv had tried to delay it to allow Bull time to negotiate with the Jordanians. But Rabin was told the men were out of contact and could not be pulled back. There was no holding them. The attack was led by Lieutenant-Colonel Asher Drizen, the commander of Battalion 161, one of four reserve units of thirty-five- to forty-year-olds in Israeli Jerusalem. Another battalion of younger men was held in reserve for counter-attacks. That Monday morning, Drizen had been hoping for a lie-in. There had been a party for the soldiers the night before. When he heard that Government House had been taken by the Jordanians, he was about a mile away in the old British Allenby Barracks, firing mortars at Jordanian positions.

The Israelis had a plan to seize Government House that they had been rehearsing for years. Drizen sent two companies there immediately, then set off himself. All day the commanders of the Jerusalem Brigade acted first and explained themselves later. They put the plan to recapture Government House into action, then told Narkiss's HQ what they were doing. Narkiss was a man in a hurry, so he was not bothered by a little free enterprise on the ground. Drizen was a man in a hurry too. When he saw the arrival of the tanks led by Aaron

Kamera (just as impatient to get on with a fight that he thought had been postponed for far too long), Drizen ran down under fire to order them into action. A few minutes later, the commander of the reconnaissance unit showed up demanding a diagram of the Israeli positions, to cut down on the risk of friendly fire. Drizen blew his top at the man's shilly-shallying. He told him he would shoot him if he did not move forward immediately. A corporal in the reconnaissance unit stepped forward and threatened to cut Drizen's throat if he did not calm down. In the end he gave them the information they needed and the attack went ahead. While Drizen led his men into the Government House compound, the Jordanians rushed for their Land Rovers which were mounted with heavy machine guns and anti-tank weapons. Drizen grabbed the heavy machine gun on his command half-track and destroyed the Land Rovers, just before a piece of shrapnel gave him a bad wound in the arm. A medic patched him up and he carried on with his right arm strapped to his side. All but three of Kamera's elderly Sherman tanks got stuck on difficult ground and could not continue the attack, but the Jordanians were unable to exploit this Israeli weakness. They tried artillery fire, but it was not accurate. Some of it fell on their own positions, and although the Jordanian infantrymen stuck to their task, they were not able to counter-attack.

An Israeli corporal called Zerach Epstein conducted his own private mopping-up operation. He was the man who had offered to cut Drizen's throat. 'They shot at me from a dugout and I shot back. I tossed a hand grenade into the trench and raced on . . . suddenly I found myself all alone among the trees. From beneath one of them a Jordanian sprang out. I shot him and went on running. Somebody called out to me. I stopped and turned back. I saw it was a Jordanian soldier standing about two metres away from me . . . we pressed the trigger almost at the same moment, but I was just a fraction quicker.' Afterwards they found the bodies of nine Jordanian soldiers lying along the route he had taken.

Just before four in the afternoon the Israelis blew open the heavy wooden doors of Government House. 'For the second time in two

154

hours,' General Bull complained, 'we found ourselves overrun. On this occasion Israel chose to cut our link with New York.' Israeli soldiers started clearing the rooms in the approved manner, tossing in a grenade and then spraying them with their Uzis. They were persuaded to stop by UN officers before they harmed any of the women and children who were sheltering there.

Abu Agheila, Sinai, 1500

Abu Agheila was on the way into central Sinai. Tanks can fight in most of the desert, but not without fuel and ammunition. Logistics go by road. War in a desert is about controlling the roads and Abu Agheila is one of the most important crossroads in the Sinai, about thirty kilometres from the border with Israel. In 1967 it was protected by four fortified positions that were connected by barbed wire and minefields. In the 1956 war Israel tried and failed repeatedly to take Abu Agheila. It fell only when the Egyptian troops were ordered to abandon it to pull back to the Suez canal. Israel mapped, surveyed and photographed the area before it pulled out after the war. In the next ten years Egypt strengthened its defences and the IDF made an intensive study of the best way to attack them. In yet another example of their thorough planning for the war, they held exercises up to divisional level, usually at night, concentrating on breaching the position.

Abu Agheila's defences hinged on a heavily fortified ridge called Um Katef. Behind a minefield 300 yards deep, Egypt had deployed around 16,000 men from its 2nd Infantry Division in three parallel lines of trenches three miles long, complete with concrete strongpoints. Egypt had reinforced the position in and around Um Katef until it had ninety tanks and self-propelled guns and six regiments of heavy artillery, all well dug in. Sharon, taking advantage of years of planning, had his attack ready. Brigadier-General Gavish at Southern Command tried to persuade him to put it off until the morning, when he would have air support. But Sharon loved fighting at night, when he believed Israeli troops had the edge. By late afternoon Sharon's division was at its start line for the attack above and below Abu Agheila, beginning at ten in the evening with the biggest artillery barrage that Israel had ever mustered.

Ramle, central Israel, 1530

General Narkiss's mobile headquarters was moving slowly, but it was in the right direction as far as he was concerned – towards Jerusalem. He had his wish. Israel was in a shooting war with Jordan. As well as counter-attacking at Government House, Narkiss had sent tanks to attack the mountain ridge that ran north-west of Jerusalem and he had been told that a crack unit of paratroopers was being sent to him to attack in the city itself. He was certain that he would be able to finish the unfinished business of 1948, and capture all of Jerusalem. 'Joy engulfed me. I knew that soon these three powerful streams would flood together into a tidal wave, to flow over and drown Jerusalem's bonds.'

Washington DC, 0715

In the Pentagon, America's huge, five-sided military headquarters, the phone rang in the office of the Secretary of Defense, Robert McNamara. It was the duty officer in the war room, who was always a general or an admiral. 'Mr Secretary, Kosygin is on the hotline and wants to talk to the president. What should I tell him?'

One of the innovations brought in after the Cuban missile crisis was the 'hotline' between Moscow and Washington. It was a secure teletype line, with American and Soviet equipment at either end. It was the first time that the hotline, which had been there since 1963, had been used in a real crisis. McNamara asked why he was calling him. The Soviet prime minister Alexei Kosygin wanted President Johnson, not the Secretary of Defense. 'Well,' the duty officer replied, 'the hotline terminates in the Pentagon.'

McNamara was aghast that the line installed by the superpowers to handle crises that could, after all, lead to a thermonuclear exchange did not reach the White House. 'General, we are spending 60 billion dollars a year on defence. Can't you take a few thousand of those dollars and get these goddam lines patched across the river to the White House? You call the Situation Room and I'll call the president and we'll decide what to do.'

They put the line through to the White House. The first sentence of the first message from the Soviet Prime Minister asked if the American president was standing near the machine. Johnson's reply was addressed to 'Comrade' Kosygin. The American hotline operators had sent a message to Moscow asking the Russian operators what was the proper way to address Kosygin. When the message went through, addressed to 'Comrade' Kosygin, the top Russians at the other end looked at it sharply. Was Johnson making fun of them?

At 0730 a presidential aide knocked on Johnson's door. The most powerful man in the world, he noted, was 'quiet – watching TV. Pres gave no indications of it being anything but a normal day – showered, shaved, dressed and left for SitRm [Situation Room].' He noted Johnson breakfasted on tea, grapefruit and chipped beef, a delicacy which GIs during the Second World War called 'shit on a shingle' when it came on toast.

Mafrak Airbase, Jordan, 1530

Hassan Sabri, a maintenance engineer at Mafrak, looked out on to the smoking wreckage that the Israelis had left behind. The runway was unusable. The stores and most of the technical areas had been destroyed. In the craters on the runway were timed bombs, set to go off at random intervals. Sabri, who spent a year at the RAF training college at Cranwell on an armament engineering course, found out they also had a mercury switch which was set to explode if they were moved. All they could do was explode them where they were.

The atmosphere on the base was transformed. Excitement and

expectation had been building up ever since the crisis had started in May. That morning most of them had believed every word of the radio reports of the triumphant progress of the Egyptian armed forces. The humiliation and dishonour of 1948 was about to be avenged. But by early afternoon, the war, for the air force at least, was lost. Officers and airmen whose families lived on the base in married quarters rushed to find them a safer place. Sabri, the engineer, knew what the Israeli raids meant. The radio reports were lies. Something similar must have happened to the air forces of Egypt and Syria. It meant the Jordanian army – and the rest of the Arabs – had been stripped of their air cover. Sabri was filled with despair. What could the army on the ground do, if Israel controlled the skies?

Jerusalem, 1600

After the capture of Government House, Israeli troops cleared the 'Sausage', a major Jordanian position that controlled access to south-east Jerusalem. Squads of men jumped into the trenches at one end, firing ahead of them and moving along until the defenders were captured. Without taking a single loss, they killed thirty Jordanians. After that they rolled up another elaborate trench system known as the 'Bell', which they were able to approach from the rear. Once again, the Jordanian infantrymen fought bravely, often to the death, but were not able to reposition themselves effectively enough to beat off an Israeli attack that was coming from an unexpected direction. But just as Lieutenant-Colonel Drizen and his men thought the entire Bell position had been cleared, they were ambushed by four or five Jordanians. Drizen, who was standing on the edge of a trench, was hit in his good hand. Two men who had been on either side of him were killed. A platoon commander was shot through the eye. Corporal Zerach Epstein fired back at the Jordanians, giving other soldiers enough time to throw grenades to kill them.

Jerusalem, 1700; Cairo, 1800; Washington DC, 1000

Teddy Kollek, mayor of Israeli Jerusalem, picked up Ruth Dayan, the wife of the defence minister, from the King David hotel, where she had been sheltering in one of West Jerusalem's more comfortable bunkers, the hotel's La Regence restaurant, two floors down and well sandbagged. They went to the Knesset, a mile-long dash by car down Jerusalem's empty streets. The corridors of the Knesset were packed with ministers, MPs and journalists. The big question was whether Israel should now take East Jerusalem. 'The mood was momentous and exciting . . . to advance on the Jordanian-held sector of Jerusalem was, of course, more of a political risk than a military one. Each of us knew in his heart that once we took the Old City we would never give it up.' People were lining up in the Knesset lobby to ask David Ben-Gurion what he thought. He wanted Israel to seize its chance.

On the Arab side of Jerusalem, Palestinians had spent the day listening to predictions of victory on Voice of the Arabs from Cairo. At a forward command post an elderly aristocrat, incapacitated by gout, was carried in dressed in breeches and armed with pistols, dagger and rifle. 'We will dine in Tel Aviv,' he announced.

Colonel Uri Ben Ari had other ideas. He commanded the mechanised brigade that Narkiss had ordered to swing round to the north of Jerusalem. He planned to have breakfast in one of the villages outside Jerusalem, if there was time. Ben Ari arrived in Israel as a young German Jew called Heinz Banner in 1939, when he was fourteen. His entire family, except an aunt who had married a German officer in the 1920s, was exterminated by the Nazis. Ben Ari had been with Narkiss and Rabin when the Jewish quarter fell in 1948. He too had unfinished business in the holy city, where he had fought with great courage. Ben Ari was one of Israel's most gifted tank commanders. He studied the theories of the German Panzer General Heinz Guderian, the man who formulated the 'blitzkrieg' – lightning war, based on fast moving armoured divisions backed up by mechanised infantry. He applied Guderian's theories with great success in the Sinai in 1956, before leaving the army prematurely to become a publisher. Narkiss called Ben Ari back in 1967. He shook up his brigade in short order, drilling them until they could move from a standing start in five minutes. On 5 June they started their decisive push to Jerusalem at five in the afternoon.

His mission was to take the high ground that ran along north of Jerusalem. If he succeeded Israel would control all the main roads to the north, east and west of the city, cutting off any chance of Jordan sending in reinforcements. But in the way were strongpoints at Sheikh Abdul Aziz, Beit Iksa and Radar Hill that had repeatedly thrown back Israeli fighters in 1948. He selected four routes for his tanks to use to climb the ridges. Instead of stopping to regroup at the foot of the hill, Ben Ari ordered them to drive straight on. It was harder to hit a moving target. Some of the routes were little more than goat tracks, heavily mined and under the Jordanian guns, but they had been carefully reconnoitred before the war. At first the fighting was hard and the going was tough. An Israeli tank commander who had done most of his training in the desert said 'we were fighting two enemies and I don't know which was worse – the Jordanians or the terrain'.

The Jordanians fired down at the advancing Israeli tanks. Soldiers riding on them had to jump down to clear the mines. All ten Centurion tanks in one Israeli unit were disabled, along with many Shermans. But Ben Ari brought his armour up behind the Jordanian positions. His unorthodox idea of splitting his force into four worked. He thought they would break through on at least two routes. In the end, they did so on all four. Many Jordanian officers abandoned the fight. Afterwards, the Israelis found no one with a higher rank than sergeant among the Jordanian dead.

By dawn on the second day of the war, Ben Ari's men were north of Jerusalem, cutting the roads, as they had planned.

The road to Al-Arish, Sinai, 1700

At about five Lieutenant Avigdor Kahalani of Israel's 7th Armoured Brigade was rolling down the road to Al-Arish. He planned to be the first into the town. First they had to get through a pass known as the Jirardi Defile. A soldier jumped out in front of him. Kahalani was about to shoot him when he realised he was Israeli. The man flagged him down, warning that Egyptian tanks were ahead. Kahalani climbed up on a ridge to take a look. Suddenly the tank bucked. It was on fire and Kahalani was burning. He could not find the strength to push himself out. 'The smell of burning and a wave of intense heat swept the tank . . . what's happening to me, I screamed, I'm coming apart.' With a final supreme effort he forced himself out and rolled out onto the engine cowling. 'Mother, I'm burning, I'm burning, I'm burning . . .' He threw himself into the sand dunes, rolling around to put the fires out. Kahalani wanted to sleep, but then realised that tanks were tearing through the sand around him and shells were exploding. All his clothes except part of his underpants and shirt were burnt off him. The sock in one of his boots was on fire. He pulled himself into the loader's compartment on a Patton tank, which took him, badly burnt and by now stark naked, to a medic.

An anti-tank gun knocked out the Patton behind Kahalani's. Two others were stopped by mines. Sergeant Dov Yam, the commander of one of the tanks in the minefield, kept on firing his gun until another anti-tank shell hit his tank and blew off his hand. He ran back to the brigade commander's half-track and collapsed on a stretcher, muttering, 'I think I did everything I could.' Major Ehud Elad, the battalion commander, took the lead, ordering his men to disperse further into the sands to try to outflank the position that was holding them back. Like all Israeli tank commanders in 1967, Elad believed he did his job best if he sat up in the turret, exposing his body but giving him an all-round view of the battle. 'Driver, faster,' he shouted through the intercom. Then the men in the tank heard a thump. Elad's body dropped down into the compartment of his tank, his head blown clean off. Before they forced some tanks through the pass with a frontal assault down the main road, the Israelis lost the battalion commander, three company commanders and their operations officer. Behind them the Jirardi Defile was still blocked. It took four hours of hard hand-to-hand fighting in the trenches that protected it to subdue the Egyptians.

At Al-Arish Brig. Gen. Tal told his brigade commanders that during the first day of fighting, through Rafah and into Egypt, they had scored a decisive victory over the Egyptian 7th Infantry Division. Before the battle Tal ordered them to throw everything into the fight. Getting the breakthrough and psychological as well as physical dominance over the Egyptians was critical, 'irrespective of the cost in casualties'. Now he told them to be more cautious, trying first what could be done with long-range gunnery, pushing only a battalion forward at a time. He did not want them taking on any more all-out battles without his express permission. Tal ordered Colonel Shmuel Gonen, the commander of the 7th Armoured Brigade, to swing south to attack B'ir Lahfan, a major Egyptian defensive zone.

Egyptian civilians were caught up in the fighting. Mrs Fathi Mohammed Hussein Ayoub was travelling to Al-Arish in the afternoon. Her car was hit, she thought by the Israelis, killing her four- and five-year-old daughters and her eight-year-old son. The driver was cut in two by the explosion.

Field Marshal Amer at GHQ in Cairo had gone from paralysis to verbal incontinence. He made call after call to his divisional commanders, all of which were monitored by Israeli intelligence. He ignored General Muhsin, the commander of the field army, and General Murtagi, the commander in chief of the front, until he needed Murtagi to send reinforcements to Abu Agheila and Al-Arish. Amer could have revived Plan Qaher, which was supposed to deal with exactly the kind of thrust that Israel had made into the Sinai, but he seemed to have forgotten about it.

State Department, Washington DC, 1000

At the State Department in Foggy Bottom the spokesman Bob McCloskey gave a briefing to correspondents. He was asked whether the US was neutral in the Middle East war. McCloskey obliged. 'We have tried to steer an even-handed course through this. Our position is neutral in thought, word and deed.'

It had seemed like a straightforward answer to a simple question. It was not. Israel's supporters were outraged. Jews at a union meeting hissed when they heard the US was calling itself neutral. The US, they believed, should support Israel. Mrs Arthur Krim, one of the president's close friends, told him that his administration looked as if it was washing its hands of the war at a time when Nasser seemed to American Jews to be a second Hitler. Mrs Krim suggested he made a ruling that the US would never re-establish diplomatic relations with a government headed by Nasser. David Brody of B'nai B'rith, the Jewish anti-defamation league, also used his access to senior officials in the Johnson administration to protest. He wanted a promise that the US would not force Israel to withdraw from any land it captured without first getting assurances of a real peace.

United Nations Security Council, New York

The Soviet delegation had heard that war had broken out before dawn, when Hans Tabor, the Danish ambassador who was taking his turn at the rotating presidency of the Security Council, called the Soviet estate at Glen Cove. Nikolai Fedorenko, the Soviet Ambassador to the UN, agreed to a meeting of the Security Council and drove to their mission in Manhattan with his arms control adviser, Arkady Shevchenko, where he was expecting to find instructions from Moscow. They waited close to their secure teletype machines. Nothing came through, so they went to their offices at the UN headquarters. The Egyptian ambassador, Mohammed el-Kony, who in Shevchenko's opinion was a 'total mediocrity', was confident, telling them that 'we deceived the Israelis. They bombed some of our false airfields, where we deliberately placed fake plywood airplane models. We shall see who wins this war.'

The Israeli ambassador to the UN, Gideon Rafael, knew how well his country's air force was doing. He had been told 'the stimulating news' in a secret cable that Israel had destroyed 250 Egyptian planes by lunchtime. Tabor, the president of the Security Council, never understood how Rafael seemed so unworried at a time when everyone else thought Israel was in great danger. Rafael's instructions were to carry out a 'diplomatic holding action. The strategic outcome of the fighting was a race between time and space. Our armoured divisions would cover the space as fast as they could and our diplomatic corps would provide the time for them to reach their objectives.' In case he needed relief Israeli foreign minister Abba Eban was on his way. As he was kissing his wife goodbye on his doorstep in Jerusalem a piece of shrapnel fizzed down to the ground near them. It took him three hours to get to the airport because tanks and troops were jamming the road. The only aircraft available was a small one designed for domestic flights. Late on Monday evening it took off from Tel Aviv and flew across the Mediterranean, almost as low as the attack jets that had bombed Egypt in the morning. By the time a queasy Eban decided it was safe to look out of the window, he saw dawn break over the Acropolis in Athens.

Millions of television viewers in the United States had been watching the Security Council debates. The superpowers' ambassadors – Goldberg from the US and Fedorenko from the Soviet Union – had become well known. Arthur Goldberg was a former union lawyer, Secretary of Labour and Justice of the Supreme Court. In private the Russians on the Soviet delegation called him 'the slick Jew who could fool the devil himself', but they respected his eloquence and intelligence and regarded him as a 'vigorous and formidable opponent'. Fedorenko had been a favourite of Stalin. He was one of the USSR's leading experts on China and spoke the language so well that he interpreted at meetings between Stalin and Mao. Andrei Gromyko, the long-serving Soviet foreign minister, disliked him. By the Soviet Union's prim standards, his hair was too long and his clothes, including the ultimate bourgeois affectation, a bow tie, were too flashy. He had been on the defensive since the crisis started, often avoiding members of the Security Council when they wanted consultations, emerging occasionally to deploy a sarcastic

Russian wit to the TV cameras. When the Canadian delegate seemed to be off beam, Fedorenko told him he was behaving like the man in an oriental proverb: when you show him the moon, all he looks at is your finger.

Fedorenko's performance in the first two days of the war served Israel's purposes admirably. It was not really his fault. Unlike Washington, Moscow had not invested heavily in cutting-edge communications, so Fedorenko and his superiors in the Soviet Union did not know how well the Israelis were doing. Initially, all they had to go on were Egypt's boasts. The Egyptian high command was already in such a state of panic and paralysis that it was not telling its own foreign ministry what was happening, let alone the people who had provided the equipment Israel was destroying. The Soviets at the UN had to fall back on their standing instructions not to allow any resolutions against Egypt, Syria or Jordan. When at last instructions arrived from Moscow 'they had a wait and see tone, while generally supportive of the Arab position. We were ordered to consult with the Arabs and condemn Israel in the strongest possible terms.'

Moscow also took military precautions. It put bomber and MiG-21 fighter units on alert in the evening. One of the officers concerned was convinced they were preparing for 'real combat'. They were moved to an airbase on the Soviet–Turkish border and were scrambled several times in the next three days. Their plan was to operate out of Syrian airbases. Working indirectly, the Iraqi government asked Turkey the next day to grant overflight rights to Soviet MiG-21s. Permission was refused.

Fedorenko and his delegation were picking up rumours, but none of the hard information they needed. The Soviet Embassy in Cairo had some around the time that New Yorkers were having breakfast, but it was not passed on. For the first few hours of the war, the Soviets in Cairo had relied on the radio like everyone else. They realised that Cairo Radio's bragging reports were inaccurate, but assumed they were exaggerations rather than outright lies. Then a group of Soviet specialists came back from Egypt's biggest airbase, Cairo West. Sergei Tarasenko, who was an attaché at the Embassy, saw them come in looking exhausted, with torn and dirty clothes. Their senior officer came to the point. 'Egypt hasn't got an air force any more, and Cairo West base has ceased to exist.' The bus carrying the Soviet technicians was just approaching the base when the first wave of Mirages attacked. They had time to pile out and take cover. After the first raid, a dozen aircraft survived. The Soviets said the pilots could have taken them into the air. But nothing happened and the next wave of attacks finished them off.

About the time that the Soviet technicians were getting back to their embassy, a call for a simple ceasefire was going nowhere. India protested about the 'wanton strafing attack' in Gaza by Israel that had killed three of its UNEF soldiers. After India tabled its own resolution saying that the ceasefire needed to be followed by a return to the positions of 4 June, the Security Council decided to take a short recess to wait for news from the battlefield. The Israelis, who knew exactly what was happening, and the Americans, who knew almost as much, kept silent. Some of the delegates stayed in their seats in the chamber of the Security Council. Others drifted out to the delegates' lounge, where reporters milled around trying to find out what was happening. The Council did not reconvene until 10:20 p.m. New York time.

Ambassador Goldberg spent hours trying to get a meeting with Fedorenko. The Soviet avoided him until late in the afternoon. For the Arabs a bitter irony was in the making. Goldberg and the Americans had concluded that they would have to soften their position. A resolution calling simply for a ceasefire did not look to be enough to get past the Soviet veto. Goldberg wanted to reach Fedorenko to offer him a ceasefire plus a withdrawal of troops, an idea that Israel opposed vehemently. Through gritted teeth the Israeli representative told the Americans that its view of the proposition was 'frigid'.

By the time Fedorenko met Goldberg, it was getting on for midnight in the Middle East. During the time that Fedorenko was mostly incommunicado, the first day of fighting had ended with Israel making big advances in the Sinai and towards Jerusalem. Goldberg offered him a new text including a demand for 'prompt withdrawal, without prejudice to rights, claims or positions of anyone, of all armed

166

personnel back to their own territories, and to take other appropriate measures to ensure disengagement of forces and to reduce tension in the area'. Fedorenko rejected it, because the reference to 'own territories' meant that the Iraqis, who had been advancing into Jordan, and other Arabs who had sent troops, would have to bring them all home. Instead, he suggested a demand to pull soldiers back behind the armistice lines. Both of them went away to think about it.

Fedorenko had stonewalled Goldberg. But in a private meeting shortly afterwards he told the Egyptian, Jordanian and Syrian ambassadors that it was the best deal they were going to get. Goldberg and Fedorenko met again at 9 p.m. New York time. By then the US had gone even further towards the Soviet position. The new American draft accepted the Soviet language that both sides should withdraw back to the armistice lines. Fedorenko stonewalled again. He could not give an answer before the morning.

In one day the United States had gone from supporting a ceasefire resolution calling simply for both sides to stop fighting, to drafting a call for a return to the positions that had been held on 4 June. Had the Soviet Union accepted it, they would have scored a diplomatic victory on behalf of their Arab allies. It would have had the added bonus for them of sowing dissension between Israel and the US. Instead, they played into Israel's hands.

White House Cabinet Room, 1130

President Johnson summoned his Special Committee of wise men that had been assembled to handle the crisis. They knew that Israel, whatever it was saying in public, had fired first. But they did not know who was winning. McGeorge Bundy, the committee's secretary, fretted about the 'awful shape we would be in if the Israelis were losing. We didn't really know anything about the situation on the ground.' The committee realised that if they were losing, the US would either have to intervene or watch Israel being 'thrown into the sea or defeated. That would have been a most painful moment and, of course, with the Soviet presence in the Middle East, a moment of great general danger.'

When, in late afternoon, they found out exactly what the Israeli air force had done, the whole atmosphere changed. Bundy was relieved that 'the fighting was the Israelis' idea and . . . the idea was working. That was a lot better than if it had been the other way around.' The Americans protected the Israelis. They knew a pre-emptive attack would be controversial, especially after Washington's loud warnings that more time should be given to diplomacy. The State Department's own legal advice was that Israel's action could be a violation of the United Nations charter. Walt Rostow thought it was best not to put on the record 'that Israel had kicked this off from a standing start'. He changed the draft of a letter from President Johnson to Britain's Prime Minister Wilson, to edit out the suggestion that Israel had moved first. The Americans were pleased that the people to whom they were drawn instinctively were on top, and that their pre-war intelligence pointing to a rapid Israeli victory had been right. But more than anything else, they were delighted that, thanks to Israel, they were off the hook. Johnson believed he had to find a way to honour the promises that Eisenhower had made in 1957 about keeping the Gulf of Aqaba open. But he did not like their only plan, for a naval operation with such limited international support that it could not have been passed off as anything other than gunboat diplomacy on Israel's behalf. Now it may be war, but at least someone else was doing the shooting.

Imwas, West Bank, 1830

Two detachments of Egyptian commandos prepared to cross the border into Israel from Imwas, a border village close to the main road from Jerusalem to Tel Aviv. Their mission was to raid the main international airport at Lod and an airforce base at Hartsour. They had Jordanian guides to get them over the border. After that all they had to rely on was a palm-sized aerial photograph and their enthusiasm. As the last of the evening light faded away, they moved quietly through fields and past farms and villages. Ali Abdul Mursi, one of the officers, realised that the whole country was at war. Most of the men were away fighting. If Egypt had been better organised, large-scale guerrilla operations inside Israel could have done a lot of damage. They trudged on through the fields.

Abu Deeb, the *moukhtar* or headman of Imwas, spent the evening sitting and talking with his brother Hikmat Deeb Ali outside their family house. Crisis or no crisis, on Monday morning Hikmat had travelled twenty miles or so by bus from his home village to get to his job on a building site in Jerusalem. He needed the money. But soon the news came through on the radio that the war had started. When they heard gunfire and shelling start in Jerusalem itself, Hikmat, like all his workmates, went back home. When he arrived, his neighbours were 'looking at each other . . . waiting. There was no sense of what was next.'

Sinai, 1830

By six, Brig. Gen. Avraham Yoffe's tanks had spent nine hours moving slowly through sand dunes that Egypt, assuming that they were impassable, had left virtually undefended. In places engineers had to dismount to clear minefields, inching their way forward with steel prods. By nightfall they were at B'ir Lahfan, where they came under fire and stopped. Yoffe's tanks blocked the road to Al-Arish from Jebel Libni and Abu Agheila. Fighting went on for most of the night, as Yoffe's men stopped reinforcements getting to Al-Arish. The confused fighting at Rafah was over by midnight. Ori Orr looked round his men who had fought there, 'trying to work out who was wounded and who was killed'. The survivors looked like 'children who have been forced to grow up in just one day'.

The commander of Israel's southern front, Brigadier General Yeshayahu Gavish, tired, with eyes bloodshot from the desert sand, flew south in a helicopter to the advanced headquarters of Brigadier General Yoffe. Amos Elon who was travelling with him, thought the camouflaged military vehicles beneath them looked like a Bedouin camp. When they landed Gavish dusted himself down and went to the war room with Yoffe. It was made of nets strung between two trucks. As the sun set, 'from the south, rolling over the darkened hills, came the thunder of cannon fire'. Rabin called Gavish, suggesting that they bomb Abu Agheila all night so they could march in when morning came. Doing that, he said, would minimise Israel's casualties. Gavish – and Sharon – disagreed. Gavish wanted to get his tanks into the position. Sharon protested that he was halfway through the attack. This was no time to break off. And he believed, correctly, that he was playing to Israel's strengths. 'The Egyptians do not like fighting at night nor do they enjoy hand-to-hand combat – we specialise in both.'

At 2200 guns from two Israeli brigades opened up on the Egyptian fortifications at Um Katef and Abu Agheila. Ariel Sharon rubbed his hands. 'Such a barrage I've never seen.' In twenty minutes 6000 shells landed on Um Katef. To the west, Israeli paratroopers, carried the first part of the way by helicopter, foot-slogged through soft sand to get behind the Egyptians, to attack their artillery. They blew up guns and shells and forced the crews to retreat. To the north, Sharon's infantry and armoured brigades, led by mine-clearing equipment, moved forward behind the barrage. Much of his infantry was transported to the battle in civilian buses, which they smeared with mud, 'not so much to camouflage them,' Sharon explained, 'but to make them appear a little more military'. They advanced the last few miles on foot, carrying coloured lights so they would not end up attacking each other.

Israeli foot soldiers worked their way through the Egyptian trenches, some men inside them, others above the parapet, shooting down into them. During the fighting at Abu Agheila, Egypt tried to send reinforcements from Jebel Libni, in the south-west. Brig. Gen. Yoffe's division was already at B'ir Lahfan to stop them getting through. The tanks fought all night. The Egyptians were overwhelmed after Israeli mechanised infantry came racing from Al-Arish to take their western flank.

Israeli wounded from the paratroop unit that was assaulting the defence lines on the road to Abu Agheila started coming in. One of their doctors 'was scared until I had to treat the first wounded . . . Soldiers lay legless, their hands crushed, a bullet in the neck, fragments in the stomach. We had only ten stretchers and some of the wounded insisted they could walk or limp along without help. The difficulty was to make sure that the infusion needles stayed in place while we advanced under fire.'

As usual, the Egyptians fought bravely in their fixed positions. But, as usual, their officers were not flexible enough to turn them around to deal with Israeli attacks from the rear. Junior officers and NCOs were also unable to organise effective counter-attacks against the Israelis who invaded their positions. But, in the end, the biggest reason for Israel's victory at Abu Agheila was Egypt's failure to commit its reserves until it was too late. They were close enough to hear the battle going on but were spectators for most of the night until Israel got round to surrounding and attacking them. Egypt had an armoured brigade in a good position to attack a task force of Israeli Centurion tanks that managed to chug its way through the supposedly impassable sand dunes north of Um Katef. But it did nothing, presumably because they did not have any orders. The Centurions' commander, Lt. Col. Natke Nir, was badly wounded in both legs, but his tanks turned the northern end of the Egyptian defences and managed to get in behind them. By eight in the morning, with smoke from burning vehicles and exploding Egyptian ammunition drifting across the sand, the battle was won. One of Yoffe's brigades was waiting to continue the advance. The road was blocked with the hundreds of civilian vehicles that had transported Sharon's infantry to the battle. They were pushed off the road and on to the sand, so Yoffe's men could continue to their next target, Jebel Libni.

Cairo, evening

Crowds poured into Cairo from the provinces to celebrate a great victory in buses and trucks provided by the Arab Socialist Union, the ruling party. Many of them had transistor radios. By 8:17 p.m. Cairo Radio was claiming that eighty-six enemy aircraft had been destroyed and that Egyptian tanks had broken into Israel. At the headquarters of the Sinai front, General Gamasy listened 'with growing horror' to what he knew was a pack of lies. At Central Command, General Hadidi slumped into his chair, convinced that the war was at least half-lost. The US Embassy did not trust the 'repetition of vague and universally victorious communiqués' on the radio. They recommended that Washington apply the 'usual coefficient of mendacity of 10, giving the total number downed as something like 9'.

Anwar El Sadat could have told them they were not being suspicious enough. Like Nasser, he had retreated to his villa, where he had spent the day ringing Nasser and Amer and trying to follow what was happening in the air and at the front. Late in the evening he rang Amer again, who told him 'drily and irritably' that the Israelis had captured Al-Arish. Sadat, at a loss, went for a long walk through the streets of Cairo. He watched Nasser's loyalists marching up and down Pyramids Road. Sadat was 'dazed and broken-hearted', as they chanted and danced to the fake reports of an imaginary victory.

Jerusalem, evening

The BBC had refused to run the world exclusive of its own correspondent, Michael Elkins. He had only just started work with the Corporation, and he was an Israeli. The editors in the newsroom in London thought that he might, as they delicately put it, have 'spoken with the tongue of the prophets'. By the evening they relented, and put out Elkins's story, which had already been broadcast coast-to-coast in the US on CBS. He beat the military censorship with careful words: '. . . less than fifteen hours after the fighting began at dawn this morning, there was every evidence that though fighting will continue, Israel has already won the war . . . I may not now report where the Israeli armed forces stand, but the place names will be familiar to anyone who has read a good account of the first five days of the 1956

Sinai campaign. This time Israel has created the nearest thing to instant victory the modern world has seen.'

The Jordanian command post on the eastern side of the city was under heavy artillery fire. The air seemed to be vibrating. Brigadier Atta Ali, the Jordanian commander, and Hazim Khalidi, a member of one of Jerusalem's aristocratic families who had been an officer in the British army, were discussing the chances of reinforcement. Messages from Amman were telling them that four brigades were coming, but they could not raise the Jordanian army's West Bank headquarters on the radio. They did not know that it was already pulling back across the river Jordan. Reinforcements that were trying to make it up the Jericho road were attacked and destroyed by the Israelis. The bunker was overcrowded. Several dozen policemen kept pushing into it to escape the shelling. No one had taught them about digging trenches to protect themselves.

Tel Aviv disappeared into a deep blackout. The British journalist James Cameron reported that it 'might seem a bit excessive in view of this claim to have rubbed out the entire Arab air threat, but the Israelis have lived so long on a razor edge that they take no chances'. The tension of not knowing what was happening at the front was still there, Cameron went on. 'It has been a day of immense sorrow and apprehension here, where virtually no one exists but has a son or a father in very serious danger.'

Washington DC, evening

Since mid-afternoon Walt Rostow, the National Security Advisor, had been talking to President Johnson about the shape of the post-war Middle East. After a long day, Rostow sat back in his chair in his office in the White House basement, dictating a message to Johnson. He beamed with pleasure and relief. The first day had been a 'turkey shoot'. He noted: 'The key to ending the war is how well the Israelis do – or don't do – on the ground.'

DAY TWO

6 June 1967

Jerusalem, 0100

The Israeli paratroops were being rushed into action. It was urban warfare, fighting house to house, close to the enemy. It was very different from their original mission to destroy the guns at Al-Arish that they had rehearsed until they had it off by heart. They had no maps of Jerusalem, nor the right equipment for street fighting. But General Narkiss wanted to get them into battle fast, in case the Jordanians counter-attacked in the morning or the Security Council passed a ceasefire resolution before they had seized East Jerusalem. Colonel Mordechai Gur, the commander of the 55th paratroop brigade, set up his headquarters in a requisitioned school. General Narkiss struggled down a dimly lit corridor, 'lined wall to wall with paratroop officers in battle dress', into the biology lab where Gur and his officers were planning their assault, next to 'jars and bottles of lizards, grasshoppers, birds, chicken eggs, a goat foetus and maybe a lamb, all swimming in formalin'.

It was decided that Battalion 66 of the paratroops would assault Ammunition Hill and the Police School, which were two connected Jordanian strongpoints blocking the way to the Israeli enclave on

Mount Scopus and the northern approaches to the Old City. Two other battalions, the 71st and the 28th, would break through into the Wadi Joz and American Colony districts of Jordanian Jerusalem. From there they would pull right towards the Old City. Narkiss was still itching with frustration that he did not have the orders to get inside the city walls, but 'we all felt that if everything went according to plan our final objective would be the Old City'.

But first they had to break through yards of barbed wire and mines to get into Jordanian Jerusalem. The high command in Tel Aviv was less impatient than Narkiss. With the paratroops at their start lines for the assault, they debated postponing it until dawn when they would get air cover. While they talked, the Jordanians spotted Battalion 28 waiting to go in and hit them with a highly accurate artillery barrage. The shelling shredded the battalion, which was made up of veterans of the wars and raids of the 1950s. At least sixty men were wounded and eight killed before they even set off. Narkiss and Gur were up on a roof, in an observation position just above Battalion 28, when the attack happened. The parapet was hit by a shell from a Jordanian twenty-five pounder. Flying shrapnel fizzed around them. Waiting in a jeep in the street below Yoel Herzl, Narkiss's adjutant, saw the roof disappear in a great cloud of dust. He was convinced the commanders had been killed. He guessed other men in the building would be trying to sort out the mess so he stuck to his orders to stay with the jeep, monitoring the radio that was their only link to GHQ in Tel Aviv. The shelling did not stop. With paratroopers shouting and running to evacuate their wounded, he crawled under the jeep, taking the radio headphones on a long cable.

Dead and wounded soldiers were lying in the street. A young officer yelled at Herzl to hand over the jeep to take casualties to the hospital. When he refused the officer, surrounded by his men, cocked his weapon and threatened to shoot him. Herzl told him that the jeep belonged to General Narkiss and its radio connected them to the general staff in Tel Aviv. Furious, the officer grabbed the headset, tore it out of the radio and stormed off. Herzl went off to borrow tools from the civilians who were sheltering in their basements. By the time Narkiss emerged, dusty but intact from the building, he had fixed it.

Battalion 28 had only a few minutes to reorganise themselves. Arie Weiner was given the sergeant major's job. His friend Shimon Cahaner became deputy battalion commander. They were both veterans of Unit 101, the irregular force founded by Ariel Sharon in 1953 to carry out cross-border reprisal raids. Weiner had escaped from Romania as a child after most of his family were killed by the Nazis. The British put strict controls on Jewish immigration to Palestine so, with thousands of other Jews who had survived the Holocaust, he was interned in a camp in Cyprus until he was smuggled into the promised land. Holocaust survivors did not get a warm welcome from most 'sabras', the native-born Israelis. The sabras saw themselves as the new, fighting Jews. They had grown up in a macho, often cruel, secular culture where self-reliance was everything. Many of them refused to understand why so many millions had gone, in the phrase that was often used, like lambs to the slaughter. Weiner saw all this and decided to join the paratroops to do what he could to break the image of the Holocaust survivor. (Thirty-five years later Cahaner, a famous Israeli fighter, heard all this and grunted his approval: 'Arie carried the image of the Diaspora Jew on his back.')

Jerusalem, 0200

Ammunition Hill was a fortress. Concentric lines of trenches ran round it, surrounded by razor wire and minefields. Dozens of well-camouflaged concrete bunkers studded the entire position, all with overlapping fields of fire. The Israeli plan was for a frontal assault, supported by tanks. Israel had good intelligence about Ammunition Hill, but it was under lock and key in the headquarters of the Jerusalem Brigade. None of it reached the paratroopers before they went into action. They assumed, wrongly, that the Police School next to it, also heavily fortified, would be their worst obstacle. Jacov Chaimowitz was 'scared to death. My throat completely dried up. We had to cross one hundred metres of minefield. I knew they could not have cleared all the mines, so I tried to run on tip-toe. There was noise, shooting, shouting, we followed the commander one by one in single file, concentrating on small jobs – checking the weapons, keeping the right distance from the others.' The Jordanians, who were from the second battalion of the King Talal Infantry Brigade, kept up a devastating rate of fire from their bunkers. Most of them were Bedouins. Their commander, Captain Sulamin Salayta, was a Palestinian. At the beginning of the battle, already lightly wounded, he told his men: 'Today is your day. Jerusalem is calling you. God is calling you. Listen and obey! Live long, but let's have hell rather than shame.'

Both sides had hell during the battle, and neither had shame. The Israelis pressed forward even though they were being cut down by accurate Jordanian fire. Most of the Jordanians fought to the death. For Colonel Gur 'this was fighting of a sort I had never experienced. The men had to break through at least five fences before they reached the emplacements . . . the fighting was going on in the trenches, in the houses, on the roofs, in the cellars, anywhere and everywhere.' Towards the end, as the Israelis closed in, the Jordanians called artillery fire down on their own positions. The sound of the battle was deafening. A mile away in the Old City, Abdullah Schliefer thought that Jerusalem's walls were being assaulted. 'No sleep for anyone,' cabled a hollow-eyed Hugh Pullar, the British consul-general. 'Very heavy rocket, mortar and automatic weapons engagements . . .'

Two hours into the battle, Chaimowitz was 'like a robot – I felt nothing – I was just thinking about fighting well to survive'. His officer had been killed and by now he had taken command of his squad. He peered round the corner of the trench, and saw the silhouettes of four men with British-style tin hats. Jordanians. He shot one. The others ducked away. Suddenly he was scared again. 'For a moment I was so frightened I felt like I was in the sea, out of my depth. I shot two bullets to make me feel more confident.' He pushed on, throwing grenades into bunkers and firing. When he ran out of grenades, he let the man behind him through to lead and dropped into a bunker to

177

look for some more. Inside was chaos. It was full of wounded Israelis. One of them said he had crawled into the bunker because he could not go any further forward as everyone else in his squad was dead. No grenades were in the bunker, but there was a Jordanian heavy machine gun. Chaimowitz had the urge to burst back into the trench firing it from the hip. 'I had seen Audie Murphy doing it in films to the Japanese. It weighed more than ten kilos. I tried to fire it in the bunker, but it wouldn't shoot and I couldn't fix it.' Chaimowitz left the bunker without the gun and for a while was on his own. Ahead of him a big concrete bunker was holding out. Some of the other Israelis had 20 kg satchel charges which they had been given to use on the guns at Al-Arish. Chaimowitz crawled with the explosives under heavy fire to the entrance of the bunker. He handed them to another soldier, who was standing behind the position. They kept firing at the bunker while they laid the charges, to stop the Jordanians getting out. Once the detonator was set, they moved back under cover and blew the charges. Firing was still coming from the ruins of the bunker. Chaimowitz charged inside and killed whoever was left alive.

When the battle was lost, Captain Salayta, the Jordanian commander, managed to break out and escape with three of his men. The last Jordanian soldier left fighting on Ammunition Hill was Staff Sergeant Ahmed al-Yamani, who kept firing and killing Israelis until he was killed. Chaimowitz went back to the discarded Jordanian machine gun and tried to work out why he could not fire it. His respect for the Jordanian's fighting qualities deepened even further when he saw that the soldier who dumped it had disabled it first.

Both sides showed great courage. In the end the decisive difference between them was the Israelis' tactical flexibility. They used initiative and daring to overcome dogged Jordanian resistance. Had the Jordanians been able to get reinforcements to the area, and had they been trained to leave their positions to counter-attack, the result might have been different – at least until daylight, when the Israelis would have brought in the air force.

After the battle, as the sun came up over Jerusalem, 106 Jordanian dead and at least as many wounded were left on the battlefield. Israel had lost 37 men. A smell of burnt flesh rose up from some of the smouldering bunkers. Major Doron Mor, the deputy commander of Battalion 66, started to collect the Israeli dead. Many of them were his friends. Paratroopers who had survived the battle sat on the ground and did not offer to help. They watched Mor and a mechanic lifting bodies into a Jordanian trailer. 'It was a very hard job. The soldiers were in shock – tired and angry, so I didn't order them to help us. It took two hours to move the bodies.'

Some Israeli officers thought their soldiers were sacrificed unnecessarily in a rushed and badly prepared attack at Ammunition Hill. Colonel Uri Ben Ari, who was heading towards Ammunition Hill from the east with his tanks, was very critical. 'Tank fire could have finished the battle of Ammunition Hill in a minute. That was the mistake, to tell them to continue and continue and continue. You have to change your plans when the battlefield develops differently than you thought. That was a mistake. The paratroopers paid dearly . . .'

At the same time that their colleagues from Battalion 66 were fighting at Ammunition Hill and the Police School, Battalions 71 and 28 broke through around half a mile closer to the Old City, into the district of Sheikh Jarrah. Once they went into action, their orders were to move along the Nablus Road towards the city walls. It was a heavily built-up area. The Jordanians made them fight house by house. If they tried by-passing houses, to go faster, they were shot from behind. Until it was light, big searchlights on the roof of the Trade Union Federation building, West Jerusalem's highest, were beamed at the area, cutting through the smoke of battle. Yoseph Schwartz, one of the paratroopers, was conscious that civilians were inside cellars and stairwells along what looked like an otherwise empty street. 'You'd approach a house, want to throw a grenade, but you'd hear a baby crying. It's very difficult when you don't want to hurt civilians.'

One of the Israeli paratroops caught up in the street fighting found himself face to face with a Jordanian soldier. He recorded the horror he felt as he killed for the first time.

We looked at each other for half a second and I knew that it was up to me, personally, to kill him, there was no one else there. The whole thing must have lasted less than a second, but it's printed on my mind like a slow-motion movie. I fired from the hip and I can still see how the bullets splashed against the wall about a metre to his left. I moved my Uzi slowly, slowly, it seemed, until I hit him in the body. He slipped to his knees, then he raised his head, with his face terrible, twisted in pain and hate, yes, such hate. I fired again and somehow got him in the head. There was so much blood . . . I vomited . . . we were all just machines for killing. Everyone's face is set in a snarl and there's a deep growl coming from your belly . . .

The Jordanians had a strongpoint in a small alley called Chaldean Street that ran into Nablus Road. They killed four Israeli soldiers and wounded several others who were trying to cross the entrance to the alley before themselves being killed by an Israeli tank. Some Israeli paratroopers called Chaldean Street 'death alley'. Yoseph Schwartz called it 'mistake junction' because so many men died. His unit started the night with 107 men. By the time they had fought their way to St George's, Jerusalem's Anglican cathedral, only thirty-four were still going. Inside, the archbishop, his staff and their families had taken to the cellars, where all night they listened to the sounds of fighting and shelling. One of them wrote: 'The noise was deafening, the electricity failed and the shelling intensified throughout the night. It was terrifying – first a distant rumble and seconds later a crash.' They heard tanks rolling along Nablus Road and soldiers talking in Hebrew. The Palestinians in the cathedral cellars were petrified, especially one of the maids, who had survived the Deir Yassin massacre in 1948. A teacher from the cathedral school was so scared he shut himself in a cupboard. When they looked out during a lull, dead soldiers lay on Nablus Road and buildings were on fire. Before the Israeli troops secured the whole area between Sheikh Jarrah and the Old City, the governor of Jerusalem, Anwar al-Khatib, Brigadier Atta Ali, the

1. Crowds line the streets of West Jerusalem on Israel's Independence Day, 15 May 1967.

2. President Nasser faces the world's press in the government's Council Chamber in Cairo on 28 May. A solemn moment, but Sandy Gall of ITN said he could turn on his dazzling smile 'like an electric light, the shiny white teeth flashing on and off'.

3. On the brink: Egypt's Field Marshal (right) greets General Murtagi at the advanced command centre in Sinai.

4. Israel Tal, the IDF's 'Mr Tank', sweating the detail at his desk before the war.

5. Brigadier-General Yeshayahu Gavish, head of Israel's Southern Command. On the eve of war, Prime Minister Eshkol offered his job to Moshe Dayan.

6. King Hussein of Jordan touring the front just before the war. He was already convinced that Israel would win – the question was whether his throne would survive what was coming.

7. Mobilising the diaspora: children in Golders Green, London, shared the concern of Jews around the world.

8. Mordechai Hod, Israeli air force commander, with cadets just before the fighting started.

9. The first battle in Jerusalem. Israeli troops capture Government House, the UN headquarters.

10. Israeli generals Haim Bar Lev, Yitzhak Rabin and Ezer Weizman early in the war.

11. Israeli troops under fire, photographed by Don McCullin as they fight their way towards the Old City's Dung Gate on 7 June.

12. Israeli soldiers celebrate the capture of the Old City at the Dome of the Rock, 7 June.

13. David Rubinger took this picture of Brigadier-General Shlomo Goren, chief rabbi of the IDF, blowing the *shofar*, a trumpet made from a ram's horn, minutes after the capture of the Wailing, or Western, Wall. Torah scrolls are tucked under Goren's left arm.

14. An Israeli soldier at the Wailing Wall, 7 June.

15. Uzi Narkiss, Moshe Dayan and Yitzhak Rabin enter the Old City through St Stephen's Gate on 7 June. Dayan, always aware of posterity, brought the photographers with him.

16. Confident Israeli soldiers move forward into Sinai in their Second World War-vintage half-tracks, 8 June.

17. The battered USS *Liberty* comes alongside in Valetta, Malta, after the Israeli attack on 8 June.

18. Palestinian prisoners in Jerusalem, photographed by Don McCullin. Note the pyjamas: some of King Hussein's soldiers changed into whatever civilian clothes they could find.

19. The Mitla Pass in Sinai, after retreating Egyptian forces were destroyed by the Israelis. A Second World War veteran who saw it said it was worse than the German retreat from El Alamein.

20. Defeat: Egyptian dead on 9 June.

21. Victory: Israeli soldiers dip their hands in the Suez Canal.

22. Palestinians clambering over the wreckage of the Allenby Bridge, across the River Jordan, and out of the newly-occupied West Bank.

23. A long walk to a harsh future. A Palestinian refugee heads for the East Bank.

24. Israeli Prime Minister Levi Eshkol (centre) visiting troops on the Syrian front line just before the ceasefire.

25. General Munam Abdul Husaini, Egyptian governor of the Gaza Strip, signs the instrument of surrender on 10 June.

26. Moshe Dayan meets Palestinian elders at Kalandiya refugee camp, between Ramallah and Jerusalem. Dayan rapidly took control of policy for the newly occupied territories.

27. Golan Heights, 12 June. Israeli soldiers investigate knocked-out Syrian tanks.

28. By October 1967, a new war was brewing along the Egypt–Israel ceasefire line. Here an Israeli soldier watches the Egyptian oil refinery at Port Suez burn. It was destroyed by the IDF after the Egyptians sank the Israeli warship *Eilat*.

29. By 1969 Palestinian armed groups were well established in the huge, sprawling new refugee camps in Jordan. These Palestinian boys were taking their first steps towards what would for many be a lifetime of violence.

Jordanian commander and Hazim Khalidi, the Palestinian who had been a British officer, managed to cross into the Old City on foot. The last twenty-five yards were under fire, in a dash towards Herod's Gate. The three of them made it. The next man who tried was killed.

Latrun, 0300

Moshe Yotvat, whose wife Ava had started the singing in their shelter in Tel Aviv, was back at Latrun, where in 1948 he had fought the bloodiest battle of his youth, and where Israel had suffered one of its worst defeats of the war. Then, the Israelis thought the position was held only by local Arab militias. Some units, including Yotvat's, rushed into a badly prepared attack. Others that were supposed to support them arrived late on the battlefield. Instead of armed villagers they came up against a well-dug-in battalion of professional infantry from Jordan's Arab Legion. The Jordanians won a decisive victory, killing scores of Israelis. Yotvat helped carry the wounded from the battlefield, among whom was a young, already heavy, Ariel Sharon. By 1967 Yotvat was forty-three and a colonel in the reserves, commanding a brigade. Three days before the war he had been ordered to 'snatch' Latrun if fighting started in Jerusalem. This was one piece of unfinished business from 1948 that Israel was determined to put right. Yotvat was certain he would end Jordan's ownership of the Latrun salient. It jutted out into the heart of Israel and commanded the main road to Jerusalem. He did not think he would be going much further. The army had only given him local maps.

Yotvat remembered the direction from which they had attacked in 1948. Assuming that the Jordanians did too, he decided to do the opposite. At 0300 a battalion of Israeli artillery opened fire on the Jordanian positions at Latrun. Then forces from the local agricultural settlements mounted a diversionary attack. Among them was Yossi Ally, a member of Kibbutz Nachshon, the nearest Israeli settlement to Latrun. At midnight he was woken up, and told to take his car to Yotvat's brigade headquarters. The idea was to make the Jordanians believe an armoured column was heading their way. Two military vehicles went first. The rest were private cars, four to five metres apart, with their headlights full on, driving from the kibbutz along a border road. Ally was driving his 'Susita', an Israeli vehicle made of fibreglass. (It was widely believed that fragile Susitas abandoned in the desert were eaten by camels.) Afterwards he wondered whether he should have felt more like cannon fodder. But at the time he was excited. Once the fake convoy had rumbled past the Jordanian positions, he drove back to the kibbutz to watch the rest of the operation from a safer distance.

Fifteen minutes after the diversion the Israelis turned large searchlights on the old British police fortress, a four-square building made of concrete and steel, of a type that they had left all over Palestine. It was the centre of the Jordanian defences. The artillery pounded the fortress and the positions on the slope behind it that led to Jerusalem and the West Bank. The monks in the Trappist monastery of Latrun, which was around half a mile from the police fortress, took cover as shells crashed into the hills around them. Hikmat Deeb Ali, who lived in Imwas, one of the three small Palestinian villages within the Latrun salient, heard the shelling too, and realised it was starting to go very wrong for the Arab side.

Yotvat's attack had hardly started when the Jordanians pulled out of their positions. Not long after the shelling started, two cars stopped in Imwas. The commander of the local Jordanian garrison got out. 'We are withdrawing,' he told them. 'Take care of yourselves.' Following him were around sixty soldiers, from the Jordanian Hashimi Brigade. They followed their commander out of the village. When the Israelis entered the old police fortress, which had been an impregnable obstacle to them in 1948, they found half-eaten plates of food. The Jordanians had left in a hurry. Colonel Yotvat, the Israeli brigade commander, radioed in to Narkiss's headquarters that after only an hour's one-sided fighting he had captured Latrun. Yotvat was surprised it had been so easy and so quick. If the Jordanians crumbled at Latrun, the West Bank must be wide open. He asked for permission to move on towards Ramallah. Narkiss told him to be careful. Yotvat asked for maps. They were delivered by helicopter.

Hikmat Deeb Ali and his brother had thought the Jordanian soldiers would protect them, just as they had in 1948. They decided it was up to them now. Nineteen years on the new war was starting to feel very different. They loaded dozens of people, their extended family and neighbours, into the village bus, to go down the road to look for sanctuary in the Trappist monastery, where they thought they would be safe. Just as the bus was about to move off, shells started crashing down. The people on the bus pushed their way off to run for cover. Not long afterwards the Israelis entered the village. Hikmat Deeb Ali, who was hiding in the church, could see them get out of their vehicles and start to sing and dance.

In Beit Nuba, the neighbouring village, Abdul Rahim Ali Ahmad's family were wide awake and could hear the sound of fighting. They decided it would be safer to leave their village for a while. The mother grabbed two blankets, folded them and balanced them on her head. There was no time to take any food. Barefoot, she led her children out of the village. Behind them they could see the lights of Israeli jeeps and tanks. They avoided roads, moving through fields as much as they could. They were terrified of the Israelis. The mother put her hand over the children's mouths when the Israelis passed, in case a cry gave them away.

Jenin, 0300

A Jordanian battle group lay in wait for the advancing Israelis in the rocky olive groves around the town. Jordanian forces were spread thinly around Jenin and in the rest of the northern part of the West Bank, but they were well organised for defence and had made the right guess about the road the Israelis would use. The day before most IDF troops in northern Israel had been deployed to fight Syria. But once Jordan entered the war and it was clear that the Syrians were going to do as little fighting as possible, a series of orders was given to move into the entire West Bank. Plans that had been in the making for years were implemented. The air force had started bombarding Jordanian positions at five the previous evening while the Israeli troops came south from the Syrian front for the attack.

Around Jenin the Jordanians set up three co-ordinated defence lines, with plenty of anti-tank guns. In the last line was a battalion of Patton tanks. They were well dug in, covering every access road. Because of the terrain, their position could not be outflanked. Israel had to mount a frontal assault. The Jordanians fought well from their positions, driving back two attacks. The decisive moment in the battle came just after dawn. Pretending to retreat, the Israelis pulled back from the battlefield, seemingly abandoning their disabled tanks. When the Jordanian tanks moved out of their positions, without infantry support, to finish them off, the Israelis turned and started firing. The Israeli Super Sherman tanks were Second World War veterans, but they had been fitted with better engines and modern 105 mm guns. They outmanoeuvred the Pattons, lining up shots against their weak points. Most of the Pattons were destroyed. The dug-in Jordanian infantry kept fighting, but they had no chance without support from armour or from the air.

Al-Arish, Sinai, 0400

After what he called a 'brutal battle' two of Israel Tal's armoured brigades were in Al-Arish. Tal's men had to overcome Egyptian anti-tank guns, which were hidden among the dunes in concrete bunkers. Tal said they always fired together. 'It was like a line of lightning across the battlefield. It was impossible to see where they were and few were destroyed by tank fire. We just advanced on the flashes with our tanks and crushed them.'

During the night Cairo ordered its 4th Armoured Division to attack the left flank of Tal's division at B'ir Lahfan. The Egyptians' Soviet-built tanks had much better night-fighting gear than anything the Israelis had. But after the 4th Armoured was given a bloody nose, losing nine tanks and destroying only one Israeli in return, they pulled back to wait for dawn. At first light they saw there were not as many Israeli tanks facing them as they had imagined the night before, so they launched a frontal attack. But the Israelis once again used their skill in manoeuvre and long-range gunnery, as well as the air force, to defeat them. They pulled back towards Bir Gifgafah, with the Israeli air force in pursuit. In the fighting Egypt's 4th Armoured Division lost between thirty and eighty tanks.

Gaza

The most impressive thing about the Palestinian Liberation Army was its title. In reality it was not an army, just around ten thousand enthusiastic but poorly trained Palestinian infantrymen supported by Egyptian tanks. Lieutenant Omar Khalil Omar, a local man from just north of Gaza City, commanded 100 men, armed mainly with a mixture of Kalashnikov automatic rifles and older semi-automatic rifles. They had nothing heavier. When Omar asked his Egyptian superior officer for anti-tank weapons, he was told to be patient, keep his chin up and stop asking questions. They had been expecting the Israelis to come from the north. When they came from the south, they were astonished. The anti-tank weapons never turned up. Neither did any orders about what to do next. The PLA fought bravely at Khan Younis, but by the time Israeli armour was penetrating north, up the Gaza Strip, Omar's men saw no point in throwing their lives away in a battle they could not win. They voted with their feet. 'My soldiers wanted to fight. But what could we do against tanks? Most of them ran away.'

Major Ibrahim El Dakhakny of Egyptian military intelligence could hear the Israelis getting closer to his office in Gaza City. It was time to get out to the beach, where he had prepared a boat with some of his colleagues. They planned to slip out to sea and head south as far as they needed to escape the advancing Israelis. But El Dakhakny had left it too late. When he tried to move through the dusty streets to the sea, he realised he had been cut off. Israeli soldiers and their tanks were between him and the beach. He radioed the men who were waiting for him and told them to get moving. He would have to find another way to escape.

In a sandy, arid valley near Gaza City, El Dakhakny linked up with fifteen Palestinian fighters who also had no plans to surrender. They told him they could get to Jordan. One night of walking, they promised, and they would be able to link up with Jordanian troops on the West Bank. El Dakhakny was not so sure. He guessed the Israelis were advancing as quickly into the West Bank as they were into Egypt. He wished them good luck, they left and he was alone again. The major went off to find somewhere quiet to hide, while he weighed up his options. He was hoping to find another boat. The sea looked like his best chance.

Ramadan Mohammed Iraqi had been on the run since his radio truck was destroyed in an air strike on the first day. He was with two other Egyptian soldiers, one of whom had lost an arm, hidden in a field next to a main road. The wounded man convinced himself that the soldiers they could see on the road were Kuwaitis. He never came back. 'When he realised they were Israelis it was too late. They shot him.' The Israelis fired into the field with a machine gun. The other man was shot in both legs. A bullet hit Ramadan's boot without wounding him. Slowly, he stood up. 'I knew they'd shoot if I tried to run,' he said. 'They shouted in Hebrew and I put my hands on my head. Then they tied my hands and blindfolded me. I thought I was going to die. I said my prayers. All I could think about was my wife, who was pregnant with our first child. We were newlyweds. They searched me for my ID and took my money and my photos. They took off the blindfold but kept my hands tied and made me run in front of the tank until we reached the place where they were assembling prisoners.' When he was being moved later in the day close to Al-Arish one Israeli soldier told them to jump off the truck and walk through the desert to Port Said. Another one cut in and said if they moved he would kill them. The prisoners stayed on the truck.

186

Amman, 0530

Jordan's ability to fight was collapsing. General Riad told King Hussein he had two choices – get a ceasefire, or pull what was left of the army out of the West Bank entirely to concentrate on defending the eastern side of the river Jordan. He went on: 'If you don't decide within the next twenty-four hours, you can kiss your army and all of Jordan goodbye! We are on the verge of losing the West Bank. All of our forces will be isolated or destroyed.' King Hussein, shaken, asked Riad to find out what President Nasser thought.

Half an hour later General Riad spoke to Nasser and then put Hussein on the line. The United Arab Command had bought the latest secure radio link for sensitive conversations between leaders. But all the equipment was still in Cairo. No one had thought about bringing it to Amman. So they talked on an ordinary telephone. The Israelis, who were intercepting the enemy's calls while keeping their own secret, recorded it and released a transcript two days later.

First General Riad confirmed to Nasser that Britain, not just America, had aircraft carriers. Then, after talk between operators, King Hussein came on the line. After a difficult exchange of pleasantries – the line was very bad – this is what they said.

NASSER: We are also fighting fiercely. We have been
    fighting on all fronts throughout the night.
HUSSEIN: (indistinct)
NASSER: However, if there is anything in the beginning,
    never mind. We will do better. God is with us. Is Your
    Majesty going to issue a statement on the subject of the
    American and British participation?
HUSSEIN: (indistinct)
NASSER: I say it would be better for us to issue a statement.
    I will issue a statement and you will issue a statement. We
    will also let the Syrians issue a statement that there are
    American and English aircraft acting against us from

aircraft carriers. We will issue a statement and thus make
the subject more emphatic, I think.

HUSSEIN: All right.

NASSER: Does Your Majesty agree?

HUSSEIN: (indistinct)

NASSER: A thousand thanks, stand firm and we are with you with all our heart. Our aircraft are over Israel today. Our aircraft have been raiding Israeli airfields since morning.

HUSSEIN: (indistinct)

NASSER: A thousand thanks.

HUSSEIN: Thank you, Abdel Nasser.

NASSER: Goodbye.

Desperate for a scapegoat, Nasser, assisted by the king, had decided to pin the blame for the impending Arab defeat on the United States and Britain. Arab suspicions were deepened by the fact that Israel seemed to be attacking with more aircraft than seemed possible. In a way, that much was correct. The Israelis had trained their ground crews to a pitch where they could turn a warplane round in ten minutes. Some aircraft did six sorties a day. Some pilots did four.

In her villa in Amman, not far from Hussein's headquarters, Leila Sharaf, the wife of the king's information minister, tuned into Voice of the Arabs from Cairo. It was transmitting a play about the heroes of a war with Israel. This time, the Arabs were winning.

Syria–Israel border, 0545

Syria staged its only ground offensive of the war. Syrian artillery shelled the Israeli frontier settlements at Shear Yusuv and Tel Dan. After a forty-five minute barrage, around a dozen T-34s (the tank that the USSR had used to beat the Germans) moved forward. At 0700 several hundred infantry men from Battalion 243 moved forward to try to invade the settlements. Their officers 'mostly pointed their men in the direction of the Israeli defences and ordered them to charge'.

The attack was stopped by the kibbutz's militia, which included farmers, shopkeepers and the local bus driver. Twenty minutes later the Israeli air force finished the job with cannon fire and napalm. The attack was all that was left of a much more ambitious plan called Operation Nasser, an attack by two divisions which had been cancelled the night before. The bigger attack would also have failed. The Syrian army was not capable of anything so complicated. After the war Israeli intelligence discovered from captured documents that the Syrians had not even checked whether the bridges over the Jordan were wide enough for their tanks – they weren't.

The Syrian army had about 70,000 soldiers, organised into ten brigades. Seven of them were infantry (half of them motorised), two had tanks and there was one artillery brigade. Syria also had an anti-aircraft artillery division, which was dispersed around the country, and a national guard, which was parcelled out among regular units on the border with Israel. Major Ibrahim Ali, the commander of a 'People's Army' of 1000 civilians, claimed it was armed and ready. An American military analysis commented that 'their effectiveness in a combat situation is questionable'.

On the eve of the war the Syrian army was still in the throes of a debilitating purge. It had started in September 1966, following the failure of yet another attempted military coup. Once the coup was crushed, Syria's ruler Salah Jadid and his right-hand man, Major-General Hafez al-Asad, the commander of the air force and defence minister, began what turned into the biggest ever purge of the Syrian armed forces. On the eve of war in 1967, it was still going on. Salim Hatum, who led the attempted coup, arrived back at the border saying that he had come home to fight. He was arrested and tortured. The head of the secret police, Colonel Abd al-Karim al-Jundi, broke his ribs before he was shot.

The other coup leaders included Major-General Fahd al-Sha'ir, graduate of a Soviet military academy, deputy chief of staff and commander of the south-west front, the only one that mattered to the Syrian army because it faced Israel. He was arrested and among other indignities reportedly had to 'get down on all fours like an animal and was ridden by his tormentors through dirty water'. Four hundred officers were dismissed. While Israel was training new officers and making sure they exercised regularly with the men they would be commanding in battle, the only Syrian manoeuvres were political.

Imwas, 0800

Hikmat Deeb Ali, from his position in the church, watched the Israeli soldiers going from house to house as the sun came up. They moved carefully. No shots were fired. Israeli jeeps fitted with loudspeakers told everyone to assemble in the centre of the village. A soldier who spoke Arabic told them: 'You have one road to leave. It's the Ramallah road. We don't want to see one of you pass by your home. You leave from here.' An old man asked the soldier if he could go home to get his shoes, because he was barefoot. 'If you do that,' the soldier told him, 'you will die. You should head for Ramallah.' No one was allowed to pack belongings or to search for missing relatives.

In Beit Nuba, Zchiya Zaid, the wife of the Moukhtar, the village headman, saw some of her neighbours coming out of their houses when the soldiers moved in. 'The soldiers did not harm civilians and they distributed food, sweets and cigarettes. The ones who wouldn't leave willingly were forced out. The soldiers called "Go to Hussein! Go to Hussein!" We couldn't take anything with us, only our children.'

The column of refugees moved off. Watching from the church, Hikmat Deeb Ali saw his own family walking between lines of soldiers. With his wife were their six children. The youngest was a week old. When they had gone Hikmat and his two cousins crept back to their family house. It was still intact. A patrol found them there and they left. On the edge of the village 'we saw hell. Young children, elderly, the ill, the handicapped, kids that couldn't walk, an old lady, all being accompanied out. Every time I think of it I want to lose my mind. Everyone left in what they stood up in, pyjamas, suit, anything you had on, that's the way you left.' He heard one of the villagers protesting to an Israeli soldier. The soldier told him that, 'If anyone remains, you will die.'

190

Cairo, 0900

Cairo Radio was still making up news and broadcasting threats. Its morning report said: 'We have defeated Israel on the first day of the battle, we will defeat it every moment and every hour. We will conquer it in the air and on the land and destroy it for ever . . . bid farewell to life, Israel.' After their disturbed night, the American journalists in the Hilton did not get any breakfast. The bell captain said Israeli planes were coming back, so meals were suspended. On every corner, loudspeakers were blaring 'strike, strike, strike'. The journalists went to the press centre and looked at the morning papers. *Al Akhbar*, one of the Cairo dailies, splashed 'Our Armoured Forces Advance Deeply Inside The Enemy Lines'. The English language *Egyptian Gazette* had a similar headline. Inside there was a shot of what the caption said was 'the wreckage of the wicked raider'. Its horoscope told readers 'to take action along technical lines if you would realise better than average gains today'.

Another air raid started at 9:05 a.m. A few minutes later the Middle East News Agency ticker 'chattered out a communiqué marked "urgent, urgent"': 'It has been definitely proved that the United States and Britain are participating in the Israeli military aggression. Some US and British aircraft carriers are undertaking large scale activities in supporting Israel . . .'

Nasser and Hussein's plan was bearing fruit. During the next two hours, similar reports were broadcast from Amman and Damascus. Dan Garcia, a diplomat from the US Embassy, promptly pinned up a press release. It said the allegation was a 'total fabrication'. As the journalists gathered round to read it, the Egyptian press officer Kamal Bakr tore it down. The reporters had pestered Bakr to meet some of the Egyptian army's senior officers. They wanted to see evidence of the military success that the communiqués were trumpeting. Now they were told there would be no briefings and they were not allowed to go out on their own. It did not matter, for the time being anyway. The allegation that the United States and Britain were involved in the war was big news. They filed their stories. But Westerners in Cairo were starting to feel very conspicuous. In Washington the CIA reported to the president: 'Cairo may be preparing to launch a campaign urging strikes against US interests in the Arab world. Both Egyptian and Syrian domestic broadcasts this morning called on the "Arab masses" to destroy all US and "imperialist" interests in the Arab homeland.'

Their stories filed, the journalists followed their professional instincts and disobeyed the official request to stay in the press centre. A man pulled up in a Land Rover and spat at them. They noticed that the police guard on the American Embassy compound had been doubled. Inside, the staff were burning their classified papers. The tension in the building went up another notch when, at 10:40 a.m., Cairo Radio broadcast that 'beyond a shadow of doubt' the US and Britain had intervened on Israel's side, flying combat missions from aircraft carriers against Israel and Jordan. They expected the crowd outside would try to break in. An hour later a mob torched the British Consulate and the US library in Alexandria.

The accusations that the British and the Americans had intervened on Israel's side raced around the world. British diplomats immediately dubbed it 'the Big Lie'. Britain's ambassador in Kuwait went to the foreign ministry to protest that it was all a fiction. He was 'dumbfounded' to discover that the ministry's most senior official believed the reports were true. After Britain's collusion with Israel and France to make war on Egypt in 1956, they seemed highly credible. Arab oil-producing countries were meeting in Baghdad. They decided to stop selling oil to any country that supported Israel. In Damascus the US ambassador Hugh Smythe went to the foreign ministry to deny the accusations. He was greeted by an official who pulled out two small pages of hand-written notes. The official read out a statement breaking off diplomatic relations because of America's 'historical' position towards the Arabs and its collusion with Israel. The Embassy staff were given forty-eight hours to leave the country. A junior administrative type was allowed a week to 'clear up'.

Amman, 0900

King Hussein was exhausted. The night had been disastrous for Jordan and he had not slept. He could not find many straws to clutch. Twenty-four hours into the war, it had already come down to limiting the size of the defeat that he always knew was coming. He warned the Americans that Egypt was going to blame them for starting the war. He did not pass on his side of the conversation with Nasser. The king was in constant contact with foreign embassies, especially the Americans and the British, his two most important foreign allies. If they could intercede with the Israelis there might be a chance of salvaging something from the mess. He told the Americans that his forces had suffered a night of 'purely punitive attacks'. If they did not stop, Jordan would be 'finished'. Reports of appalling losses were coming in from his field commanders. Casualty reports were, in fact, consistently inflated, perhaps because of the confusion of battle, perhaps because they wanted an excuse for Israeli success.

Ordinary Jordanians still had no idea how badly the war was going. Leila Sharaf went to give blood with her friend Mrs Shakir. Jordan still had a bad case of war fever. The streets were full of excitement, overwrought chatter and wild rumours. Claims that Israel had destroyed most of the Egyptian air force were laughed off as propaganda. Someone told Mrs Sharaf that Nasser had built underground airstrips, which would soon be launching a new wave of attacks on the Jews. Someone else said the Syrian army had penetrated deep into northern Israel. Mrs Sharaf listened with horror. Her husband, the minister of information, who was in the operations room most of the time, had told her what was really happening. But not one of the people she overheard exchanging excited gossip, stories and speculation doubted what they were hearing on the radio about an Arab victory. The message that Voice of the Arabs in Cairo had pumped out to the rest of the Arab world – that Nasser, their inspiration, had created a mighty army – was deeply ingrained. The mood was so unreal that when Leila Sharaf heard bangs and explosions near her house she assumed they came from fireworks, let off in honour of a victory that would come if only Arabs believed in it hard enough. Her husband had to pull her inside. It was not fireworks, it was anti-aircraft fire, and Israeli planes were coming in low.

Thanks to Voice of the Arabs, the Arab delegations at the UN in New York were as ill-informed as the people on Amman's streets. Since they had heard that fighting had started on Monday, all of them kept their short-wave radios tuned to Cairo. They believed what they heard, rejoicing as the Arab victory seemed to unfold. In Amman the Jordanian foreign minister Ahmed Toukan realised very early on that the fighting had to be stopped as soon as possible or Jordan would lose Jerusalem and the West Bank. But Dr Muhammad al-Farra, Jordan's ambassador to the UN, would not believe him when he called. At first he refused to press for a ceasefire because Cairo Radio was telling him that what they really needed to organise was a victory party.

The British military attaché in Amman, Colonel J. F. Weston-Simons, had been watching events over the previous three weeks with something approaching disgust. Arab propaganda had tried to 'lift its listeners with ever increasing speed to a sublime state of religious intoxication. Martial music, interspersed with stirring words encouraging the holy war, blared from radios. The Jordanian armed services prepared to ride on white and chivalrous steeds to battle.' General Khammash, the chief of staff, was one of very few 'sophisticated and far thinking officers'. The rest, 'intoxicated' by the pact with Nasser and 'blinded by their infinite capacity for self-deception . . . simply assumed without any justification, that they were more than a match for the Israelis'.

But by the second morning of the war, there were no more illusions left at army headquarters. The war was lost and the king was in despair. What made matters even more complicated was that he did not feel ready to tell the people the truth. 'We must stop the fighting, but for God's sake the Israelis must not announce anything publicly, or there would be anarchy here,' he told the American ambassador.

Jerusalem, 1000

Narkiss was keeping the pressure on the Israeli general staff to authorise an attack on the Old City. He told them that they would be blamed for the failure if they did not do it. The Israelis were mopping up most of the built-up part of East Jerusalem outside the city walls. There was still isolated, freelance resistance, from soldiers who had been cut off from their units who stayed to fight and die, or from a few handfuls of Palestinian men who were using the weapons that had been distributed at the last minute. Around 100 armed Palestinian civilians died in the fighting. Soldiers and a few volunteers still manned the city walls, and put down deadly fire on the Israelis below them.

Rubi Gat, an eight-year old Israeli boy, was with his family in their basement. He was excited. Now he would have a war, his war, to talk about. He had always been jealous of the way that his older sisters told stories about the 1956 war, about how their father looked when he went off to join his unit. In the last few weeks Rubi and his friends at school had been told what to do when the fighting started. They had rehearsed how they would walk home, as quickly as they could, keeping close to the walls in case shells fell. The day before a Jordanian shell had landed close to Rubi's house. He had picked up fragments of shrapnel afterwards. He fingered them as he listened to the muffled explosions coming from the Mount of Olives.

On the Jordanian side of Jerusalem the American journalist Abdullah Schliefer had moved his family into three small rooms off the stairwell of his building in the Old City. The streets were almost empty. Sometimes he would see an army patrol, or a civil defence team racing boxes of ammunition to where they were needed. Inside the ancient walled city it felt medieval, like 'an old-fashioned garrison under siege in a war fought with supersonic jets, napalm and tanks'.

Amman, 1230

General Riad and King Hussein agreed they had three choices. First, hope the UN Security Council or one of the big powers could stop the fighting; second, evacuate the West Bank in the coming night; or third, hang on to the West Bank for another twenty-four hours, which would lead to 'the total destruction of the Jordanian army'. It was a grim menu. Riad put it into a telegram for Nasser, while the king sent one of his own. 'The situation is deteriorating rapidly. In Jerusalem it is critical. In addition to our very heavy losses in men and equipment, for lack of air protection, our tanks are being disabled at the rate of one every ten minutes.' Rightly, the king did not trust Nasser. He wanted him to be implicated in any decision he had to take, not just through General Riad, but personally. Just as his coded message was being transmitted to Cairo, the answer to Riad's telegram arrived from Field Marshal Amer: 'We agree to the retreat from the West Bank, and the arming of the civilian population.' Hussein and his chief of staff Amer Khammash suspected a trick. Khammash warned the king that the Egyptians might pounce on a Jordanian withdrawal as an excuse to pull out of the Sinai. The Egyptians might then try to present their defeat as a Jordanian betrayal. If a story like that stuck, Hussein's throne would be in even more jeopardy. The sad truth for the Jordanians was that withdrawal from the West Bank was looking like the least bad option. But to pull out on Cairo's orders could be a serious error. They decided to hang on longer. Even at moments of great crisis, the Arab leaders could not trust each other

Hussein summoned the ambassadors of the UK, USA, France and the Soviet Union to give them the same message he had sent Nasser. He begged them, on their own or through the Security Council, to arrange a ceasefire. The king said he would still prefer the ceasefire not to be announced. But if the Israelis wanted it done publicly, then that was fine too. On the way out of the palace, the American ambassador had to take cover as the air-raid sirens sounded. The Israelis were back again.

Jerusalem, 1230

Generals Narkiss, Dayan and Weizman arrived in East Jerusalem in a convoy of two half-tracks and a jeep. As usual on a windy open-top journey, Dayan had taken off his black eyepatch and put on a pair of dark glasses. Narkiss greeted Major Doron Mor, second in command of Battalion 66 of the paratroopers, who was an old friend. He told Mor they wanted to go to Mount Scopus. Mor told him they had not sent troops up to clear the road yet. Narkiss said, 'So clear it now.' But all Mor's men were committed elsewhere. He took a risk. All he had were two jeeps mounted with recoilless rifles. Narkiss, Dayan and Weizman got into one of them. Mor, in the other, 'took some grenades and told the driver to go as fast as he could. Narkiss and the others followed. It took a minute. The road was empty. No one shot at us. When we got to the barrier at Mount Scopus the soldiers started to kiss us.'

As Mor stood admiring the view, the first time he had seen Jerusalem from the east, he heard Narkiss and Dayan talking about capturing the Old City.

Dayan was also enraptured by what he could see. Narkiss thought his moment had come. With the two of them looking down on the breathtaking sight of Jerusalem on a beautiful day in early summer, Narkiss said softly, 'Moshe, we must go into the Old City.' Dayan snapped back to business. 'Under no circumstances.' He was not a man for small talk. He wanted to surround it and wait for it to surrender 'like a ripe fruit'. He ordered Narkiss to take the heights behind Jerusalem that commanded the north and east sides of the Old City.

Israeli troops were also advancing on the Old City from the south. The district of Abu Tor, which straddled the border between East and West Jerusalem close to Government House, fell in the afternoon. The Jordanians fought hard as they retreated. A company of men from Israel's Jerusalem Brigade was caught in a bombardment as they crossed Hebron Road, near Jerusalem railway station. Casualties were left all over the street. Then a sniper killed all four members of a machine gun team as they crossed the road. When a bazooka man was sent to try to blast the sniper out of his position, which was only ten metres away, the sniper killed him while he was aiming. It took a grenade tossed in through the firing slits of his position to silence the sniper. As they pushed into Abu Tor, the battalion commander, Lt. Col. Michael Paikes, led his command group into a Jordanian trench that supposedly had been captured. Suddenly a Jordanian with a rifle dropped down next to them. He was as surprised as they were. The battalion's intelligence officer, Johnny Heiman, grabbed the man's rifle. Three more Jordanians jumped into the trench. Two saw what was happening and ran. The third shot Paikes dead before escaping and attacking Heiman. They grappled together on the floor of the trench until Heiman managed to empty his Uzi into his assailant.

Jenin, northern West Bank, 1300

It took until the afternoon to subdue the last Jordanian and Palestinian resistance in Jenin. Israeli troops had been in the town since 0730, after a night of hard and confused fighting. Sherman tanks, following standard Israeli doctrine for fighting in a built-up area, moved up and down firing in all directions, followed by infantry. Then, south of Jenin, Jordan's best commander, Brigadier-General Rakan al-Jazi and his 40th Armoured Brigade arrived. They were returning from a wild-goose chase to Jericho, where they had been sent to relieve the 60th, Jordan's other armoured brigade while it went to take part in the Egyptian offensive that never was against Beersheba. The Jordanians reoccupied the positions they had abandoned for their unscheduled trip to Jericho, controlling an important road junction at Qabitiyah.

Most of Jenin's civilians took to caves and hills around the town. But not all of them. Haj Arif Abdullah took his Bren gun and five armed men and went out to the 40th Brigade to continue the fight. He was a big and burly man, forty-five years old, with seventeen children. During the British occupation he had served with the RAF police. The Jordanians made him commander of the local national guard but he had a stormy relationship with the king's men because of his strong nationalist views. He supported the Ba'th party, the pan-Arab, left-wing political movement that swept through Syria and Iraq in the fifties and threatened to do the same in Jordan. Between 1957 and 1961 he was in and out of prison. The longest spell was two years, for trying to overthrow the monarchy. He was pardoned when tensions in the Middle East were rising, so he decided that his real enemy was Israel, not King Hussein. A year before the war, recognising that Haj Arif Abdullah was a necessary man in Jenin, the local Jordanian commander sent him his own Bren light machine gun and twelve boxes of ammunition.

The 40th Armoured Brigade was ready twelve hours before the Israelis expected them. They hit Brig. Gen. Elad Peled's armoured brigade with an ambush. Back in Jenin they heard the roar of tank fire. It inspired the defenders who were still fighting to counter-attack. Peled sent a relief column to rescue his tanks, which were trapped and low on fuel and ammunition. Al-Jazi's scouts told him that they were coming. Fifty to sixty Pattons were ready, hull down on a ridge, and blasted another batch of Israeli tanks when they came down the road towards them. Israel lost seventeen Super Shermans. Haj Arif Abdullah was disappointed that the Israelis did not send infantry with the tanks. He fired at the Israeli tank commanders, who as usual were fighting with their bodies exposed in their turrets. Another thrust from the Israelis was beaten off later in the afternoon. The Jordanians tried to chase them, but were pushed back by artillery and air strikes. By nightfall, the Jordanians still controlled the crossroads, cutting the main north–south road through the highlands of the West Bank and a major east–west artery.

Amman, afternoon

General Riad was calm enough in the face of the disaster to take regular naps in a special room set aside for him at the headquarters building. King Hussein was wide awake, though he felt the day was 'like a dream, or worse yet, a nightmare'. He felt out of his depth at the headquarters in Amman: 'Standing in front of maps in the operations centre, everything [seemed] abstract, vague and not very convincing.' So, driving a jeep with a two-way radio, the king left with his bodyguards for the Jordan valley. He saw for himself just how bad it was.

> . . . I will never forget the hallucinating sight of that defeat. Roads clogged with trucks, jeeps and all kinds of vehicles twisted, disembowelled, dented, still smoking, giving off that particular smell of metal and paint burned by exploding bombs – a stink that only powder can make. In the midst of this charnel house were men. In groups of thirty to forty, wounded, exhausted, they were trying to clear a path under the monstrous coup de grace being dealt them by a horde of Israeli Mirages screaming in a cloudless blue sky seared with sun.

When he returned to Amman King Hussein was back on the phone to Findley Burns, the American ambassador, straight away. What had Israel said about the ceasefire? Burns went immediately to the palace to pass on the bad news from the Israelis. They were not interested in a ceasefire. Hussein had been given his chance to avoid the war on Monday morning. He had chosen to ignore Israel's warning. Now he was reaping his reward. The king was now more convinced than ever that the Israelis wanted to destroy his army. He told Burns about his own tour of the front lines that afternoon. The army had virtually ceased to exist. Some units were still fighting, even though they had been without air cover for the last twenty-four hours. The big question now was whether to abandon the West Bank. 'If I evacuate tonight, I am told I will lose 50 per cent of my men and only limited equipment could be evacuated. If we do not withdraw tonight we will be chewed up. Tomorrow will leave only the choice of ordering the destruction of our equipment and leaving every soldier to look after himself.' General Riad, 'who had been pretty much running the whole show', was telling him to withdraw. The decision had to be taken soon.

Gaza

Egyptians and Palestinians had fought hard and killed scores of Israeli soldiers. But two Israeli brigades had mastered an urban battlefield which, on the first day of the war, had been defended by 10,000 armed men. Now Israeli troops were mopping up scattered resistance. Much of it came from Palestinian civilians, who had been given arms by the Egyptian authorities. Some fought to the death. Some were shot out of hand after they surrendered. Twenty-eight young men from the Abu Rass family in Gaza's Zaytoun district were captured, taken away and summarily executed. Their bodies were dug up from a mass grave by their family and reburied after the war.

But, according to their families, men of military age who had not taken up arms were also deliberately killed. In Khan Younis, where fighting had been especially bitter, Shara Abu Shakrah, a woman of forty, was at home with her husband Zaid Salim Abu Nahia. He made his living selling tomatoes, potatoes and okra from a stall. Zaid's thirty-year-old brother Mustafa and his wife were there too, with Ghanem, another brother, and Mohammed, Zaid's son from an earlier marriage. They had all been sheltering inside, hoping that the fighting would pass them by.

Suddenly they heard loud voices outside the house, calling in broken Arabic for the men to come out. The men complied. The women were terrified. Their first thought was that the Israelis wanted to kill their men. Their fears were based on what had happened in the 1956 war. Then, on 3 November, the invading Israeli troops carried out a series of massacres in Khan Younis. They started in the centre of the town, then moved out into the suburbs. Between 500 and 700 Palestinians, mainly civilians, were summarily executed. The dead included children and the elderly. In one case, twenty-one members of a single family died together.

Shara and the other women in the house screamed and tried to push their way out into the yard outside. They thought it was happening again. The Israeli soldiers pushed them back inside and blocked the door. Inside, the women heard shooting. They pushed harder against the door, trying to get out. In a few minutes the door opened and they spilled out into the yard.

Mustafa was lying dead in the dust. He had three sons and two daughters. Next to him Mohammed was badly wounded, with a hole in his stomach which was bleeding profusely. A few yards further on, they found Ghanem's body. Shara could not see Zaid, her husband. She found his body on the other side of the house. He had been shot through the head.

The women washed and wrapped the bodies, preparing them for burial. But under Muslim law, they could not bury them. They waited three days for the curfew to be lifted long enough for neighbours to come round to do the job. Before that happened, while the bodies were decomposing rapidly in the heat and humidity of Gaza in early summer, more Israeli soldiers came to the house, asking Shara where the men had gone. 'We screamed and threw sand at them, and scooped sand from the ground on to our faces. We said come to see them, they're dead.' Mohammed took two days to die. His stomach wound kept on bleeding. 'We had no doctor, no medical treatment. We were all women, we didn't know what to do.'

Cairo, 1630

By Tuesday afternoon, a day and a half after the fighting started, news of the defeats in the desert overnight was coming in to Amer at GHQ in Cairo. It seemed to General Fawzi, the Egyptian army chief of staff, that Field Marshal Amer was 'psychologically worn out . . . on the verge of nervous collapse'. Suddenly, he called Fawzi into his office and gave him twenty minutes to make a plan to pull the Egyptian army out of Sinai to the west bank of the Suez canal. It was the first direct order that Amer had given to his chief of staff since the war began. A fighting withdrawal is a legitimate and effective military tactic. It takes good organisation and a brave rearguard that will keep on shooting until the rest of the forces can pull back to a defensible position. At their military academy and staff college, Egyptian officers learnt about Britain's withdrawal to El-Alamein in 1942, when Montgomery and his commanders rallied their troops and forced them to hold on until they had rebuilt their strength for the offensive that turned the tide of war in North Africa. Some senior Egyptian officers even met Montgomery himself in Egypt in May 1967, when he came for the commemoration of the twenty-fifth anniversary of the battle of El-Alamein. Many Egyptian units, though battered, were still largely intact. A fighting withdrawal should have been possible.

After the order from Amer, Fawzi dashed off and with two other generals came up with a plan and a timetable for a withdrawal to the canal that would take four days and three nights. In his memoirs Fawzi describes what happened when they presented the plan to Amer and told him how long it would take. 'He raised his voice and addressing me said, "Four days and three nights, Fawzi? I have already given the order to withdraw and that's that." His face had become very red and he left, looking somewhat hysterical, for his bedroom, which was behind his office. The three of us were left completely taken aback by his condition.'

Amer claimed that Nasser had approved the decision. Nasser claimed the decision was Amer's. Whoever was finally responsible, Amer passed the order on in what had become his signature haphazard manner, mentioning it to everyone he spoke to in the field. According to Vice-President Abdul Latif Boghdady, Amer told them to dump their heavy weapons and pull out during the night, to try to get to the west side of the canal before dawn. When Boghdady visited Amer on Tuesday evening and heard what was happening he told Amer it was 'a disgrace'. Amer replied, 'It is not a matter of honour or bravery, but a matter of saving our boys. The enemy has destroyed two of our divisions.' Apart from getting involved in the war in the first place, Egypt's worst error in June 1967 was its shambolic withdrawal from Sinai, which led to the deaths of thousands of

Egyptian soldiers and the loss of millions of dollars' worth of equipment.

Field Marshal Amer, the obvious scapegoat for what was happening in Sinai, grabbed at the accusations against Britain and the United States. He summoned the Soviet ambassador for a dressing-down. Why, he demanded, hadn't the USSR done for Egypt what the West was doing for Israel? Was it because of 'détente' between Washington and Moscow? If that was the case, the Soviets were, effectively, colluding with Israel too. What about the incident in the early hours of 26 May, when the Soviet ambassador had woken Nasser at 3 a.m. with an urgent message from Kosygin, warning Egypt not to attack? Moscow had practically condemned Egypt to defeat. 'It is you who prevented us from making the first strike,' Amer went on, desperate to blame anyone other than himself. 'You deprived us of the initiative. That is collusion!'

The Egyptians sent out official messages to their embassies abroad containing evidence they said proved the allegations. A captured Israeli pilot had 'freely confessed' that British aircraft had used the airbase from which he had taken off. Syrian radio had intercepted messages in English appealing for help from US aircraft carriers. French fighter planes had been brought back from South Africa and delivered to Israel. King Hussein had personally seen British warplanes in action. The reports were believed, an Egyptian diplomat claimed, 'in the highest Arab circles'.

At the headquarters of the Cairo military district, the head of Egypt's Central Command, General Salahadeen Hadidi, had long since stopped believing what he was hearing on the radio. He was spending most of his time on the phone to other senior officers, trying to find out what was really happening on the battlefield in Sinai. A deserter was brought to his office, a private soldier who had been arrested at Cairo's main railway station by the military police. Hadidi had been in charge of Eastern Command – the Sinai desert – from 1964 to 1966. He knew about the Qaher plan for the defence of the area. The general interrogated the exhausted private about his unit, where he had been and what had happened. The soldier had been on the front line. He gave a bleak account of a hellish landscape dominated by swooping, predatory Israeli warplanes. Nothing, he said, could be done to stop them. His unit had been broken and so had the units around him. Everybody was in retreat, trying to get away from the Israeli jets. It was every bit as bad as the general had feared. The soldier was court-martialled and sent to the military prison. General Hadidi spent the rest of the war trying to reconstruct recognisable units from the exhausted and demoralised individuals who were streaming in from the desert. 'I was very shocked. The whole country was very shocked.'

By 8 p.m. the US press corps had retreated to the Nile Hilton for dinner. Kamal Bakr, the head of the press centre, rushed into the dining room and told them he had very important news. Courteously, the American newsmen asked him to join them for something to eat. Bakr replied, 'It is impossible. You have to leave the country – tonight.' They were told to call their embassy, which advised them to stay where they were. The air-raid sirens wailed again. Flashes and explosions seemed to be coming from the direction of the pyramids. Egyptian air defence batteries were shooting back.

Sinai

The Egyptian army in Sinai was collapsing so quickly that no one really noticed an expeditionary force of 1250 men that had been sent by the ruler of Kuwait. More than half of them were kept safely in reserve in the Suez canal zone. But 550 commandos were sent into Sinai by train. They were bombed by the Israelis as they were unloading their gear from the train in Al-Arish. During the night of 5 June they tried and failed to phone the Egyptian gunner regiment to which they were supposed to be linked. On the morning of the 6th they drove to where the Egyptians were supposed to be. They had gone. In the absence of a war to fight and an ally to fight it with, the

Kuwaitis decided to pull back to the canal as well. Two weeks later, between 100 and 150 of them were still missing in Sinai. General Mubarak, their commander, told a British diplomat in Kuwait that he was 'quite relaxed about their fate, because they are Bedouin and will, he is sure, be able to survive. Understandably, however, he has little good to say about the Egyptians.'

Lieutenant Mohammed Shaiki el-Bagori was part of the Egyptian 6th Division, in the desert not far from where the Kuwaitis had been supposed to deploy. All day his division's armoured vehicles and supply trucks were hammered by the Israeli air force. He lay on the ground, trying to find some cover, listening to a small transistor radio he had brought from home. As he tried to make himself smaller, and the Israelis ripped his unit to shreds, he listened to Cairo Radio predicting victory. 'The Egyptian army has been storming the Zionist concentrations . . . advance and strike the enemy.' Someone, he realised, was lying to them. He could not believe it could have been Nasser.

By 5 p.m. the Egyptian garrison at El Kuntilla had destroyed or buried what was left of their equipment. An hour before they had been ordered to retreat. Corporal Kamal Mahrouss, a professional soldier, felt a strong sense of personal humiliation. The soldiers got into trucks which drove slowly away, trying to get to Ismailiya on the Suez canal. They were sitting ducks. After dark they were picked out by searchlights. Israeli tanks started firing. Another Egyptian column was under attack ahead of them. More Israeli tanks were behind them. The men who still could leapt out of the trucks and ran away.

Near the front of the Israeli advance, Brig. Gen. Gavish now realised that the Egyptians were retreating. 'It took a day and a half for the Egyptians to understand that their air force had gone and we had three divisions in the Sinai. Now we had two problems – stopping them getting out of Sinai and fighting tanks that were scattered all over the desert.' Gavish and his divisional commanders decided the best way to destroy the Egyptian army in Sinai would be to overtake it in the race to the passes through the mountains in western Sinai. That would mean sending armoured spearheads down the three main roads across the desert, driving right through the Egyptians to set up blocking positions at the entrance to the passes before they got there. The rest of the Israeli forces would advance on a broad front, driving the Egyptians on to the guns that would be waiting for them.

Moscow

An unexpected message came through to the Austrian Embassy in Moscow. First deputy foreign minister Kuznetsov wanted to take up an invitation that had been discussed vaguely a couple of weeks earlier to lunch with the ambassador. It was a surprise. Impromptu lunches with senior Soviet officials were not the norm in Moscow in the sixties. They spent two and a half hours together. The Soviet minister confided that when he arrived at his office on Monday morning (Moscow is in the same time zone as Cairo) the news of the fighting had taken him totally by surprise, especially since he had thought a deal on the Gulf of Aqaba was close. He could not believe that the Israelis would have attacked without assurances from the Americans. The question now, though, was how to end it. Kuznetsov, who seemed in a confident mood, was hoping that the Security Council in New York would call for a ceasefire followed by a withdrawal. The Russian hoped 'this unfortunate matter' would not stop progress towards East–West détente.

Moscow was sending out a deliberate message. In 1967 Austria was a neutral central European state that was sometimes seen as a point of contact between East and West. Kuznetsov did not seem to know that he was using an informal back channel to the West to push for the kind of deal that the US was offering at the UN, and which the Soviet ambassador, without firm instructions from Moscow, was in the process of turning down.

United Nations, New York, 1000 (1700 Israel, 1800 Cairo)

The US ambassador Arthur Goldberg had another meeting with his Soviet counterpart Nikolai Fedorenko. Once again he rejected Goldberg's offer of a Security Council resolution demanding a ceasefire and withdrawal to the positions both sides held on Sunday 4 June, before war broke out. This time the problem was that Goldberg said a disengagement of forces had to include ending the blockade of the Straits of Tiran. A report to the White House at 1:15 p.m. said 'the continuing delay in convening the Security Council is very much in Israel's interest so long as Israeli forces continue their spectacular military success ... The Russians suffer a genuine disadvantage in having slower and more distant communications than we do. They have shown signs of trying to adjust their position to the changing situation on the ground in the Mid-East, but their adjustments have not caught up with the deteriorating position of their allies . . .'

Fifteen minutes later, Fedorenko called Goldberg. He had received a telephone call on an open line from Moscow, which in itself was 'an extraordinary occurrence'. It came from the deputy foreign minister, Vladimir Semyonov. New instructions were on their way. As soon as they arrived, he stressed, Fedorenko had to arrange a meeting with Goldberg. Finally, and very belatedly, the Soviets had realised what was being done to the Arabs, now that Israel's troops were racing towards the Suez canal and closing in on Jerusalem. When the new instructions arrived, Fedorenko was told to accept the US plan for a ceasefire plus withdrawal. If for any reason that was not feasible, he was to go back to the original Security Council resolution calling for a simple ceasefire.

Following his orders, he tried to find Goldberg. But now the Americans were making themselves scarce. At 3 p.m. they met again. Fedorenko said again he would support the American resolution, but could not accept that it would apply to the Straits of Tiran. Goldberg's compromise was ceasefire followed by 'urgent consultations' on withdrawal. Fedorenko said that was even worse.

Then he suggested going back to the original resolution that had been first put to the Security Council on Monday morning. It called only for a ceasefire and a cessation of all military activity. In the resolution only the phrase that it was 'a first step' suggested that other matters might have to follow. A withdrawal to the positions of 4 June was not mentioned. It was adopted unanimously at 6:30 p.m.

There was one more twist. In the morning, at 10:02 a.m., Johnson had sent a hotline message to Kosygin, urging him to accept the US resolution calling for a prompt ceasefire and withdrawal to the armistice lines. Kosygin took eight hours to reply. When he did, he told Johnson that he agreed and that instructions had been sent to Fedorenko to accept the resolution that Johnson had described. Kosygin's acceptance of Johnson's formula had come over the Washington end of the 'Molink', the hotline's nickname, just after six. The Americans had a rough translation of the message, taken off the printer, by 6:12. It was in the hands of the president three minutes later. But as they read the incoming message, Johnson's advisers could see on their televisions the Security Council preparing to vote for a plain ceasefire without withdrawal. In the Situation Room there was a rapid discussion of whether they should stick to Johnson's offer, or let events at the UN take their course. Everyone agreed they should take advantage of what looked like a first-class Soviet diplomatic foul-up. There was time to get a call to Goldberg at the Security Council. In the Situation Room they sat back, watched the TV and waited for Fedorenko to vote. When he did, they cheered, then wondered whether Fedorenko would end up in Siberia.

The Americans had offered the USSR much more than the Israelis wanted them to give. But Moscow's incompetence made sure the Israelis had exactly what they needed. Once Egypt's air force had been destroyed, much more troubling for Israel than the fight in the desert was its fear that diplomatic pressure in the UN would stop it before it had achieved its military objectives. Worst of all would have been a rerun of what happened after the war in 1956, when they were forced to pull out of occupied territory in the Sinai. But the Kremlin's bungling neutralised the weapon the Israelis feared most. By the end of Tuesday, the second day, they still controlled around a quarter of Sinai, though they were hours away from conquering Jerusalem. Had the Soviet Union not turned down the chance of a ceasefire and a withdrawal of forces to the positions they had held until 4 June, significant parts of the Egyptian army might have survived in the Sinai. Egypt would have had to lift the blockade of the straits, but in the circumstances, it would not have been a high price.

Realistic American officials at the UN reported that 'nobody expects the call to be heeded or this to be the decisive Security Council resolution'. Israel would probably have ignored a ceasefire resolution it did not like for as long as it could. But other stronger resolutions would have followed, increasing the international pressure on Israel and when the war ended it would most likely have been impossible for them to hang on to what they had captured for very long. As the Security Council showed when Israel ignored the call for a ceasefire on the Syrian front later in the week, it was capable of piling on the pressure when it lost patience.

Gaza Strip

In Khan Younis, some Israeli soldiers were still killing civilians. About 100 yards away from the house of the Abu Nahia family, where four Palestinian men had been shot in cold blood, Abd al-Majeed al Farah and his wife Faika, who were both in their late thirties, had spent two days hiding in their basement with their six sons and six daughters. Then the Israelis came and ordered Abd al-Majeed to go with all the other local men to the school, where they would be interrogated. They walked there in single file, at gunpoint.

'Some soldiers were good,' he remembers. 'Others were bad and aggressive. One of us who knew a little Hebrew heard one of them saying, "these are military, we should shoot them." Another one said, "We can't do that, we have to call the headquarters in Beersheba."'

Some of the prisoners at the school were taken out and shot, including his brother's son. The rest were kept at the school, chained together. They were not unchained when they needed to use the lavatory. They all went together. One of the prisoners was untied so he could open the men's trousers to let them urinate. After three days most of the men were released. When Abd al-Majeed al Farah arrived home he found the women crying and the bodies of twelve members of his extended family dead in their farmyard. They were all boys and young men, aged between fourteen and eighteen. They seemed to have been shot because they had not obeyed the order to report to the school. One of the women had tried to hide her seventeen-year-old son, but he was dragged out of the basement and shot dead in the street by an Israeli soldier. Abd al-Majeed says none of the dead was a fighter. Because of the curfew, they were not allowed to bury the twelve dead teenagers, or the four dead soldiers who had also been killed on their property. From their house they could smell the bodies as they started to rot. After three days, when the smell was getting very strong, they were allowed out to bury the men. The Israelis returned every day to count the people who were left in the house. Some of the soldiers let them go to their neighbour's well to get water. One of the women was allowed to leave the house to get food for her children.

As the fighting in Gaza went on shells smashed into the UNEF headquarters building. When the fighting started UNEF peacekeepers had still been trying to pack up and get out. After first light the UNEF commander, General Rikhye, tried to get back into his badly damaged HQ to collect secret United Nations documents. He was stopped by one of the advancing Israeli tank units. Some of Rikhye's peacekeepers were being killed. Three Indian soldiers died south of Khan Younis when they were strafed by Israeli aircraft. Five more Indians were killed and more than a dozen wounded, by IDF artillery fire later in the day.

Qalqilya

In the mountains above Qalqilya, where most of the town's population had fled, ten-year-old Maa'rouf Zahran's parents were frantic.

Somehow, in the confusion, they had lost their nine-year-old daughter. They started moving towards Nablus, hoping that another family was looking after her. Maa'rouf was tired and hungry and frightened. And his feet hurt. Somehow, his shoes had gone missing. He walked to Nablus, like many others, barefoot.

Memdour Nufel, the young Palestinian with aspirations to be a guerrilla leader, could see the war was lost. He never fired his elderly Karl-Gustav at the Israeli tanks. He could not see the point. His mother and sister, who he had been visiting in the olive grove above the town where they were sheltering, begged him to get rid of the gun. So he smothered it in grease, wrapped it and then buried it in a cave. (In 1969 he told fighters from the Popular Front for the Liberation of Palestine where to go to dig it up.) Before Nufel and his family joined the long trek of refugees across the mountains to Nablus, he went back into Qalqilya to collect clothes and supplies from the family's home. His grandmother had been too weak to join the exodus to the mountains. Like many old people she had stayed in the house throughout the fighting. Nufel found her weeping and terrified. The house had been ransacked. Nothing of value was left. The old lady said the looters had been Israelis. When the Israelis took full control of the town they told people who were left to assemble at the mosque, where they found buses to take them to the river Jordan.

Fayek Abdul Mezied, the seventeen-year-old boy who had been so enthusiastic about the war, left Qalqilya with his mother, four brothers and sister and friends and neighbours. In all there were nineteen of them. 'As we left the town it was one of the saddest and most despairing moments of my life. We were overwhelmed by a feeling of humiliation and loss. We felt there was no place for us under the sun.'

They walked up the steep path to the high ground where they thought they would be safe. Hundreds of people were dragging themselves up it. An old man close by was carrying his transistor radio. Fayek could hear Ahmed Said broadcasting from Cairo reporting huge Israeli losses and still predicting victory for the Arabs and disaster for the Jews. The old man swore and threw his radio into a cactus bush. The mountain paths were safer than the road. East of Qalqilya, near the village of Azoun, a truck full of refugees was attacked by the Israeli air force. Twelve people were killed, mostly women and children. Heavy bombing and artillery fire killed old people who could not leave and others who had refused to go. Their bodies were buried in the rubble of their destroyed homes. In all seventy-four people from Qalqilya were killed.

Sharm al Sheikh, Egypt

Red light from the setting sun was spreading out over the Red Sea. Brigadier Abdel Moneim Khalil, commander of the Egyptian paratroops at Sharm al Sheikh, stood on a low hill overlooking some of his troops' positions. He had no idea how the war was going. The day before his regular morning helicopter from Hurgada on the other side of the Red Sea had not turned up. Nothing had been heard from Cairo. All they had to go on were the radio news reports, reporting overwhelming Egyptian successes, until on the morning of the 6th a message had arrived out of the blue from Field Marshal Amer. It said that Egyptian airfields had been hit, but gave no details. Khalil was deeply suspicious. He sensed something bad was happening, but he had no more information than his private soldiers who, like him, were listening to the radio. Khalil had deployed his men to fight an Israeli move against Sharm, but could not shake the feeling that they might have to leave in a hurry, just as Egyptian troops had had to do in 1956. He told his men to be ready to move at a moment's notice.

He had been there with his paratroops since 19 May. Their presence at the small settlement overlooking the Straits of Tiran had caused an international crisis. Yet it had been one of the strangest deployments of Khalil's military career. To start with, his force of 4000 men was not, he believed, suitable for the job. They were paratroops, trained to spearhead an assault, not create a remote coastal garrison. Their biggest problem was not preparing to fight Israel, but finding water. Sharm al Sheikh had none. The UNEF

213

troops had destroyed their desalination equipment before they left. The Egyptians had nothing like that themselves, and not even any water tankers. They had to fetch water for 4000 men from an oasis 100 miles away. Driving 100 miles to fill up hundreds of jerry cans and then driving 100 miles back tied up almost all Khalil's vehicles every day. He begged Cairo to send a him a floating water tanker. All he received, to his dismay and entirely without warning, were two American-built transport planes, flown by Saudi pilots which had landed in Sharm on 28 May. Out came several hundred Egyptian special forces, armed only with their personal weapons. Amer had sent them without telling him. All Khalil saw were more thirsty men who needed water he did not have.

The message from Amer ordering a withdrawal arrived just after the sun had set. Khalil called his officers together to tell them that they had to move that night to El Tour, a logistics base at an oasis where they had been collecting water every day, and then back to the west bank of the Suez canal. One of the officers, Mohamed Abd-el Hafiz, a veteran who was so badly wounded in Yemen that he needed eleven operations on his leg after a four-day evacuation on a donkey, said, 'We were shocked, depressed and sad. The radio was still broadcasting songs of victory and big claims. One I heard said that our forces would soon be in Tel Aviv.' Some of the officers urged Khalil not to retreat but to attack Eilat instead. They were well equipped, ready to go with naval support waiting. If the attack failed they could always pull back to Aqaba, the Jordanian port which was only a few miles from Eilat. Khalil refused. They would follow orders.

Before they could withdraw they had to dispose of fifteen thousand tons of ammunition that had been delivered by ship a few days earlier. It included the mines which were intended for the Straits of Tiran but somehow had never been laid. When they blew it up some of the soldiers thought the Israelis were attacking and panicked. Order was restored with difficulty. Brigadier Khalil was the last to leave Sharm al Sheikh, just before first light, hours after the first of his troops had gone. Because they had come into Sharm al Sheikh by air they did not have vehicles for all the men. To make matters worse, some of the trucks were away on the daily water run. His men were crammed in every available vehicle. Hafiz travelled on a jeep designed for five men that was carrying twelve and a heavy mortar. More soldiers were perched on top of another 120 mm mortar in a trailer pulled behind them. Other soldiers were clinging to three amphibious transporters that lumbered along at not much faster than walking pace. As the sun rose, Khalil hoped that the fact that his paratroopers were strung out over many miles would help them avoid the attentions of the Israeli air force, to which they were utterly exposed. A detachment of men that had been sent to the island of Tiran by helicopter was left behind. They were rescued by a fisherman who took them back to Sharm al Sheikh instead of Hurgada, on the other side of the Red Sea. Israeli forces landed in Sharm al Sheikh at 1100 on Wednesday morning. The soldiers and the fisherman were taken prisoner.

Jerusalem

Just outside Jerusalem Colonel Moshe Yotvat's brigade took the city's small airport without a fight. They moved towards what they thought was the road to Ramallah. Yotvat ordered an old Palestinian man to come with him in his command half-track, to show them the way. Behind them the roads were packed with Israeli troops. Caught in the traffic jam were at least a battalion of armour and a battalion of paratroopers. Yotvat was frustrated he could not get his hands on them. He pushed forward towards Ramallah with his reconnaissance company while he waited for the rest of his brigade to catch up.

Then Yotvat was badly wounded in the arm and shoulder and lost consciousness. He came round lying on the road. His first thought was that he must be dead. If this is death, he thought, it's not too bad.

Uzi Narkiss, meanwhile, was feeling very good about what was happening. He composed an order of the day to be circulated the following morning. 'Today Jerusalem is to be liberated. In the south and in the north the city of our ancestors is in our hands. Our army is still poised. Men of this regional command, be resolute. Do not waver.'

Israeli forces from Central Command were pushing north from Jerusalem. That evening they captured the West Bank town of Ramallah, fifteen miles north of the Old City. Uri Ben Ari was getting impatient and sent his force into the town without waiting for a bombardment to soften it up. Capturing a big town in the dark was not an easy military task. A tank battalion went first, followed by the reconnaissance company. Colonel Ben Ari said afterwards, 'We decided to go into Ramallah with a battalion of tanks, shooting at all sides as far as possible. We crossed and recrossed the city several times and it slowly fell silent.' They cleared out for the rest of the night. By the morning there was no resistance.

In the evening, towards midnight, there was a fierce encounter at the foot of the Mount of Olives, near the Garden of Gethsemane, the place where the Bible says Jesus sweated blood in the night before his arrest. A steep road runs up the hill past the Garden gates, just after a bridge over a dry river valley. Battalion 71 of the Israeli paratroop brigade, reinforced by tanks, were supposed to attack the heights above the Old City. But they took a wrong turning and found themselves being shot at from both sides, from Jordanians on the Mount of Olives and on the walls of the Old City, who put flares down on to the road to light up the tanks and opened up with everything they had. The commander of the lead tank was hit in the forehead. His eyes were so choked with blood that he could not see and ordered the tank behind him to take the lead.

Then for the Israelis it went from bad to worse. Soldiers in jeeps from the reconnaissance unit were cut to pieces when they tried to reach the tanks to guide them back to safety. When the tanks tried to pull out on their own, one was blown up and another crashed off a bridge. The crew inside were knocked cold but survived. During more frantic rescue operations, under heavy fire from the city walls, a medical orderly called Shindler dashed forward to get to a man who was screaming in agony as the uniform burned on his back. The wounded man was hit again and shot dead as Shindler tried to beat the flames out with his hands. Then, with more bullets slamming into the roadway around him, Shindler saved himself by jumping off the side of the bridge into the darkness. Fortunately for him the drop was not far. He escaped with a sprained ankle and scorches on his face and hands.

Micha Kapusta, the commander of the reconnaissance unit, managed to get to the bottom of the bridge where he was in dead ground and out of sight of the Jordanians. With him was Meir Har Zion, believed by many Israeli soldiers to be the apotheosis of the fighting Jew. Moshe Dayan said he was the finest Jewish warrior since Bar Kochba, the man who led the second revolt against the Romans in the second century. In the 1950s Har Zion was a close comrade of Ariel Sharon: 'Laconically killing Arab soldiers, peasants and townspeople in a kind of fury without hatred, he remained cold-blooded and thoroughly efficient, simply doing a job and doing it well, twice or three times a week for months.' Although he had suffered lasting damage from severe wounds, including the consequences of a battlefield tracheotomy with a penknife, he was back as a volunteer with the unit he once commanded. Har Zion and Kapusta shinned up a pipe on the side of the bridge to try to get to the men they thought were trapped on it. The tank on the bridge was burning, giving off enough light for them to see three men who were lying on the bridge. They could not get near them because the tank's ammunition was exploding and Jordanians were still firing at the bridge. Kapusta 'crawled as close as I could and called out the names of my men. Not one responded.'

DAY THREE

7 June 1967

Jerusalem, 0030

The terrifying sound and light of battle was close enough to be seen and heard clearly in Jerusalem. Israeli artillery, tanks and air strikes were destroying a Jordanian column that was making a late and desperate attempt to climb the steep road from Jericho to Jerusalem. Jordanian soldiers and armed Palestinian civilian volunteers took it all in from their posts on the walls of the Old City. For two hours, confronted with Israel's power, they chanted '*Allahu Akbar, Allahu Akbar*', God alone is great. On the Mount of Olives more than 100 civilians, mostly Muslims, crowded into the Apostolic Delegation, the official residence of the Pope's representative in Jerusalem. But the soldiers on the city walls were abandoned by most of their officers, who slipped away during the night. At half past midnight Brigadier Atta Ali, the Jordanian commander, went to the offices of the Waqf, the Islamic religious authority, where the Governor of Jerusalem Anwar al Khatib had set up his headquarters. The brigadier told him that nothing more could be done. The men on the walls were demoralised, hungry and exhausted. The army had given them no food since the battle for Jerusalem started. There was only

218

ammunition in the Old City but it was not reaching their positions. There was no resupply. On the first day of the war, Jordanian soldiers had knocked on the front door of the house of Anwar Nusseibeh, a leading Palestinian, to tell him that they had run out of ammunition. By the third day the situation was critical. Communications had broken down throughout the Jordanian army. After the first day the batteries on their radios had gone flat and were not recharged or replaced. Around Jerusalem they used ordinary telephones, which the Israelis easily intercepted, until they stopped working. In Jordanian Jerusalem there was no electricity and very little water. Most of the army had pulled back across the river Jordan to the East Bank. The governor refused to believe it was over. Surely, he asked, the people of Jerusalem could take up arms to continue the fight. If they needed officers the sons of the notable Palestinian families were available.

The brigadier was against it. 'All you'll be doing is destroying Jerusalem. Jerusalem will definitely be assaulted by dawn, and my troops are in no condition to resist.' He was leaving too. He offered to escort the governor to safety. Khatib refused. 'You are the military commander and you decide military behaviour, but Jerusalem is my adopted city and I'm not ready to leave it that way. If it is the will of God that I should die, I would not want to die anywhere else.'

Jordan's hold over Jerusalem, which had lasted nineteen years, was slipping away. At one in the morning Jordanian NCOs came into the room to report to Atta Ali that, with the officers gone, some of their men were deserting. The brigadier told them to come back with him to their positions. He did not want several dozen Palestinian civilians who had congregated at the offices of the Waqf to hear what he was going to say next. When they were clear of the building, which is on the edge of the holy compound that encloses Jerusalem's great mosques, he told them, discreetly, to take their men to Dung Gate in the southern wall, where they would start their journeys home. Not long afterwards Palestinian volunteers burst into the Waqf with the news that the Jordanians were leaving. Governor Khatib was so stunned that one of his aides worried he was heaving a heart attack. Some of the volunteers went back to their posts on the city walls. A few Jordanians stayed behind, to fight to the death. But throughout the night, more policemen and civilians handed in their weapons.

At Dung Gate, the brigadier gave the order for 'all ranks get out as best they can and make for east of the Jordan'. The withdrawal was not organised. An officer from Aden who was attached to Jordan's Jerusalem Brigade walked more than thirty miles to get to safety. At the Inn of the Good Samaritan, about half way between Jerusalem and the river Jordan, he passed the remains of an Iraqi brigade which had been bombed. The Iraqis, like him on foot, were 'fleeing east', without, the major believed, ever firing a shot. Brigadier Atta Ali, his officers and men, were blaming Nasser for the defeat as they trudged home – but they also kept accusing Britain and America of providing air support for the Israelis.

By dawn in Jerusalem the sound of shelling and machine gun fire had faded. It seemed unnaturally calm. Then 'a tremendous stentorian voice' called in Arabic over a loudspeaker for the Jordanians to surrender. The British foreign correspondent James Cameron had not had much sleep. 'All through last night it was remarkably like the old days of the London blitz, the same stumbling around unfamiliar streets in total darkness, the same crump and thud of explosive, the same trying to write by the glimmer of a single candle.' In Amman the minister of information, Abd al-Hamid Sharaf, ordered Jordanian Radio to start preparing the people for the fall of Jerusalem. His instructions were to emphasise heroic resistance, and slowly introduce the idea that martyrs were sacrificing themselves as the enemy pushed forward.

Sinai

The first Israeli forces reached the Suez canal in the early hours of Wednesday morning. They had driven straight down the coast road from Al-Arish. Dayan immediately ordered them to pull back twenty kilometres, perhaps because he did not want reports of the Israelis washing their feet in the canal to hurry up progress towards a ceasefire.

After the disasters of Tuesday, the generals at Egypt's Advanced Command Centre decided to move their headquarters back towards the Suez canal, travelling west through the Giddi Pass. The road was packed with troops and vehicles moving away from the fighting. The generals became more and more alarmed. Amer had not got round to telling them about his decision to order a general withdrawal. By 3 a.m. they had found out what was happening. The military police chief told them that the Egyptian army had been ordered to get out of Sinai. It was the first they had heard of it. They were 'amazed, and became even more' when they heard that Lieutenant-General Salah Muhsin, the commander of the Sinai field army, had also retreated to the other side of the Suez canal. General Murtagi crossed the canal to find Muhsin. He asked him why he had not asked permission to pull back his command. Murtagi was incensed when Muhsin muttered something about not being able to raise him on the telephone.

Yahya Saad, whose reconnaissance unit was destroyed by Israeli tanks on the first day, found his way back to the Suez canal by walking and hitching lifts on Egyptian vehicles. On the road to the Mitla Pass the burnt bodies of the crews of self-propelled anti-aircraft batteries were frozen in their seats. On the road there was 'total destruction and many corpses . . . when I reached the Suez canal bank I saw General Murtagi staring at the soldiers who had lost their boots walking barefoot. When I got there I threw myself on to the ground and went into deep sleep.'

Back in Sinai, General Gamasy stood outside the Advanced Command Centre's new site, watching 'completely disorganised' Egyptian troops pouring down the road to Suez. Gamasy knew that a retreat from a battle against an advancing enemy was desperately dangerous. It needed discipline, planning and a fighting rearguard to cover them and aggressively to keep the Israelis back. Nothing like that was being done. A military setback was about to turn into a disaster. 'I waited and watched on the morning of 7 June and saw the troops withdraw in the most pathetic way from Giddi and Mitla under continuous enemy air attacks, which had turned the Mitla passes into an enormous graveyard of scattered corpses, burning equipment and exploding ammunition.'

When the British defence attaché, a veteran of the campaign in the desert against the Germans in the Second World War, was flown over the Mitla Pass by the Israelis he saw destruction that was 'devastating over a four- to five-mile stretch of road running through the defile. All vehicles were nose to tail and in places double and treble banked. There was considerably more destruction than I had seen after the Axis retreat from Alamein. So far as can be ascertained, this destruction was the result of continuous air attack.' Along the route of the retreat the British foreign correspondent James Cameron saw hundreds of wrecked tanks 'strewn across the miles of wilderness like broken toys'. The Mitla Pass was even worse. 'A couple of miles of road suddenly looks like a thin strip of hell. Anything up to a couple of hundred vehicles, caught in the Mitla Pass, are trapped, burned, exploded, demolished; they are strung along in a caterpillar of ruination, upside down, inside out, fragmented, terrible. Some – desperately leaving the road altogether – have been delicately picked out on the desert.'

Yoffe's tanks drove all night, going headlong towards the Giddi Pass. They fought a series of running battles with any Egyptian who got in the way, blasting their way through and pushing on. In the darkness so many Egyptian vehicles were on fire that some of the advancing Israelis saw that 'as far as you could see, burning Egyptian vehicles were turning the night into day, with a noise that was a terrible symphony of destruction'. The wreckage was on both sides of the road and in a wadi below it. Away from the fires, there were vicious encounters along the dark desert road. An Israeli tank crew, heavily outnumbered, attacked a truckload of Egyptian soldiers with their Uzis. It turned into a hand-to-hand fight after the Israelis' ammunition ran low and the Egyptians managed to climb on to the tank. 'We began to hit with the butts of our Uzis on the heads that stuck out and the hands that grasped the sides of our tank . . . All one could hear were a few shouts, groans, and the dull sounds of butts on bodies. One of our men broke the butt of his Uzi and drew a knife.' In the confusion the survivors on both sides disengaged.

The Israelis set up a blocking position at the entrance to the Mitla

Pass. Egyptian tanks 'came up fast – escaping from the death behind them into the death that was lying in ambush for them . . . all the morning we continued pouring fire on hundreds of vehicles that were streaming past from all directions . . .'

At dawn air strikes against the retreating columns resumed. One of the pilots was Uri Gil. He had felt no pity and had not hesitated to shoot down a Syrian in a dogfight on the first day of the war. But this felt different. 'It was the greatest vehicle cemetery I ever saw. I was not happy about the situation. They looked like humans, like victims. I blew up a fuel tanker at close range. There was no fire from the ground. It was slaughter. I didn't think it was necessary. The war against Egypt was finished. I think they wanted to destroy as much as possible to teach the Egyptians the price of war. That was a mistake.'

The general staff in Cairo tried to salvage something from the chaos that was sweeping across the Egyptian army in Sinai. Belatedly, they tried to improvise rearguards. Part of the 3rd Infantry Division was told to stay in its trenches and bunkers at Jebel Libni. The infantrymen fought hard before they were 'outflanked and obliterated'. What was left of the 4th Armoured Division was ordered to fight a delaying action at the Bir Gifgafah crossroads. They had some success against a small blocking force of Israeli AMX tanks, whose shells bounced off the armour of the Egyptian T-54s. An Israeli paratrooper was woken around midnight 'by a groaning clanking sound of tanks approaching. Then suddenly we saw more than forty Egyptian tanks with their headlights blazing.' In the end, though, Tal encircled the Egyptians and his tanks destroyed an entire brigade. But the fight bought time for the Egyptians. The rest of the division – about a third of the force that started the war three days before – escaped relatively intact across the canal.

Jerusalem, 0530

Finally, General Narkiss was ordered to capture the Old City. Israel's deputy chief of staff, Haim Bar Lev, told him: 'We are already being pressed for a ceasefire. We are at the canal. The Egyptians have been carved up – don't let the Old City remain an enclave.' It was a moment for which Narkiss had waited since 1948, when he could not stop the Jewish quarter falling to the Jordanians. His war room was 'completely awake and tense with excitement'.

0600

David Rubinger, a photographer for *Time* magazine, let himself into his family home in Jerusalem. Until the night before he had been with the Israeli troops in the Sinai. He had been there right through the three weeks before the war, but he was disappointed with the pictures he had shot in the first forty-eight hours. Ironically, he had been too close to the action, where it was hard to capture what was happening. What he needed to photograph, he decided, was not all-out war, but the consequences of war. On Tuesday evening he had heard rumours that Jerusalem was about to fall. It sounded promising. He jumped on a helicopter that was evacuating wounded soldiers, ignored an airman shouting at him to get off, and made it back to Israel. He picked up his car and a hitchhiker to do the driving so he could sleep, and headed for Jerusalem. As Rubinger finished breakfast with his family he heard from the rumble of the guns that the war was picking up again. As he kissed them goodbye, shrapnel was pinging into the roof of the house. He drove as close as he could to the Old City then set off to walk down to Dung Gate, which was the closest to the Wailing Wall.

0800

From his garden the American journalist Abdullah Schliefer could see Israeli aircraft bombing the Jordanian positions around the Augusta Victoria, a towering and beefy piece of Prussian architecture that had been built by the Kaiser while he was eyeing Jerusalem hungrily at the end of the nineteenth century. It commanded the ridge of land that connected Mount Scopus to the Mount of Olives. By 1967 it was a hospital. Two hundred Palestinian doctors, nurses and patients retreated to its cellars, hoping that the building's heavy bones were strong enough to protect them. They could feel the building shaking around them. When the air raids ended, Schliefer saw Israeli paratroops advancing under heavy artillery cover towards the Augusta Victoria from Mount Scopus and straight up the Mount of Olives road from Wadi Joz.

Hamadi Dajani, a Palestinian trader, had moved his family into the Indian Hospice, a solid two-storey stone building in the densely populated Muslim quarter of the Old City. The hospice is on a rare patch of open ground just inside Herod's Gate, a narrow opening close to the north-east corner of the city walls. It was built by the Muslim authorities for pilgrims from the Indian sub-continent. The Dajanis could still hear the sounds of the battle, Israeli planes were overhead, but it was well organised and felt safe. They were welcomed because Hamadi's wife Amina was half Indian. They had three children, a daughter Manal, who was five, and two sons, Mohammed, who was four, and Ahmed, three. More than a dozen other people were sheltering there. The women had brought food. They prepared a meal of Palestinian salads. Thirty-five years later Ahmed fancied that he could still taste it.

At the Indian Hospice the Dajani children had pestered their parents to let them play just outside the door to the solid stone building that was being used as a shelter. The boys were wearing white shorts. Their sister Manal wore a white dress. Then they heard jet engines screaming. The children's father yelled at them to run inside. Before they could even turn, the first bomb crashed through the roof of the hospice and exploded. The Dajani family were very close to the explosion. Shrapnel and shards of Jerusalem stone torn out of the walls of the hospice blasted them. Mohammed Dajani, the four year old, was killed. His grandmother, who had been nursing another child on her lap, was decapitated. The child was unharmed. In the yard Ahmed and Manal lay close to the door in pools of blood.

Ahmed's left hand was smashed and his body was covered with shrapnel wounds. Manal was much worse off, with a badly damaged arm. Their father Hamadi was unconscious, with serious shrapnel wounds. Amina Dajani saw her mother and son killed and her husband and two other children badly wounded. She rushed into the courtyard to help them. Another bomb fell, and she was killed. A Jordanian mortar position close by seemed to have been the target of the Israeli attack. The surviving Dajanis – and other witnesses – claim its crew had abandoned the position nine hours before it was bombed.

0830

The sun had come up over the Judean desert and crept across the Mount of Olives. It was burning away the shadows around the minarets of Jerusalem's mosques and the towers of its churches. Colonel Mordechai Gur, commander of the Israeli paratroop brigade, looked down from his position on the Mount of Olives. The Old City, the ancient walled heart of Jerusalem, was laid out below him. Gur's view of the Old City was dominated by a great mosque, the Dome of the Rock. Muslims believe it marks the spot where the prophet Mohammed ascended to paradise on a staircase of light. The Dome had been the first sight of Jerusalem for every traveller coming over the crest of the Mount of Olives since it was built at the end of the seventh century – and for every invader. The Crusaders, the Ottomans and the British had all stood on the Mount of Olives, coveting the holy city laid out below them. And now, on another beautiful June morning, it was the turn of Colonel Gur and his paratroopers.

Gur had just sent three companies of men down to the walls of the city. His main objective lay deep inside the Old City, just beyond the Dome of the Rock. It was a narrow lane in the Moroccan quarter. Muslims called it al-Buraq road because they believed it was where Mohammed had tethered the winged horse of that name that had brought him to Jerusalem from Mecca. A high wall ran along one side of the lane. It was built of massive, evenly cut smooth stones. It is known as the Wailing Wall. For Jews it was the holiest place in the world to pray. Two thousand years earlier it was the western wall of the compound surrounding King Herod's second Jewish temple. It was torn down and most of Jerusalem's Jews dispersed by the Romans after a revolt in the first century. But detailed descriptions of the temple survived in Jewish holy writings. It had been a splendid place, massive, stone-built and decorated with gold. Now, in 1967, the Jews were fighting their way back. The founding generation of Israelis were mainly secular socialists. Ancient symbols had not, at first, meant that much to them. But as they drew closer to the heart of Jerusalem, they seemed to matter more and more.

Velni and Ronen, two journalists from Israeli army radio, were on the roof of the trade union building in Jerusalem, monitoring the battlefield radio traffic on army walkie-talkies. Suddenly they recognised Gur's voice, giving orders to occupy the Old City: 'Come in all battalion commanders. We are sitting on the mountain range which looks down on the Old City and are about to enter it. All our generations have been striving and dreaming about the Old City . . . We will be the first to enter it . . . tanks will enter the Lion's Gate. Move to the gate! Rendezvous on the open square above it.'

With them was the chief rabbi of the Israeli army, Shlomo Goren. He had arrived back from the fighting in Gaza the day before, his face covered in soot, telling Narkiss: 'Who cares about the south? Jerusalem and the Temple Mount, they are what count! You'll make history!' Now Goren dashed to his car to catch up with the soldiers. The two young reporters jumped in behind him.

Opposite the Mount of Olives is St Stephen's Gate, one of the seven great entrances to Jerusalem. It is also known as Lion's Gate because the king of the beasts is carved into its stone portico. Gur could see his men running up the steep road behind the tanks. He got into his half-track, and raced down to join them.

'I told my driver, Ben Zur, a bearded fellow weighing some fifteen stone, to speed on ahead. We passed the tanks and saw the gate before us with a car burning outside it. There wasn't a lot of room but I told him to drive on and so we passed the burning car and saw the gate half-open in front.' Gur wondered for a second whether the gate was booby-trapped. Then he gave another order: 'Ben Zur, move! He stepped on the gas, flung the door sideways and to hell and we crunched on over all the stones that had fallen from above and blocked our way.' The Israelis were inside the Old City.

The *Sunday Times* photographer Don McCullin was playing catch-up. He was tearing up the road to Jerusalem with a reporter called Colin Simpson. Now that Israel was close to an historic victory, it had given up its strategy of blacking out the news. McCullin, Simpson and a few others had been picked up by an elderly Israeli De Havilland Rapide in Cyprus and flown into Tel Aviv. The Jerusalem road was so peaceful that they started to worry that they had missed the war completely. On the radio the BBC quoted reports that the Old City had already been taken. In Jerusalem McCullin and Simpson bumped into a group of soldiers from the 1st Jerusalem Regiment. They explained to the forward company commander that, 'If he was set upon making Jewish history, it was only fit and proper that the *Sunday Times* should be with him to record it. We were accepted right away, and moved off with them through the olive groves.'

Also driving up from Tel Aviv was Ava Yotvat, whose husband Moshe had been wounded outside Ramallah. The road felt quiet and tense. At midnight an officer had knocked on her door to tell her the bad news. She found her husband at Hadassah hospital at Ein Karem in West Jerusalem. It was treating so many casualties from the street fighting that she thought he was being ignored. She took him back to Tel Aviv, where the main hospital had prepared hundreds of beds for casualties who had never materialised. Delighted to be doing something, doctors swarmed around him.

McCullin followed the soldiers from the Jerusalem Regiment as they advanced towards Dung Gate, one of the southern entrances to the Old City.

We took a lot of casualties in that first hundred yards inside the gate, coming under heavy sniper fire, bullets ricocheting in all directions as we fanned out . . . So exposed were we that if the Arabs had used mortars we would not have stood a chance . . . suddenly a Jordanian soldier ran out in front of us with his hands up. He did not appear to be armed, but everybody was jittery because of the snipers, as we all hit the ground. The Jordanian was blown to bits . . . the unit was moving further down the street when the lead man was shot dead, and a few yards later the next man received a bullet through his chest. A doctor came up to me and started screaming for a knife to cut away the man's clothing, though I failed to understand the torrent of Hebrew until someone said 'knife' in English and I fumbled for mine while the man died.'

The streets of West Jerusalem were almost deserted, except for occasional army jeeps careering round corners and up the empty avenues. One of them was Goren's jeep. They raced through the city towards the Mandelbaum gate, the crossing point between the two sides of Jerusalem, where they abandoned the jeep. Goren was carrying scrolls of the Jewish bible, the Torah, and a *shofar*, a bugle made from ram's horn which Jewish tradition dictated should be blown at auspicious occasions. The two journalists followed, ducked along the line of the city wall, working their way down to St Stephen's Gate.

At Dung Gate the Israelis were winning. Palestinians and some of the Jordanians who had not left started to surrender. Some of the soldiers threw away their uniforms and changed into civilian clothes, even suits of striped pyjamas. Don McCullin saw the Israelis obeying orders that been issued not to harm the holy places. 'On more than one occasion I watched Israelis hold their fire when sniped at from the roofs of religious buildings of any persuasion.'

The Palestinian dentist John Tleel peered out from under the pillows, blankets and thick sticking plaster he had used to block up the windows of his house in the Christian quarter. He saw Israeli paratroopers advancing, cautiously. At first, like many others in and around the Old City, he thought they might be Iraqis. Then for the first time since the city was divided in 1948, he realised that he was listening to Hebrew. The soldiers kept their backs to the walls and 'were advancing with extreme caution, watching their steps . . . with guns pointed out in front of them, they were on extreme alert'. He went back into his house to tell his friends and family what was happening. At first, they did not believe it could be possible.

After Colonel Gur, the commander of Israel's 55th Paratroop Brigade, led his men into the Old City through St Stephen's Gate, his driver Ben Zur swung their half-track to the left, flattening a motorcycle that stood in the way. They drove into the compound that encloses the great mosques and the site of the ancient Jewish temple. Anwar al Khatib, the Jordanian governor of Jerusalem, was waiting with the mayor. They told Gur that the army had withdrawn and there would be no more resistance.

Coming up not far behind Gur and his men were Uzi Narkiss and the IDF's deputy chief of staff, Chaim Bar Lev. As they were about to follow his troops through St Stephen's Gate into the Old City, Narkiss radioed Gur to find out where he was. Gur came up with what, for Israelis, are the most famous few lines of the 1967 war. 'The Temple Mount is ours!' Narkiss did not believe him. 'I repeat,' said Gur, 'the Temple Mount is ours. I'm standing next to the Mosque of Omar [the Dome of the Rock] now. The Wailing Wall is a minute away.'

Narkiss and Bar Lev drove fast up the slope that led to St Stephen's Gate. Paratroopers were still exchanging fire with men on the battlements. Dead bodies lay around the street. They abandoned their jeep, Narkiss threw a smoke grenade to give them some cover and they went forward on foot. They climbed over a tank that was stuck in the arch.

Yoel Herzl, Narkiss's adjutant, caught up with the generals a few minutes later. They were lying on the ground, pinned down by a sniper. Herzl noticed that a cloth on a second floor window in a building opposite was twitching. Asking the paratroopers to cover him, he ran over to the entrance. Moving as quietly as he could, he went up the stairs. Through an open door, he saw a red keffiyeh, the distinctive headscarf worn by Jordanian soldiers. It was the sniper.

'I emptied a clip from my Uzi into him. Until today I feel bad about it. It was a split-second thing. That's war. The fastest stays alive. If you think, you're dead.

'After that things moved very fast. Everyone was looking round for the way to the Wall, running like crazy, but we couldn't find the way. Rabbi Goren was there. He said follow me. He was carrying a Bible. We kept on running and we got to the Wall. Of the people who liberated it, I was the seventh.'

Yossi Ronen, the young reporter from army radio who was with Goren, said the Rabbi 'did not stop blowing the shofar and reciting prayers. His enthusiasm affected the soldiers and from every direction came cries of "Amen!" The paratroopers burst into song, and I forgot I was supposed to be an objective reporter and joined them in singing "Jerusalem of Gold" ... the commanders gave short, emotional speeches.' Narkiss remembered his failure to capture the Old City in 1948. 'Never has there been such a thing, for those standing here right now ... We all kneel before history.'

For Israelis it was the emotional climax not just of the war, but of their first nineteen years of independence. All the men there were deeply moved by the capture of the Jewish people's most evocative and holy place. Many of them wept. The photographer David Rubinger and the BBC correspondent Michael Elkins, highly secular Israelis who had followed the first troops to the Wall, were swept up in it. 'We were all crying. It wasn't religious weeping. It was relief. We had felt doomed, sentenced to death. Then someone took off the noose and said you're not just free, you're King. It seemed like a miracle.' They still had jobs to do. Rubinger lay on the floor of the narrow alley that ran along the wall to get some sense of the wall's height, and then with tears pouring down his face started taking pictures of stunned, awed and exhausted paratroopers.

Major Doron Mor, second in command of Battalion 66, started worrying when he saw the narrow lane in front of the Wall full of soldiers 'in ecstasy'. He had already lost thirty-six men in the battle for Jerusalem and did not want to lose any more. 'I was afraid one Jordanian sniper in one window would shoot all of them. We started to push the soldiers out, because it was very dangerous.'

Sinai

Herzl Bodinger, the Israeli pilot, was returning from another attack on Bir Tamada. He tuned his radio to Voice of Israel, so his direction-finding equipment could zero in on the signal to get him home, while he caught up with the news. They announced that the Temple Mount was in Israeli hands, and played 'Jerusalem of Gold'. Bodinger, not a religious man, was surprised that he was so overjoyed. General Yeshayahu Gavish, commander of Israel's forces in the Sinai, was in a half-track at Bir Gifgafah when he heard the same news. It was his biggest thrill of the war. 'Then I thought, Oh shit, they stole all the glory.'

Nablus, West Bank

Around eleven o'clock Palestinians ran through the streets, shouting that the Algerians were coming. A crowd on the edge of Nablus was throwing rice at an armoured column that was rolling into the town from the east, from the direction of Tubas and the East Bank of the Jordan. If they weren't Algerians, perhaps they were Iraqis. The people in the crowd didn't mind. Cairo Radio had been full of the contributions to the war effort made by Arab brothers. Now their saviours were coming.

But the tanks were Israeli, from General Peled's division. The troops were bemused by their reception. 'Thousands stood at the entrance to Nablus, waving white handkerchiefs and applauding . . . we entered the town and were surprised . . . the population was friendly.'

When an Israeli soldier tried to disarm one of the Palestinians, shooting started. More Israeli tanks arrived later from the west, after they had finally scattered the 40th Armoured Brigade at the Qabatiya crossroads, where fighting had started again at dawn. While the Israeli tanks were manoeuvring, armed Palestinian civilians opened fire. For six hours there was a confused gun battle. Jordanian tanks that had been at the other end of the town got involved. Outside Nablus other Jordanian tanks managed to break out towards the Damiya bridge over the river Jordan, to get to the relative safety of the East Bank. Raymonda Hawa Tawil, a middle-class Palestinian housewife, was in the cellar with her children, who were petrified as explosions and gunfire came closer and grew louder. 'Mama, what's happening? Mama will we die? What do Jews look like?' Around seven in the evening Tawil heard a voice speak through a loudspeaker. 'The town has surrendered. We will not harm you if you put up white flags. Anyone who goes outside does so at the risk of his life. The Mayor of Nablus requests you to surrender.' The announcement was in literary Arabic. It reminded Tawil of when, as a child, she heard Israelis making the same sort of announcement when Nazareth surrendered in 1948. King Hussein came on the radio, exhorting them to defend themselves tooth and nail. An old man in the shelter tried to cheer them all up. 'My false teeth are barely sharp enough to eat a sandwich . . . bite 'em with your own teeth!' Now, in 1967, fighting and sniping went on into the night.

By mid-afternoon Israel was fighting the clock as well as what was left of the Jordanian army. It always knew that once the Security Council passed a ceasefire resolution, the time for military action started running out. Israel wanted the entire West Bank as well as Jerusalem by the time it stopped shooting. Both sides blamed each other for breaking the ceasefire, which King Hussein had accepted in the early hours of the morning. Certainly, Israel had a greater interest in continuing the fight. It pressed home fierce attacks against columns of Jordanian forces that were retreating down from the high mountains of the West Bank into the Jordan valley, the lowest place on earth, on their way out of the West Bank. Israeli warplanes – at least 100 according to the Jordanians – strafed and bombed them and, in some places, they were shelled by Israeli tanks. Without air cover, they were at the Israelis' mercy.

The Israeli air force flew 597 sorties against Jordan during the war, 549 of them for ground attack. Sharif Zaid Ben Shaker, the cousin of King Hussein, felt like he had been on the wrong end of most of them. He commanded the 60th Armoured Brigade which lost forty of its eighty tanks, mainly to air attack. 'When you're strafed you have to jump out of your vehicle – I was in a Land Rover – and throw yourself into a ditch. They hit the wireless car behind me. They used a lot of napalm. A napalm bomb ricocheted on the asphalt near me, went about 200 yards and exploded. God was on my side.'

Even though King Hussein had long since dropped his desire for a secret ceasefire, broadcasting his acceptance of the UN resolution on Radio Jordan, the Israelis continued to press home their attacks. A few Jordanian units kept on fighting. Most were trying to cross to the East Bank or to melt away into the west. The US ambassador, Findley Burns, in Amman, feared that the Israelis were trying to destroy the Jordanian army completely. He was so concerned about what that could do to the stability of Jordan that he urged President Johnson to phone Prime Minister Eshkol to push Israel to respect the ceasefire. Burns was also acutely aware that almost every Jordanian believed the United States could stop the Israeli onslaught if it wanted to – and if it did not, he feared some of the thousand-plus Americans in Jordan could face 'mob violence'.

Bethlehem, 1500

When the war started Badial Raheb, a young mother, was better prepared than most of her neighbours in Milk Grotto Street in Bethlehem. It is a narrow lane that runs along the side of the Church of the Nativity, which Christians believe was built on the place where Jesus was born. Her husband Bishara Raheb owned a bookshop. He followed the news closely. When he was in the house the radio was always on, especially Saut al Arab, the Voice of the Arabs from Cairo. Bishara discounted most of its bragging, bloodthirsty propaganda, but he hoped that the Arabs were strong enough to win the war that he was convinced was coming. Badial was not sure. It was clear to her that the Arabs were more than simply disunited. They were ready to betray each other, which was much worse. How could they fight Israel in such a state? She was worried. She had a four-year-old son, Mitri, and she was expecting another child. Together, Badial and Bishara prepared for the war, stockpiling food.

Jordan's Hittin Infantry Brigade pulled out of Bethlehem at midday without a fight. The Mayor of Bethlehem surrendered the town to a task force from the Jerusalem Infantry Brigade, which entered Bethlehem at three in the afternoon. By then the Rahebs had covered the windows of their house with cardboard. They wanted to make the place look empty, so they would be ignored by the invaders. The family retreated down to a basement room that was protected by a thick stone wall. The electricity and the water were cut but they had candles and there was a well. In their basement they could hear the sounds of war. The prospect of Israeli soldiers coming to their town was terrifying. People were talking about the massacre of Deir Yasin in 1948. Some of the Rahebs' neighbours who thought it would happen again left for Jordan. Badial started to feel very unsafe, even in their well-protected stone cellar. She decided to cross the road to take refuge in the Church of the Nativity. Getting to its door was agonising, even though it was no more than two dozen yards away. Her little boy Mitri had a leg in plaster from an accident just before the war. With them as well was Bishara's old aunt, well into her eighties and barely able to walk.

The ancient church was full. It was very dark. The electricity had been cut and the people were frightened to light candles, which might have attracted attention. As her eyes got used to the dark, Badial Raheb saw that hundreds had gathered there, so many that she struggled to find somewhere for her family to sit down.

Cairo

The Soviet military attaché was granted an audience with Field Marshal Amer at his headquarters, in the brand new defence ministry building in Nasser City, one of Cairo's newest suburbs. Sergei Tarasenko, an attaché at the Embassy, was with him as interpreter.

The atmosphere around the ministry was not what Tarasenko expected – no checkpoints, no barriers and no guards. The first soldiers that they saw were at the entrance to the building. An immaculately turned-out officer opened the door for the Soviet party. Somewhere in the background there were three soldiers with a light anti-aircraft gun.

They went down in a lift what seemed to be a long way and were shown into a big room. Around ten senior officers were sitting there. Tarasenko was bemused. 'I was expecting to see them extremely active, messengers running in all directions, to hear orders and reprimands shouted into the telephone or walkie-talkies. Instead there was complete stillness and quiet. The officers were sipping coffee and exchanging quiet remarks. Some of them were listening to small transistor radios.'

Amer's office was just off the big, quiet room. He was in an armchair next to a small table. Tarasenko's attention was caught by a six-inch split in a seam in the usually immaculate Amer's uniform. The Russians knew already it was going badly for Egypt. Now they started to think it could be even worse. Over Arabic coffee the military attaché asked Amer what was happening at the front. Amer, 'with unsuppressed irritation', said the main item on his agenda at that precise moment was Nasser's decision to close the Suez canal, which Amer seemed convinced had turned the war into an international conflict. The Soviet military attaché started asking specific questions. Where was the front line? What happened to particular units? What was happening in Ishmalia? Amer did not answer the questions. 'It was obvious that Amer himself had no idea of what was happening on the battlefields. My impression was that he had been taking drugs, or just switched off.'

Amer livened up only when he insisted that Egypt was now fighting the United States as well as Israel. The Israeli air force, Amer claimed, more preposterously than ever, had been destroyed by the air forces of Egypt, Syria and Jordan. The war was being continued by the Americans, who were flying operations from their aircraft carriers in the Mediterranean. In the circumstances, Egypt expected the

236

Soviet Union to offer its support. The military attaché asked for proof. Had they shot down an American plane? Or captured an American pilot? Amer was 'almost rude'. He explained to the two Russians that it was all so well known and obvious that no proof was needed. Besides, the downed aircraft had all fallen into the sea and sunk. With that, he called the meeting to a halt.

Outside Amer's bunker, in the real world, Cairo had a quiet morning, after a night of air raids on factories and on the Cairo West military airbase. Rumours that a disaster had occurred in Sinai was spreading around the capital. Local journalists at the official Middle East News Agency were accusing the Soviets of betraying Egypt. Why hadn't they intervened? Why was the army surprised that the Americans and the British helped Israel? Some were suggesting that it would be just as bad if London and Washington's denials were true, because it meant that the Egyptian army had disastrously underestimated the Israelis. Even Nasser was being criticised. One reporter from his regime's favourite newspaper, *al-Ahram*, said Nasser had two choices left: to kill himself or leave the country.

'Despair settled over the city,' according to Trevor Armbrister, one of the twenty-two American reporters in Cairo covering the war. Even the Nile was quiet. A few feluccas drifted downstream with their sails furled. Troops in combat fatigues with bayonets fixed guarded the bridges. Just past midday Armbrister and his twenty-two colleagues were 'rounded up and taken to the Nile hotel, a dingy establishment facing the Corniche. As we milled around the entrance, a convoy of military vehicles rumbled by loaded with sand bags and artillery shells. We'd seen such convoys before, and the troops had always been singing. Now they were silent. The Egyptians made it clear that we were under house arrest. A blue-gowned Nubian called Mahatma guarded the hotel entrance, thrusting a thick black arm in front of anyone who attempted even to peer outside.' The hotel restaurant had been moved to the boiler room, 'a smelly cavern abuzz with flies'. For lunch they were served some dried meat they thought had come from a camel. 'Waiters in filthy galabias plopped six bottles of beer on the table. There would be no more until the war was over. The beer factory was closed.' They listened to reports from the BBC and Voice of America on shortwave radios and wondered how long their internment would last.

Gaza

After three days sheltering with his family in some farm buildings south of his home town of Deir al Balah, the 25-year-old Gaza schoolteacher Kamel Sulaiman Shaheen decided it was safe to take them home. A police station was behind their house in Deir al Balah. While they had been away, it had been occupied by the Israeli army. Shaheen heard a burst of machine gun fire coming from some open ground near the police station. Later he went out with some neighbours to try to see what had happened. The bodies of five executed Egyptian soldiers lay in the dust. Civilians picked up the bodies and buried them. Most of the time, Deir al Balah was under curfew. The Israelis conducted aggressive searches of houses. Sometimes they pulled young men away from terrified women and children, took them outside and shot them. Mr Shaheen helped bury five local men who had been killed by the Israelis. Thirty-five years later, now a headmaster a few weeks from retirement, he sat in his school in Deir al Balah and as the younger teachers listened he went through their names.

'Mahmoud Ashur, Abd al Rahim Ashur, Ali Ashur, Ahmed Shaheen, who was my cousin, Abd al Marti Ziada . . . I saw their bodies. I heard about others but I didn't know their names. Many people were killed. They killed people who broke the curfew. It wasn't clear to people what the rules were. They made announcements in very bad Arabic . . . and went into alleys and very narrow streets, where people had thought it was safe to move . . . They were very hard and painful days. We had very little food, and no electricity or water.'

'After six or seven days the Israelis started to arrest people rather than shoot them. We had been sheltering some Egyptian soldiers, given them civilian clothes. After a while they thought it was safe to surrender, so they gave themselves up.'

Jerusalem

Moshe Dayan broadcast to the nation. 'We have united Jerusalem . . . We have returned to the holiest of our holy places, never to part from it again.'

A few hours after the Israelis had captured the Temple Mount, Rabbi Goren went up to General Narkiss, who was lost in thought.

'Uzi,' said the rabbi, 'now is the time to put 100 kilos of explosives into the Mosque of Omar so that we might rid ourselves of it once and for all . . . you will go down in history if you do it.'

'My name will already be written in the history books of Jerusalem.'

'You don't grasp what tremendous significance this would have. This is an opportunity that can be taken advantage of now, at this moment. Tomorrow it will be too late.'

Narkiss tried to shut the rabbi up by threatening him with jail.

One of the paratroopers got to the top of the Dome and hung out a big Israeli flag. By the weekend Moshe Dayan ordered them to take it down. He also pulled Israeli troops out of the compound of the Haram al Sharif, though they stayed on its gates. Day-to-day administration of the site was handed back to the Muslim authorities. Jews would be allowed in, but not to pray. Later in 1967, in a speech to a military convention, Rabbi Goren called Dayan's actions a 'tragedy for generations . . . I myself would have gone up there and wiped it off the ground completely, so that there would be no trace that there was ever a Mosque of Omar there.'

Israeli soldiers went from house to house in the Old City, searching for pockets of resistance. Haifa Khalidi was an eighteen-year-old Palestinian schoolgirl. She had been expecting a great victory. Like everyone she knew, she believed the Arab propaganda. When the shelling was at its loudest, she assumed that Israeli West Jerusalem was being destroyed. Some of her neighbours had looked out of their windows and seen soldiers in camouflage uniforms they thought were Iraqis. Haifa's mother, who remembered the Jews from before 1948, told her to get away from the windows, because the soldiers were Israelis. They banged on the Khalidis' front door, shouting in English, 'Open up, we don't hurt innocents.' But before they could decide whether or not to let them in, there was an explosion as the soldiers blew the door open. 'They came in to search the place. They saw we were educated so they were polite and behaved correctly. The soldiers spoke English with American accents.'

At nine in the evening, for the first time since the first morning of the war, Israeli civilians in Jerusalem were allowed out of their shelters. In three days of war fourteen Israeli civilians were killed and 500 wounded. No one has accurate casualty figures for Palestinians.

Jericho

Thousands of Palestinians were leaving like their friends and family had nineteen years before, fleeing in front of an advancing Israeli army. They walked down the steep road from Jerusalem, some of the women balancing suitcases on their heads, leading dirty, tearful, barefoot children towards the Dead Sea and the river Jordan. The bridge across the river had been blown by the Israelis. It was an old steel crossing, named by the British after General Allenby who captured Jerusalem for them in 1917. Jordan had renamed it the King Hussein bridge. Now it lolled down into the Jordan's muddy water. The long line of refugees crawled across the wreckage to get across to where they thought they would be safe.

Bombing continued in and around Jericho. Sami Oweida, who worked for the local council, saw what it could do. Iraqi soldiers attacked by napalm 'threw themselves in front of the water hoses. But they kept burning, uttering piercing screams.' Still, he thought he was safer at home. Oweida's seventeen-year-old daughter Adla, who had just graduated from high school, begged her father to change his mind. They left home at half past two.

> On the way to the bridge we saw no less than 200 bodies of soldiers and civilians. Whoever could do so covered the bodies with any kind of cover available.
>
> We crossed the King Hussein bridge, walking . . . We tried to avoid big crowds, thinking that the planes would bomb the crowds. At that moment, about four o'clock, I saw a plane coming down like a hawk directly at us. Directly. We threw ourselves on the ground and found ourselves in the midst of fire. Children were on fire. Myself, my two daughters, my son and two children of my cousin . . . I tried, but I couldn't do anything. Fire was all around. I carried my burning child outside the fire. The burning people became naked. Fire stuck to my hands and face. I rolled over. The fire rolled with me.
>
> At that moment another plane was coming directly at us, coming down. I thought it was the end of us. I could not lie on my face. My hands and face were burning. I saw the plane come down over me. I thought the wheels of the plane would hit me. I saw the pilot lean over and look at me.

Sami Oweida and his family had been hit by napalm, a highly flammable jelly which is made by mixing a thickening agent with petrol. They picked up their wounded children, and kept walking towards Amman. Oweida's four-year-old daughter Labiba died that night. Adla died four days later. His son was also badly burnt, but survived.

The Israeli air force used napalm extensively in 1967. As the Americans proved in Vietnam in the 1960s, and NATO proved again in Kosovo in 1999, bombing moving traffic on the roads is an inexact science. It is very easy for high-performance aircraft to destroy what is below them. It is harder, though by no means impossible, for pilots to work out if they are killing soldiers or civilians. Sharif Zaid Ben Shaker, the cousin of King Hussein who commanded one of Jordan's two armoured brigades in the thick of the air attacks, believed until his death in 2002 that Israel did not differentiate between civilian and military traffic on the roads. As he was retreating to the East Bank on the day before Sami Oweida's family was attacked by napalm, he saw a bus full of civilians coming out of Jericho and heading for the Allenby bridge. He saw the bus again about ten minutes later, after it had been attacked from the air with napalm. 'Women, men and children – there were no soldiers on that bus – were all sitting in their places all burnt up – and you could see the driver with his hands on the steering wheel. They didn't differentiate at all. I will never forget the smell when I passed them . . . They used everything they had without differentiation . . . they had all the time to look. They were having fun. They were overhead and choosing their targets.'

The first wave of refugees – around 125,000 people – crossed the Jordan from the first day of the war to 15 June. The Jordanian government was horrified by the arrival of so many people whom it had no way of supporting. The government, British diplomats reported, was as 'stunned and disoriented' as its people, 'incapable of organising the reception and distribution of relief supplies'. Radio Amman kept telling Palestinians on the West Bank to stay in their homes or their camps. When the director of public security was ordered to stop them coming, if necessary by force, he refused. The Jordanian government and UNRWA, the United Nations agency for Palestinian refugees, ran out of places to house so many people. A serious health hazard developed in UNRWA schools, where five or six families were living in every room. Camps, most of which had almost no facilities, started to spring up.

When they crossed the Jordan, people searched for news of their families and friends. All conventional communications with the West Bank were cut, so they had only alarming rumours. Exaggerated stories of military and civilian deaths in Jenin, Jerusalem, Jericho and Ramallah raced around, ratcheting up the anxiety and tension. Enterprising boys made money carrying messages to the West Bank by swimming or fording the Jordan. Palestinians abroad inundated foreign consulates in Jerusalem asking for help in tracing West Bank families who had fled.

Save the Children's senior nurse in Jordan, Mary Hawkins, was consumed by frustration. Reports of what was happening at the crossing points of the river Jordan were reaching Amman and she wanted to act. Hawkins was a vastly experienced British woman of fifty-five, for whom the word indomitable could have been invented. At the siege of Monte Cassino in the Second World War she was awarded the Croix de Guerre by the Free French forces after three days and nights under fire treating the wounded. In 1948 she worked with the first wave of Palestinian refugees, the 750,000 who lost their homes in Israel's war of independence. In 1956 she left Jordan's refugees to go to Austria. Soviet forces had crushed the Hungarian uprising. In midwinter families were being shot at by border guards and Soviet troops as they tried to get through the Iron Curtain to Austria. Some of them took their chances swimming the freezing Einser canal or crossing on rubber dinghies or inflated inner tubes. The refugees gave their children heavy doses of bromide so they kept quiet when they were passing border guards and Soviet troops. Hawkins treated the people who got over for frostbite and gave the drugged children sweet coffee to keep them conscious.

But Hawkins and the British staff of the Save the Children fund in Jordan had been under what amounted to self-imposed house arrest since the second day of the war. They had been warned that going out in public was dangerous, because so many people believed the story that British and American aircraft had intervened decisively on Israel's side. Their local colleagues had kept their operations going. They spent 'two endless days' playing Scrabble in one of their flats in Amman.

London

The British and the Americans started an immediate propaganda counter-offensive against the accusation that they were fighting on the same side as the Israelis. Thirty years before Western governments became obsessed with the twenty-four-hour news cycle, one official complained bitterly when the Ministry of Defence in London took fourteen hours to come up with a rebuttal. Official denials were circulated widely to radio and TV stations. Conscious that denials alone would not do the job, they decided to do all they could to attack Nasser – discreetly, or their words would rebound on them. Nasser had to be shown to be responsible for the disaster that was enveloping the Arabs. The Americans had similar ideas. An official called Chet Cooper was given the job of countering the Arab accusations. He wanted to find 'a prominent Arab willing to expose Egyptian mendacity for what it was'. Failing that, he suggested that 'greatly increased publicity for the Egyptian use of poison gas in the Yemen might help to discredit Nasser in Arab eyes'.

In London an official recommended ways of spinning the news to give the impression that Britain was more sympathetic to the Arab side than was actually the case. Israel's official account of the way that the war started – an Egyptian attack to which it responded – should be subtly challenged. Although the British and the Americans knew that Israel's statement that it attacked on 5 June in response to an Egyptian strike was untrue, they had not publicly questioned Israel's version. Now the BBC should be urged to quote unofficial British sources reporting that the Israelis crossed the frontier first. The BBC should, the official went on, also stress Britain's arms embargo and Israel's protest against it. (In fact Britain was delivering arms to Israel until the morning the war started.)

But it was all a little late for that. The 'big lie' stuck. By the last day of the war it was still believed firmly by almost every Arab who read the papers or listened to the radio. In Saudi Arabia senior foreign ministry officials, receiving politely formal written and spoken denials from diplomats, 'profess to believe them but nevertheless appear sceptical'. Within two weeks some of the dust settled when the movements of British and American aircraft carriers were made public, showing they had not been involved. King Hussein accepted that he had no proof that American and British warplanes had intervened on the Israeli side. But Nasser's accusations were widely believed on the Arab street. Among many older people they still are, even though Nasser withdrew his accusations in March 1968. He told the American magazine *Look* that they had been based on 'suspicion and faulty information'.

What was certain was that Britain and America were hoping for an Israeli victory and relaxed about Israel's intentions and even plans they might have to extend their territory. Britain's Prime Minister Harold Wilson telephoned Lester Pearson, his counterpart in Canada, on Wednesday 7 June. After expressing his surprise that the Russians had voted for the ceasefire resolution in the UN, this is how the conversation went:

> WILSON: Well, there are rumours of a *coup d'état* in Cairo. I
> don't know if it's true.
> PEARSON: Really.
> WILSON: It's only in the newspapers so far . . . What I feel is
> that there is a good chance now that the Israelis are
> generous and pretty magnanimous. They want to be
> settled there with everyone recognising their existence
> and right to live, and obviously they want Aqaba. [It is
> unclear whether he means access to the Gulf of Aqaba or
> capturing the Jordanian port of Aqaba itself.] But I
> understand now that they are prepared to settle the
> refugee problem once and for all.
> PEARSON: Well, that would be a step forward.
> WILSON: And this would help the Arabs not to lose too
> much face and the Israelis are conscious of this . . .

West Bank

By the evening Israel's job was done. Jerusalem and the West Bank were captured. The war against Jordan was over. At first the Jordanians claimed they had lost 6094 killed and missing. Later Jordanian army figures were much lower. The best estimate is around 700 dead and 2500 wounded. Israel lost 550 killed against Jordan with 2400 wounded. King Hussein, who had lived on cigarettes, caffeine and adrenaline since the war started, was exhausted. He went on Amman radio to acknowledge the defeat. 'Our soldiers have defended every inch of our earth with their precious blood. It is not yet dry, but our country honours the stain . . . If in the end you were not rewarded with glory, it was not because you lacked courage but because it was the will of God.'

The speed of the Israeli advance into the West Bank was breathtaking for some of the men who took part in it. After the war an Israeli journalist called Igal Lev turned the experiences of the unit he commanded into a novel called *Jordan Patrol*. It is a revealing snapshot of the self-image of what seems to have been a typical Israeli reserve unit. In his preface Lev writes: 'Wars were what I was born to. That is why I hate them.' War, he accepts, is foul and violent, but necessary for Israel's survival and for the construction and expansion of the state. As they advance, the soldiers are struck with the realisation that the land they are occupying was theirs.

> We penetrated into the heart of the West Bank like a knife cutting into a loaf of bread . . . the vastness of the area and the swiftness of our advance were intoxicating. Only as we moved ahead did it occur to us how artificial and compressed Israel was. We who were born there and had never travelled overseas had looked upon the size and extent of Israel as the infinite. All of a sudden we came upon other vistas and so discovered our country anew – a lovely green land of hills and dales with pastures in between. Our country.

As the men move forward they come upon Arab villages, which they search for weapons and soldiers. They are humane, standing in 'awkward confusion' when a baby bursts into tears, 'frightened by the sight of our sweaty figures, our steel helmets and Uzis at the ready'. Lev recognises the child's tears as a 'protest against the madness'. They demand that the village headman finds the baby's mother so it can be cared for properly. But moments later they show their strength, which is as important to the way they see themselves as their embarrassed reaction to the baby. One of the soldiers, 'with nerves of steel and great strength' interrogates the village elders to find where they keep their weapons. '. . . at first I was surprised by the brutality with which he carried out the searches.' But then, as the soldier beats the truth out of 'a sweating, pale frightened man' and 'a yellowish stain' spreads out on the front of the Arab's robe, the violence is shown to be necessary. He confesses that they do have weapons and blurts out where they are. The soldier gives him a final blow – then rushes out of the Arab's house, 'retching horribly . . . I realised then what a strain the searches and the interrogations were for him.'

Washington DC

The Americans were turning their minds to what would happen after the war. A State Department paper stated that the US needed peace in the Middle East and 'reasonably friendly relations with both Israel and the Arab states'. But any US peace plan faced big obstacles. There was the 'stubborn Arab refusal to recognise that Israel is here to stay'. The Arabs regarded the Americans as Israel's ally and their 'imperialistic arch enemies'. But Israel's attitude was another obstacle. 'Through years of experience, the Israelis have come to believe that the Arabs understand only force and that it is hopeless to negotiate with them on any other basis. While they talk of an overall peace settlement with the Arabs, they have understandably been reluctant to offer serious concessions for that purpose. Their leverage in US domestic politics can limit our flexibility.'

President Johnson was not as exhilarated about Israel's rapid-fire victories as some of his subordinates. Glumly, he told them he was 'not sure we were out of our troubles'. America's objective should be to 'develop as few heroes and as few heels as we can . . . It is important for everyone to know we are not for aggression. We are sorry this has taken place.' He warned them that by the time the US had finished, 'with all the festering problems we are going to wish the war had not happened'.

DAY 4

8 June 1967

Sinai

Sharon's division, minus his infantry brigade, had a difficult journey south to Nakhl, which is in the centre of the Sinai desert. They slept 'like the dead' for two hours just before dawn while the engineers cleared mines. After first light they moved on until they saw an entire brigade of Egyptian Stalin tanks, reinforced by self-propelled guns. When the Israelis went forward to engage them, the Stalins did not move. They had been abandoned intact. Their commander Brigadier Abd el-Naby was captured a little later. He said he had left them the way they were because 'my orders did not say to destroy my tanks . . . if I had blown up my tanks the Jews would have heard me. It makes a lot of noise to destroy a tank.'

Sharon sent an officer up in a helicopter. He saw a column of Egyptian armour approaching. Sharon hurriedly set up an ambush. Fighting started at ten in the morning, with the Israelis destroying around 60 Egyptian tanks, around 100 guns and more than 300 other vehicles. Hundred of Egyptians were killed and wounded. At least 5000 more managed to escape the carnage and moved away into the desert. Many of them died of exhaustion, heat stroke and thirst. When the fighting stopped at around 2:30 p.m., Sharon surveyed the battlefield. 'This was a valley of death. I came out of it like an old man. Hundreds were killed. There were burning tanks everywhere. One had the feeling that man was nothing. A sand-storm had been churned up by the tanks. The noise was tremendous . . . vehicles loaded with ammunition were exploding all along the line. The dead lay all around.'

After the war Ariel Sharon offered a blunt assessment:

I think the Egyptian soldiers are very good. They are simple and ignorant but they are strong and disciplined. They are good gunners, good diggers and good shooters – but their officers are shit, they can fight only according to what they planned before. Once we had broken through, except for the minefield between Bir Hassneh and Nakhl, which was probably there before the war, the Egyptian officers placed no mines and laid no ambushes to block our line of advance, but some soldiers, particularly at the Mitla [Pass] where we blocked their line of retreat, fought to the death in an attempt to break westwards towards the canal.

Brigadier Abdel Moneim Khalil's paratroopers had lost men throughout Wednesday to Israeli air raids, but they were dug in and dispersed while they were under attack and it could have been worse. By the early hours of Thursday they were on the move towards the Suez canal, still a relatively intact fighting unit. All along the horizon black smoke was rising from dozens of fires. Coming in the opposite direction was an envoy from Field Marshal Amer in Cairo, sent to check rumours that the brigadier had abandoned his men. Khalil pointed to his troops, still armed and well disciplined. The envoy relaxed and told him about what had been happening at Amer's headquarters since Monday. Like most of the Egyptian officer corps, Khalil liked Amer, who had promoted him. But he had always thought he would crack up under pressure. Once, during the war in Yemen, they had been discussing a plan for an offensive that was likely to cost many Egyptian lives. Amer had withdrawn from the meeting to return to his bedroom. Khalil went to see what had happened to the field marshal. 'I went into Amer's bedroom. He was sitting down, with his head tilted back. You could see the veins in his temples pounding. I told him he was tired and gave him an aspirin and some water.' Amer was grateful for the attention. When Khalil suggested it would be more efficient to cancel the offensive and bribe the local tribesmen instead, Amer agreed.

Standing in the desert, Khalil wondered what state Amer was in by now. At dawn, Khalil and his men started to cross the Suez canal. As they moved over to the west bank of the canal, engineers were dismantling the bridge beneath them. By the time their self-propelled guns arrived the bridge was down. They had to push the guns into the canal. Khalil was pleased. He had extracted his men successfully, with only moderate losses. But all around them was chaos. Officers were stopping convoys and frantically redeploying every soldier they could see to the town of Suez, which they were certain was Israel's next target. Khalil rang Amer when he arrived at Suez. 'He gave me orders that were puzzling, confusing and unexpected, to sack the head of the 1st Armoured Brigade, take over the command and take them back to the Mitla Pass, where Amer said Israeli paratroops were landing.'

It was 0500. Khalil had no intention of obeying Amer's order. As a paratroop commander, he thought it was madness to take over an armoured unit at a moment's notice and then lead it into battle. Instead, he crossed to the east bank of the canal, found the general he was supposed to replace, did not tell him he was sacked, only that he had to take his men to the pass. 'When I got back to Suez, I called Amer from the Governor's office, who gave me another weird order. He said, have you gone to Mitla? I said, I'm getting ready. He said, good, now you're also commander of a mechanised infantry brigade . . . take that to Mitla too. I went to the brigade's commander, Suad Hassan, and told him to follow the other armoured brigade to the Mitla. I'll stay here to supervise. It was ridiculous.'

Another Egyptian commander determined not to obey Amer's orders was Major-General Saad el Shazli. He had been hunkered down since Monday with his force of 1500 men in an L-shaped defile just inside Israel. 'There were some long-distance skirmishes, but during that time we were not in a war.' He had heard nothing from Cairo until seven on Wednesday evening. Shazli says they yelled at him: 'What are you doing there? The troops have pulled out, you have to withdraw immediately. I knew I'd be attacked if I followed orders. So I said yes, but I didn't do it. We waited until it was dark and started moving across the desert. We moved cross country all night.' By dawn on Thursday 8 June, when they had crossed 100 kilometres, they were discovered by the Israeli air force and attacked. 'We only had machine guns against the aircraft. When the soldiers saw they weren't doing anything they stopped firing. I shouted at them to keep firing. It was good for morale. They didn't feel so powerless.'

Shazli's unit took casualties of 15 per cent. By the standards of the Egyptian army in the Sinai that week, that left him with a formation that was almost intact. They crossed the Suez canal at dusk. Six years later Shazli was chief of staff of the Egyptian army. He was responsible for the assault across the Suez canal at the start of the 1973 war, which was Egypt's greatest modern military feat and Israel's rudest military shock.

Cairo

Cairo had become very uncomfortable for Americans. A siege mentality developed inside the US Embassy in Cairo as reports came in from across the Arab world that demonstrators were gathering almost everywhere that the United States had posts or property. In Dharan, the oil capital of Saudi Arabia, mobs attacked US-owned installations. In Syria the US Consulate in Aleppo was attacked and burned. Ambassador Nolte cabled: 'Almost total defeat UAR [Egyptian] armed forces is beginning to sink in on populace . . . we think there is a danger situation here may deteriorate rapidly and that even if the government willing to protect us it may be unable to do so.' A liner was already on its way from Greece to evacuate 800

Americans, but Nolte was worried that it would be too slow. Edgily, he added a note for the commander of the Sixth Fleet. If necessary, did he have enough landing craft to pick them up from 'some beach west of Alexandria'?

The CIA produced a grim summary of what was happening for President Johnson. Americans in Jordan could become the targets of angry refugees from the West Bank. Nasser was refusing to accept the UN's ceasefire order. Israel seemed to be ignoring it on the Jordanian front. In Cairo the Egyptian leadership was in a state of panic. Nasser was 'desperate and might do almost anything to maintain his position'.

The English language *Egyptian Gazette* was still insisting that 'Arab Forces Inflict Big Losses on the Israelis' on its front page. The BBC was reporting that Jordan had accepted a ceasefire and Israel had reached the Suez canal, but Cairo Radio was still making the best of it. It claimed that UAR forces had regrouped at Sharm el Sheikh and had annihilated a regiment of Israeli paratroopers: 'Today Moshe Dayan, the mouse of the desert, is speechless . . . Our forces in Sinai have minced his armoured brigade, destroyed it and turned it into fragments and shambles of burnt iron.' In the streets radios blasted out military music in between news bulletins.

Moscow

The Egyptians had never been the most satisfactory allies for the Russians. For a start they found the West attractive, which made the Soviets feel second-best. A member of the Central Committee of the Soviet Communist Party remonstrated with Mohamed Heikal, Nasser's favourite journalist. 'We give you all this aid,' he said, 'but what do we get out of it? You still talk, and sometimes even write, like Westerners. Why, for example, are there no Soviet films on show in Cairo, but only American ones?'

Heikal replied that most Soviet films were mainly crude efforts about the Second World War, which Egyptians would not go to see.

The Russian was insistent. 'But if you used the right propaganda and educated people, they would be persuaded to go to them. In any case, even granting that people don't want to see our films, why should you let them see American films? These are poison. The result of showing them is that whenever the West chose to beckon, you'll go running to them.'

The Americans, on the other hand, were starting to look at Israel with new eyes. They were delighted that their ally was stronger than Russia's. Western weapons had beaten Soviet weapons. Richard Helms, the director of Central Intelligence, noted with relish that backing Egypt had turned into a bigger miscalculation for the Soviets than the Cuban missile crisis.

In Moscow post-mortems were starting about why Egypt had fallen apart so quickly. Before the war even started one Soviet ambassador was saying loudly enough for the CIA to overhear that the Arabs would lose because 'they are cowards'. He also could not understand why the USSR had given Egypt so many weapons. Another Soviet official grumbled to the CIA that Moscow had overestimated the Arabs and underestimated the Israelis. He claimed that the USSR had wanted to create another Vietnam for the Americans, but the plan backfired because the Egyptians were so incompetent. But most of the evidence from the Kremlin suggests it was reacting to events it could not control. The Russians were not asked about reimposing a blockade on Eilat. They tried to contain the war once it started, which was difficult because the Egyptians would not tell them the truth about what was happening. The Russians warned Nasser not to count on direct Soviet intervention.

The flip side of Egypt's untrue tale about British and American aircraft bombing them was anger at the Russians for not providing the same service against the Israelis. A columnist in the Cairo newspaper *Al Akhbar* dreamt of being able to turn every word he wrote into a deadly poison 'to pour down the throats' of Kosygin, Johnson and Harold Wilson.

Nablus

Qalqilya's population started arriving in Nablus during the night. Raymonda Hawa Tawil emerged from her cellar 'to find our house an island in a human sea. Astonished, I gaze out of the window at one of the most amazing, horrifying scenes I have ever beheld. Outside our house, in the road, in the olive groves, there are literally thousands of people – old, young, families with children, pregnant women, cripples. In their arms or on their backs they carry bundles with a few possessions. Young women clutch babies. Everywhere, the same exhausted broken figures, the stunned, desperate faces . . . people are sitting there weeping from misery, horror and frustration. Parents beg bread for their children.' She drove into Nablus in a car marked with a red cross to approach the Israelis for food for the refugees. 'Everywhere we see tanks, roadblocks, barbed wire. Some houses are on fire.' One of the women who were begging for food was the mother of Fayek Abdul Mezied. 'It was so humiliating for her to be reduced to begging. But she did it for us. I felt dispossessed and lost in my own homeland.' Thirty-five years later, remembering it made him weep.

Tawfik Mahmud Afaneh, the commander of Qalqilya's battered national guard detachment, had hung on in the town until Wednesday morning. Until one of his men found their positions empty, he had no idea that the remains of the Jordanian garrison had slipped away on Tuesday evening. They certainly had not told him. It was hopeless to carry on. He told his surviving men to save themselves and headed for the hills on foot with three of his fighters to try to find their families. They still carried their weapons and their last few magazines of bullets. The four men walked towards Nablus, stopping in villages along the way, asking if anyone had seen their wives and children. Once the villagers told them that the Israelis had smashed the Jordanian army, they buried their weapons. After eight days Tawfik found his family, hungry but unharmed, in a village south of Nablus. When he was with them, he started thinking about everything that had gone wrong. He had fought in Qalqilya to be part of what he had believed would be an Arab victory to avenge the catastrophe of 1948. He thought the Arab forces were strong. After all, Cairo Radio praised them almost every day. Tawfik was shocked by all the lies that the defeat had exposed, lies that Arab leaders told to their own people. He had done his best, he was happy to be back with his family, but he felt beaten and desperate.

Eleven-year-old Maa'rouf Zahran was with his family in Nablus. They had left Qalqilya on Monday, after loudspeakers from the Israeli side of the border told civilians to get out. On the way out, they found his lost sister. Until the shooting died away, Maa'rouf watched Jordanian soldiers and the national guardsmen firing at Israeli warplanes coming in low to attack. Then they hid in caves until it felt safe to move.

Bethlehem

On the first full day of the occupation, Israel was trying to win hearts and minds. Jeeps with loudspeakers toured the streets offering an amnesty for all weapons that were surrendered voluntarily. Samir Khouri, the owner of a restaurant, handed in his old revolver at the Town Hall. For him the beginning of the occupation was not painful. 'The first Israelis behaved well, distributed food and some of the soldiers spoke Arabic. Before the war there were demonstrations almost every week against the king. The Jordanians weren't bad – we felt we lived in peace and Jordanians and Palestinians married each other – but the government was a different matter. At first many people thought the Israelis were better than the Jordanians. It wasn't too bad until the 1973 war, tourists came, life was good, but the Israelis put up taxes and made life harder. Then we started to think in a different way about the occupation.'

Fifteen miles to the south Lieutenant-Colonel Zvi Ofer, the commander of the battalion of the Jerusalem Brigade that captured Hebron, was trying to set up a local military government. First he organised a ceremony for the mayor formally to surrender the town. Details of the curfews were sent to the mosques so that the muezzins could proclaim them from the minarets.

Jerusalem

Nazmi Al-Ju'beh, a studious twelve-year-old Palestinian boy, looked down from his grandfather's house on to the Moroccan quarter. The district was right next to the Wailing Wall, which was supposed to be off-limits to Israeli civilians. Soldiers flouted the rule, bringing in their friends and families to line up alongside official parties of VIPs to marvel at Israel's new possession. As far as Nazmi could see, soldiers were everywhere, in the alleys and on the flat roofs of the old houses. His older relatives were jumpy and miserable. The sight of the Israeli flag flying on the Dome of the Rock brought home to them what had happened. But Nazmi was fascinated and intrigued by the Israeli soldiers. They were the first Jews he had ever seen. Like so many others, some of his neighbours thought they were Iraqis when they appeared in the Old City. One old neighbour of his grandfather's prepared a pot of tea for the men who he assumed were his liberators. With a smile and a spring in his step for a man of his age, he arranged it on a tray with some glasses and took it out to them. Just as he was preparing to welcome his Iraqi saviours, the soldiers yelled at him in broken Arabic to go home. They spoke with rasping Hebrew accents. The old man retreated, confused and still carrying the tray of tea. He sat on his step with the tray next to him muttering 'go home, go home', as if the phrase could help him understand what had gone wrong.

Among the euphoric Israelis at the Wall that morning was a party led by Mayor Kollek. He believed Israel should and would never give up what it had captured, and he dreamt of peace, on the grounds that 'the Arabs will have learned that they cannot fight us and win'. Kollek invited his group, including Ben-Gurion and a member of the Rothschild banking family, which had been among the Jewish state's strongest supporters, back to lunch at his home. There, Ben-Gurion punctured his host's mood. 'This is not the end of the war,' he said. 'The Arabs cannot take such a defeat and such humiliation. They will never accept it.' Ben-Gurion wanted Kollek to demolish the city walls, to integrate it properly into Jewish Jerusalem. If the walls stayed up he warned it would always feel like a place apart, tempting the Palestinians to think they could get it back. His suggestion was not taken up.

Suez canal, 1200

Tanks from Tal's division reached the Suez canal. The Egyptians had tried to delay them, their tanks opening fire from behind sand dunes with just their guns and turrets showing. Other tanks were deployed further away from the roads to ambush the Israelis if they tried to outflank them. But Colonel Shmuel Gonen, the commander of the lead brigade, saw what was happening. He sent two companies of tanks through the dunes while a battalion moved ahead in a column down the road. Once again the Israelis used their skills in long-range gunnery to blast the Egyptians. By the end of the morning the Israelis had lost five tanks and knocked out fifty. Among Israel's dead was Major Shamai Kaplan, the accordion-playing tank commander who back in 1964 had made his men sing to warm themselves up when they were waiting to attack the Syrians.

Sinai coast, 1230

It was another beautiful early summer morning. Visibility was perfect. Around twenty miles from the coast in international waters was an American naval spy ship called the USS *Liberty*. The officers on the bridge could just see the minaret on the mosque at Al-Arish on the horizon. As usual reveille had sounded at 6:00 a.m., but for an hour before that, since just after dawn, Israeli planes had been flying close to the *Liberty*, taking a strong interest in a ship that was dangerously close to the Sinai war zone. James Ennes was officer of the deck for the morning watch, from eight to midday, responsible for the ship's log. He reckoned the Israelis flew directly over the ship six to eight times, once at less than 200 feet. Before he went off watch he noted the Israeli overflights and, according to US Navy regulations, signed and dated the entry.

The *Liberty* was loosely attached to the American Sixth Fleet, the most formidable naval force in the Mediterranean. But its two aircraft carriers with all their support ships were 500 miles away, well away from the action. The *Liberty* was on her own, and unarmed, except for four .50 calibre Browning machine guns, but its crew was not worried. Lieutenant Lloyd Painter, a young American naval officer, felt reassured by the presence of the Israelis. He looked out over one of the upper decks. It was a peaceful scene. Off-duty officers were sunbathing. He felt 'good and warm inside that we were safe, that we weren't strangers here'. On 8 June the *Liberty* was steaming in what the US Navy called a 'modified condition of readiness three'. That meant its normal watch was on deck, plus one man standing at the forward gun mounts. Men from the bridge would run to man the two after guns if, in an emergency, general quarters sounded.

The *Liberty* had started life as a freighter in the Second World War. But by 1967 it had been comprehensively rebuilt into one of the most advanced spy ships in the world, one of about a dozen that the United States always had cruising the oceans. It listened in to radio transmissions. According to one of its crewmen, 'If it was broadcast on a radio wave, we could receive it, on any frequency.' The *Liberty* was a highly distinctive, unusual-looking ship, festooned with aerials and an ultra-modern microwave dish.

The *Liberty* had been redeployed from a patrol along the West African coast when the crisis in the Middle East blew up. On 8 June it had just arrived on its new station, sailing slowly up and down the coast of Sinai, shuttling roughly between Al-Arish and Port Said. The *Liberty* took its orders from the US Navy, but the technicians it carried were under the control of the National Security Agency. The NSA is one of the most secret parts of the US government. It eavesdrops on the world's communications. In the 1960s it was a vital part of the Cold War with the USSR and the hot war in Vietnam. On 8 June 294 men were on board the *Liberty*. Around two-thirds of them had very little to do with sailing the ship. They were technical experts – linguists, radio engineers, cryptographers. While they were on duty they stayed below in front of a great array of scopes, scanners and monitors. There were also three civilians from the NSA, including an Arabic linguist, and three US Marines who were specialists in Arabic and Russian.

Just after 1300 the *Liberty*'s captain, William McGonagle, sounded general quarters. It was a drill. The crew ran to take up the posts they would man in an emergency. They were patrolling at five knots, which was the best speed for their technical gear to suck intelligence out of the radio waves. But Captain McGonagle did not want them to have the idea that this was some sort of leisurely Mediterranean cruise. After all, they were only twenty miles from a war zone. Once the exercise was over, though, off-duty men went back to sunbathing. The crew of the *Liberty* prided themselves on the fact that they were different. They enjoyed their posting and were proud of their ship. There was a cook-out on the ship's fan-tail every Sunday. For young conscripts who had friends who were foot soldiers in Vietnam it seemed a pretty good way of doing their national duty.

That morning, orders were sent from Washington for the *Liberty* to move further away from the coast. But there was an error in transmission. Before they arrived, the *Liberty* was destroyed by Israel's air force and navy. Between 1400 and 1430 around two-thirds of the ship's company became casualties. Thirty-four men were killed and 172 wounded. How it happened is well documented. Why it happened is still a matter of bitter dispute.

At 1350 a flight of two Israeli Mirages, codenamed Kursa, was contacted by Colonel Shmuel Kislev, the chief air controller at the military headquarters in Tel Aviv. (Their exchanges were taped.) He told Yigal, one of the pilots, that he had a ship at 'location 26. Take Kursa over there. If it's a warship, blast it.' In the Israeli air control room there were some doubts about their target's identity. Three minutes later another officer, a weapons controller, can be heard asking, 'What is it? An American?' In later testimony the officer said that he was convinced the Egyptians would not send a solitary warship so close to a coastline now held by Israel. According to Aaron Bregman, an Israeli scholar who has listened to the tapes, Colonel Kislev is then heard picking up a phone and calling an unnamed superior officer. Referring to the suggestion that the ship could be American, he asks, 'What do you say?' The answer is, 'I don't say.' The tone, according to Bregman, is 'I don't want to know'. Another three minutes later, at 1356, the leader of the two Mirages asks permission to attack. Colonel Kislev does not order them to establish its identity. All he says, impatiently, is, 'I have already said: if this is a warship . . . to attack.'

Lookouts on the *Liberty* saw the Mirages. They were not worried, assuming it was another reconnaissance flight. Using radar, the ship's position was fixed as 25.5 nautical miles away from the minaret at Al-Arish, which was to the south-east. It was in international waters. Commander McGonagle believed they were safe. The *Liberty*'s name and identification numbers were clearly marked, a stars and stripes flag measuring five feet by eight was flying and it had been identified by the earlier overflights. Lloyd Painter, who had been so reassured earlier by the Israeli presence, was looking at them through a porthole when he realised that they had levelled off and were approaching the ship as if they were attacking. Red flashes were coming from under their wings. The shells from the Mirages' 30 mm cannon exploded into the ship. Painter's porthole was blown out into his chest. The man looking through the next one along was hit in the face. Most of the men on the bridge were knocked off their feet. The helmsman was badly wounded. Quartermaster third class Troy Brown immediately took the wheel. Later, he was killed. Commander McGonagle grabbed the engine room telegraph and rang up all ahead flank, the order for maximum speed.

The *Liberty*'s radio operators were trying to get an SOS to the Sixth Fleet. They had two big problems. The Israelis were jamming them, and the ship's complex system of antennas was being blasted away. James Halman, one of the radio operators, kept repeating the message, using the *Liberty*'s call sign. 'Any station, this is Rockstar, we are under attack by unidentified jet aircraft and require assistance.'

At 1359 the leader of the Kursa flight reported back to Tel Aviv: 'We have hit her very hard. Black smoke is coming out. Oil is spilling out of her into the water. Splendid . . . extraordinary. She is burning. She is burning.' Two minutes later: 'OK, I have finished. I have just finished my ammunition. The ship is burning . . . very big and black smoke.'

The *Liberty* was still trying to send an SOS. Lieutenant Commander Dave Lewis, in charge of the NSA operation on board, believes the Israelis targeted their communications gear. 'The only reason we got an SOS out was that my crazy troops were climbing the deck stringing long wires while they were being shot at.' USS *Saratoga*, one of the Sixth Fleet's two aircraft carriers, acknowledged their distress calls at 1409. The *Liberty*'s radio operators repeated their message: 'Schematic, this is Rockstar. We are still under attack by unidentified jet aircraft and require immediate assistance.' *Saratoga* wanted an authentication code that had been destroyed. 'Listen to the goddamn rockets, you son of a bitch!' the radio operator yelled back.

In Tel Aviv the air controller Kislev ordered another flight, this time of two Super Mysteres to take up the attack. 'You can sink her,' he told them. They raked the decks and the antennas and dropped canisters of napalm, which exploded throwing out burning jelly and clouds of thick black smoke. Fuel tanks on the ship's whaler exploded. At 1414 one of the pilots asks about the ship's nationality. They had read the ship's markings which were marked in Western numbers, not Arabic ones. Kislev says twice that it is 'probably American'. Twelve minutes later, at 1426, three Israeli motor torpedo boats arrived. The *Liberty* is identified again as Egyptian and they attack it with five torpedoes. From the bridge Captain McGonagle screamed a warning into the public address system. Gary Brummett was below decks. 'When we received word that a torpedo was going to hit us starboard side and stand by to abandon ship, I personally knew I would never see my friends in Louisiana again or drink another cold beer. At twenty, those are important events. I blew my life vest up . . . and awaited what

I thought would be somewhat like a crawfish boil and [we] were the crawfish.' Only one torpedo hit, which probably saved the ship. The force of the explosion picked the *Liberty* out of the water. When it came down it was listing to starboard with a huge hole in its side. The five-feet-by-eight stars and stripes that the *Liberty* was flying was shredded with most of the ship. It was replaced five minutes before the torpedo attack by an even bigger one, seven feet by thirteen.

Washington DC, 0950 (1750 Egypt, 1650 Israel)

Walt Rostow dictated a message for President Johnson, warning there was a 'flash report . . . a US elint [electronics intelligence] ship, the LIBERTY, has been torpedoed in the Mediterranean . . . we have no knowledge of the submarine or surface vessel which committed this act.' An hour or so later the US defence attaché in Tel Aviv told them Israel had carried out the attack. Drily, the last line of Rostow's note to Johnson said that the 'Tel Aviv message appears to be apology for mistaken action'.

After the initial SOS, radio operators in the Sixth Fleet could not get through to the *Liberty*. The fleet prepared to take action. Pilots were mustered in their briefing room. The assumption was that the ship was being attacked by Soviet forces. The pilots were told the *Liberty* was right on the edge of the Egyptian twelve-mile limit. Rules of engagement were issued. They ordered them to 'use force including destruction as necessary to control the situation. Do not use more force than required. Do not pursue any unit toward land for reprisal purposes . . . counter-attack is to protect *Liberty* only.'

Washington DC, 1013

The commander of the Sixth Fleet reported to Washington that he was launching four armed A-4 bombers from the USS *America* and four A-1s with fighter cover from USS *Saratoga*. Two destroyers were also ordered to get to the *Liberty* at full speed. USS *America*'s ready aircraft, A-4 bombers, were armed with nuclear weapons. They were recalled soon after they were launched. The fleet commander asked permission to send other, conventionally armed aircraft. Permission was refused. Secretary of Defense Robert McNamara came on the line from Washington to give the order.

Cairo, 1845; Washington DC, 1045

In the US Embassy in Cairo it was about the worst news they could get. They assumed the *Liberty* had been feeding information to the Israelis. After the allegations of collusion with Israel on air strikes, Ambassador Nolte already felt that every American in town was in danger from the Cairo mob. Tersely, he cabled: 'We had better get out our story on the torpedoing of USS *Liberty* fast and it had better be good.' The Egyptians seized on the attack as evidence that they had been right all along. On Cairo Radio Ahmed Said accepted Israel's story that the destruction of the *Liberty* had been an accident, because it proved one thing: 'Arabs . . . we are fighting against the USA.'

Washington DC, 1645

In the Situation Room at the White House a soldier called Baker scrawled the latest information on the *Liberty* from the National Military Command Center on a telephone pad. '10 killed, about 100 wounded – (1 doctor aboard, just hasn't been able to complete rounds on all) 15–25 wounded seriously (so far) Liberty should rendevouz [sic] with elements 6th Fleet around midnight EDT.'

The next morning the NSC Special Committee met in angry mood to discuss what happened to the *Liberty*. Clark Clifford, a Washington lawyer who had been a presidential adviser since the 1940s, was concerned that the US was not being tough enough on Israel. It was an 'egregious' attack. It was, he told them, 'inconceivable that it was an accident'. There were three strafing passes and three torpedo boats in attendance. The Israelis responsible should be punished. In the sheaf of handwritten notes torn from a legal pad that records the meeting, 'President subscribed 100%' is noted in the margin. Ambassador Lucius Battle thought the attack 'incomprehensible'. Secretary of State Rusk said the US should 'do what is normal'. Israel needed to pay reparations, punish those responsible and ensure there was no repetition of the attack. Dean Rusk always believed the *Liberty* had been attacked in the full knowledge that it was an American ship. Before he died, he said that 'the sustained attack to disable and sink *Liberty* precluded an assault by accident or by some trigger-happy local commander . . . I didn't believe them then, and I don't believe them to this day. The attack was outrageous.'

Letters of apology from the Israeli diplomats started to arrive for the president. Ambassador Avraham Harman expressed 'heartfelt sorrow at the tragic accident for which my countrymen were responsible . . . I write to you in desolation.' Abba Eban was 'deeply mortified and grieved by the tragic accident'. Secretary of State Rusk replied tersely that the attack was 'quite literally incomprehensible, an act of military recklessness reflecting wanton disregard for human life'. Israel's first response to Rusk's note was considered by the Americans to be so aggressive that they told the Israelis that they wanted it withdrawn and rewritten 'in a more moderate vein'. It contained statements 'they might find it hard to live with if the text some day became public'. It is still secret.

Israel accepted full responsibility for what had happened, insisting that regrettable but honest mistakes, made in the heat of battle, came together to cause the incident. It started, they said, with a series of what turned out to be false reports from the navy and air force that Israeli positions in Al-Arish were being shelled from the sea. Then, somehow they lost track of the *Liberty* after it had been positively identified as American earlier in the day. Mistakenly, they thought the ship was travelling at thirty knots, not five knots, leading to the wrong conclusion that it was an enemy warship. It was then mistaken for the Egyptian transport *Quseir*.

A fierce controversy about the *Liberty* still goes on, fuelled by the fact that many documents about what happened have still not been declassified. Some of Israel's supporters have dismissed claims made by the survivors of the attack as sad delusions of traumatised ex-servicemen. Clark Clifford, who was one of Israel's staunchest supporters in US administrations from the 1940s to the 1970s, wrote a report on the incident for Johnson that was kept secret for thirty-four years. On the face of it, it upheld the Israeli position that there had been a series of terrible of mistakes, though Clark put it more strongly, condemning 'gross and inexcusable failures ... the unprovoked attack on the *Liberty* constitutes a flagrant act of gross negligence for which the Israeli government should be completely responsible, and the Israeli military personnel involved should be punished.' But Clark's analysis of Israel's explanations raises more questions than it answers. He did not have any evidence that top people in the Israeli government knew an American ship was being attacked. But, he implies, that did not mean that they did not know. 'To disprove such a theory would necessitate a degree of access to Israeli personnel and information which in all likelihood can never be achieved.' This was more than a Washington lawyer choosing his words carefully. In his memoirs he wrote that it was 'unlikely that the full truth will ever come out. Having been for so long a staunch supporter of Israel, I was particularly troubled by this incident; I could not bring myself to believe that such an action could have been authorized by Levi Eshkol. Yet somewhere inside the Israeli government, somewhere along the chain of command, something had gone terribly wrong – and then had been covered up. I never felt the Israelis made adequate restitution or explanation for their actions.'

In July 1967, three days after Clark's report was delivered to Johnson, an inquiry by an Israeli military judge, Colonel Yeshayahu Yerushalami decided there were no grounds for disciplinary action against the Israeli officers connected with the attack on the *Liberty*. His report reads like a legal closing of ranks, the product of a system going through the motions to satisfy its obligations to the United States rather than one driven by a desire to get to the bottom of what really happened. Yerushalami's report had a generous, even elastic interpretation of 'reasonable' behaviour from a soldier in wartime. For example, the divisional commander who directed the torpedo attack from one of the boats, told the judge that he had not received an order at 1420 stating, 'Do not attack. It is possible that the aircraft have not identified correctly.' Yerushalami observed that the order was entered into the log book of the divisional commander's vessel and into the war diary of the Naval Operations Branch. His deputy commander testified that he received the order and passed it to him. Yet the torpedo attack went ahead.

As well as Rusk and Clifford, many other senior American officials did not buy Israel's explanations. Richard Helms, the director of Central Intelligence in 1967, believed the attack was intentional: 'No excuse can be found for saying it was just a mistake.' Lucius Battle, an assistant secretary of state in the Johnson administration, concluded there was a cover-up. Admiral Thomas Moorer, who later became chairman of the US Joint Chiefs of Staff, wrote that responsibility for the cover-up should be shared between the US government and the Israelis. He could not accept the Israeli claim of mistaken identity: 'I have flown for many years in both war and peace on surveillance flights over the ocean, and my opinion is supported by a full career of locating and identifying ships at sea.'

Many of their doubts are based on the fact that the IDF seemed so efficient in everything else it did that it was inconceivable that it could make such a grotesque series of 'mistakes' in broad daylight. Perhaps their view of the IDF in 1967 was wrong. It was daring, well organised and highly motivated. It was also used to fighting appallingly prepared and ill-led armies, which allowed it to get away with mistakes when they were made. Israeli fire discipline is another factor. It has always been sloppy. A serviceman on one of the motor torpedo boats that attacked the *Liberty* now accepts they were 'inexperienced and probably a little trigger happy and it was a war zone'.

266

Still, if Israel did in fact know what it was doing when it destroyed an American ship, as so many veterans of the Johnson administration believed, why did it do what it did? Some theories revolve around the theme of collusion between Israel and the United States. They speculate that pro-Israel elements in the United States military had plotted with Israelis to create an incident that could draw the US into the war. Greg Reight, a former US air force man, claimed on a BBC documentary that he was part of a US photo-reconnaissance team that flew covert missions on behalf of the Israelis from a base in the Negev desert. The crews wore uniforms without badges and 'there was a hurry-up paint job done to the aircraft so they would be like Israeli aircraft'. If his allegations are true, it means that Nasser's accusations of collusion between Israel and the US were correct.

For Assistant Secretary of State Lucius Battle the most likely explanation is that Israel feared the *Liberty* was 'listening in to some conversations and other things that were going on that they didn't want us to know about . . . they had been engaged in some pretty outlandish stuff in the course of the war. I don't think they wanted us to know the detail of that.'

Kuwait

As the size of the defeat became clearer, Arab leaders started to feel vulnerable. The Amir of Kuwait seemed dazed when he received G. C. Arthur, the British ambassador. Arthur asked him for the latest on the fate of the Kuwaiti troops who had been sent to Egypt. 'He said he had no idea. He did not seem to care.' Instead, he 'kept asking what I thought would happen to King Hussein.' The Saudi ruling family had similar fears. The Amir said he did not believe that the British and the Americans had intervened on Israel's behalf. Perhaps he was starting to feel the need for Britain's well-established role as guarantor of his family's power. Kuwait had a big and hard-working Palestinian population. In the 1950s it included Yasser Arafat, who founded his faction Fatah there in 1957. Wealthy native Kuwaitis needed them but the Palestinians made them nervous. Before the fighting started, a serious suggestion was made in the National Assembly that Kuwait's contribution to the war effort could be to conscript its Palestinians and to send them into battle. British diplomats asked who would run the country in their absence. Twenty-four years later, after the Gulf War in 1991, the Kuwaitis seized their chance to expel thousands of Palestinians who had spent their lives in Kuwait, because of Yasser Arafat's support for Saddam Hussein.

Tel Aviv, 1900

General David Elazar, head of Israel's Northern Command, was 'beside himself with anger and frustration'. On Thursday evening he went to Tel Aviv to see Rabin, to press yet again for the order to do to Syria what was being done to Egypt and Jordan. Elazar could not believe that Syria, Israel's most bitter enemy before the war, had not been attacked. It was now or never. If Syria was not dealt with, the war was over. Prime Minister Eshkol summoned the cabinet defence committee. They had to decide. Eshkol and most of the cabinet were in favour. Moshe Dayan argued the case against attacking Syria in what he called 'the most extreme terms'. If Israel attacked Syria, he told them, it risked a war with the Soviet Union. Moscow would protect its friends in Damascus. A less than veiled threat had been made by the Soviet ambassador Sergei Chuvakhin on 6 June. He told the West German ambassador in Tel Aviv that Israel should stop its attacks immediately. If the Israelis, 'drunk with success', did not, 'the future of this little country will be a very sad one'. The West German, worried, passed the information straight to the Israelis, with a warning not to do anything more than seize the high ground near the border. America's ambassador Barbour thought the West Germans were getting over anxious. He thought the Israelis would penetrate twenty-five kilometres into Syria.

Much to Dayan's irritation, a deputation from the thirty-one front-line Jewish settlements close to the border with Syria was ushered into the cabinet room. They had been lobbying hard for war with Syria and now had the chance to argue their case in person. Dayan pretended they were not there. He 'went to sit in the back of the room, put his feet up and fell asleep'. Yaakov Eshkoli, one of the kibbutz leaders, could see it would be risky to attack Moscow's closest ally in the region. But it was a risk worth taking. He told the cabinet that if the IDF did not push the Syrians out of the Heights that overlooked their settlements, he would tell all his people to pack their bags and leave. Levi Eshkol, the prime minister, and most of the other elderly men around the cabinet table were Zionists who had come to Palestine when they were young men fresh out of Eastern Europe. Many of them had spent their lives pushing out the frontier of the Jewish settlement by establishing pioneering communities in hostile areas that they made their own. The settlers' words hit home. Eshkoli saw some of the ministers wiping away tears after he and the others had spoken emotionally about how their families had been forced by shelling to spend days in shelters. But Dayan refused to allow an attack on Syria. He was not persuaded by the settlers, who he said later were just interested in grabbing good farmland.

Elazar was astounded when Rabin told him there would be no attack on Syria. 'What has happened to this country? How will we ever be able to face ourselves, the people, the settlements? After all the trouble they've caused, are those arrogant bastards going to be left on top of the hills riding on our backs?' Rabin, on Dayan's orders, denied his request to evacuate non-combatants from the border, though he allowed children out of the front line.

Late on Thursday evening a frustrated David Elazar called Elad Peled, who was supposed to command the main effort in the attack on Syria. Elazar had been pushing hard for permission to start the offensive, but now he was ready to give up. He told Peled to sleep in his headquarters in Nablus. The war is nearly over, he told him, they've decided not to attack Syria. Just before dawn, Yaakov Eshkoli stopped at Elazar's bunker on his way home and told him about the meeting with the cabinet.

Eshkol was starting to relax. During the day he made a euphoric speech to the leaders of Mapai, his political party. He agreed with a newspaper headline that said 'Israel Reborn', only he hoped not to have to go through such a traumatic rebirth again. 'Maybe it's a decisive time from which a new order should be born . . . so we'll be able to sit safely in our homes on our land.' But the war was not over yet. Moshe Dayan had other ideas.

New York, 2035

Egypt accepted the terms of the ceasefire resolution passed by the Security Council the day before. At least 10,000 Egyptian soldiers and 1500 officers became casualties, probably split evenly between men killed and wounded in battle and those who died of heat stroke or thirst in the desert. Eighty per cent of the Egyptian army's equipment was destroyed or captured. That included 10,000 trucks, 400 field guns, 50 self-propelled guns, 30 155 mm guns and 700 tanks.

DAY 5

9 June 1967

Ministry of Defence, Tel Aviv

After the cabinet meeting, Moshe Dayan went to the army headquarters. He spent most of the night in the Pit, the underground war room. It was quiet. None of the senior commanders was there. The war seemed almost over. Dayan was still holding forth about why Syria should be left alone. But sometime around 0600 he read a telegram intercepted by Israeli intelligence on its way from Cairo to Damascus, in which Nasser told Syria's President Atassi that he was about to accept the UN ceasefire and he recommended that Syria do the same. Other intelligence reports said that the Syrian army was collapsing, and that Damascus was grabbing at the chance of a ceasefire so it could avoid what had happened to Jordan and Egypt. Dayan debated the point for a few minutes with some of the junior officers, who told him not to miss a historic chance.

Dayan changed his mind. Without bothering to tell Prime Minister Eshkol or Chief of Staff Rabin, he picked up a secure phone and called Brigadier-General Elazar direct. When Dayan asked him if he could attack, he nearly fell out of his chair. Elazar said he could, 'right now'. 'Then attack,' Dayan ordered.

Rabin never knew exactly what was going through Dayan's mind that night. Assuming that the cabinet decision not to attack Syria meant the war was more or less over, he had gone home to sleep. The first he knew of Dayan's conversion was when Ezer Weizman phoned him at seven in the morning to tell him that, fifteen minutes earlier, Dayan had ordered Elazar on to the offensive. As minister of defence, Dayan should have told his chief of staff first. But even if the decision had been taken the wrong way, Rabin had 'no desire to quibble when the Syrians were about to get their just deserts for malicious aggression and arrogance'. Eshkol also found out at seven. He was angry. Dayan had violated the agreement they had made when he was appointed that was supposed to rein him in. But since Eshkol had wanted to capture the Golan Heights all along, he accepted it.

Nonetheless, when the cabinet defence committee assembled at 9:30, Dayan had some explaining to do. The interior minister Haim Moshe Shapira fiercely criticised Dayan and demanded the attack be stopped immediately. But however much the rest of the committee resented Dayan's high-handed decision-making, they liked the decision too much to try to unpick it. Later, Dayan said it was one of the worst decisions he ever made. (The other was allowing Jewish settlers into the West Bank town of Hebron.)

Elazar passed what for him was the best news he had heard all week to Peled's divisional headquarters in Nablus. Peled told him he would move north as quickly as he could. It was going to take a few hours to get his forces to their start lines. His men were going to take the southern sector. Two other thrusts would come further north. Israeli sappers were already clearing paths through minefields on the border. It was harder on their own side. The heavy rain that fell every winter washed the mines away, so in spring they had to be replaced. The Israelis had been more conscientious about doing it than the Syrians, who had left great holes.

All week the Syrians had shelled Israeli border settlements. By Thursday evening they had hit 205 houses, 9 chicken coops, 2 tractor sheds, 3 clubhouses, a dining-hall, 6 barns, 30 tractors and 15 cars. They had also managed to burn down 175 acres of fruit orchards and

75 acres of grain. Two Israelis had been killed and sixteen wounded. But since Syria had accepted the UN ceasefire at 5:20 p.m. the previous day, there had been a lull. Orders had gone out from Damascus to cease fire. Armour was pulled back from the front towards Damascus. The danger from Israel seemed to be receding, so the Syrian regime returned to its standard operating procedure of guarding against the actions of its own people or discontented officers.

Israel was going to have to violate the ceasefire to attack Syria, but no-one on their side minded. One Israeli paratrooper commented: 'We all wanted to have a go at the Syrians. We didn't much mind about the Egyptians. We have a certain respect for the Jordanians, but our biggest score was with the Syrians – they had been shelling our kibbutzim for the past nineteen years.' The air strikes restarted, and so, in response, did the Syrian shelling. Elazar's forces had been kept in the rear, out of range of Syrian artillery. On Friday morning they moved forward towards their start lines for the attack.

Suez, 0800

The town of Suez was in a state of complete confusion. The remnants of units that had escaped from the Sinai were mixed up with individual soldiers who had somehow found their own way back to relative safety. Brigadier Abdel Moneim Khalil, commander of a brigade of paratroops that he had pulled out, relatively intact, from the Sinai, called Field Marshal Amer at GHQ in Cairo. Only twenty-four hours earlier Amer, panicked and desperately improvising, had tried to give him the command of two brigades, one armoured and the other of mechanised infantry. Khalil had ignored Amer's orders, which now seemed to have been forgotten by the field marshal. When Khalil described the chaos in Suez, Amer immediately told him he was in command. Khalil decided that not much was to be gained by more conversations with Amer. He deployed his paratroops in defensive positions around the town and called the chief of staff General Fawzi to tell him what he had done.

273

Cairo Radio was playing emotional, sad music. Song after song was about tragic love of country, about the place reserved for Egypt in the blood and hearts of its people. Abd al-Hamid Sharaf, the Jordanian information minister, heard the broadcast in Amman. 'Listen to what they're playing,' he told his wife Leila. 'They're preparing the people.' He was convinced Nasser had killed himself. For millions of Arabs across the Middle East who idolised Nasser, the reality was almost as bad. He was going to resign. Mohamed Heikal, the editor of *al-Ahram* and Nasser's long-serving voice, was already writing the resignation speech. Nasser's advisers were horrified. In the Arab world, when the leader goes, his court tends to go with him. Around midday an announcement was made that the president would address his people at 7:30. Across the Arab world people turned on their televisions and tuned in their radios, prepared for something momentous.

Sinai

Winston Churchill, grandson of Britain's wartime leader, who was covering the war for the London *Evening News* and the *News of the World*, was flown to Bir Gifgafah to visit Brigadier General Sharon. After lunch, Sharon took him on a tour of his positions in the desert, his driver racing at the highest speeds possible along bumpy desert tracks. Suddenly, in the distance, they saw a line of exhausted-looking Egyptians walking in the general direction of the Suez canal. Sharon leapt to the heavy machine gun that was mounted on the jeep. 'He was like a demon possessed . . . firing as we careered over the desert. We were bumping so much that he probably didn't connect . . . but the intention was there . . .' Later, an ebullient Sharon tried a pun: 'Winston, we have peace – a piece of Egypt . . .'

Thousands of Egyptians surrendered. Many were released to find their own way back to the Suez canal. Some injured men were well treated. A few weeks after the war, Uri Oren wrote a piece for Israel's mass circulation daily, *Yediot Ahronoth*, describing how he came upon a wounded Egyptian soldier who had been abandoned by his unit. (Every Israeli reader knew that the IDF had an unshakeable policy of never leaving their wounded on the battlefield.) The wounded man looked at Oren 'in supplication', begging for his life. 'I knew immediately,' Oren wrote, 'that I would not dare to cut it off. There were too many corpses lying around, and the man – the odour of decay already came from him. I had no greater desire than to return him to life. It was not "one soldier less", the slogan of battle, but "one corpse less", the rule of life.' Oren rescued the man and turned him over to the medics. A few days later, when he tried to visit him in hospital, he was told that the man had been transferred to the Red Cross for repatriation. He had left for Oren the photographs of his wife and children, which had kept him going for three days while he was waiting to be rescued. On the back he dedicated them to 'my brother fighters, restorers of life'.

But according to Israeli witnesses and historians, and Egyptian survivors, Oren's new friend was an exception rather than the rule. Aryeh Yitzhaki, an Israeli historian, said that after the war, while he was working in the army's history department, he collected testimonies from dozens of soldiers who admitted killing prisoners. Yitzhaki claimed around 900 Egyptian and Palestinians were killed after they surrendered. The worst massacre, Yitzhaki says, was on Friday and Saturday, the fifth and sixth days of the war, at Al-Arish. He says it started when Egyptian prisoners opened fire after they had surrendered, killing two Israeli soldiers. That made the Israeli soldiers angry. They 'fired at every Egyptian and Palestinian for several hours. Commanders lost control over the force.' Yitzhaki says his evidence is locked in a safe at Israeli military headquarters. 'The whole leadership, including defence minister Moshe Dayan and chief of staff Rabin and the generals knew about these things. No one bothered to denounce them.' Some of the soldiers alleged to have taken part in the massacre were in a unit commanded by Binyamin Ben Eliezer, who became the leader of the Israeli Labour Party and defence minister in Ariel Sharon's first coalition government in 2001. Another Israeli historian, Uri Milstein, said many Egyptians were killed in other incidents after they had surrendered. 'It was not official policy, but there was an atmosphere that it was OK to do it. Some commanders decided to do it, others refused. But everyone knew about it.'

Declassified IDF documents show that the operations branch of the general staff felt it necessary on 11 June, the day after the war ended, to issue new orders about the treatment of prisoners. The order read: 'Since existing orders are contradictory, here are binding instructions. a) Soldiers and civilians who give themselves up are not to be hurt in any way. b) Soldiers and civilians who carry a weapon and do not surrender will be killed.' The order concluded: 'Soldiers who are caught disobeying this order by killing prisoners will be punished severely. Make sure this order is brought to the attention of all IDF soldiers.' Meir Pail, who was General Tal's number two in the Sinai, said men who killed prisoners or civilians were sentenced secretly by military courts and sent to prison. 'The idea was that it is better to deal with this in the closed circle of the military.'

An Israeli journalist called Gabby Bron, who was a reservist in the 1967 war, saw hundreds of Egyptian prisoners of war being held at the airfield at Al-Arish. On 7 June around 150 of them were in a sandbagged enclosure inside an aircraft hangar, packed in tight and sitting on the ground with their hands on the back of their necks. Next to the compound sat two Israeli soldiers at a table. They were wearing steel helmets and sunglasses, and most of their faces were covered by khaki-coloured handkerchiefs. Every few minutes, military police brought a prisoner out of the compound. Bron watched what was happening.

'The POW was escorted to a distance of about 100 metres from the building and given a spade. I watched the POW digging a big pit which took about fifteen minutes. Then the policemen ordered him to throw out the spade. When he did so one of them pointed his Uzi machine gun inside the pit and shot two bursts, consisting mainly of three to four bullets each. The POW fell dead. After a few minutes another POW was escorted to the same pit, forced to go into it and also shot dead.' An officer, a Colonel Eshel, appeared and shouted at Bron and other soldiers who were watching. When they did not move he pulled out his revolver. They moved. Later Bron was told that the soldiers at the table were identifying Palestinian fedayeen who had murdered Jews and disguised themselves as Egyptians.

After Egypt regained Sinai as a result of the Camp David peace agreements, a number of mass graves were discovered in Sinai. Bahjat Farag, a police general, discovered a grave outside Ras Sudr hospital which contained the remains of fifteen soldiers in special forces uniforms. In Al-Arish a former prisoner called Abdel Salam Mohammed Ibrahim Moussa claimed to have buried twenty prisoners who had been shot. Human rights organisations in Egypt have collected dozens of testimonies from former soldiers and civilians which accuse the Israelis of ill-treating prisoners and shooting some of them dead. Ironically it was something the Egyptian government had never pursued. It took the publication of the Israeli stories of killing to start them looking.

Syria–Israel border, 1130

Colonel Albert Mendler's armoured brigade, followed later by infantrymen from the Golani Brigade, crossed the northern end of the border into Syria near the settlement of Kfar Szold. Like every Israeli attack, the plan had been worked on, refined and perfected for years. It was helped enormously by intelligence from Eli Cohen, a Mossad agent who infiltrated the heart of the Syrian regime. He was executed in the centre of Damascus in 1965, but the damage was done. Their assault was up some of the most difficult terrain in the area. It looked nearby impassable, so the Syrians had concentrated more of their troops further south. The Israeli force had to work their way up steep, rocky slopes to get to a ridge 1500 feet above them.

Mendler's armour followed eight unarmoured bulldozers. They zigzagged up the slope, clearing the way for the tanks and the infantry who were following in half-tracks. The Syrians had no air cover and they faced the heaviest air attacks of the entire war. Israeli warplanes flew 1077 ground attack assaults against the Syrians, more than against Jordan and Egypt. But the Syrian bunkers were well protected, with grooves in the concrete that funnelled napalm away. The Syrian gunners kept up heavy fire, causing serious Israeli casualties. Three of the bulldozers were destroyed. All of them lost crews. Tanks were knocked out. A battalion commander was killed leading his troops. So was the second in command who replaced him.

By all the laws of war, Syria should have stopped the Israeli assault easily. The Israeli attack was not a surprise. Jordan and Egypt had been polished off, so the Syrians knew there was a very good chance they would be next on the menu. Israel chose an uphill, frontal attack in broad daylight against well-prepared positions. They were losing vehicles and men to Syrian fire. Boulders were stopping their advance and jamming the tracks of the Israeli armour. Some vehicles slipped away backwards or sideways because the unstable slopes of gravel and basalt were so steep. Some of the Israeli forces, who had been transferred in a hurry from the Sinai, did not know the terrain and took wrong turnings. But the Israelis did not stop. Infantrymen knocked out Syrian tanks that had been buried so only their gun and their turret protruded.

The Syrians were badly trained and badly led, though individuals fought bravely. Their most serious error was to keep their main armoured forces in reserve. Their front line defences were relatively light, supported by some tanks dug into the hillsides and some anti-tank guns. There were only a few narrow tracks up the steep sides of the escarpment, but the Israeli tanks, protected by unchallenged air power, were able to use them, in full view of the Syrians. They would have lost tanks to Israeli air attacks if they had committed them, but they might have stopped the slow Israeli advance up a treacherous and steep slope.

Savage fighting started when the Israelis reached the first line of Syrian fortifications and stormed inside. After the battle General Elazar said that at the position of Tel Fahr 'at the post and in the trenches there were at least sixty bodies spread about. There was hand-to-hand fighting there, fighting with fists, knives, teeth and rifle butts. The battle for the objective lasted three hours.' Sixty Syrians were killed and twenty captured. Israel lost thirty killed and about seventy wounded. Further south, around midday, light Israeli AMX tanks crossed the border without infantry support. They took the Syrians by surprise and made rapid progress. Sloppy radio security betrayed the Syrians. When they asked for support, they disclosed the location of the tanks they hoped would come to their rescue. The Israelis, who were monitoring their radio channels, promptly found the tanks and destroyed them.

Amman

The Americans wanted to see how much damage the allegations of collusion with Israel had done them with King Hussein. On the streets everyone believed that Britain and the US had attacked the Arab air forces. Findley Burns, the ambassador in Amman, and Jack O'Connel, the CIA station chief, went to see the king in his palace in the afternoon. They were worried that Hussein was so 'deeply entrapped with Nasser' that he too would start to blame the US and Britain for the Arab defeat. But Hussein had not lost his ability to charm Westerners. They went away reassured. Hussein promised he would try to get Nasser to tone down his attacks. Better still, the king told them Nasser had asked him specifically not to break diplomatic relations with Britain and the US. Egypt wanted to keep open a channel to the West.

Hussein's biggest problem was the enormous influx of refugees who had fled the fighting on the West Bank. Jordan accused Israel of forcing them out. Britain tended to agree. The Israelis 'were up to their old tricks', going round Palestinian villages with loudspeaker trucks broadcasting that, 'If you remain quiet you can stay here but if you want to go we will arrange safe conduct through the lines.'

In Tulkarem on the West Bank, Israeli soldiers came knocking on the door of the house that Ghuzlan Yusuf Hamdan, a 23-year-old Palestinian woman, shared with her family. When the war started they had been determined not to leave their home, which was less than a mile from the border with Israel. Fifty relations and neighbours gathered together in the three strongest-looking houses in their district, 'the old men in one house, the young men in another, and the women and children were in the third house . . . We stayed like this for three days, in one night the firing didn't stop, children were sick and women were tired but we all helped each other.' Like all Palestinians, they thought of the massacre at Deir Yassin in 1948 when the Israeli tanks and helicopters were close: 'The earth shook like an earthquake, we were lying on the ground and we wouldn't dare lift our heads up and look out the window because we were afraid we would be hit. Those were the most frightening moments of my life because I was afraid they would come in and kill us indiscriminately. We weren't armed. We turned on the radio to listen to the Israeli station and there was an announcement ordering us to put out white flags and surrender. So we did.'

That Friday morning the Israelis who were banging on their door came into the house and ordered the family to come with them to the town centre. 'Each one of them was carrying a machine gun and hand grenades, so we got out and when we arrived we found it packed with people. On the rooftops there were Israeli soldiers carrying weapons. No one dared say a word because they were afraid.'

Ghuzlan Yusuf Hamdan and her family, like hundreds of others, were thoroughly intimidated. They did not protest when Israeli soldiers loaded them on to buses. She managed to persuade one of them to let her go home to grab a suitcase with a few things. Everything else was left behind. The buses took them to the river Jordan, where they arrived between three and four in the afternoon. 'An Israeli soldier told us not to stay by the bridge because Israeli war planes might launch an air raid. So we had to cross but the bridge was blown up and parts of it had sunk in the water, so we had to climb across. I remember seeing a family where the young men were carrying their grandmother on a blanket. We saw people from wealthy families in a very poor state . . . It was desperate. Lots of people were walking around the country looking for relatives who got lost along the way.'

Refugees were pouring over from the West Bank after the ceasefire. A French television journalist described 'terrible scenes of thousands of refugees fording the river Jordan with their livestock under the indifferent eyes of the Israeli soldiers and without any evidence that the Jordanian authorities were doing anything to cope with the disaster'. No Jordanian officials were trying to help them. Sightseers in cars from Amman were gawping at the spectacle alongside other Jordanians who had driven down to the river to look for information about relatives on the West Bank. The refugees were in 'appalling' condition, 'at the end of their tether'. When the journalist went with Jordanian officials to the camp at Zerka, which housed 5000 refugees with very poor facilities, they had to be protected by a 'very large' military guard. 'The refugees hurled insults at them and appeared extremely excitable.'

The Jordanian authorities were overwhelmed and their first instinct was to keep foreigners away. But Mary Hawkins of Save the Children knew the Jordanian director of public security. She persuaded him to let her travel to the edge of the Syrian desert, to a place called Wadi Dhuleil. Five thousand refugees were there in a miserable state, with hundreds more arriving every day. She went to work immediately. Refugees 'pour in daily faster than the tents can be erected and there are always pathetic little groups of people camping under the cruel sun and sleeping in the cold desert night with the heavy dew'. Babies of less than a week old, born on the journey from the West Bank, were lying in the open. Hawkins called them 'children of the dust . . . Five days out of seven the wind starts at about 10.00 a.m. and blows till evening. The dust chokes and blinds the refugees and the workers . . . all the time it is in one's food, water, clothes hair and bedding . . . one man said to me, "My children are eating dust all the time."'

Most people had no way to cook. On the worst days there was only a single water tanker for the refugees. The police – who had set up the camp – had to use force to keep the desperate refugees back when Hawkins and her team wanted to get water from the tankers to mix powdered milk for the children. More and more arrived until there were between 14,000 and 15,000 refugees there. They were filthy and starving. The camp had no sanitation and most of the refugees had dysentery or worms. Human faeces were everywhere and so were millions of flies. Hawkins managed to get her hands on some clothes, shoes, soap, blankets, water containers, cups, washing bowls and hurricane lamps. But there were not enough: 'It is almost impossible to make any kind of distribution without a riot.' A month later she reported that, 'after 30 days of living and working in this hell, it seems like a timeless nightmare'. Remembering the camps in 1948, with deep mud and uncovered latrines in which children sometimes drowned, she felt 'the greatest apprehension about the fate of these refugees during the coming winter'.

One of the best UNRWA camps was at Suf. It was still grossly overcrowded. Even by late July, 12,500 people were living there. Most of the refugees were peasant farmers, who are usually tough and resourceful with well-developed survival skills, unlike the middle classes, who often die first in refugee camps. The peasant refugees at Suf improvised ovens, built mud walls round their tents, and used camel thorn to rig up shelters against the brutal sun. They had brought goats, sheep and chickens from the West Bank, which grazed and picked around the tents. But the latrines were completely inadequate for so many people, and the medical centre had only two doctors and four nurses. They were overworked, mainly because so many children had malnutrition.

Any Arabs who tuned into the radio news from Cairo could still persuade themselves that nothing was going wrong. Kuwait, which had sent troops to Egypt, refused to accept a ceasefire. 'I suppose all Arabs live in a dream world,' commented G. C. Arthur, Britain's man in Kuwait wearily, 'but the inhabitants of Kuwait seem further removed from reality than most just now. They and their brethren are still winning great victories over the Zionist gangs . . . what I fear most now is the delayed shock of reality . . . the whale is at its most dangerous when it whips its tail before expiring.'

Syria–Israel border, 1630

It was time for the Israelis to let the Americans know what was happening. The Israeli foreign ministry told them that the time had come 'to weed out the people who have been shelling our settlements for the last two years. This effort is now under way and is proceeding satisfactorily.' But it was taking longer than expected. The Syrians were still fighting despite an intensive air bombardment from the Israeli air force. Brigadier General Hod recalled: 'We attacked with everything we had . . . we dropped rockets, bombs and napalm.' When Israeli soldiers were airlifted on to the Syrian positions in the southern sector, they found a shell-shocked Syrian gunner still sitting at the controls of his anti-aircraft gun. All he could say was 'aircraft, aircraft'.

Syrian soldiers were weak because their officers were too busy with politics to train them properly. Before the war a small group of Soviet advisers did their best to fill in the gaps, but without officers that wanted to listen and take part, and without the creation of a solid core of NCOs, the Syrians had no chance. Some of the Soviet advisers were very close to the fighting. In some of the captured bunkers Israeli soldiers found a copy of one of Balzac's works, translated into Russian.

As darkness fell casualties were still scattered around the steep slopes of the heights. An Israeli doctor called Yitzhak Glick, who had been treating the wounded all day, found six injured men next to a couple of knocked-out tanks. One of them was in a critical condition. 'I worked on him by torchlight for almost an hour. I tried artificial respiration, put an injection direct into his heart, did external massage. The others walked around and said: "Just half an hour ago he was talking, still telling us all kinds of things." They had the feeling that I had arrived too late, that they had been abandoned. When I told them [he was dead] they cried . . . there was also a terrible feeling of isolation – we were alone in the world. It was quiet and completely dark.'

By the evening Israeli troops were outside Kuneitra, the main town in the Golan, fifteen miles inside Syria and only forty miles from Damascus.

Jerusalem

For 3000 years Jerusalem has been looted by its conquerors. The Israeli army was following in an ancient tradition. Holy places were protected by the new occupiers and in most cases escaped unscathed. But a huge amount of private property was removed. As the front-line combat troops moved out, systematic looting of Palestinian and Jordanian property in the newly occupied territories began. During the fighting a Catholic nun called Sister Marie-Therese treated the wounded in a convent on the Via Dolorosa in the Old City. After Jerusalem fell a sympathetic Israeli officer gave her a permit to move freely in Jerusalem and the West Bank to do humanitarian work. 'It is necessary to state unambiguously that the first wave of Israeli soldiers were decent, humane and courageous, doing as little damage as possible,' she wrote after the war. 'The second wave was made up of thieves, looters, and sometimes killers, and the third was even more disturbing since it seemed to act from a resolute desire for systematic destruction.'

Major-General Chaim Herzog, who was appointed Israeli governor of the West Bank, was deeply concerned about the chaos that followed the withdrawal of the paratroopers and their replacement by reservists from the Jerusalem Brigade. 'There was no order or discipline. All the wives and sweethearts were allowed to roam around the area. All of Jerusalem was coming in, destroying and looting.' Herzog complained and was given the security detail from the Israeli parliament to try to stop it. Various orders were issued to stop the looting, but they were widely ignored. Some of the fighting units did not like what the rear-echelon troops were doing. Paratroopers who were sitting on the walls of the Old City waiting to be relieved saw Israeli soldiers with sacks on their backs moving about the Arab village below them. 'I took a rifle from one of the boys and began shooting, not at them, but just in front of them. They got a terrific shock. We shouted down: "Bring everything you've got!" So they emptied the sacks by the wall, and we shot again – just missing their hands – and they scuttled back to their camp.' Another combat soldier was shocked, when he came into the village in the West Bank where his unit had based itself, to find 'the storemen and cooks – all that lot – absolutely rolling in things that they'd looted from the village. Wrapped up in carpets, women's jewellery – it was a horrible scene.' His commander, who was religious, read the looters passages from the Bible prohibiting what they had done.

Fifty paratroopers who were billeted in the American Colony hotel in East Jerusalem were very well behaved. They brought their own rations and only needed water, which they took from the rainwater cistern. They borrowed mattresses to sleep on the floor. Everything was returned and the soldiers left the rooms swept and clean. An officer tried to commandeer an Austin 1100 belonging to the family who owned the hotel. Frieda Ward, a member of the family, was about to open it when she saw the paratroopers taking cover in case it was booby-trapped. She thought they would never see it again. They brought it back a few hours later, because they could not work out how to disable the immobiliser. But by Friday, as the tail of the army moved in, they had to post watchmen to try to keep looters away.

Every army has more soldiers at the rear than at the sharp end. Abdullah Schleifer, the American journalist who lived in the Old City, saw the second wave in action. They were 'shooting the locks off the metal shutters and smashing their way into empty houses whose occupants had fled. They took radios, jewellery, TV sets, cigarettes, canned food and clothes. On the sidewalk outside the king's Jerusalem palace a young Israeli girl soldier danced about in an evening gown while her comrades ripped into Hussein's liquor stores in the basement.' Soldiers backed trucks up to shops in East Jerusalem's main shopping streets and took stoves, refrigerators, furniture and clothing.

One of the looted houses belonged to Um Sa'ad. She lived on the north-eastern side of Jerusalem, near the airport. She had fled to Ramallah when the fighting started, with her child and her husband, who ran a successful building company. They stayed in Ramallah the whole six days. 'After the war was ended, somebody came and told me, "We saw your doors wide open." I lost everything in that house.

I found a couch that was slashed all up and down, no curtains, nothing in the house that you could use. Our wedding pictures were just stabbed. They left clothes under the bed or under the table. And there was a curfew. Nobody could leave his house to steal or to do something like this. It had to be Israeli soldiers who did it.' When Palestinian shops eventually reopened in the Old City, a British diplomat reported that their owners were 'afraid to show much in the windows' because so much had been stolen and added his own gripe that 'some of my staff were fired at by Israeli soldiers when sitting in a garden at 5 p.m. The Israelis cannot count among their qualities an ability to make friends.'

Israeli troops in Gaza were also compulsive looters. UNRWA, the UN agency that looked after Palestinian refugees, carried out a comprehensive survey of looting after the war. The survey documented scores of thefts, carefully separating incidents in which Israeli soldiers stole UN property from looting by locals, which in places was also very thorough. On one occasion the UNRWA director of operations was threatened with a submachine gun and told to make himself scarce when he went to a UN food store in Gaza City that was being emptied by Israeli troops. At times more than fifty soldiers were involved, loading army trucks which were then driven away into Israel. Any safes that were discovered were blown open and robbed. UNRWA lost two complete operating theatres, one from Gaza and one from the West Bank. The stores at Rafah refugee camp were stripped. An UNRWA guard saw an Israeli car outside the camp loaded with timber and pipes. After Israeli troops left the Gaza YMCA and its hostel, which they occupied for two weeks, George Rishmawi, the YMCA chairman, discovered they had taken all its typewriters, its encyclopedia, its safe, television and radio and all its beds, blankets and mattresses. UNRWA schools were occupied by Israeli troops up and down the Gaza Strip. When they left, they often took with them anything that looked valuable – everything from sewing machines to sports equipment to desks and chairs, even doors and door-frames. On several occasions soldiers sold looted food and goods to Palestinians for cigarettes or Egyptian currency. What was not taken was often smashed. The latrines in the girls elementary school in Deir al Balah were vandalised. The soldiers used the rooms of the toddlers' play centre instead. There are several reports of text books being piled up and burnt. Maps of the area showing a complete Palestine without Israel were shot up. After the war UNRWA presented a bill of $708,610.43 to the Israeli government for the damage done by its troops.

The peacekeeping troops of UNEF had left in such a hurry that they could not take a stockpile of vehicles, communications equipment and other substantial stores of military and logistical equipment. It was looted on a grand scale by the Israeli army, which has a department of war booty. The UN had intended to transport the UNEF stores to Pisa where they would become the nucleus of a UN stockpile that could be used at short notice for peacekeeping operations, something that the UN has never had, before or since 1967.

Archaeological treasures became spoils of war. The parts of the Dead Sea scrolls that were held by Jordan were taken from the Palestine Archaeological Museum while the fighting was still going on. They are still in the Israel Museum in West Jerusalem. Also taken to Israel were the Lachish Letters, messages sent by the garrison commander of a small fortress to his commanding officer in palaeo-Hebrew script written on small pieces of pottery. When Jordanian Jerusalem was annexed the entire museum was declared an Israeli institution. So many Egyptian artefacts were taken from the Sinai that their return was made part of the peace deal between Israel and Egypt that was thrashed out at Camp David in 1979. Hundreds of cases of antiquities were returned to Egypt. Moshe Dayan was an obsessive collector of ancient artefacts. While he was touring Israeli army positions in the Negev desert in the last days before the war started, he dropped in on Colonel Yekutiel Adam, who showed him some ancient arrowheads and a flint axe that he had just found on the border with Sinai. Dayan sympathised with his friend's frustration that he was not able to use the army bulldozers at his disposal to do some more digging. Dayan took his leave of the colonel promising to find an untouched tomb that they would open together. The Egyptians complained that, archaeologically speaking, Dayan had far too good a war. They say that his activities in Sinai amounted to 'the theft of hundreds of Egyptian antiquities'. They are still demanding the return of forty bronze statues, among many other items. They claim he removed entire columns from the Temple of Sarabeit El-Khadem in Sinai, which he displayed in his garden in Tel Aviv.

Cairo, evening

The minister of information, Mohamed Fayek, sent an outside broadcast unit to the El Koba palace for President Nasser's broadcast. He sat down in his office at the TV centre to watch it. He did not know what was coming. In the morning Nasser had given orders that his name must not be mentioned in news broadcasts. Fayek assumed the president had decided to take the spotlight off himself for a few days, but now it was starting to look serious. The American journalists under house arrest at the Nile hotel found a TV set and at 7:30 p.m. they sat down in front of it too. The speech started at 7:43. According to Eric Rouleau of *Le Monde*, Nasser's 'features were drawn, his expression tormented. He appeared to be overwhelmingly depressed. Speaking haltingly and hesitatingly, he read a text, stumbling over his words.' Throughout his career Nasser had been a fluent, charismatic public speaker. The contrast with his mood less than a week before could not have been clearer.

He told them that they had all suffered 'a grave setback in the last few days'. Just as he said that the air-raid sirens wailed. Among the watching American reporters in front of the Nile hotel's TV, Trevor Armbrister thought he saw tears in Nasser's eyes. 'It was all very convincing.' Nasser did not go into the scale of what had happened, or even use the word 'defeat'. He used the Arabic word *naksa*, which means setback, to describe the calamity that had befallen Egypt in the previous five days. (His description stuck. The 1967 defeat is often still described euphemistically in Arabic as the 'setback', while 1948 is always called the 'catastrophe'.) Nasser said they would get over the 'setback'. Once again, he blamed the West for intervening on Israel's side:

> 'In the morning of last Monday, 5 June, the enemy struck. If we say now it was a stronger blow than we had expected, we must say at the same time and with complete certainty that it was bigger than the potential at his disposal. It became very clear from the first moment that there were other powers behind the enemy – they came to settle accounts with the Arab national movement.
>
> '[The army had fought] most violent and brave battles in the open desert . . . without adequate air cover in face of the decisive superiority of the enemy forces. Indeed it can be said without emotion or exaggeration, that the enemy was operating with an air force three times stronger than his normal force . . .
>
> 'Now we arrive at an important point in this heart-searching by asking ourselves: does that mean that we do not bear the responsibility for the consequences of the setback? . . . I tell you truthfully and despite any factors on which I might have based my attitude during the crisis, that I am ready to bear the whole responsibility . . .
>
> 'I have taken a decision in which I want you all to help me. I have decided to give up completely and finally every official post and every political role and to return to the ranks of the masses and do my duty with them like every other citizen . . .'

When he had finished, the announcer came back on the air and broke down. The microphones picked up the sound of weeping elsewhere in the studio. Heikal's words and the sight of the wounded giant all struck a deep chord in Egyptians and in Arabs across the Middle East.

General Salahadeen Hadidi, the head of Central Command, was watching the speech at the headquarters of the Cairo military district. He was disgusted. 'Nasser had got us into the mess. It was up to him to get us out.' Amin Howedi, a minister trusted by Nasser, saw him half an hour after the speech. 'His face was pale. His eyes were wide open and staring straight ahead.' At the Broadcasting Centre, the information minister Mohamed Fayek started receiving agitated visitors as soon as Nasser had finished. Egypt's greatest musical diva, the singer Umm Kulthum demanded the right to go on air to make a statement of her own about Nasser's greatness. Field Marshal Amer wanted his own broadcast to clarify his own position. The head of the Egyptian trade unions had to be physically stopped from battering his way into the studio to hijack the microphone. Luckily for Fayek, who refused all their requests, Egyptian TV was due to go off air at nine. But it took him another two hours to make it clear that they were not going on the radio either. A survival instinct told him that Nasser's message should not be diluted by others.

High above Cairo's streets, in a twelfth-floor apartment, Eric Rouleau of *Le Monde* heard a noise that sounded like the approach of a storm, even though the weather was perfect. He went out on to the balcony. 'From all sides,' he remembers, 'we saw people coming out of their houses like ants and heads leaning out of windows. We went down. It was dusk and the city was half immersed in the darkness of the black-out. It was an extraordinary spectacle to see people hurrying from all sides, shouting, weeping, some wearing pyjamas, some barefoot, women in night dresses, all tormented by a suffering beyond endurance and imploring "Nasser, do not leave us, we need you."'

Gunfire started. 'The crazy Egyptians were firing ack-ack and rockets at the stars – and some of the bursts seemed close,' an American reporter, held with the rest of the US press corps in the down-at-heel Nile hotel, noted with alarm. By now they were all thoroughly spooked. One of them thought he remembered that Europeans were dragged from their hotels in Baghdad during the coup in 1958 and butchered in the streets. At one point an Egyptian army captain shouted at the Americans, 'Rush to your rooms. They are coming.' After trooping upstairs they were escorted back downstairs for dinner at ten. 'A few demonstrators, someone explained, had tried to set fire to the hotel, but they had been stopped by police.' Some hotheads wanted to burn down the US Embassy but the police kept them back. Others gathered outside the USSR's Embassy to chant anti-Soviet slogans. For Sergei Tarasenko it was the most frightening night of the war. It seemed as if ten million people were chanting a single word: 'Nass-er! Nass-er!' The Soviets lay low and waited for the night to be over.

Nasser had been the dominating personality in the Arab world for the best part of 15 years. He was a gigantic figure who was loved and hero-worshipped by millions. Nasser had given Arabs their pride back after the humiliations of colonialism and the disaster of 1948. Young people in their twenties had grown up listening to Cairo Radio's accounts of his exploits, from the expulsion of the British, to the rhetoric about the rights of dispossessed Palestinians and what had seemed, until only a few days before, to be a heroic stand against Israel and its Western allies. Until a few hours before Nasser's resignation, Cairo Radio had still been reporting the triumphs of the Arab armies. Now that familiar voice, coming from the same place on the dials of their radios (and on the television too), was shattering everything that had seemed certain in their lives. Nasser, the good son, the big brother, the father of the Arab nation, was going. No wonder they came out on the streets. Observers at the time reckoned there were hundreds of thousands of people on the streets of Cairo. In Egypt's second city Alexandria there were also mass demonstrations. In Port Said, on the Suez canal, the governor had to intervene to stop the population decamping for Cairo to add their voices to the crowd in the capital.

Whether Nasser's plan to resign was sincere or not is still widely debated in Egypt. Many people believe the speech was a piece of political theatre. The truth is probably that he felt he had no other choice. The scale of the Egyptian defeat was so vast that his best guess on Wednesday and Thursday was that a popular rebellion would kick him out of office. Before the broadcast, Mohamed Fayek, the information minister, claims Nasser told him: 'They'll put me on trial and hang me in the middle of Cairo.' Perhaps resignation was not only more dignified, but it offered the chance to return at some time in the future. What he could never have guessed at was the reaction of the people. A huge crowd gathered outside his villa, where he had returned after the broadcast. The wife of Amin Howedi, who was about to be appointed minister of defence, was so stricken with grief that she left her house in her dressing gown to join the crowd. Fayek arrived at Nasser's villa in his official car. When the crowd was too thick to drive through, he got out to move forward on foot. Suddenly people started shouting that he was Zakkaria Mohieddin, the vice-president that Nasser had nominated as his successor. They turned on him, jostling him and ripping his clothes for having the temerity to take their hero's job. Fayek was rescued by the presidential guard and entered Nasser's residence badly shaken and dishevelled. Inside, he was received by Nasser, who was sitting alone. Fayek told him that a woman had killed herself with grief.

Some of the demonstrations were organised. The ruling party, the Arab Socialist Union, told 20,000 hard-core activists in Cairo to expect instructions once the speech was over. According to the official Yugoslav news agency, they directed the demonstrators once they were on the streets. But there was a massive element of spontaneity. If party activists were organising elements of the demonstrations they did not do the job across the country. Some hapless officials of the ASU refused to provide vehicles to take the faithful to Cairo, saying they were waiting for an order. The faithful responded by burning down the party offices. Gamal Haddad, the governor of a province in the Nile Delta, was asked by the ASU to provide transport on the morning of the 10th to take demonstrators to Cairo. He was convinced their grief was spontaneous, because in his province the ASU was not capable of organising anything remotely so big. The same evening, after Cairo Radio broadcast that Nasser would be appearing the next day at the National Assembly, the Cairo office of the Socialist Youth Organisation of the ASU sent out a circular to its members telling them to seal off the National Assembly building 'and not let Nasser go out unless he has gone back on his resignation'.

Damascus

Nasser's announcement was as big a bombshell to the Syrians as it was elsewhere in the Arab world. In Damascus the government panicked. Jordan was defeated, Nasser's resignation meant Egypt must be too – which left only one Arab country for the Israelis to knock over. They were already attacking. If a leader like Nasser could not resist them, who could? Self-preservation became the government's priority. Orders were issued for the army to disengage and fall back to Damascus, only forty miles or so from the border. Key members of the government left the capital. The army command was infuriated by the order to pull back, which at first it refused to obey. But during the night General Suwaydani, the Syrian chief of staff, was told by Ahmad al-Mir, the commander of the front, that Israel was close to trapping the Syrian army by outflanking its defences. Suwaydani ordered them to fall back to Kuneitra, the main town of the Golan, which controls the road to Damascus.

DAY 6

10 June 1967

Syria–Israel border, 0826

Israel had used the night to regroup and resupply its forces – and to brace themselves for a counter-attack which never came. Instead the Syrian army was pulling back. Its soldiers were being shelled and bombed from the air. But in the end they broke because of a piece of Syrian propaganda. A defence ministry communiqué was read out on Damascus Radio, saying that Kuneitra, the provincial capital, had fallen. It was untrue. Perhaps they hoped a false report would put more pressure on the UN Security Council or the USSR to stop the Israelis. Or perhaps it was a mistake, a sign of panic and confusion. Two hours later General Hafez al-Asad, the Syrian minister of defence, ordered a correction to be broadcast. But by then the damage had been done. Syrian troops facing the Israelis ran for their lives. Ahmad al-Mir, the commander of the front, escaped on horseback. Some reserve officers changed into civilian clothes and headed for the Syrian capital. Damascus Radio tried to make up for its mistake by, once again, claiming that America and Britain were helping Israel. 'The enemy's air force,' it reported, 'covered the sky in numbers which can only be possessed by a major power.' Later, Ba'th party officials claimed the premature announcement about Kuneitra was a clever tactic which saved the lives of thousands of soldiers.

The Israelis pushed on, not always fast enough to catch up with the retreating Syrians. A senior Israeli officer grumbled, 'It was very difficult to make contact with the retreating enemy. Whenever we arrived, they had withdrawn their forces and we could not make contact. We fired on a number of tanks only to discover that they had been deserted. Their crews had abandoned them.'

Cairo

Nasser withdrew his resignation. Senior Egyptian officers wanted Nasser back as much as the weeping crowds in the streets, but not for emotional reasons. They wanted Nasser to get them out of the mess he had got them into. They wanted Amer back too, not because they rated his military skills, but because if he was purged anyone could be. And, remarkably, he still inspired loyalty, even though his incompetence had been proved beyond doubt. General Fawzi, the chief of staff, announced that Amer would be appearing at GHQ to say farewell to his officers. Five hundred of them gathered in a hall inside the building to honour their chief. When Amer did not appear, the officers started to chant his name. The atmosphere was getting tense and ugly. General Hadidi, the commander of the Cairo military district, left the hall and went down into the basement complex of bunkers to find Fawzi. He told him he had to face the men upstairs, or 'there would be a revolution'. When Fawzi reappeared, saying that Amer had telephoned to say he was not coming, there was uproar. Officers started to insult Fawzi, yelling at him to get out of their sight. He left. The demonstration, with some leadership, could have turned into a threat to the regime. But no leaders emerged. After another hour or so of shouting, the disheartened officers started to drift away.

On the radio news at 2:30 p.m. Nasser started to reassert himself, striking out at the potentially disloyal. The announcer read out a communiqué announcing the retirement of a dozen officers. More names, with more sackings, came in bulletins later in the afternoon. If there was going to be a coup against Nasser, this was the moment. He was very vulnerable. But it was a step that nobody was prepared to take. General Hadidi had no more troops left in Cairo to protect him. Every spare man had been sent to the Sinai. Nasser had the Presidential Guard, which would have been an obstacle.

But his best defence, which was formidable, was his aura. Nasser was still Nasser, the only leader the Arabs had. He was also protected by the convenient fact that the people who had wept for him in the streets still did not know the full extent of the disaster. As the survivors of the beaten divisions in the Sinai trailed back, the truth was spreading, but it would take weeks to filter through the barrage of propaganda that was coming from the official media. Newspapers, radio and television redoubled their accusations of collusion between Israel, the United States and Britain. They continued to hide the truth about the defeat. 'Setback', the word used by Nasser in his resignation speech, was the only way it was described. A week later, Michael Wall of the *Guardian* could still report that 'the Egyptian people have no conception of the disaster that has overtaken their country'. But the news was leaking out. Soldiers back from the front were telling 'appalling stories of casualties, of wounded being left where they fell, of the hundred mile struggle back in the burning sun, of Israeli planes trying to mow down each individual staggering towards the canal'.

In his office opposite Nasser's residence, Sami Sharaf was sitting with Amin Howedi, the new minister of defence and head of general intelligence. Two officers came in to report to Sharaf that Egypt had 100 tanks left. Sharaf got up, threw his arms around Howedi and said they should give thanks that something had been saved. Howedi shook his head and pulled away. He told Sharaf that he seemed to have forgotten that a week earlier Egypt had more than one thousand tanks. 'Amer's got to go,' he said, 'or we'll never sort this out.' If there was going to be a fall guy, it was going to be Field Marshal Amer, not Nasser.

Nasser was back in power, but he was never the same man again. On the eve of the war he still hoped he had scored his greatest political victory, a bloodless defeat of Israel. After his armed forces were smashed he kept his job' because there was no other convincing candidate. No one else had any chance of inspiring public confidence. In Cairo the CIA was told that if Nasser had simply disappeared there would have been 'chaos and the collapse of the Cairo government'. Egypt, though, was now like a sinking ship. 'The morale of the ship's crew may be maintained by giving the appearance that the captain remains in command; however, the ship sinks and the captain sinks with it.'

Gaza

Major Ibrahim El Dakhakny had been in hiding since 6 June, in a hut near a dried up river valley called Wadi Gaza. Local Palestinians kept him fed and watered and tipped him off when the Israelis were about. On a small transistor radio they had given him, he heard that Nasser had resigned. Dakhakny was as angry as his brother officers in Cairo. Nasser, he thought, could not go because he had to face his responsibilities. He might have been responsible for the defeat, but there was no one else to replace him.

The Palestinians had put Dakhakny in touch with three of his soldiers, who were also on the run from the Israelis. As the resident chief of Egyptian military intelligence in Gaza he assumed the Israelis knew his name and were looking for him, along with their pilot who was downed by anti-aircraft fire on the first day of the fighting. The Israeli pilot had been sent to Cairo in one of the last cars to make it through Al-Arish before the Israeli takeover. Dakhakny was stuck. He was hearing stories from the Palestinians that the Israelis were shooting prisoners and civilians. Some of them claimed that the victims had been forced to dig their own graves before they were killed. He was determined not to be captured.

Dakhakny bought a camel from a Palestinian farmer. With his three soldiers, and the camel's help, he was going to cross the Sinai and get home. They loaded the beast with water, flour, sugar and tea, enough they hoped to keep them going until they reached Egypt. They left after dark, moving down the Gaza Strip and into Sinai, avoiding Israeli patrols by staying off the roads and walking through fields and groves of oranges, bananas and olives. Dakhakny always liked to keep a low profile by dressing in civilian clothes, so he had not been wearing a uniform when the war started. His three soldiers had dumped their uniforms and been given new outfits by friendly Palestinians. They had all kept their Kalashnikov assault rifles.

Their plan, once they had slipped into the vastness of the Sinai desert, was to find a Bedouin guide. Luckily they had just been paid when the Israelis invaded, but most of their cash had gone on the camel. But they found a man who would take what was left. He even brought another camel. They stayed at least ten kilometres away from roads, moving at night because of the heat. 'It was very, very hard. The sand was very hot. So was the air. We had no tents or shelter when we stopped during the day. We just covered our heads and sat and tried to rest.' They walked for nearly three weeks, following their camels and their guide along a meandering route. Sometimes they had to turn back and take a looping detour when they met Bedouin who told them that the Israelis were ahead. As time went by, and more and more Israelis were demobilised and sent home, the desert seemed emptier.

With their supplies almost gone, they reached the territory of the Bayardia tribe of Bedouin, around forty kilometres from Suez. The tribe had made a camp from palm branches, a custom that went back to biblical times. (During the Jewish religious holiday of Sukkot, the faithful build small shelters of palm branches to commemorate the wanderings of Jews in the Sinai in the time of Moses.) Dakhakny and his party had passed other Egyptians as they moved through Sinai, all trying to evade the Israelis and get back home. Quite a few of them had been swept up by the Bedouin and brought to the camp made of palms. The Bedouin were in contact with the Egyptian military. They took small groups of fugitives to the beach at night, where they were picked up by boats that Egypt had sent from Port Said. The boats came full of flour and other staples the Bedouin needed, were unloaded and filled again with the thin, sunburnt and exhausted Egyptians. Dakhakny gave his camel to the guide who had saved him. 'I felt I was already in the grave. Sinai was a grave, and I was reborn when I left it.'

Once the ceasefire held, the atmosphere along the canal was more relaxed, though still wary. Israeli soldiers who spoke Arabic sometimes shouted over to the Egyptians, bartering prisoners for watermelon. A rope was stretched between the two banks for prisoners who could not swim. Watermelon floats, so the Egyptians pushed them across.

Sinai

Amos Elon drove back north through an eerily silent desert after the ceasefire came into effect. Israeli salvage crews were going through the wreckage at the side of the roads. In the opposite direction were jams of huge supply convoys going south, further into Egypt. It felt odd to drive towards the back of Hebrew signs warning about mines and the approaching frontier. He did not reach Jerusalem until late in the evening. The city's lights were blazing. It had been three days since they had had a black-out. Later, Elon looked back on 'a victory notable for its lack of hate, but marked by more than a trace of arrogance'. Elon may have felt no hate, but that was not how it seemed to Egyptian prisoners.

Ramadan Mohammed Iraqi was captured on the second day of the war. With several hundred other prisoners he was forced to lie down in a number of long lines. The Egyptians were convinced they were going to be shot. Ramadan always believed their lives were saved by a passing Israeli officer who saw what was happening and ordered their captors not to execute them. They were taken to Al-Arish airfield, where they were kept in aircraft hangars. Eventually they were transferred to a prison camp in Beersheba and then to another in Atlit, south of Haifa. Ramadan, like a number of other prisoners, says that they were moved in open lorries. Some civilians would throw stones at them, spit and yell abuse. Conditions in Atlit were especially bad. The prisoners were given very little food, mainly bread and onions. Some prisoners were shot by guards in the first few weeks, before they were registered by the International Committee of the Red Cross (ICRC). Conditions improved slightly once ICRC visits began. There was more food and no more killing, except one man who was killed when the prisoners rioted in August. The prisoners were not allowed to leave their sheds between 4 p.m. and 9 a.m. They snapped when guards fired at a prisoner needing water who broke the rules by stepping out of one of the sheds at the wrong time. The prisoners broke out of the sheds, tearing at the wire and throwing stones at the watchtowers. The Israelis brought an Egyptian general who spoke to them through a loudhailer and told them that he had been promised that conditions would be improved. There was a little more food and they received parcels from the Egyptian Red Crescent containing new underwear and pyjamas. Ramadan Mohammed Iraqi was able to send messages back to his family through the ICRC during the seven months he was a prisoner of war. One says, 'Don't worry, I'm alive, one day I'll be home.'

Jerusalem

It was the Jewish Sabbath. General Narkiss, Mayor Kollek and General Herzog, the new governor of the West Bank, went together to the Wailing Wall, where Sabbath prayers were being said by Jews for the first time since 1948. When the Wall was captured they discovered a urinal had been installed along part of it, which was immediately removed. Now they were eyeing the Moroccan quarter, an area of small, densely packed houses that stood between the Wall and the Jewish quarter. The quarter's history went back 700 years, when the Ayyubids and the Mamluks, who were the dominant powers in Jerusalem, set aside land for immigrants from North Africa. Many of the 150 families – more than a thousand people – who lived in its small houses and narrow alleys in 1967 had North African connections. The following Wednesday was an important Jewish festival. Hundreds of thousands of Israelis were expected to come to pray and to celebrate the victory. What Kollek called the Moroccan quarter's 'small slum houses' would be in the way. Kollek, Narkiss and Herzog decided they had 'an historic opportunity' to pull them down. They decided to send in bulldozers as soon as the Sabbath ended at sunset. Herzog later said some with some pride, 'We hadn't been authorised by anyone and we didn't seek authorisation.' They were worried that if they did not act decisively it would become politically impossible to knock down the houses of so many civilians. 'We were concerned about losing time and the government's difficulty in making a decision. We knew that in a few days it would be too late.'

Abd el-Latif Sayyed was a twenty-year-old trainee teacher who had been born in the Moroccan quarter. In 1967 eighteen people from his family shared a five-room house, which was around fifteen yards from the Wall. His maternal great grandfather, an immigrant from Morocco, had been granted it around 1810 by the Moroccan religious authorities in Jerusalem. Not long after dark they were given half an hour to leave. Abd el-Latif's family were very frightened. They guessed the house was going to be searched, but no one dared to ask the soldiers. They were too scared of the new occupiers to question their orders. The family assumed they would be allowed back in a couple of hours, so they left all their possessions in the house. At an aunt's house, about a hundred yards away, on the other side of the Moroccan quarter, they waited for the order to go home. They could hear bulldozers grinding and squealing. Nervously, they tried to work out what the noise was all about. They told each other that the Israelis were building a road, but as the night went on they became more and more concerned. When they tried to go out to take a look soldiers, who were patrolling the alleys, ordered them back inside.

Nazmi Al-Ju'beh had a much better view. From the roof of his grandfather's house he could see the bulldozers working away at the edges of the Moroccan quarter. Steadily, they started to flatten the buildings, then move deeper into the quarter. Lorries came to take away the rubble. It went on all night. Major Eitan Ben Moshe, an engineer officer from Central Command, who was in charge of the

301

work, went about his job with gusto – and anger, because of the urinal the Jordanians had set up to desecrate the Wall, which he had already removed. A small mosque called al-Buraq, after the winged horse that brought Mohammed to Jerusalem from Mecca, stood near the wall. 'I said, if the horse ascended to the sky, why shouldn't the mosque ascend too? So I crushed it until nothing was left.'

The next morning Abd el-Latif Sayyed went down to where his home had stood. All that was left among piles of bulldozed rubble was a palm tree that had stood in their back yard. The family's possessions were somewhere under the rubble. Nazmi's parents decided it was safer for them to return to their house outside the city walls. They moved at first light, picking up bales of bedding then walking, as usual, down a narrow passage and a flight of steps to get to the Moroccan quarter. They turned the last corner. In front of them, instead of the narrow, congested streets they had been walking through for years, was a broad and open space. At one end the Wailing Wall had been exposed. Hundreds of soldiers and bearded, black-clad ultra-orthodox Jews had linked arms and were dancing on the ruins of houses that had been bulldozed flat. His mother and father stumbled in shock. 'I started to shout, where's Mohammed, where's Abed – these were my friends from the Moroccan quarter. The soldiers came and gave me candy and then arrested my two older brothers. One was a teacher and one was a lawyer. They were held for two days, with hundreds of other young men, at the Aqsa mosque, then at a military base. They were released after a week. We walked on, across the ruined houses of our friends.'

A middle-aged woman called Rasmiyyah Ali Taba'ki was found in the rubble, badly injured. Her neighbours assumed she had not heard the orders to leave. An Israeli engineer who was supervising the demolition tried to revive her, but she was already dead. Major Ben Moshe told an Israeli journalist that he found at least three bodies 'of people who refused to leave their homes'.

On Sunday morning the site was visited by cabinet ministers. According to Chaim Herzog, 'they were astounded. All they saw was ruin and dust. Warhaftig, the minister of religion, who was also a jurist, claimed our actions were against the law. At any rate, what was done was done.' Teddy Kollek was proud of the destruction of the Moroccan quarter and the creation of the great open air plaza that is there now. It was a decisive act to create new facts on the ground in the classic tradition of Zionism. 'It was the best thing we did and it's good we did [it] immediately. The old place had a *galut* [Diaspora] character; it was a place for wailing. Perhaps this made sense in the past. It isn't what we want in the future.' His men worked fast. 'In two days it was done – finished, clean.' Kollek claimed that all the evicted families were found decent alternative accommodation, something they deny. They received backdated eviction notices in 1968, along with an offer of compensation of 100 Jordanian dinars. Around half the families took the money. The rest, in a small gesture against the occupation, refused what was anyway a paltry sum.

Syria–Israel border

Rabin had ordered Elazar to press on to Kuneitra, the regional capital of the Syrian border province. But then, in the morning, perhaps having second thoughts about his sudden decision to attack Syria, Dayan ordered that all military operations were to stop. When Rabin passed the order on, Elazar claimed it was too late to recall an airborne brigade, which was already going into action. After Dayan repeated his order, Rabin called Elazar again, who said, 'Sorry, following your previous order, they began to move off and I can't stop them.' Rabin knew that Elazar 'didn't feel an ounce of regret'. But something in his tone made the chief of staff suspicious. After the war he discovered that when Elazar told him the airborne brigade could not be recalled, it was still waiting for orders miles from the border. Elazar's desire to move as far forward as fast as he could was shared by his commanders. Rabin admitted he did not try very hard to check whether Elazar was telling the truth about the airborne brigade or not, and whatever Dayan's later regrets about the wisdom of taking the Golan Heights, during the fighting he turned his blind eye to Israel's ceasefire violations.

The first Israeli troops entered Kuneitra at two in the afternoon. One of the commanders reported: 'We arrived almost without hindrance to the gates of Kuneitra . . . All around us there were huge quantities of booty. Everything was in working order. Tanks with their engines still running, communication equipment still in operation had been abandoned. We captured Kuneitra without a fight.'

The riches left behind by the Syrians were too much of a temptation. After it fell to the Israelis, the entire city of Kuneitra was sacked. When Nils-Goran Gussing, the UN special representative, visited in July he observed 'nearly every shop and every house seemed to have been broken into and looted'. Some buildings had been set on fire after they had been stripped. Israeli spokesmen told Gussing philosophically that 'looting is often associated with warfare'. They claimed that because Syria had announced the loss of Kuneitra twenty-four hours before it was captured, fleeing Syrian soldiers had a whole day to loot the place themselves. Gussing listened politely and concluded that 'responsibility for this extensive looting of the town of Kuneitra lay to a great extent with the Israeli forces'. Gussing's version seems most logical. There were only five and a half hours between the false announcement on Damascus Radio at 0826 and the fall of the city at 1400. Troops so panic stricken that they abandoned tanks without even turning off their engines were unlikely to have stopped to clear out the shops.

New York, 0850

From the outset, the fact that Syria had accepted the UN ceasefire on Thursday night was irrelevant to Israel. They planned to keep going until they had what they wanted, or until they were stopped by one of the superpowers. But time was running out for the Israelis. They knew it, and so did the diplomats at the Security Council, who were getting impatient with what looked like a blatant land grab. They sat into the early hours of Saturday morning, waiting for news from the Syrian front. The attack on Kuneitra was the last straw. Lord

Caradon, the UK ambassador, believed there was a 'clearly deliberate Israeli campaign' to attack the town after the council had twice asked it to respect the ceasefire. Like the French ambassador Seydoux, he saw 'no justification' in taking Kuneitra, since the fighting had stopped elsewhere. A report of bombing close to Damascus was 'still more deserving of condemnation'. Abba Eban, who was at the UN, tried to call Eshkol at his flat. Eshkol's wife Miriam answered. She told Eban that Eshkol was with the troops in the north. Eban said, 'Tell Eshkol to stop the war. The United Nations is putting pressure on me.' Mrs Eshkol called her husband, who had a radio telephone in his car. According to her, Eshkol was in a fine mood. 'He started telling me how beautiful the Golan is and so on and then he said, "You do hear me, darling?" I said yes, yes, yes. Listen. Aubrey [they always used Eban's original first name, rather than the Hebrew one he adopted] said you have to stop. Then Eshkol says, "I can't hear you." So I said, you could a minute ago . . . so he said, that's it. I'll talk to you when I get home.'

Washington, 0900

Walt Rostow, President Johnson's National Security Advisor, had given up tennis for the Six-Day War. But, this Saturday morning, he knew they were working on a ceasefire in New York, so he thought it was safe to play. He was on the court when a message arrived from the White House. He had to get to work, fast. The Soviets had activated the hotline. If Israel did not desist, they would take military action. 'They called me off the court. I was still in tennis clothes.'

The translation of Kosygin's message was with Johnson five minutes after the teleprinter had gone quiet. Without mentioning its advance into Syria, Kosygin said, 'A crucial moment has now arrived.' Israel was ignoring the resolutions of the Security Council. The US must tell Israel unconditionally to stop military action in the next few hours. The Soviet Union would do the same. If not, 'these actions may bring us into a clash, which will lead to a grave catastrophe'. If

Israel did not comply, 'necessary actions would be taken, including military'.

Rostow had time to change into a suit before he joined the rest of the president's top advisers in the basement of the White House, around the mahogany table in the Situation Room. Everyone was speaking quietly. Most of them had gathered in the same room in 1962 after the Soviet Union deployed nuclear missiles in Cuba. It felt like the most dangerous moment since then. Richard Helms, the director of Central Intelligence, had never heard such low voices in a meeting of that kind. Johnson, studiously calm, was eating his breakfast. Under Secretary of State Nicholas Katzenbach left the Situation Room to call in the Israeli ambassador to put pressure on him to accept a ceasefire. Russian speakers, including Llewellyn Thompson, the ambassador to the Soviet Union who happened to be in Washington, studied the text of the hotline message, to make sure that the phrase 'including military' really was there. It was. Intelligence from Syria was sketchy. Richard Helms was reduced to ringing friendly countries that still had missions in Damascus to try to find out what was really happening.

The gravity of the crisis depended on how soon Israel stopped shooting. In London, Britain's Joint Intelligence Committee, the prime minister's main intelligence advisers, believed that the Russians were bluffing. Moscow, they thought, would not risk a confrontation with the United States. The JIC believed the ceasefire would start to stick once Israel had completed its conquest of the Heights, which would be wrapped up by the end of the day. The Soviet Union, the British thought, was just trying to save some face with its Arab clients, trying to convince them, very late in the war, that their toughness and determination had rescued Syria.

But most of the Americans in the Situation Room thought that the Israelis wanted to press on to Damascus, which made it a big crisis. The main voice raised against was McGeorge Bundy's. He shared the British line that the Soviets 'were doing their damnedest verbally to protect their friends in Damascus'. The Americans had information that the Israelis had discussed taking the battle all the way to the

306

Syrian capital. Before the offensive even began, West German diplomats in Tel Aviv passed on the word from their contacts in the IDF that an advance to Damascus might be necessary to destroy the Syrian armed forces.

They had urgently to reply to Kosygin. Getting the tone right on a teleprinter was a very delicate business. The Russians seemed to be testing them out. Their worry was that if their message was too polite, they might look intimidated, as if they were backing down. Johnson approved his reply at 0930. It was transmitted at 0939. He chose not to up the ante by making threats of his own. Instead, he assured Kosygin that he was also pressing for a ceasefire. Kosygin replied insistently that, 'We have constant and uninterrupted communications with Damascus. Israel, employing all types of weapons, aviation and artillery, tanks, is conducting an offensive towards Damascus . . . it is urgently necessary to avoid further bloodshed. The matter cannot be postponed.'

After an hour or so, while Johnson was out of the Situation Room, McNamara, the Secretary of Defense, turned to Thompson and said, still in a low voice, 'Don't you think it might be useful if the Sixth Fleet which is simply orbiting around Sicily, in the light of this Russian threat . . . wouldn't it be a good idea to simply turn the Sixth Fleet and head those two aircraft carriers and their accompanying ships to the Eastern Mediterranean?'

Llewellyn Thompson and Richard Helms thought it would be a very good idea. Helms said, 'The Soviets will get the message straight away because they've got some fleet units in the Mediterranean and they're sure watching that Sixth Fleet like a hawk with their various electronic devices and others. Once they line up and start to go in that direction, the message is going to get back to Moscow in a hurry.' When Johnson came back into the room, McNamara made the recommendation. The Sixth Fleet should head east. Johnson smiled and agreed.

McNamara picked up a secure telephone and gave the order. Since 20 May, elements of the Sixth Fleet had been ordered to stay within two days' steaming time of the Mediterranean coast of Israel and Egypt. In practice, because different ships move at different speeds, that meant 200 to 600 miles away, to the west of Cyprus, mainly near Crete and Rhodes. After McNamara's order, they moved to around 100 miles closer to the eastern littoral of the Mediterranean. Without hard intelligence from Syria, the Americans were improvising. For Helms, the 'momentous' decision to move the Sixth Fleet 'in a very assertive direction . . . [was] made literally from one minute to the next. There were no papers. There was no direct organisation. There was no estimate. There was no contingency plan, there was nothing!'

The Americans handled the crisis neatly. The tension dissipated as quickly as it had built up when it became clear that Israel had achieved its objectives in Syria, was not going to capture Damascus and was ready to honour a ceasefire. Before that happened, the presidential advisers in the Situation Room talked a great deal about what the Soviets were capable of doing. Bundy's view was that 'the Russians' possibilities were not really that impressive'. Recent evidence suggests that did not stop Moscow making plans. The Soviet Union had sent its Black Sea naval squadron into the Mediterranean in May and early June. It was not a match for American naval power, but it was still a big force. By the time the war started, as well as the surface fleet, the Soviets had eight or nine submarines in or near the Mediterranean.

But the Soviet Union did contemplate military action. General Vassily Reshetnikov, commander of the Strategic Aviation Corps, was ordered 'to prepare a regiment of strategic aviation to fly to Israel to bomb a number of military targets. We started the preparation, studied the maps, examined Israeli air defence systems . . . It was a real rush . . . we loaded the bombs and were awaiting the signal to go.' An Israeli journalist, Isabella Ginor, has uncovered evidence that the Kremlin intervened to stop hawks in the military taking action. Once Israel started moving into Syria, a plan was put together to land a raiding party of about 1000 men and 40 tanks from an amphibious landing ship at or to the north of Haifa, Israel's main port and naval base. Soviet Arabic language interpreters had been on board since 11

May. They were told they would liaise with Arabs inside Israel after a landing in Haifa. The raiding party was roughly improvised, but it might have been able to do some damage. Although most of the Israeli army was a long way from Haifa, on the front lines against Egypt, Syria and Jordan, battle-ready forces could have reached Haifa within twenty-four hours, and the Israeli air force would have bombarded the raiders without mercy from the first moment. But the USSR would have been directly involved, which would have taken the crisis on to lethal new ground. Some of the men told to 'volunteer' for the operation knew what was being risked. 'What then,' one of them told Ginor, 'we land our force and world war three begins?' At a Communist party politburo meeting in the Kremlin on 10 June hawks led by the acting defence minister, Andrei Grechko, and Yuri Andropov, the head of the KGB, pressed for action. They were overruled by more cautious civilian leaders, who 'realised that half an hour after we landed the world would be in ruins'. The foreign minister Andrei Gromyko suggested breaking off diplomatic relations instead. One of Andropov's military advisers, Nikolai Ogarkov, said in 1991, 'Thank God, that under the [Soviet] feudal regime we only had Afghanistan. There might have been Poland, the Middle East and . . . frightening to contemplate, nuclear war.'

Imwas

Some of the Palestinians who had been expelled from the three West Bank villages of Imwas, Beit Nuba and Yalu were given shelter by the great Trappist monastery of Latrun. A local official from the nearby Israeli settlement, Kibbutz Nachshon, was ordered to 'transfer' them all to Ramallah. The idea of 'transferring' Arabs out of the land needed for the Jewish state was well established in Zionist thought. Various schemes had been discussed since the 1930s. It is still an attractive idea to right-wing extremists in Israel. But as the official recalled a year later in a mimeographed newsletter on the kibbutz, 'transfer' may sound painless, but what it meant was uprooting people from their homes. He wrote that 'an order is an order but to go physically to take out children and people and transfer them on buses . . . even though I tried to keep it as humane as possible it was hard to digest. It was much harder than killing someone or dealing with those already dead.'

Hikmat Deeb Ali found his family in a village nearby. They joined the long column of refugees on the road to Ramallah. Just outside the town, Israeli soldiers stopped them and arrested twenty-five men of military age. Hikmat had a child in each arm and one on his shoulders. After some argument between themselves, the soldiers let him stay with his family.

One of the soldiers who was guarding the village of Beit Nuba was an army reservist called Amos Kenan. He was struck by the beauty of the stone houses, which stood in orchards of olives, apricots and grapevines. There were carefully watered cypresses and other trees that had been grown for their beauty and shade. Between the trees were neatly hoed and weeded rows of vegetables. In Beit Nuba, Kenan and his fellow soldiers found a wounded Egyptian commando officer and some old women. The soldiers were told to take up positions around the villages. Israel Radio had been broadcasting assurances in Arabic that it was safe for Palestinian villagers to return home. But if anyone tried to get into Yalu, Beit Nuba and Imwas, the soldiers were to shoot over their heads to keep them out. Kenan and the other soldiers in the villages had been told why. Imwas, Yalu and Beit Nuba were to be destroyed. The houses would be blown up and the rubble bulldozed flat. There were good reasons, the platoon commander told his men; to straighten out the Latroun 'finger' in the confrontation line between Israel and Jordan; to punish 'dens of murderers'; and to deprive infiltrators of a base in future.

At noon the first bulldozer arrived and set about uprooting the trees and destroying the houses and everything that was inside them. Then a column of refugees arrived, trying to get back into their village. Kenan's platoon tried to explain in Arabic what they had been ordered to do. They ignored their orders to shoot over the civilians' heads to drive them away. Many of the soldiers were veterans of the 1948 war. Kenan had fought in the extremist Stern Gang against the British. They were experienced fighters who did not like the look of what seemed to them to be an operation against peaceful farmers.

Kenan wrote and almost immediately published an account of what happened.

There were old men hardly able to walk, old women mumbling to themselves, babies in their mothers' arms, small children weeping, begging for water. They waved white flags. We told them to move on to Beit Sira. They said that wherever they went, they were driven away, that nowhere were they allowed to stay. They said they had been on the road for four days – without food or water. Some had perished along the way. They asked only to be allowed back into their own village and said we would do better to kill them. Some had brought with them a goat, a sheep, a camel or a donkey. A father crunched grains of wheat in his hand to soften so that his four children might have something to eat. On the horizon, we spotted the next line approaching. One man was carrying a 50 kilo sack of flour on his back and that was how he walked mile after mile. More old men, more women, more babies. They flopped down exhausted at the spot where they were told to sit . . . we did not allow them into the village to pick up the belongings, because the order was that they must not be allowed to see their homes being destroyed. The children wept and some of the soldiers wept too. We went to look for water but found none. We stopped an army vehicle in which sat a lieutenant colonel, two captains and a woman. We took a jerry can of water from them and tried to make it go round the refugees. We handed out sweets and cigarettes. More of our soldiers wept. We asked the officers why the refugees were being sent back and forth and driven away from everywhere they went. The officers said it would do them good to walk

311

and asked, 'Why worry about them, they're only Arabs?' We were glad to hear that half an hour later they were arrested by the military police, who found their car stacked with loot.

In the refugee camp in Jordan where they ended up after the war, a family from Beit Nuba told a researcher that they saw red soil being put over the place where the houses had been. It felt 'just like a dream. It's as if we had never been there.'

Refugees in Ramallah on the West Bank had heard Israeli proclamations that it was safe to go home. Hikmat Deeb Ali did not try to return. With six children, it was impossible to walk back. The people who tried made it as far as Kenan and his colleagues. They saw Israeli trucks taking away the old heavy stones that had been their houses. What was left of their possessions was taken away to be dumped in a landfill. They were never allowed back to rebuild their homes. The sites of the villages were turned into a forest called Canada Park. Thirty-six years later, it is a popular Israeli picnic spot.

UN Security Council, New York

Goldberg, the American ambassador to the UN, asked Rafael, his Israeli counterpart, to join him in the delegates' lounge. Goldberg was direct. 'The situation has reached a point where you must immediately make a statement that Israel has ceased all operations on the Syrian front. Fedorenko [the Soviet ambassador] any minute now, is going to make a statement in the form of an ultimatum. He will declare that "the Soviet government is prepared to use every available means to make Israel respect the ceasefire resolution".' Goldberg said he was speaking on the specific and urgent instructions of President Johnson, who did not want the war to end with a Soviet ultimatum. It would be 'disastrous for the future of not only Israel, but of us all'. Rafael was, once again, playing for time, arguing that he could not do anything without the authorisation of his government, when he was called to the phone. It was the foreign ministry in Jerusalem. There was a show of reluctance. They would stop even though their position 'will not provide future protection for Israeli border settlements'. But Rafael took down a statement accepting the ceasefire, which went into effect at six-thirty in the evening, Israel time.

Israel had destroyed its enemies, just as its generals and the intelligence services in Washington and London had predicted. The victory was greeted with huge relief by the Israeli people. Because of strict censorship, they had never known how confident their generals were of victory. Instead they had listened to blood-curdling Arab propaganda, which they had no choice other than to take seriously. Twenty-two years after the end of the European Holocaust, many Israeli civilians believed they had been delivered from an evil that could have turned into another genocide. If the Arab armies could have destroyed the Jewish state, millions of Arabs would have been delighted. But as the commanders of the IDF knew, they would never have the chance. Israel was too strong.

Reaction to the victory in Western Europe and North America was summed up by the journalist Martha Gellhorn, one of the great reporters of the twentieth century's wars. 'In June 1967, Israel was the hero of the western world. The Six-Day War was a famous victory, unmatched in modern warfare. The David and Goliath aspect of this conflict aroused great admiration. Considering Goliath's superior force, it looked beforehand as if David might not make it.' The truth, of course, that was demonstrated so well by the IDF during six days of war, was that if any country in the Middle East was Goliath, it was Israel. But Abba Eban, its foreign minister, sensed and seized skilfully the prevailing mood in the West. On the second day of the war, in a speech at the United Nations in New York that reflected the genuine fears of Israeli civilians, he described the previous fortnight as a time of 'peril for Israel wherever it looked. Its manpower had been hastily mobilised, its economy and commerce were beating with feeble pulse, its streets were dark and empty – there was an apocalyptic air of approaching peril, and Israel faced this danger alone . . .'

The idea that the story of David and Goliath was being replayed in the 1960s was easy to understand, and enormously attractive in

Israel and the West. It was also a deadly political weapon, as effective in its own way as the IDF had been on the battlefield. It helped turn a military victory into a political one. Eshkol, Eban and the rest of the Israeli government were determined to avoid a repeat of what Eban called the 'nightmare' of 1956, when Israel 'won a glorious victory and then . . . [was] forced back by political pressure without any concrete gain'. Just as important as David and Goliath to Eshkol and Eban was their successful resistance to the demands of the Israeli generals and their cabinet allies for an immediate military response to Egypt's adventurism. By not going for immediate war, and by dropping the problem in the lap of Lyndon Johnson, they gained the moral high ground. Once the Americans realised that the only way to stop a Middle East war was to risk starting one themselves, something they were not prepared to do, Israel's politicians were free to turn to their superbly confident and competent generals without paying an international political price. By the time Eban addressed the UN Security Council on 6 June, President Johnson's most influential advisers were already telling him that Israel should be allowed to hold on to the land they had captured until a broader peace settlement could be negotiated. The Sinai was returned to Egypt after the Camp David peace agreement in 1979. The West Bank, Golan Heights and Gaza are still under Israeli control.

The Israeli newspapers that were being prepared on the evening the war ended talked about the Messiah walking behind advancing Israeli tanks. Even to secular Israelis, victory felt miraculous. But it was no miracle. Israel won because of a generation of hard work. In 1972 some of Israel's commanders in the Six-Day War were starting to enter politics and were in no mood to minimise their role in one of the most overwhelming military victories of the twentieth century. Future president Ezer Weizman, blunt as ever, told an Israeli newspaper that 'there was never a danger of extermination. This hypothesis had never been considered in any serious meeting.' Chaim Herzog, another future president, agreed: 'There was never any danger of annihilation.' General Matityahu Peled, a pioneer of the peace movement said that, 'To pretend that the Egyptian forces concentrated on our borders were capable of threatening Israel's existence not only insults the intelligence of any person capable of analysing this kind of situation, but is more than anything an insult to the Israeli army.'

So if Israel did not face extermination in 1967, why was it fighting? Fifteen years later, Menachem Begin, by then Israel's prime minister, told the *New York Times*: 'In June 1967 we had a choice. The Egyptian army concentrations in the Sinai approaches do not prove that Nasser was really about to attack us. We must be honest with ourselves. We decided to attack him.' The choice was about going to war or letting Nasser inflict Israel's most serious political defeat since independence in 1948. Losing the port of Eilat's connection to the Red Sea, Africa and Iranian oil would not put the existence of the Jewish state in danger. It would have been a serious economic blow, but even worse for Israel's leaders, it would have been a genuine Arab political victory. Nasser risked everything in pursuit of that political victory. He did not want a war. But he convinced himself that if he took a military crisis to the brink, he could force Zionism into its first backward step. His gamble was based on the delusion that Israel would not fight, and the illusion that his forces would at least hold the IDF until the superpowers forced a ceasefire. Both the Arabs and the Israelis are bad at reading each other's motives, but Nasser could not have got it more wrong. In 1967, Israel's own rules of behaviour told it clearly that if Nasser did not back down, it would go to war, to defeat the Arabs in the way that it had been planning since the early 1950s. Eshkol and Eban did not embrace war willingly. But they were prepared to fight rather than hand Nasser and the Arabs any sort of victory, bloodless or bloody. The generals and their fire-breathing political allies would have fought much sooner. They regarded war as a part of Israel's life in the Middle East. For them, the dangers lay in hesitation. But Eshkol, Eban, Allon, Dayan and the rest of them were agreed. An Arab victory, political or military, whether or not he attacked, was simply unthinkable.

On the Arab side post-mortems started. One condemned the way that 'foolish and irresponsible' Arab governments 'allowed themselves to appear as the aggressor instead of the victims. While they talked of war and conquest, Israel prepared for it.' Amer Ali, a retired Iraqi major-general, submitted a devastating analysis of Arab military failure to heads of state of the Arab League. He ripped into weak political and military leadership, faulty strategy and inadequate logistics. The fundamental aim of warfare, he wrote, is the complete operational destruction of the enemy until 'he is neither willing nor able to continue resistance. This aim can only be achieved by persistence and by taking the initiative, qualities which the Arab leaders have lacked for nineteen years, and the lack of which has been aggravated by the lying propaganda broadcast by all Arab radio stations.' The Arabs, the general went on, also ignored the power of surprise, 'one of the most effective weapons available'. Instead, they 'publicised their own movements, used conventional plans against which the enemy had already taken precautions and depended on foreign newspapers and periodicals for information about the enemy's movements'.

In every department of warfare in which the Arab armies failed, Israel excelled. The Israelis were clear about what they had to do. The Arabs were confused. Another Arab military critic warned that if his side did not improve its coordination and manoeuvrability and seize the element of surprise Israel would always win 'even if we arm ourselves with nuclear bombs'. But criticism went much deeper than the conduct of military affairs. Even the way that the Arabic language was used to create and then embroider Arab dreams and illusions was attacked. Writers called for a more honest use of words. The rhetoric about revolution, reform and rebirth that had surged around the Arab world in the 1950s and '60s was shown by the defeat to be hollow. The debate among intellectuals was passionate. Much of what they said is still valid in the twenty-first century. But because most Arabs lived in police states, not much of it penetrated to the masses. In the years ahead, they started listening intently to a message that was much stronger, that came loud and clear from the mosques.

A few days after he emerged with his camel from the Sinai desert,

Major Ibrahim El Dakhakny left Port Said for Cairo by car. To his horror, an artillery exchange started as they drove along the Egyptian side of the Suez canal. Shells landed near them. It was his most frightening moment since he left Gaza. 'Oh God, I thought, to get this far, and die here! But two days later I was back in my office in Cairo . . . We had to start work to rebuild.'

Consequences

Operation Johnson

Nasser called in the Egyptian general staff and exploded with fury. They were 'cowards and bastards'. Nasser's entourage was full of talk of reprisals against senior officers. In the end there were trials, but no executions. He huffed and puffed about restarting the war, but the Israelis were not impressed. Even though Egypt was re-arming, they believed the damage they had inflicted made war impossible 'for quite some time to come'. By the end of July morale in Egypt was at a very low ebb. The full implications of defeat had sunk in. More people were prepared openly to oppose the government and fiercely to criticise the 'bourgeois lifestyle' of the officer class that sustained Nasser's regime.

Nasser's biggest problem, though, was Field Marshal Amer, who was refusing to accept his dismissal as commander-in-chief. It was a direct challenge to Nasser's authority. The president's old fears about Amer leading a coup against him resurfaced. The field marshal was officially under house arrest in his villa in Giza, a suburb of Cairo near the pyramids. But he had surrounded himself with around two hundred loyal officers and kinsmen from his village in Upper Egypt, all of whom he had looked after royally in the fat years. They turned the house into a fortress.

Across the city, around the pool in an exclusive club in Heliopolis, three close advisers of Nasser met on his orders. They were Amin Howedi, the new minister of defence and director of general intelligence, Sami Sharaf, Nasser's chief fixer and private one-man intelligence agency, and Sha'rawi Goma, the interior minister. They hatched a plan to bring Amer to heel that, sardonically, they called Operation Johnson. Arresting him at his villa was no good because it could turn into a bloodbath. Stopping Amer's limousine in the centre of the capital when he was out defying his house arrest, touring his old haunts in Cairo, could also be bloody. They came up with something much more discreet. Nasser would invite Amer to dinner at his home. At the same time troops would surround Amer's house. Amer would then be told that the game was up. They hoped he – and his men – would come quietly. Nasser wanted the job done by 29 August, when he was due to go to Khartoum for the Arabs' official inquest into the June disaster.

Amer leapt at the chance to have dinner with Nasser again. On 25 August he arrived at the president's house, which was much more modest than his own. Minutes after he went inside, his car was seized. There were going to be no quick exits. Waiting with Nasser were the vice-presidents Zakkaria Mohieddin and Hussein el Shafei and Anwar El Sadat, the speaker of the national assembly. When Amer was sacked at the end of the war Nasser sent Sadat to offer him a moneyed exile. Amer sent Sadat back to his master with a flea in his ear. This time, nothing nearly as tempting was on the table.

Howedi watched Amer going in, confirmed that his house in Giza had been ringed with troops, then went into the reception area outside the sitting room to wait. He could hear raised voices. After a while, Nasser came out. He was furious, 'smoking like a refinery'. He stamped up the stairs to his bedroom. Howedi went into the sitting room, to join Amer and the three vice-presidents. He could feel the tension in the air. Sadat seemed to be close to tears.

Amer exclaimed mockingly, 'Look, the minister of defence has arrived. You've really been cooking something up here, haven't you?' Then he went into the bathroom, which was off the main hall. After a few minutes he came out with a half-full glass of water in his hand. He threw it on the floor and said, 'Go tell the president that Amer has taken poison.' Howedi ran up the stairs. Nasser had changed into slippers and a T-shirt. Howedi blurted out the message. Nasser did not believe it. 'If he was going to do that he would have after what happened in Sinai,' he said sarcastically.

Downstairs doctors were arriving for Amer, who was showing no signs of expiring. In fact he had perked up, and was protesting loudly that he was not the only one to blame for what had happened. At Amer's house his people were burning documents in the garden. By 4:00 a.m. General Fawzi reported in from Giza. The house had surrendered. Three lorry-loads of weapons had been removed.

Amer returned home. On 13 September he was sitting with his eleven-year-old son, Salah, in his grand drawing room. Now he had lost his arsenal and his private army, he was surrounded by Nasser's men. General Fawzi, who had succeeded him as head of the army, and General Riad, who had presided over Jordan's defeat, entered the room. They informed Amer he was to be moved from his house. He refused. Guards grabbed him to take him by force. The field marshal was a big man, over six feet tall and well built. His son saw him struggling with the guards as they dragged him out of the room. It was Salah's last sight of his father. Amer, the authorities made it known, was under observation for his own protection because he had tried to kill himself again. Doctors, his family say, found no evidence of poison when they pumped his stomach. Fawzi moved him to a villa owned by the secret police in Mariotya, not far from the pyramids. He was closely guarded, and checked every six hours by doctors.

The next morning, 14 September, he sent a message to his family asking for books and for medical preparations he needed for toothache. They heard nothing more until the next day, when a messenger arrived telling them to travel to Minya, Amer's home village in Upper Egypt. As his wife, four daughters and three sons drove into the village they were greeted by crowds of wailing women.

They realised Amer must be dead. They were taken to the graveyard, where he had already been buried. Eleven-year-old Salah never forgot that the cement on the stone over the grave was still wet. An official communiqué was issued. Field Marshal Amer had taken poison and killed himself.

Operation Johnson had succeeded. Amer was no longer a threat to Nasser's regime. The question is whether Amer was murdered, as his family believe, or whether he killed himself. Certainly, Amer had reasons to end his life. He faced personal and professional ruin. He was being blamed for a catastrophic defeat. He faced trial for the capital crime of conspiring to bring down the government. And Cairo's drawing rooms were buzzing with the scandal, which had just leaked out, that he had secretly made his mistress, a famous actress, into his second wife. Thirty-five years on, Howedi and Sharaf, surviving members of the team that ran Operation Johnson, insist that the field marshal obtained a deadly poison called Aonitine from stocks held by the army. Howedi says that when Amer's body was examined, unused capsules of the poison were found taped behind his testicles. He claims that on 26 August, the day after his house arrest began, Amer was visited by the head of the army's poisons department who later confessed he prepared capsules of Aonitine for the field marshal.

Amer's family insist that he was murdered on the orders of Nasser. They say he collapsed after drinking a glass of guava juice that had been spiked with Aonitine. A week before he died, on 7 September, Amer completed a last political testament, which was smuggled out of Egypt to Lebanon after his death and published in *Life* magazine. In it he wrote that his enemies were closing in. He said he no longer felt safe from Nasser, his 'friend and brother . . . I am receiving threats because I asked for a public trial. Some two hours ago I was visited by an intelligence officer whom I would not bother to look at in the time of my glory. He threatened to silence me forever if I ventured to talk. When I said I wanted to contact the president he said: if you think your friendship with the president can protect you, you are mistaken. I tried to contact the president by telephone . . . for three days I was told that he was busy. I feel sure that a conspiracy is being prepared against me . . .'

Aonitine was found in Amer's body at the autopsy. The question is how it got there. The saga, his family insist, has all the signs of a cover-up. If he was planning suicide, they say, why did he ask his family a few hours before he allegedly killed himself to send him books and ointment for toothache and sore gums? It took six hours for Nasser's men to tell the attorney-general that Amer was dead. It was another six hours before forensic scientists came to the villa where he died. By then, his corpse had been dressed in clean pyjamas, and the glass that his family believe contained a lethal cocktail of guava juice and poison had been washed, dried and put away.

The official report into his death, signed by the Egyptian attorney-general, said that Amer had killed himself with two doses of poison, on the day he died and the day before. But in 1975 Anwar El Sadat, who assumed the presidency of Egypt after Nasser died in 1970, reopened the files. Dr Ali Diab, a professor and toxicologist at Egypt's top institute for scientific research, re-examined all the evidence. He said it was physically impossible for Amer to have taken two separate doses of Aonitine a night apart. A fraction of the dose contained in one of the capsules would have killed him instantly. Dr Diab concluded that Amer could not have killed himself. Someone must have administered the poison.

Even without Amer, the CIA believed that the Egyptian army was Nasser's 'main source of danger'. Even his life could be at stake. Nasser was prepared to take the risk. It was good for him to have Amer out of the way. The remaining Amer loyalists were purged from the army. The creeping fear of a coup led by his old friend left him for the first time since at least 1961. General Fawzi, who owed Nasser everything and who was lacking even an ounce of the charm and charisma that had made Amer so popular, was firmly in control of the army. Nasser travelled to the Arab summit in Khartoum at the end of August knowing that he would have a job to which he would be able to return. Even though he had led Egypt and millions of Arabs who idolised him to disaster, he was more secure than he had been in years.

The new Goliath

The British foreign correspondent James Cameron was exhilarated by Israel's victory. The following Monday he reported that 'many are saying that Zion was born not nineteen years ago with the birth of the state of Israel, but today, in its great and rather frightening exultation, with the Jewish nation suddenly translated from David into Goliath'. In fact Israel had been Goliath for years. It simply had not had the chance to use its strength properly.

Washington suddenly found Israel much more attractive. The 1967 war transformed its entire approach to the Middle East. Israel had always come first. But the United States had tried, not always successfully, to have a relationship with Arab countries too. It was prepared to restrain Israel, to criticise it in public and even vote to censure it in the UN Security Council. The Eisenhower administration made Israel disgorge the land it captured in the 1956 war. All that changed after the lightning victory in 1967. Some senior officials in the Johnson White House realised what was happening. On 31 May, before a shot had been fired, Harold Saunders, a senior national security aide, warned that in the two weeks since Nasser mobilised, 'We have reversed the policy of twenty years . . . Israel may really be the big winner. For twenty years Israel has sought a special relationship – even a private security guarantee – with us. We have steadfastly refused in order to preserve our other interests in the Middle East.' Now the US had emphatically and irreversibly taken sides.

The Americans expected Israel would win quickly. But when they saw it happening, Israel became a much more interesting prospect as an ally. Vietnam was bleeding the Johnson administration to death and the Israelis were making war look simple. Better still, they had used Western weapons to crush Soviet allies and Soviet weapons. The president's envoy Harry McPherson wrote to Johnson that 'after the doubts, confusions and ambiguities of Vietnam, it was deeply moving to see people whose commitment is total and unquestioning'. Like most Westerners in 1967, he was deeply impressed by the macho, self-reliant sabras. 'Israel at war destroys the prototype of the pale, scrawny Jew; the soldiers I saw were tough, muscular and sunburned. There is also an extraordinary combination of discipline and democracy among officers and enlisted men; the latter rarely salute and frequently argue, but there is no doubt about who will prevail.' In the US, Israel had enormous public support. America fell in love with its tough young friend.

The US had always had enemies in the Arab world. But now it took on the role Britain had filled earlier in the century, as the Arabs' bogey-man, the cause of all their problems. The CIA's exceptionally well-connected staff in Amman reported that 'the time has passed when it would have been easy for the US government to recoup its prestige with the Arabs by uttering a few proper phrases . . . The US government should make no mistake, it is hated in the Arab world; innate courtesy, apathy from the shock of defeat, and the memory of kindnesses by individual American friends lead most educated Jordanians to conceal this hate, but it is there.' The only way to reverse matters would be to force Israel to leave the conquered territory.

The risks of a long occupation were clear to Secretary of State Rusk. On 14 June, four days after the war ended, Dean Rusk warned the special committee of the NSC at the White House that if Israel held on to the West Bank 'it would create a revanchism for the rest of the twentieth century'. At the beginning of the twenty-first, revanchism, the desire of the Palestinians to regain lost territory, is stronger than ever.

But Johnson, even though he saw 'festering problems' ahead, made his choice. On 19 June he delivered a speech accepting Israel's view that a return to the situation as it was on 4 June was 'not a prescription for peace, but for renewed hostilities'. Before the war Israel had feared that they might, as in 1956, be forced to give up the spoils of victory. But Eshkol and Eban's patience and restraint in the weeks before the war paid off. Until there was a peace deal, Israel could stay where it was.

Occupation

A 25-year-old Israeli soldier back from the war predicted that Israel was going to be changed irrevocably by the huge territories it had captured. He told his comrades, 'We've lost something terribly precious. We've lost our little country . . . our little country seems to get lost in this vast land.' All the issues that are now depressingly familiar to anyone who sees news reports about the Arabs and the Israelis – violence, occupation, settlements, the future of Jerusalem – took their current form as a result of the war. The shape of the occupation emerged very quickly. Warnings about the dangers that lay ahead were ignored.

Just after the war ended, David Ben-Gurion, Israel's first prime minister, warned Israel against the seductive charms of victory. In a speech at Beit Berl, the think-tank of the Israeli left, he said that staying in the territories would distort the Jewish state and might even destroy it. Israel must keep Jerusalem, but everything else should go back to the Arabs immediately, with or without a peace agreement. But Ben-Gurion, the architect of Israeli independence, seemed way out of touch. He was old, bad tempered and ignored. Abba Eban, the foreign minister, was alarmed by new maps of Israel that showed it stretching from the Golan to Suez and running along the entire length of the river Jordan. They were 'not a guarantee of peace but an invitation to early war'. Eban believed that Israel's legitimacy derived from the fact that it had accepted that British-ruled Palestine would be partitioned between the Jews and the Arabs. He wanted to use the captured territory as a bargaining chip for negotiation, not as a place for expansion or settlement.

But the mood in Israel blew away any suggestion of caution as decisively as the Israeli army had dealt with the Arabs. In just under a week of war the Israeli public went from despair to the joy of deliverance. Israelis were never in as much danger as they thought they were, thanks to their military strength and the Arabs' weakness. But although Israeli generals knew it, the public did not. Abba Eban, more and more worried about the way the new post-war Middle East was developing, felt as if he was 'in an isolated realm of anxiety while the noise of unconfined joy kept intruding through the window'.

The 1967 war made Israel into an occupier, which more than anything is why it still matters. Overnight it gained control of the lives of more than one million Palestinians in the West Bank and Gaza. The experience has been a disaster for Israelis and Palestinians. By 2003 Israel had become a coloniser of land in which the Palestinian population had trebled. Abba Eban predicted that Palestinians would not lose their 'taste for flags, honour, pride, and independence', but the Israeli occupation still seeks to make them into a subject people. The occupation has created a culture of violence that cheapens life and brutalises the people who enforce and impose the occupation and those who fight it. Human rights and self-determination are denied to Palestinians. With nowhere else to go, more and more of them have turned to the extremists.

The signs were there from the beginning. After Israel's victory was secured, some of the fighting soldiers found occupation duties distasteful. Being a conqueror, one complained, 'destroys human dignity . . . I felt it happening to me, felt myself losing respect for people's lives.' When they were relieved, they were just as dismayed by the effect that occupation had on rear-echelon soldiers who 'suddenly considered themselves tough . . . [and] found this a good opportunity to play top dog'. In November 1967 a British reporter visited the burial place of Abraham, Isaac, Jacob and their wives in Hebron. It is a holy place for both Jews and Muslims. The soldier on the door asked him to cover his head, out of respect for the Jewish faith. When the reporter offered to take off his shoes too, in deference to Muslim sensibilities, the soldier told him not to bother. The mutual hatred has deepened ever since. Anyone who doubts how little respect most Israeli soldiers have for Palestinians after nearly forty years as occupiers – and how much sullen hatred they receive in return – need only spend a couple of hours at a checkpoint. Of course there was hatred on both sides before the war. The difference afterwards was that the two sides came into daily contact.

In June 1967, with a political career still only a gleam in his eye,

General Ariel Sharon left his headquarters in Sinai and flew back to Israel in a small helicopter. He told the pilot to sweep low along the coast. As they passed places Israel had captured – Jebel Libni, Al-Arish, Rafah, Gaza – Sharon tried to shout something over the thumping of the engine to his travelling companions, who included Yael Dayan, the daughter of the minister of defence. 'He was stretching one hand as if showing us the view, in case we hadn't noticed it, and murmuring something. On a piece of paper – as it was obvious we couldn't hear – he wrote, "All of this is ours", and he was smiling like a proud boy.' While they were still in the desert, they had all talked about what the scale of the victory meant. They agreed that 'the previous borders and armistice agreements were annulled by the war'. Yael Dayan, who went on to become a Labour politician closely identified with the peace movement, concluded at the end of the war that Israel had become 'something new, safer, larger, stronger and happier'. Sharon was part of the government that presided over the return of Sinai to the Egyptians after the two countries made peace. The biggest question about his time as prime minister, which began in 2001, is whether he will do the same for the West Bank, Gaza and the Golan Heights.

Another cock-a-hoop general was Ezer Weizman, who created the air force that won the war. He had always been open about his belief that Israel had the right to 'Hebron and Nablus and all of Jerusalem', even though his views were politically incorrect for most of his colleagues who, unlike Weizman, were from the Israeli left. When he was air force commander the straight-talking Weizman used to lecture his subordinates that the Arabs living on the hills of the West Bank saw Israel as a tantalizing stripper of a country, 'green, flourishing, prosperous, twinkling at night with a mass of lights . . . And you know what happens to a healthy man when he watches a rousing striptease act? Right, that's exactly what happens to him! Therefore there won't be any choice. The Arab will have to be moved away from Israel's naked borders. It's the only way of knocking these exciting ideas of a masculine conquest of Israel out of his head!'

327

Jerusalem

Just after the war the Holocaust survivor Elie Wiesel wrote a story of redemption set around Israel's victory called 'A Beggar in Jerusalem'. It ends with the beggar, a symbol of exile, standing at the Wailing Wall preaching that victory came from the Jews' own tragedy. The lost communities of Eastern Europe 'emptied of their Jews, these names severed from their life source, had joined forces and built a safety curtain – an *Amud Esh*, a pillar of fire – around the city which had given them a home. Sighet and Lodz, Vilna and Warsaw, Riga and Bialystock, Drancy and Bratzlav: Jerusalem had once again become the memory of an entire people.

'"And the dead", the preacher was saying in a vibrant voice. "The messenger who is alive today, the victor of today, would be wrong to forget the dead. Israel defeated its enemies – do you know why? I'll tell you. Israel won because its army, its people, could deploy six million more names in battle."'

The novelist Amos Oz, who fought as a paratrooper in the Sinai, was one of the few Israelis who questioned Israel's right to all of Jerusalem. Oz saw the mother of a soldier from his kibbutz who was killed in the fighting for Jerusalem weeping for her dead son. The young man's name was Micha Hyman. One of her neighbours, trying to comfort her, said, 'Look, after all, we've liberated Jerusalem, he didn't die for nothing.' Mrs Hyman burst out, 'The whole of the Wailing Wall isn't worth Micha's little finger as far as I'm concerned . . .' Oz concluded: 'If what you're telling me is that we fought for our existence, then I'd say it was worth Micha Hyman's little finger. But if you tell me it was the Wall we fought for, then it wasn't worth his little finger. Say what you like – I do have a feeling for those stones – but they're only stones. And Micha was a person. A man. If dynamiting the Wall today would bring Micha back to life, then I'd say blow it up!'

But Oz was in a small minority. Israel's possession of the stones of the Wailing Wall sent shivers up and down the whole country, among the religious, the secular, even the atheists. They all believed the sacrifices of the men who had died fighting for Jerusalem were well worth it. Israel seemed more complete. The historic capital of the Jewish people was in Jewish hands and they planned to keep it that way. 'Jerusalem is beyond discussion' was the way Yael Dayan and her friends at General Sharon's headquarters put it in the desert, and their view was shared by almost every Israeli. Some suggestions emerged that the holy places in the Old City might be in some sort of international framework, but always under overall Israeli control.

Standing at the Wall, close to its stones, minutes after it was captured, Yoel Herzl felt an emotional connection with Israel for the first time in his life. Until then, he had always felt like an outsider, though he idolised Uzi Narkiss, who was standing not far from him, the general who had given him his chance and made him his adjutant. Herzl was born in Romania, where the Nazis killed his father. In 1947, Herzl and his family decided to escape the new communist regime to get to Palestine. On the first leg of the journey Soviet soldiers opened fire at them as they tried to cross into Hungary. In a confused few minutes in a dark forest the young boy, barely a teenager, was separated from his mother and brothers. The Russians put him in an orphanage. Four years later, the local communist party boss, a Jew who had known his father, took pity on Herzl. He let him join his family who had made it to what had become Israel.

As soon as he could, Herzl joined the IDF. 'It's hard to understand, a small Jewish boy, always being hit and in the corner, coming to be an officer in your own land.' Herzl decided that no one was going to hit him again. But it was not easy. He never felt accepted by the native-born kibbutzniks who dominated the army. 'It all came so easily to them. They didn't understand what it was like outside, with no rights and no self-esteem . . . People like me weren't accepted. They used to laugh at me when I studied at night. I finished high school after I became an officer. Even when I was an officer, I was never accepted in the group. But I didn't care what they said.' But it all changed at the Wall. Herzl felt a rush of emotion. Israel – Jerusalem – felt like a part of him for the first time. 'People had no heartfelt connection with Jerusalem until they arrived and saw the

Wall. From that second Jerusalem took a big part of my heart. I will always be ready to fight for it, not because it was our ancient capital, but because of the way the Jordanians treated it. They tried to destroy our Jewish holy places.'

Many religious Jews believed that the victory was a miracle that had been given to them by God. Hanan Porat, the devout paratrooper who fought at Ammunition Hill with Battalion 66, never forgot the sight of his secular comrades weeping at the Wall a few minutes after they captured it: 'I had the sense that here in Jerusalem the inner truth of the Jewish nation was revealed. It was a miracle because the truth of the Bible was combined with the truth of life. An electric current ran right through the people of Israel. I'm talking about soldiers in Sinai who jumped off their tanks and danced when they heard or the Jews in Russia or the United States who also felt it. No one imagined how strong it could be. The connection between the pain of losing friends who were killed and the happiness of the return created a critical mass of feelings that had never existed before.' For Rabbi Zvi Yehuda Kook, Porat's teacher and mentor, the Israeli army was doing God's work. 'The IDF is total sanctity. It represents the rule of the people of the Lord over his land.'

Some Jews looked at their scriptures and deduced that the time of the Messiah was upon them. One rabbi wrote that the war was 'an astounding divine miracle . . . through conquest the whole of Israel has been redeemed from oppression, from Satan's camp. It has entered the realm of sanctity.' The gift had strings: 'If, God forbid, we should return even a tiny strip of land we would thereby give control to the evil forces, to the camp of Satan.' Not all religious Jews agreed. Some believed that the best theological response to the victory would be to make enemies into friends. Gershom Scholem, one of the greatest Jewish thinkers of the twentieth century who pioneered the study of *kabbalah*, Jewish mysticism, warned against the abuse of scripture for political reasons. The upsurge in messianism, he feared, would lead to catastrophe.

But the warnings were ignored. The 'electric current' that Hanan Porat and his friends felt as they captured the Old City powered the movement of Jewish settlers into occupied land, especially the West Bank. Religious fervour combined with a Zionist imperative to settle new land created one of the most dynamic and powerful political movements in Israel, that opposes the return of even a grain of sand.

Israel's occupation of East Jerusalem matters because it has deepened its conflict with the Palestinians and the wider Islamic world. Once again, there were warnings. Bob Anderson, President Johnson's trusted adviser on Arab attitudes and his go-between with Nasser, told him on 6 July 1967 that Jerusalem had a special significance for Arabs: 'The Old City of Jerusalem is capable of stirring mobs in the streets to the point where the fate of our most moderate friends in the Middle East will be in jeopardy and the basis laid for a later holy war.' But Israel insisted it had the only legitimate claim to Jerusalem. It came from the ancient Jewish kingdom which had its capital in Jerusalem 2,000 years before and the prayers and dreams of generations of Jews that one day they would return from an exile that started when the Romans destroyed their Temple in AD 70. But history does not stop. Muslim and Christian claims to Jerusalem had developed in the 1,897 years between the destruction of the Jewish Temple and the Israeli Paratroop Brigade's return to the Temple Mount in 1967, which General Narkiss calculated was the thirty-seventh time that the Old City had been overrun.

Amos Oz felt the strength of the Palestinian link with Jerusalem the day after the war ended, when he arrived there from Al-Arish in his paratrooper's uniform, still carrying his submachine gun. He wrote immediately afterwards that 'with all my soul, I desired to feel in Jerusalem as a man who has dispossessed his enemies and returned to the patrimony of his ancestors'. But then he saw that for the Arabs it was home. 'I passed through the streets of East Jerusalem like a man breaking into some forbidden place. Depression filled my soul. City of my birth. City of my dreams. City of my ancestors' and my people's yearnings. And I was condemned to walk through its streets armed with a sub-machine gun like one of the characters from my childhood nightmares.'

After the war the common wisdom in Israel was that the war had been forced on them and they had not sought territory. For some people that became a good enough reason to keep what had been captured. As a soldier called Asher explained: 'Jerusalem is ours, it's got to be ours and it'll remain ours . . . Because I conquered it, and because I had every right to do so, because I didn't start the war. Everyone knows Israel didn't want territorial gains. It's a good thing we had the chance, and a good thing that we took Jerusalem and other places. There's every justification for hanging on to it all.'

On 28 June Israel annexed the Jordanian side of Jerusalem, around 6 square kilometres, and 65 square kilometres of the West Bank that had never been part of the city. The extra land belonged to twenty-eight Palestinian villages. Israel euphemistically called the annexation 'municipal fusion'. The new areas were added to Jerusalem's boundary. They were mainly intended for Jewish settlement. By the end of the century, most of them were built on. Palestinian community leaders who led fierce local protests were banished from Jerusalem. In Washington the State Department disapproved: 'The over hasty administrative action taken today cannot be regarded as determining the future of the holy places or status of Jerusalem in relation to them. The United States has never recognised such unilateral action by any state in the area as governing the status of Jerusalem.' George Brown, the British foreign secretary, had already warned Remez, the Israeli ambassador in London, that 'the annexation of the Old City by Israel could never be acceptable to the Arabs and would be likely to block any general settlement . . . [It] would be both unwise and unjust.' Most countries in the world, including the United States and the countries of the European Union, still do not recognise Israel's claim to East Jerusalem.

Land

When I was reporting on the thirtieth anniversary of the war in Jerusalem in 1997, an Israeli friend sat me down and explained how all the territory captured in the war, except Jerusalem, would have been handed back immediately if the Arabs had accepted Israel's offers of peace. Lots of Israelis share his view. But it is only partly true.

Israel's first breezy assumption was that all it had to do was sit tight and wait for the Arabs to sue for peace. Israelis wanted to believe that their enemies had been taught such a painful lesson that they had no choice other than to accept Israel on its terms. A few voices called for international help to hurry the process along. But no one on either side tried in a serious way to make peace. Shlomo Gazit, who became co-ordinator of Israeli government operations in the territories, believes Israel should have done more. It missed an opportunity 'as it waited for the Arabs to come begging'.

After only a few weeks, Israelis had a rude awakening. The UN convened an emergency session of the General Assembly on 19 June. Israelis had been overwhelmed by the huge support they had received from the West during the war. But at the UN, according to Michael Hadow, Britain's man in Tel Aviv, they saw that the Arabs 'seemed capable of getting their second wind: that it was not generally accepted that the vanquished must sue for peace: and that the victors had merely been put on a par with the vanquished in a squabble which the world found dangerous and embarrassing'. Israel responded 'with a self-righteous stubbornness and a nation-wide hardening of opinion against friend and foe alike'. By August Gideon Rafael, the Israeli ambassador at the UN, was talking about 'digging in for peace'. Speaking privately to diplomats, he gave the impression 'that the Israelis seemed to be ready to sit tight for years'. By November the cabinet secretary Ya'acov Herzog told the White House that 'Israeli leaders are deeply divided over whether they should risk a political settlement, if the right terms can be negotiated, or sit tight on their expanded boundaries and rely for survival on the added military security that they provide.' By the end of the year, according to Hadow, 'there is virtually unanimous feeling now, not about peace, but about the need to attain maximum security'. The *New York Times* agreed: 'The overwhelming sentiment of Israeli public favours Israel keeping all the territory acquired during the war . . . a peace treaty with the Arab countries would not be worth the sacrifice of land and security.' Moshe Dayan said he was waiting for the Arabs to phone him. But as early as 11 June he told the American TV network CBS that Gaza would not be returning to Egypt, nor the West Bank to Jordan.

The key post-war meeting of the Israeli cabinet on the future of the occupied territories was held in the run-up to the General Assembly session over four days from 16 to 19 June. Prime Minister Levi Eshkol and his leading cabinet ministers agreed to return captured Syrian and Egyptian land, as long as it was demilitarised under a proper peace treaty. But the West Bank was different. At no time did they want to return it to Jordan. From the very beginning, there were powerful pressures to absorb all or most of it. It was seen as a different kind of land, to which Israel had rights, part of the unfinished business of 1948 that could have been captured any time since if it had been prepared to go to war with Jordan.

Westerners tried to understand Israeli politicians by classifying them as 'hawks' or 'doves'. It was a false distinction. 'Doves' like Eshkol had almost identical instincts to 'hawks' like Yigal Allon, especially when it came to the West Bank. Both were in favour of Jewish settlement. Eshkol, Allon and the entire cabinet wanted Israel's eastern border to be along the river Jordan. Abba Eban explained that Israel's desire for security and peace meant it had to keep land: 'No one at all in Israel was ready to return all of Jordan's territories. They would not redivide Jerusalem nor would they again expose Israel's narrow waist to the danger of shelling from Jordanian guns.' Beyond that, there were differences. Eban talked of 'security men', led by Allon, who would not return any land in return for a settlement with King Hussein. The 'politicians' in the cabinet believed Israel would have serious problems if it tried to absorb the Palestinians. Some of them wanted to carve an autonomous Palestinian entity out of the West Bank and the Gaza Strip. Eban was against the idea because he thought it would become an independent state. The justice minister Ya'acov Shimshon Shapiro protested that it was wrong to talk about colonising occupied territory, at a time when the rest of the world was decolonising.

Realising that trying to resolve the matter would cause a damaging public split, the cabinet made no final decisions and postponed any more debate. The government's first instinct was to keep what it was contemplating secret. After all, Israel's spokesmen had said repeatedly that they had no territorial ambitions in the war and absorbing Palestinian land might not go down well in Washington. When, on 18 June, two Israeli papers tried to report a plan to create a Palestinian canton that would eventually be absorbed into Israel, the military censor tried to hold up publication, a decision overturned the next day after furious protests from newspaper editors.

Various schemes for the future of the West Bank existed. Forty-eight hours after the final ceasefire, the army produced two. Three days later a memo was prepared for the prime minister about using water from the occupied territories for agriculture. In the parched Middle East, water is a critical strategic resource. In Gaza, the memo said, they were using too much. The most influential plan was put forward by Yigal Allon. It was never formally approved by the cabinet, but it is more or less what happened. Today's Israeli ideas to enclose Palestinians in small cantons are the direct descendants of what is still known in Israel as the 'Allon Plan'. He wanted Israel's eastern border on the river Jordan, to give the country's defences strategic depth and to enclose the Palestinians in the West Bank. They would live in autonomous districts centred on their main towns, the most important of which would be surrounded by a ring of Jewish settlements and army bases, on land that Israel would annex as part of its sovereign territory. Gaza would also be absorbed by Israel once its refugees had been moved out.

Allon pressed hard for his plan to be approved because, he argued, Israel faced dangers if it did not make the running in the territories. In 1948 'political considerations' had stopped it finishing the job and capturing all of the West Bank and Jerusalem. Now it had to work fast or the Americans might try to impose a peace plan. Worse still, 'the Arabs in the West Bank are recovering from their shock and they may start deluding themselves about bringing Israel back to its former borders'. Allon complained that Israel was not asserting itself enough in East Jerusalem. If it showed weakness by letting refugees back or hesitating over building settlements in the territories it would send a signal that it would pull back from the land it had captured, damaging its own bargaining position. In fact Israel had already annexed East Jerusalem and it was letting only a trickle of refugees back. Authorisation for building settlements was only two months away.

Egypt and Syria did not respond to Israel's overtures, not just because they did not take them seriously. To do so would have been political and perhaps personal suicide for an Arab leader in 1967. Even Nasser believed he would be ousted if he negotiated. Israel's insistence on direct talks was rejected on principle. Face-to-face meetings implied recognition of the Jewish state, which was why Israel wanted them and the Arabs did not. And as for the Israeli assumption that they had finally learnt their lesson, the Arabs were, the CIA warned, 'absolutely unwilling to face reality in the Western sense, i.e., that they, as losers of the war, must pay some price and make the best deal they can with the victors'.

The leaders of Egypt and Syria might have made progress had they been prepared to swallow their pride, risk the fury of their own people and negotiate with Israel. But King Hussein would not have got very far if he had taken up Dayan's offer to pick up the phone and talk about the West Bank and Jerusalem. In late July Abba Eban told George Brown, the British foreign secretary, that 'there was no firm Israeli government decision about the terms that could be offered to Hussein, nor even whether it was in their interests to negotiate seriously with him at all'. Brown concluded from Eban's comments that 'if Hussein embarks on separate negotiations with Israel at this moment, through whatever channel and however discreetly, the odds are that he will not get a settlement he can live with and may well destroy himself and his regime in the process'. A CIA informant said that he would be 'absolutely alone, nobody would support him and he would be killed as his grandfather was killed'. The British ambassador in Amman agreed. Hussein was risking 'an assassin's bullet'. Only Nasser was capable of making a deal with Israel. 'If he takes the lead in seeking peace, Jordan could and would come along, and the radical Arabs would be helpless.'

At the end of August the Arabs held their official inquest into the disaster at a summit in Khartoum. The Sudanese capital, which stands at the place where the Blue Nile meets the White Nile, almost cut off from the outside world by exceptional summer rains, was running out of food, petrol and aviation fuel. The people were cheerful, though. Everywhere Nasser went, he was greeted as a hero by chanting crowds. The first item on the summit's agenda called for a resumption of the war. The conference room went silent as Nasser brought a little reality to the discussion. Looking round the room he said Egypt was in no position to fight. Which other country, he asked, would like to take up arms? No one replied.

They produced a communiqué that, among other things, agreed there would be no peace with Israel, no recognition of Israel and no negotiations with Israel. Western diplomats in Khartoum saw the 'three noes' as the usual ritualistic sloganeering. Britain's representative in Khartoum, Norman Reddaway, did not even mention them directly in his report to London. Nasser, he said, was being forced by economic and military weakness 'to seek a peaceful solution and try to rebuild his country's shattered strength'. Arabs still hated Israel, but seemed prepared for negotiations through the United Nations: 'It is a step forward that the Arabs are ready to seek a political solution short of a direct settlement with the Israelis.'

The UN Security Council hoped Resolution 242, which it passed on 22 November 1967, would become the basis for peacemaking in the Middle East. It emphasised 'the inadmissibility of the acquisition of territory by war'. Israel would give up occupied territory in return for peace deals with the Arabs. A crucial piece of drafting, by the British permanent representative at the UN, Lord Caradon, was vague about the amount of land to be given up by Israel. The English language version of the resolution spoke of 'territories' to be given up, rather than 'the territories' or even 'all the territories'. Caradon wanted it vague to 'to leave room for negotiation on frontier adjustments'. Withdrawal had to be linked to a 'just and lasting peace'. But it was not, Caradon believed, a licence for Israel to keep large amounts of land. He had been 'greatly concerned' about the question of withdrawal since the war ended. As early as 12 June, he wrote: 'In these days we surely cannot defend acquisition of territory by conquest . . . The Israelis themselves said at the beginning of their campaign that they had no aim of territorial conquest. It seems to me clear that we must say nothing which could possibly be regarded as an admission from us that they are entitled to keep what they have won by force of arms.'

The Arabs signed up to 242, fully realising that it was a tacit acknowledgement of Israel's right to exist. But Israel held up the 'three noes' of Khartoum as proof that the Arabs did not want any settlement at all. Anyway, Israel did not take the beaten Arab leaders very seriously. A CIA source in Israel, whose name is still classified, expected Nasser to be ousted in six months while King Hussein did not 'merit respect'. Israel needed to 'call their bluff, stand firm and keep its nerve. Thereafter new Arab regimes must appear which can approach problems realistically.' In the meantime, the Palestinians would be useful workers. 'A new Arab population would be superior as raw material to Iranian and Turkish peasants.'

Resolution 242 might have had immediate results if President Johnson had put his weight behind it. Making a push for peace was discussed inside the White House. Pessimists said there was no point. The Israelis were already, according to LBJ's national security aide Harold Saunders, running a 'campaign to blacken Hussein's image and paint the bleakest picture of Nasser's intentions'. They would scuttle any settlement – and even if they did not, the Arabs would not make the compromises that were necessary for it to work. The other school of thought said that Johnson should try, even if it ended in 'honest failure'. But Israel would have to be pressed 'pretty hard' to get a fair settlement and 1968 was an election year. Johnson's Democrats could suffer at the polls. Saunders reflected that 'a lot of people here and in the Arab world doubt we have the heart to try when it means leaning on Israel'. In the end there was no American peace plan. The war in Vietnam and the convulsions it was causing at home took all President Johnson's waning political energy. In March 1968, exhausted and disheartened, he decided to leave politics.

As ever in the conflict between the Jews and the Arabs, the leaders on both sides failed to display any empathy with or real understanding of the other's position. Neither side was really serious about starting a dialogue and paying the price peace entailed. Israel's destruction of the Arab armies gave it enormous confidence. They might have done a deal if it was on their terms. But, as victors, they were not prepared to make concessions of the kind that Arab leaders would need to sell peace agreements to their sullen and humiliated people – or even to try secret negotiations through an intermediary. By the end of the year, Hadow in Tel Aviv believed that, 'If the Arabs were suddenly to announce their readiness for "direct negotiations", the wrangling at the conference table would be as nothing to the convulsions which would shake and even split the Israeli cabinet.'

For both sides, it was still a game of winner takes all. Arab propaganda before the war about destroying the state of Israel was only fantasy because the Arab armies could not do it, not because they didn't want to. Israelis usually expressed the idea more subtly to Western listeners than the Arabs did, but the same idea, that they could only prosper if the other lot suffered, was still there. The unsubtle General Ezer Weizman laid it out to the British journalist Winston Churchill. 'Don't allow yourself to be fed bullshit about Israel not being built at the expense of the Arabs. If I was a Palestinian Tel Aviv would be blowing up every ten minutes.'

Israel digs in

The Israeli cabinet's decision not to set a firm and public policy on the territories left a vacuum. It allowed people with strong beliefs to push hard for what they wanted. One such person was Hanan Porat, who had fought with the Israeli paratroopers from Ammunition Hill to the Wailing Wall. He wanted to return to his first home, a kibbutz called Kfar Etzion. Its ruins were deep in the West Bank, between

Bethlehem and Hebron. The kibbutz was started by religious nationalists in the 1930s who bought land in an area that the UN later allocated to Arabs in its plan to partition Palestine. During the 1948 war 151 Jews died in a long siege of what was known as the Etzion bloc. Before the end, the women and children, including a six-month-old Hanan Porat, were evacuated. The kibbutz and neighbouring Jewish settlements were looted and destroyed. For the Israelis, it was a catastrophe. Hanan Porat's father only survived because he had been sent out to organise supply convoys from Jerusalem.

The children were brought up to believe that they would return. In the fifties and sixties they went to summer camps together. They would travel to a spot overlooking the West Bank where they could see a tree that stood near their old home. When Israel captured the West Bank, their first thought was to go back. Victory had filled Hanan Porat and the others with religious zeal. They did not regard themselves as occupiers. The biblical heartland of the Jews was not Tel Aviv and the coast. It was the mountains of Judea and Samaria – in other words, the West Bank – and now, through God's will, it was back in Jewish hands. The Arabs could stay if they lived by Jewish consent in a Jewish state, or they could get out.

Within Israel a noisy public debate started about the territories. Ten thousand Israelis signed a petition calling on the government to keep the land. A new political movement started to campaign for the annexation of the 'liberated' areas. Groups calling themselves 'Action Staff for the Retention of the Territories' and 'Movement for the Annexation of the Liberated Territories' called for 'the immediate settlement of the entire West Bank'. Fifty-seven prominent Israelis, including reserve generals, rabbis, the Nobel laureate for literature S. Y. Agnon and well-known kibbutz leaders formed the 'Movement for a Greater Israel'. They published a declaration on 22 September that stated that the victory had brought Israel into 'a new and fateful era'. The land of Israel was 'indivisible' and no government had the right to divide it again.

The same day the advertisement appeared in the papers, Eshkol met Hanan Porat and the other would-be settlers. He told them that the future of the West Bank was not decided. But with instinctive sympathy for them, he promised to help. Two days later, on 24 September, Eshkol told the cabinet that the Etzion bloc would be resettled. Other settlements were to be set up at Kfar Banyas, east of the old frontier with Syria, and Beit Ha-Arava, at the northern end of the Dead Sea. All were classified as special cases because their roots went back before 1948. But the principle was established. Jews could live in the Occupied Territories.

The Americans and the British tried, half-heartedly, to dissuade the Israelis. They believed that Jewish settlement in the territories would put peace even further out of reach. In Washington the State Department said, 'The plans for the establishment of permanent Israeli settlements would be inconsistent with the Israeli position as we understand it – that they regard occupied territories and all other issues arising out of the fighting in June to be matters for negotiation.' The Americans sent their ambassador in Tel Aviv a quotation from a treatise on international law, stating that a military occupant has a duty to administer the country according to its existing laws and rules. But the State Department was not optimistic that it would have any effect on the Israelis. In London the Israeli ambassador explained the settlements were 'only temporary military holding operations . . . to counter subversive activity without setting up a strong military regime, and simultaneously to hold internal pressure for the reoccupation of Israeli settlements destroyed by the Jordanians in 1948'.

At the foreign ministry in Jerusalem the veteran Israeli diplomat Arthur Lourie complained that Eshkol had agreed to the establishment of the settlements 'without thinking', and without consulting the cabinet, and as a result he had 'pulled the rug out' from under foreign minister Abba Eban at the UN in New York. The settlements, he said, meant there was less chance that the West Bank would be surrendered in peace talks. The emotional reaction to Eshkol's decision in the press meant 'this was just one more item which the Israel government could plead that it was unable to reverse without dire consequences to itself from the voting public'. Eban himself feared the 'great gusts of theological emotion' that were sweeping across Israel. A new religious dimension had appeared in what had been entirely secular calculations about the security of the state.

If, as Arthur Lourie said, Eshkol had not had to think too hard about allowing the first settlements in the West Bank, that was because the development felt entirely natural to the founding generation of Israelis. In mainstream Zionism, settlement was a sacred duty. As Yigal Allon put it, 'The true frontier of the State of Israel moves and forms according to the movement and location of Jewish workers of the earth. Without Jewish settlement, defence of the country isn't possible, even if we double the size of the army.' Pushing out the frontier by settling Jews in Arab areas had been a fundamental and highly effective tool in the construction of the Jewish state. What started with a few toeholds in the dust and swamp of Palestine in the years before the First World War had, in a few generations, become an independent country and regional superpower, capable of beating all its enemies in less than a week. By 1967 the job of settling the land within the 1948 ceasefire lines was almost over. The organisations responsible for the process were running out of work. Now suddenly there was a vast new territory for them to get their teeth into. The only problem was that the Palestinians who lived there already thought it was theirs.

The new settlements were built by a branch of the army called Nahal, a Hebrew acronym for Fighting Pioneer Youth. Pushing out the frontier was their job. Since 1948 Nahal had created military outposts in the border lands, which were eventually turned over to civilians. Most of the settlements that have been built in the Occupied Territories since 1967 started out as Nahal outposts. Some Israelis saw the dangers ahead. Shlomo Gazit, the co-ordinator of government operations in the territories, whose own plan for a demilitarised Palestinian state in the West Bank and Gaza never took off, described the Nahal outposts as 'inevitable time bombs because of the way they turned into permanent civilian settlements'. On 15 December 250 intellectuals placed a newspaper advertisement warning that 'the

Jewish features of the state as well as its humane and democratic character' were in danger. In London *The Times* welcomed the advertisement as an 'encouraging note of dissent' against what was becoming a mainstream view that the territories, especially the West Bank, were Israel's to keep.

On Israeli state radio, the newly Occupied Territories were included in the weather forecasts. Arabic place names were changed to Hebrew versions. Sharm al Sheikh, for example, was referred to as 'Solomon's Bay'. The right-winger Menachem Begin said it was unthinkable that any of 'Eastern Israel' – the West Bank – be returned to Jordan. By July 1967 Hebrew street signs were appearing in East Jerusalem. So were branches of Israeli banks and post offices. The tourist industry was getting excited about the money that could be made from the attractions they captured from Jordan. 'If our dreams come true – Jerusalem, Bethlehem, Jericho – they'll all be terrific,' one official told a reporter from the *Wall Street Journal*, whose story was headlined 'Israel Digs In, Victor in Mideast War Plainly Plans Long Stay in Captured Arab Lands'.

Journalists had started noticing what was happening. Rowland Evans and Robert Novak wrote in the *Washington Post* on 22 October that 'no matter what they say publicly, the Israelis are performing exactly as though they plan a permanent occupation of the historic lands west of the Jordan River'. In November 1967 Michael Wolfers of *The Times* toured the Occupied Territories and saw that Greater Israel was 'fast becoming a reality . . . the statement "other places we can give back but this place never", which I first heard in Jerusalem in June, is now being heard from Israelis standing on what less than six months ago the world regarded as Syrian and Jordanian soil'. Money was pouring into infrastructure investments, from the settlements themselves to new roads and phone lines. New bus shelters and traffic signs on the Golan seemed to be 'a thorough bid to turn a Syrian landscape into the usual Israeli urban scene . . . [W]ith the speed and efficiency that the Israelis bring to this kind of pioneering it cannot be long before the Israeli occupation of the Golan becomes as difficult to unscramble as its hold on Jerusalem already is.'

The *Washington Post* visited the settlers in the Etzion bloc and concluded that it would 'never peacefully return to Jordan'. It added that it will be a 'near miracle if the Israeli government, which has no clear idea of what West Bank settlement it really wants, can withstand domestic political pressures for many more Etzions'. Hanan Porat and the others Etzion returnees had sworn at the gravesides of the settlers who were killed in 1948 that they were going home, never to leave again. They returned in a convoy led by an armoured car that had evacuated them in 1948. Porat went on to become one of the leaders of the settler movement. The settlements have expanded enormously: more than 400,000 Israelis now live on land occupied in 1967. They are heavily defended, at great cost, and are the focus for violent Palestinian action against the occupation.

Successive Israeli governments have not accepted that they are occupiers at all. They say that the West Bank and Gaza were not part of any sovereign state before 1967. The territories, therefore, are administered, not occupied. Israel's interpretation is not accepted by the UN Security Council, the International Red Cross and most of the rest of the world. But Israel defends its position fiercely because if the territories are legally classified as occupied land, its settlement activities since the end of the Six-Day War amount to multiple, serial violations of the Fourth Geneva Convention. It is one of the main planks of international humanitarian law, which forbids the colonisation of occupied territory. Israel argues the Fourth Geneva Convention does not apply to its activities in its 'administered' territories, though it says it applies the 'humanitarian' provisions of the Convention, without saying which ones it means. Even so, Israel has violated other aspects of international law during the years of occupation, by torturing suspected terrorists, demolishing houses, jailing suspects without trial and deporting people it says are dangers to the Jewish state. Sooner or later serious peace talks will start again. They will fail if they cannot find a fair way of fixing the mess the 1967 war left behind.

Refugees

Refugees continued to pour out of the West Bank into Jordan after the war ended. Finding justice for the refugees was – and is – at the centre of Middle East peacemaking. As early as the second day of the war, Walt Rostow, the White House National Security Advisor, said that a definitive Middle East peace settlement depended on 'a broad and imaginative movement by Israel on the question of refugees'. In his speech on 19 June President Johnson said 'there will be no peace for any party in the Middle East unless this problem is attacked with new energy by all, and, certainly, primarily by those who are immediately concerned'. The same week, something similar came from Britain's foreign secretary George Brown: 'The hopes for any enduring settlement will depend to a large extent on Israel's actions now. The generous and humane treatment of the Arab population in the occupied areas could contribute to a breaking down of the barriers of hatred and hopes of a reconciliation at some date, however remote.'

Moshe Dayan, by now seen as the authoritative voice on the Occupied Territories, told a news conference in Jerusalem on 25 June that the vast majority of the refugees would not be allowed back. They were the people who wanted to exterminate Israel only twenty days earlier, so it was what they deserved. Dayan brushed aside earlier government claims that the 'extent of the movement was greatly exaggerated' and accepted that 100,000 Palestinians had crossed to the East Bank. Even that was a major underestimate. The next day UNRWA put the figure at 413,000. Dayan was not sympathetic. He said most of the refugees were landless people from camps who had nothing to lose and would continue to get their UNRWA rations wherever they were, or otherwise they needed to go to Jordan to pick up the remittances they lived off from relations in other Arab states.

By the time Dayan made his views on the refugees clear, Israel was at the start of an organised process of encouraging Palestinians to leave the West Bank that went on for the rest of the year and into 1968. The first wave of refugees, who had left home in a panic because of the war and the new occupation, stopped crossing by around 15 June. For almost a week, that seemed to be that. Then, from 20 June, a second wave started arriving on the East Bank. They were transported from Hebron, Bethlehem, Nablus, Jenin and Qalqilya to the river Jordan by the Israeli army in trucks and buses. Israel did not repeat the forcible evictions that happened in Qalqilya, Tulkarem, the Latrun villages and in some of the villages around Hebron during the war. The second wave left 'voluntarily', taking up an offer that was usually broadcast from loudspeakers mounted on jeeps moving slowly up and down streets that had been emptied by curfews. In Bethlehem, for instance, Samir Elias Khouri says Israel 'started asking people to leave about a week after the occupation started. They brought buses to Manger Square and many people went, especially if they had relatives in Jordan. My brother gave them his ID and left.' They were given 'every facility to leave . . . none to return home'. Israel also stopped the limited amount of two-way traffic that it had been allowing across the Jordan.

Israelis in favour of absorbing the West Bank realised it would be easier if there were fewer Palestinians. Eshkol's advisers told him on 13 September that West Bank Palestinians would have to be encouraged to emigrate to have any chance of even keeping population growth to the pre-war rate of 1 per cent a year. Israelis feared the Palestinian birth rate. It was one area in which they could not overtake the Arabs. Some politicians in 1967, like Justice Minister Shapiro, warned that the Jewish nature of the state would be in danger if it tried to absorb an area populated by Arabs. If Israel did not give up territory, he warned, 'the whole Zionist enterprise is over. We'll be in a ghetto.' Since Israel's reoccupation of the West Bank in 2002, fears about a Palestinian majority between the river Jordan and the Mediterranean have resurfaced. The latest predictions say it is around a generation away.

Israel denied vehemently that it was putting pressure on the Arab population to leave, an accusation that its minister in London described as 'a colossal propaganda campaign of defamation'. Palestinians, though, were complaining that they were being made offers of 'assisted emigration' that came when they were so intimidated that they did not dare to refuse. Their accusations were corroborated by British diplomats. Ambassador Hadow in Tel Aviv, whose telegrams consistently gave Israel the benefit of the doubt or actively defended it against Arab accusations, told the Israeli foreign ministry that 'if the Israeli Government went on like this even her friends would have to believe that she was trying to get rid of the Arab population on the West Bank in order to Israelise it'.

Dayan told journalists on 25 June that life was returning to normal on the West Bank, that curfews were being reduced, services were being reinstated and food and fuel supplies restored. But the same day 'responsible witnesses' reported to the British Embassy in Amman that Israeli searches, looting, 'facilities to leave' and other 'selective' pressures, particularly in the Old City of Jerusalem, were forcing out well-established middle-class Palestinians. Any hopes the Palestinians had of 'a reasonable life there' were being destroyed. By mid-June many Arabs were leaving Jerusalem every day from Damascus Gate, the main entrance to the Old City from newly captured Jordanian Jerusalem. A British diplomat's 'houseboy' was among them, because life in his home village of Issawiya, close to Mount Scopus, was difficult, 'with Israelis shooting off guns in the middle of the night', and also because he was worried that he would not be able to get his Jordanian army pension any more.

The way that the process worked was witnessed by Jesse Lewis, a reporter from the *Washington Post*. Just inside Damascus Gate, Israeli soldiers set up a table, taking names and giving numbers to people who wanted to go to Jordan. A queue had formed, which Lewis joined. When he said he lived in the Old City and wanted to get out, the soldiers gave him a refugee number too. Nearly half the refugees were children. Men were outnumbered by women, who were wearing traditional Palestinian embroidered dresses. Many of them were becoming refugees for the second time. In 1948 a woman called Rashidah Raghib Saadeddin had left her home in Lifta, a village at the western entrance to Jerusalem. (It still stands, as a ruin, at the beginning of the twenty-first century.) Now, with her frail and wrinkled mother and her fifteen-year-old son, she was moving again.

She said the Israelis did not want them to live in peace. Another passenger, a man called Abdul Latif Husseini, had come to Jerusalem from Jaffa, which had been the main Palestinian town on the coast, in 1948, when he was eleven. He had planned to get married at the end of June. But the bank where he worked had closed, the house he had rented had been damaged and nearly $1000 worth of furnishings had been stolen or ruined by looters. He told Lewis, 'I can forget you slapping my face but I will pass this on to my children.'

Just after half-past two in the afternoon trucks and four buses pulled up in front of Damascus Gate. The adults scrambled for places. Babies were passed up afterwards like 'sacks of rice or sand'. Lewis found a space in the back of one of the trucks. 'As the convoy left Jerusalem, no one in the truck had much to say except the babies, who were crying. It was after 3 o'clock and there were no Arabs on the street and there wouldn't be until 9 the next morning when the 18-hour curfew ended.' When the Israeli soldiers who were driving the buses and trucks missed the turning to Jericho and went on towards the Dead Sea, one of the women said, 'See, this is not the way. They are going to kill us.' But, eventually, they made it to the Allenby bridge, which formed a 'grotesque V in the middle of the river', broken-backed since it was blown up by retreating Jordanian troops. 'The incline of the bridge was so steep that improvised ladders had been placed along its slanting floor and a rope was strung taut to prevent refugees from falling.'

UNRWA, the UN agency responsible for Palestinian refugees, faced its biggest ever challenge. Before the war it already had 332,000 Palestinian refugees from the 1948 war on its books in Jordan. By mid-June they had been joined by 140,000 more refugees from UNRWA camps in the West Bank and 33,000 from camps in Gaza. In addition, there were 240,000 more displaced Palestinians who had never been refugees before. Suddenly Jordan, a country with almost no natural resources, was dealing with 745,000 refugees.

Levi Eshkol, echoing Dayan's 25 June assertions, told the International Committee of the Red Cross that the refugees left the West Bank 'deliberately and of their own free will, long after the fighting had stopped. As a rule, it was because of family links or to pick up an official salary or pension, or remittances sent from people who had left to work in the Arab countries that produced oil.' The truth was much more complicated. Some refugees, like the British diplomat's houseboy, were worried about their pensions. But most of the 240,000 'new refugees' were peasant farmers and their families from the West Bank. They came from tightly knit traditional communities, which had barely changed in hundreds of years. A survey of 122 families from 45 different villages in the West Bank was carried out by researchers from the American University of Beirut (AUB) in September 1967. It found that a large proportion of them had lived in their home villages all their lives. Four-fifths of them had owned good plots of land, of more than two and a half acres. In other words, they had every reason to stay. Sitting stunned by what had happened to them eight to ten weeks after the event, they showed deep attachment to the people, homes and land they had been forced to leave behind.

Most of them left because they were terrified – 57 per cent said because of air attacks. Around half of them left because of the direct actions of Israeli troops, including 'the eviction of civilians from their homes, looting, the destruction of houses, the rounding up and detention of male civilians, the deliberate shaming of older persons and of women and the shooting of persons suspected of being soldiers or guerrilla fighters'. Shaming was especially important. Palestinian society in the 1960s, in the towns as well as the country, was deeply traditional. Honour, dignity and pride were valued above all else. The obligation to protect and uphold the honour of the family, especially of the women, was paramount. Nineteen years after the massacre at Deir Yassin, it was still mentioned by some families as an example of what Israelis were capable of doing. But simply being refugees fed their feelings of humiliation. The AUB researchers found that 'they cannot live with the idea that they have lost their country, honour, pride and still not being able to do anything about it . . . this is their greatest source of aggression against themselves, their leaders, Israel and the great powers.' Children who were born during the exodus or in the camp were given names like Jihad (struggle), Harb (war) and A'ida (one who will return).

Nils-Goran Gussing, the special representative of the UN secretary general, investigated why people had fled the West Bank, Gaza and the Golan Heights. The CIA described his report as 'the most authoritative available'. Before 5 June some 115,000 Syrians lived on the Golan Heights. A week later only around 6000 were left. Gussing investigated Syrian claims that Israel had made 'systematic efforts to expel the entire original population'. The report concluded that, whatever the policy of the government on the matter, 'certain actions authorised or allowed by local military commanders were an important cause of flight'. In a dusty refugee camp outside Damascus thirty years later, where refugees from the Heights still live, village headmen told me they were evicted at gunpoint from homes that were then destroyed. On the West Bank, Gussing found there had been acts of intimidation by the Israeli army and that Israel had made attempts, using loudspeakers, to suggest to the local population that 'they might be better off on the East Bank'. The report's conclusion was that the main reasons why Palestinians left were the impact of war and occupation, particularly because the Israelis made no effort to reassure local Palestinians.

Many young men in Gaza had no choice in the matter. They were rounded up and bussed out to Egypt. By late June they were crossing the Suez canal at the rate of 1000 a day. A group of students from Gaza City, who were being taken across the canal in a fleet of small boats, told a British reporter that they had been 'taken forcibly from their families and driven by truck to a collection point near Beersheba'. Many complained they had been beaten up and robbed by the Israeli soldiers and that they were not given any water on the journey across the desert. The flow out of Gaza continued. The CIA pointed out that 'Israel would like to retain Gaza, if the bulk of its Arab population went elsewhere'. In October around 500 new refugees were crossing into Jordan every day. Many of them came from Gaza.

The news that Jews were moving into the West Bank plunged

refugees into even deeper gloom. They had been hoping that international pressure would force Israel to allow them back. The return of settlers to the Etzion bloc near Bethlehem took those hopes away. Some of the bitterness and anger that was brewing was taken out in nasty incidents in the camps.

Since there were no legitimate ways of crossing the Jordan into the West Bank, many people tried to use clandestine methods. By September 1967 the Mayor of Jericho claimed that 100 people from his area had been shot trying to cross the Jordan illegally. In a single incident on 6 September fifty civilians tried to cross the river near Damia. Eight were shot dead and the rest sent back to the East Bank except for one man who hid and later made it to Jerusalem. It was difficult, though, accurately to assess the numbers killed, because the Israeli soldiers had a tendency to bury the people they had shot without informing their relatives or even finding out who they had killed.

Despite Dayan's insistence in June that most of the refugees would not be allowed back, the Israeli government raised expectations that it might change its mind when, in August, it agreed to a scheme supervised by the International Committee of the Red Cross. After difficult negotiations – one problem was Jordan's objection to the form Israel provided for the refugees to fill in, because it was headed 'Government of Israel' – 167,500 refugees applied from 9 to 17 August.

Then Israel announced the scheme would end on 31 August. When the ICRC representative protested that it would be impossible to get 100,000 refugees across the bridge by the end of the month, his Israeli interlocutor's only comment was that the word 'impossible' did not exist in the Hebrew language. On 30 August the ICRC in Geneva sent an urgent telegram to Eshkol, asking him to extend the deadline 'to permit continuation of return operations and to avoid creating undue hardships and discrimination among returnees'. Eshkol ignored the ICRC's appeal. He did not reply to it for nearly two months. Israel gave permission to only 5102 to cross. By the time it reached its own 31 August deadline, it had not processed thousands of the forms it had issued through the ICRC. No permission was given to anyone from refugee camps on the West Bank, or from Jerusalem or Bethlehem. At 10 Downing Street, the British foreign secretary reported to the cabinet that Israel's rejection of applications from people displaced from those areas 'may signify that they are thinking in terms of a long stay on the West Bank and wish to limit their own refugee commitment there'. In the end only 3824 of those 5102 returned in the time allotted, mainly because of extra restrictions imposed by the Israelis. In some cases families were not allowed to bring back their older children, so they stayed put. No one was allowed to come back with a car. No livestock were allowed back, which ruled out shepherds and small farmers who had driven their flocks into Jordan. In Amman the British ambassador thought Israel's performance had been 'half-hearted and dilatory'.

Once the deadline had passed, the facts were clear. Israel had blocked some 150,000 Palestinians who had wanted to return home. A campaign in the Israeli press said it was all because King Hussein was out to exploit the refugees for 'political ends'. It was dismissed as 'irrelevant . . . argument about petty details' by Michael Hadow, who had defended Israel's insistence on controlling the rate of return of the refugees for security reasons. If Israel, he said, was worried about letting Hussein score political points because of the suffering of displaced Palestinian civilians then there was an obvious answer – offer to take back all the refugees so the king would have none left to exploit. But the refugee crisis was useful for Israel. It kept Hussein off-balance. Israel put even more pressure on the Jordanians and the international agencies that were struggling to cope with the refugees by denying a right of return to the big, well-equipped refugee camps that were lying empty in Jericho. The Palestinians who had lived in them since 1948 had left at the height of the fighting. Most of them were living in desperate conditions a few miles away on the other side of the river Jordan. New camps had to be built, at huge expense.

By the end of the year the outlook was bleak for the refugees. Violent resistance to the occupation had started, making it even less likely that Israel would take them back. None of the 150,000 refugees who were turned down by Israel after they filled in an International Red Cross repatriation form had been allowed home. Around forty people were allowed back under Israel's own scheme for family reunification. And it seemed to be getting worse. British diplomats in Jerusalem believed Israel was using security as an excuse to force more Palestinians out, reporting 'increasing evidence of Israeli efforts to swell the numbers of refugees on the East Bank by wholesale evictions of people on the ground that they had been involved in sabotage – for example the eviction of 195 members of the Arab al Nasariah tribe in the Arja area on 6 December'.

Israel seized on statements on Radio Amman that returning refugees would join the struggle against occupation. The Israeli ambassador in London explained that his government 'did not want to find itself forced into a campaign of repression to deal with the attempts of a deliberately introduced fifth column to disturb the peace on the West Bank'. Israel would suffer a damaging loss of face among the local Arab population if it admitted 'a disruptive element which would disturb the present tranquillity of life'.

But life was not tranquil.

Violence

The occupation generated bloodshed from the outset. Israel used violence to maintain and deepen its occupation. Palestinians soon realised that if they wanted to resist the occupation, they would have to do it for themselves. Arab governments were not going help them. Armed groups and political movements stopped looking to Nasser or to Ba'thism. Instead, they developed a distinctly Palestinian identity. Moshe Dayan, in keeping with his view that the Israelis and Palestinians were in a perpetual war, saw what was coming. He predicted to foreign minister Abba Eban that the Palestinians would use terrorism to fight Israeli rule. When Eban asked him how he knew, he said, 'because that is exactly what I would do if I were in their place'.

The occupation's capacity to create violence was there for everyone who chose to see it. An editorial in the *Washington Post* on 22 October 1967 said it was a 'bitter pill' for Israel to swallow to 'to have taken territory to assure security, and then to learn that the security menace has merely been shifted from outside to inside one's borders . . . [N]o more than any other nation which harbors an alien people and denies them the right of self-determination, Israel cannot expect to avoid the embarrassment and harassment of local Arab resistance.'

There were forty-eight attacks that were considered to be serious terrorist incidents from July to the end of the year along with many more minor ones, as well as eighty-four serious incidents involving Jordanian, Egyptian or Syrian troops. A typical night was spent by paratroopers from Battalion 202 racing round the town of Khan Younis in Gaza on 7–8 July. Earlier in the day they had captured a Palestinian 'informer' who was with them. At 8:15 p.m. they saw a group of men moving towards the beach. Seven were arrested. One was shot 'while charging' at one of the soldiers. At 11:30 the informer took them to a house where they found a cache of weapons. At 4:44 a.m. they caught an Egyptian second lieutenant who had been in hiding. At 5:00 the informer tried to take them to an Egyptian captain, but when his house was raided he was gone. From 5:30 to 7:30 a.m. the paratroopers searched an orchard where the informer said fedayeen were hiding. One man escaped, one was captured. At 8:00 a.m. the informer took them to another Egyptian, who they found hiding in a stable. Fifteen minutes later, as they were on their way back to their camp at Gaza City, the informer pointed out another 'Egyptian', who was arrested.

There were many more serious incidents. September 1967 was much worse for Israelis than many of the months before the war. On the 8th a mine killed an Israeli officer and wounded four soldiers. On the 15th an Israeli train was derailed by sabotage close to the border of the West Bank near Tulkarem. On the 19th a bomb in West Jerusalem wounded seven civilians. There was more sabotage on 21, 22 and 23 of September. On 24 September, the day Eshkol announced the start of settlement in the Occupied Territories, thirteen guerrillas from Fatah, Yasser Arafat's faction, were captured after a gunfight near Nablus. The next day Fatah blew up a house at a farming cooperative in Israel, killing a child and wounding the parents. On 27 September, the day that settlers returned to Kfar Etzion, two border policemen were killed and one wounded in a shoot-out with Fatah, a train was derailed near Gaza by sabotage and three unprimed hand grenades were found outside the prime minister's house.

Casualty figures show clearly how the dangers to Israelis increased after the occupation began. Between June 1965 and February 1967 twelve Israelis were killed and sixty-one wounded in what Israel classified as terrorist attacks. From February until the outbreak of war, when tension was very high, four Israelis were killed and six wounded. But Israeli casualties rose sharply after the occupation began. Between the end of the war and February 1968 twenty-eight Israelis were killed and eighty-five wounded by terrorists. During the same period Israel said it killed forty-five Palestinian gunmen, wounded thirty and detained more than a thousand. By November more than a thousand Palestinian homes had been bulldozed in reprisals. In some refugee camps, all males between the ages of sixteen and seventy were lined up and paraded past men whose heads were disguised by sacks with only their eyes visible through slits. Every time one of them nodded towards a refugee, he was taken away for questioning. The result, according to a British diplomat, was 'to persuade more families to pack up and trek off to the east'. The spokesman for Brigadier-General Narkiss told a *Sunday Times* reporter, 'If you know the Arab mentality, you know this toughness is probably good. I don't think they really understand any other language.'

Israel went back to attacking Jordan in reprisals for attacks by Palestinians. The huge and miserable refugee camps in Jordan were the best recruiting and training grounds Yasser Arafat and the other guerrilla leaders ever had. With the West Bank gone a weakened King Hussein had no inclination to rein the Palestinians in. Israel responded by shelling the refugee camps. On 20 November, for example, the Karameh camp in the Jordan valley was attacked by 120 mm mortars and field artillery. The bombardment happened in mid-afternoon on a fine day, when the streets of the camp were crowded and children were returning from school. The casualties were taken to a hospital nearby. Twelve people were dead, including three children, one woman, two Jordanian policemen and six other men. The defence attaché from the British Embassy in Amman, a professional soldier, inspected the corpses and concluded they had been killed by the fragmentation of shells. The wounded included seven children (two of whom were unlikely to live), three women, three policemen and sixteen men, one of whom had both legs amputated while another lost an arm. Israel finally sent tanks and infantry into Karameh, which had become a major base for Fatah, on 21 March 1968. They ran into much heavier opposition than they expected from Arafat's guerrillas and the Jordanian army which had learnt from its traumatic experience of the previous summer. After a day of fierce fighting, 28 Israelis, 61 Jordanians and around 100 Palestinians were killed. For Palestinians the most important legacy of the battle was that it established the legend of Yasser Arafat. Even though most of his men were killed, wounded or taken prisoner, they had stood up to the Israelis in a way that Arab regulars had singularly failed to do nine months earlier.

Some Israelis predicted the shape of the violence to come. In March 1968 an Israeli who had been transported by the British to a Kenyan jail between the ages of seventeen and twenty-one for resisting their occupation told the British ambassador, 'It would be all too easy to run a truck into the middle of Dizengoff Circle in Tel Aviv in the rush hour and explode a heavy charge causing some 200–300 Jewish casualties.' He thought it was unlikely to happen because the Palestinians were not up to it. In 1968 suicide bombers were still twenty-five years away.

Many Israelis believed that Palestinians would never be capable of organised resistance. A year after the 1967 war, the British journalist Winston Churchill had lunch with an Israeli who had been part of the group that bombed the King David hotel in Jerusalem in 1946. When asked whether Palestinians could ever do something similar to Israelis, he replied, 'Not a chance.' Unfortunately for Israel's own future, one of the by-products of their crushing victory in 1967 was overconfidence and complacency, and not just about their ability to stop Palestinian terror. Hubris almost led to disaster in 1973 when they ignored warnings that Egypt and Syria were going to attack. It took nearly three weeks of hard fighting and many casualties before the superpowers ended the war. The 1973 war led to the return of the Sinai and peace with Egypt. Israel's relations with Egypt ever since have been cold but correct. Israel stayed in the Golan Heights, Syria is still an implacable enemy, but the 1973 war was followed by a disengagement of forces agreement that has kept the border quiet ever since. When they needed a battlefield in the 1980s, they used Lebanon.

Legacy

Every year on the anniversary of the 1967 war, Israel celebrates what it calls 'Jerusalem Day'. Several thousand young people assemble, many sporting the tribal symbols of right-wing religious nationalism, T-shirts printed with political slogans, skullcaps made of coloured, knitted cotton for the men and long skirts for the women. They parade around the walls of Jerusalem's Old City, which is mainly populated by Palestinians, waving Israeli flags and chanting and singing patriotic songs. Quite a few of them are armed. Hundreds of paramilitary border police are deployed to protect them. The intention is to celebrate Jerusalem as the unified, eternal capital of Israel. But it demonstrates the opposite, that Jerusalem is deeply divided. A few weeks after the victory in 1967, Israel pulled down the concrete walls that physically divided the city. But they are still standing in people's heads. Most Palestinians keep out of the way when the march is going on, but their sullen, unseen presence is always in the air.

Jerusalem repelled me when I first lived there. I loathed the place. Hatred and conflict seemed as pervasive as the dust, noise and the blinding sun. But Jerusalem gradually pulled me in, as it does with most people in the end. Part of it was the light, bright and hard at midday, soft on the rocky hills in the evening. It was also that history is alive in Jerusalem. Events that in most places are safely tucked away in books belong to everybody's present, and not always in a good way.

When the sun was going down and the jackals were starting to howl in the hills, the pink and gold walls around where I lived let go of the heat that had been blasted into them all day. For Israelis and Palestinians, the stones of Jerusalem also give off power. The two sides share a unrequited desire to possess them absolutely. Palestinians love to tell you that they have outstayed the Jordanians, the British, the Ottomans and the Crusaders and they will do the same for the Israelis. Israelis warn their enemies not to underestimate their attachment to their only home. A religious Jew, an immigrant from Latin America, on an isolated settlement near the fiercely nationalistic Palestinian city of Nablus, told me that he had returned to live on land that was a gift from God. He talked about how Jews had been driven out by the Romans and fought their way back as if it was a personal trauma that happened last week, rather than a saga that had unfolded over almost two thousand years.

When two rabbis from Vienna came to Palestine on a fact-finding mission in 1897, they sent back a telegram: 'The bride is beautiful, but she is married to another man.' Arabs and Israelis were fighting over the land long before 1967. But decisive victories change conflicts decisively. The 1967 war made the Arab–Israeli conflict what it is today. The only way to make peace is to unravel what 1967 left behind.

Israelis call it the Six-Day War. Arabs call it the June War. Whichever name you prefer, it was one of the greatest military victories of the twentieth century. Across the world it made the reputation of the Israeli Defence Forces. Most, though not all, of the Israeli veterans of 1967 I spoke to when I was doing my research believed that their victory had been squandered. Palestinians I met in the West Bank and Gaza lived lives so dominated by the grinding misery of the occupation that sometimes it was difficult to jerk them out of the present long enough to talk about the past.

Jerusalem

In Jerusalem, at three minutes to eight on the morning of Thursday, 28 September 2000, Ariel Sharon, seventy-two years old, retired Israeli general-turned-politician, walked through a stone arch in one of Jerusalem's ancient walls. Sharon's squat, heavy frame was almost lost in a thick crowd of bodyguards. Israeli sharpshooters were deployed on rooftops. He was entering the walled compound around the Aqsa mosque and the Dome of the Rock, since 1967 the most contested piece of land in the Middle East. Sharon has always denied that he was out to provoke Palestinians who had gathered there to protest about his visit. In a way, he is telling the truth. His target that day was Binyamin Netanyahu, a rival for the leadership of the Israeli right, who he planned to upstage by demonstrating that Israelis can go wherever they like in Jerusalem. What Palestinians thought about his walk in the September sun was not the issue. In his long career, the feelings of Arabs had never been Ariel Sharon's greatest concern.

But Palestinians regard the territory upon which he was stepping as their own. It is the holiest site in the Islamic world after Mecca and Medina. The Israeli authorities were so certain that Palestinians would give Sharon a rough ride that they deployed 1500 heavily armed police to protect him. Under Jerusalem's two holy mosques, the remains of the Jewish Temple lie unseen and unexcavated. The Temple is at the heart of modern Israel's claim to Jerusalem. For almost 2000 years after the Romans destroyed it and expelled the Jews from the holy city, they prayed for their return. Refugees in the Palestinian Diaspora put images of the Dome of the Rock and of al-Aqsa on the walls of their homes, just as Jews, also removed by war from Jerusalem, remembered the Temple. For Palestinians the mosques have become national symbols that are every bit as potent as the memory of Jerusalem was during the Jews' exile.

Riots started as Sharon left the compound at 8:31 a.m., thirty-four minutes after he had entered it. Since then, the violence has not stopped. In 2002, in response to savage attacks by Palestinians on Israeli civilians, Israel smashed Yasser Arafat's Palestinian Authority and reoccupied the areas in and around the main Palestinian towns. Since then millions of Palestinian men, women and children have suffered harsh collective punishments and been imprisoned in their homes by curfews for months. The Palestinian economy has collapsed. Israelis have had periods of relative quiet, but the suicide bombers have always returned to kill more civilians.

Afula

Doron Mor was waiting for me in a café in a shopping mall in Afula, a town in northern Israel on the border with the West Bank. He had brought his grandson with him. Indulgently, he gave him cash to play video games and to buy a burger and an ice cream. Piped music tinkled around us. A pretty girl delivered a menu. Most Israeli towns, even small ones like Afula, have malls. They show just how far Israel has come in the lifetime of a man like Doron, who grew up when Israel was small, poor and ambitious. When developers built malls in the eighties and nineties, shoppers liked them because they were modern, Western, a little bit flashy, just like the places where Israelis, who love shopping, visited on holidays abroad. Israelis still like them – not because they feel like America or Europe, but because malls are a little safer than traditional markets and high streets. They have a limited number of doors. Security people at the mall in Afula search everyone who comes in. The man who frisked me concentrated on the places where bombs could be strapped.

Doron Mor is a sun-tanned, fit-looking man, who lives on a kibbutz. In 1967 he was a major in the Israeli paratroop brigade, the deputy commander of the battalion that fought in the battle of Ammunition Hill. He is proud of what his generation achieved – and sad about what happened afterwards. 'In 1967 we were in real danger. We were surrounded by three nations. It was the first time we proved that we were strong. We were shocked we won so quickly. It made us think we were supermen and we paid for it . . . We're still making the same mistakes. Since the *intifada* [Palestinian uprising] started we

361

have proved we can't stop terror. For true peace I'd give up all the territories and also Jerusalem. If it's true peace, you could go there freely anyway.'

Jacov Chaimowitz fought with Doron Mor at Ammunition Hill. After the war he took the Hebrew name Hetz. Now he is an engineer living with his wife and eight children in a relatively peaceful corner of northern Israel. After the war Hetz, who was decorated for his bravery, went on to become an officer and to command the unit he fought with in 1967. He showed classic signs of 'survivor's guilt' that is often suffered by people who have seen their friends die. 'I felt desperate because of so many dead. I took many months to understand what had happened. I was upset because some of my friends were killed and I just had scratches from shrapnel and blast, and a gashed hand from when I tried to open an ammunition box with a bayonet . . . I felt like a robot most of the time in battle. It was him or me. I thought it was tough, but I also thought it was the last battle in the Middle East.' Now he knows it was not. Like all Israelis and Palestinians, his life has been dominated by the way 1967 changed the Middle East. I met him a day or two after yet another suicide attack in Jerusalem. 'We need a proper border. A year after the war I realised that the only solution was peace. I would swap the West Bank for peace any time. The settlers have to leave the Occupied Territory, so we can have a border we can defend.'

Before I met Mor and Hetz, I had been on the West Bank, in Jenin. It used to be easy to drive the few miles between Jenin and Afula, across the border, which is known as the green line. The first time I went that way was on a cold night in November 1995, straight from a huge commemorative rally in Tel Aviv for Israel's prime minister Yitzhak Rabin, who had been assassinated a week before.

Rabin knew a lot about the occupied territories. More than any other Israeli, he was responsible for Israel's stunning victory in 1967. But years later Rabin had realised that however many tanks and helicopter gunships Israel possessed, it would never have peace while it tried to control the lives of four million Palestinians. Peace meant dismantling the territorial legacy of the 1967 war. Since it was his greatest victory, a majority of Israelis trusted him to do it. Some did not. For months before he was killed, a poisonous cascade of hatred was directed at Rabin and his family. Rabbis cursed him. Extreme right-wingers waved pictures of him dressed in a Nazi uniform. Some of them believed Israel needed the land to be safe from the Arabs. Others believed it was God's miraculous gift to the Jewish people, the restoration of the sacred territory that the Romans took from them in the first century AD. How, they asked, can a Jew return what God intends him to have?

No one knows how far he would have taken the process of disengaging from occupied land, because on 4 November 1995 he was assassinated by a Jewish fanatic called Yigal Amir. It was one of the most effective acts of political violence in modern history. Eight years after Rabin's assassination, more Jews than ever were settled on the occupied land. Terrible violence was part of daily life. Israel was mired in an unwinnable colonial war.

A week after Rabin was murdered, when young Israelis were lighting candles and weeping for everything that Amir had taken away, I watched the last Israeli troops leaving Jenin. A few minutes later, after their jeeps had headed off towards Afula, uniformed Palestinians arrived, hanging off the sides of their vehicles and firing guns into the air. Everyone who was there rambled around the old Israeli base, looking at the cells in which some of them said they had been held. On other freezing nights that winter most of the major towns on the West Bank were handed over to Palestinian self-rule. Israel continued to control the roads in and out of the towns and to take land by force to build Jewish settlements. But, at first, a majority of Palestinians and Israelis thought they were on a one-way street to peace.

Some Israelis say that the roots of today's conflict are not in the occupation, but in the Arabs' desire to destroy the Jewish state. It is true that Palestinian extremists swear that they will fight until the Jewish state has been destroyed.

But the violence of the occupation has given them a prominence they would not otherwise have. During the time that Palestinians hoped the Oslo process was working, the extremists were in the fringes where they belong. Violence pushes the extremists from both sides into the mainstream. Palestinian extremists found more people prepared to listen to their bloodthirsty dreams, while Ariel Sharon appointed ministers to his cabinet who believed that Palestinians in the West Bank should be expelled. When, in Rabin's time, Palestinians thought the occupation was ending, suicide bombers were deeply unpopular in the West Bank and Gaza. Now that Israeli tanks are back on their streets, the bombers' approval ratings are very high.

Bethlehem

Mrs Badial Raheb was sitting in a smart jacket in a beautiful vaulted room in her house opposite the Church of the Nativity. Framed pieces of Palestinian embroidery hung on the walls. Less than a hundred yards away in Manger Square, an Israeli tank was parked outside the Nativity church, its turret moving back and forth across the square every few minutes. Palestinian boys peered round the corners of the church at the tank, and ducked back every time the barrel came their way. In her serene sitting room, Mrs Raheb was embarrassed and upset to talk about the past. When the Israelis were advancing into Bethlehem, she had taken her son to hide with hundreds of others in the church.

'My husband came to get us. He took one look at the people sheltering there and said if we're going to die, we'll die at home. I was pregnant and the next day I had a miscarriage – I suppose it was because I was so afraid. It was ten days before they could get me a doctor.

'After the war the Israelis used to drive round with loudspeakers telling everyone not to be afraid. For days people were under curfew. They said they wouldn't hurt us. They brought in basic essentials and sold them very cheap. They were trying to get us to like them.'

She laughed. 'They fed us honey and then onions.' There were no massacres in Bethlehem when Israel moved in. But the neighbours who left for Jordan never came back.

Another Israeli armoured column was grinding its way through Bethlehem. On a rooftop not far from Mrs Raheb's house, Raja Zacharia cocked an expert ear. That's not a tank, he said. It's an armoured personnel carrier. Raja is an expert diagnostician of the sounds that steel tracks make on the roads on his home town because he has heard them many times since 7 June 1967, the day the occupation started. It was also the day when his father was killed trying to protect him from an Israeli shell. Sometimes it feels as if he has heard Israeli armour every day since then, although that is not strictly true. The first Israeli occupation ended on Christmas Eve 1995. For seven years after that there was relative freedom. Israeli soldiers stood at the gates of Bethlehem and controlled who left and who came in, but it was the closest thing to independence that the people of Bethlehem had ever had. Before the Israelis, the Jordanians were in charge, who had succeeded the British who had followed the Turks and a long time before that were the Romans. In May 2002 the Israelis came back, because the government was under pressure to act and because the army believed its tanks could stop young Palestinians turning themselves into human bombs. The Israelis administered a stern collective punishment to a town that overwhelmingly supported armed resistance. Before the first of what turned into a series of temporary withdrawals, they destroyed millions of pounds' worth of renovations that had been paid for by the European Union and Japan for the Millennium celebrations, as well as the livelihoods of Palestinians who had invested their life savings in businesses during the years of self-rule.

Raja was standing on his roof listening to the clanking, screeching steel tracks because at four that morning the Israelis had come back again. The day before a Palestinian who was living in Bethlehem had blown himself up in Jerusalem, which is only a few miles down the road. May's collective punishment had not had the deterrent effect for which the Israelis had hoped. As soon as Raja and everyone else in Bethlehem heard that the suicide bomber had come from their town they knew what would happen. They checked their stocks of food and water and candles and went out to buy what they did not have. Now the whole town was under curfew and would be for the foreseeable future. That meant nobody was allowed out of their houses, though in practice Raja could stand on his roof and some of the children, when the tanks were not around, played in the streets close to their front doors.

Raja Zacharia was six years old in 1967. He was not aware that a war was coming until he heard the shelling. He was his parents' only child, born after they had been married for fifteen years. His father, Farah, a silversmith, was a talented and versatile man. He wrote, in English, a book of homespun moral philosophy called *A Call from the Wilderness*. Raja has a picture of him in an illustrated book from the 1960s about a young Swedish girl's trip through the holy land. Farah is showing the grinning little blonde child how he could turn a lump of silver into an elegant crucifix. On Wednesday 7 June 1967 he was outside with the neighbours, on the roof where Raja was standing thirty-five years later, when shells started to land near them. Farah rushed inside to tell his wife and child to take cover. Raja had been asleep. His father grabbed him and lay with him as more shells exploded outside. Then one hit the Greek Catholic church, which was next door to their house. The force of the explosion blew a hole in their wall. Farah, cradling his son, took the force of the blast. Raja was unhurt. The neighbours took Farah out into the street when the shelling stopped to try to find someone to take him to hospital. His wife Natalie was terrified and weeping, almost paralysed with dread at the thought that her husband would die, which he did, two hours later.

'When the Israelis came back this year, it was much worse than 1967. In '67 there was no resistance, we had no weapons. It was different this time. I feel very sorry for the people who were killed on that bus in Jerusalem yesterday, but blood brings blood and we're in a violent circle that never stops. Now we live in a box and there's no hope. We all want the land of 1967. Israel wants peace and the land. It can't have both. They signed agreements in front of kings and presidents and now they've just torn them up.'

Gaza

Kamel Sulaiman Shaheen sat behind his desk in the headmaster's office in his school and talked about all the years of occupation. In the winter sun outside hundreds of boys tore around the playground, yelling, punching each other, playing football. Gaza has one of the highest birth rates in the world. The biggest thing that hits you when you walk down any street in Gaza is not occupation, or resistance, or destruction, but children, thousands and thousands of them. Halfway down the Gaza Strip, near Mr Shaheen's school, the Israelis have built a checkpoint that can cut the territory in half. Actually it is more of a chokepoint than a checkpoint. Closing the checkpoint stops the traffic along Gaza's only north–south road. Thousands of people stew in the jams until it reopens. Even when the checkpoint is open, progress is still very slow. At either end you move slowly up the line until it is your turn to be examined by invisible Israelis, who are behind bullet-proof reflective glass in thick concrete bunkers. Palestinians believe that the fuller their car is, the more likely they are to be let through. The Israelis, Palestinian logic goes, believe a full car is less likely to contain suicide bombers. Young Palestinians work the queues, offering themselves as passengers to drivers with too many empty seats. They ride back and forth all day, earning a shekel every time.

Mr Shaheen would prefer to see them going to school. He is the headmaster of Deir al Balah Elementary. Its 945 boys use the buildings in the mornings. In the afternoons another school moves in, one of dozens that are run for refugee children by UNRWA. They had their own buildings, close to Kfar Darom, a Jewish settlement nearby. But the Israeli army decided the UNRWA school was too close for comfort, so they told them to get out. Mr Shaheen is a mild and polite man. He hates the occupation that has gone on for most of his adult life.

'We're still suffering from what happened in 1967. We're occupied. They kill people and demolish houses nearly every day. A stranger comes and kicks me out of the land where I was born. It's miserable and the world watches and doesn't do anything, especially the strong countries. But we are still hopeful, to be steadfast and achieve victory, which would be the liberation of Gaza, the West Bank and Jerusalem. I believe in two states. It's the best political solution.

'The children hear the stories of what's happened in the occupation and they're well aware of the situation. They see killing and demolition and uprooting. When a child hears his family talk about their history and they see what the Israelis do, they start to hate. Most people in this part of Gaza have lost a member of their family, or property, or trees. It makes us think we should be persistent in resisting, to defend our land until they find a just solution.'

Down the road from Deir al Balah is Shara Abu Shakrah's house in Khan Younis. After her husband and the other men in the family were killed in 1967, Shara was left alone in a society that did not value lone women, with four daughters and three sons. The eldest was eleven. She still yearns for the life they had before the war, when her husband, who was called Zaid, made a good living selling tomatoes, potatoes and okra. The widow of her husband's brother Mustafa, who was also killed by the Israelis, lives next door. Between them the two women raised twelve children.

She is still terrified of Israeli soldiers. When she heard the night prayer coming from the mosques, she felt sick with fear. Sometimes, she says, the soldiers came during the night to search her house. 'They used to say don't scream, you'll wake the children. They beat me, they pushed me around every time they came, they knocked me down to the floor.

'My daughter once said to me, "Wake me when the Israelis come, Mummy, so I can be with you." I have no idea how I raised my kids. Many people helped me. No men were left in the family. We depended on alms for the poor.'

She insists that her family's dead men were not involved in politics or resistance. 'The men were kind, decent, lived good lives, kept themselves to themselves.'

No one from her family is in politics, she says, or in prison, even after two intifadas. Now her sons have grown up and married and had their own children, she is terrified that the Israelis will come back and hurt them or kill them. One of her sons left to go to study in Poland at the beginning of the first intifada. In sixteen years, he has never been in touch. Perhaps he could no longer stand the strain of living in a house so full of poverty and grief.

Shara Abu Shakrah, who is now seventy-five years old, must have been a woman of great strength. She sits on a plastic chair in the doorway of her house. Children are everywhere, as usual in Gaza. Shara has thirty-five grandchildren. As she told her story, she was joined by her only daughter who never married, who was around forty years old. Unlike her mother, who wore a loosely knotted traditional Palestinian headscarf, she was fully veiled. She must have heard her mother talk about 1967 many times, but as she listened tears blotted through the black crepe of her veil in two dark lines. Shara wept too, for everything that has happened to her, for her dead husband and her lost son and a life that she never expected would be easy, but which became brutally harsh.

Qalqilya

I tried to get into Qalqilya on one of the West Bank's biblical winter days. If you are on foot, which you will be if you are not riding in an Israeli jeep or tank, the only way in is along a barbed wire passageway. Rain lashed at the Israeli sentries, wind howled through the barbed wire and lightning crashed into the hills. It feels like paying a visit to a prison, which is about right, because that is what Qalqilya is now. Israel treats the 42,000 Palestinian men, women and children as convicts, even though the vast majority of them have never been convicted of anything. They need special permission to leave, even to visit one of the outlying villages which used to be a couple of minutes away by car. Unemployment stands at 80 per cent. Procreating children and watching television are two of the main pastimes left to Qalqilya's people. When the curfews are in force, sometimes for weeks at a time, even the procreation of children is difficult in the town's chronically overcrowded homes. That leaves watching the television. In the last few years satellite channels like al-Jazeera, the Qatar-based station which is one of the few Arab forums for free speech, have become very popular. From Qalqilya the news of the last few years looks like a consistent campaign of Western aggression against Muslims.

Their jailers are the Israeli border policemen who guard the gate of the town. If the Israeli authorities judge the Palestinians inside are in need of discipline, soldiers and tanks from the regular army help the paramilitary border police administer collective punishment. I was not the only person visiting Qalqilya on a foul Friday during the holy month of Ramadan. Families and friends from other parts of the West Bank who had been granted visiting rights were queuing up either side of the barbed wire to go in or come out. The border police were having some fun. They were Israelis of Russian origin who were much less worried by the winter weather than the Palestinians.

One of the Russians, a burly blond six-footer, stopped a man and woman and their five children. The youngest was a tiny baby wrapped in a shawl. He stood in front of them in the narrow wire tunnel, his M-16 assault rifle across his chest. He put his face close to the Palestinian father. 'Where are you from?' he bellowed in Hebrew. The wind was strong but he was not raising his voice to make sure his message was heard. He was raising his voice to show who was boss. The man said he was from Bidya, which is one of the local villages. 'You're from Bidya? You say you're from Bidya?' The Russian yelled again, successfully frightening and humiliating the man in front of his family. 'Bidya? Bidya?' He stared at them. 'OK. Pass.' He moved aside and let them through. The woman tugged the shawl tighter around her baby. The Russian guard grinned at his comrades. It was the best entertainment on offer on a wet day.

I had an appointment with Maa'rouf Zahran, who was a boy in June 1967 when his family joined the lines of people who had either been expelled or fled in terror across the hills to Nablus. Now he is mayor of Qalqilya. He sat in his office in the shuttered and quiet town hall. Two portraits hung from the walls on either side of his vast, Wurlitzer-like desk. One was Yasser Arafat. The other was Walid

Ishreen. In 1967 he was the most glamorous fighter in Qalqilya, a little older than the others. Ever since Fatah had sent him to a training camp in Algeria he had used the *nom de guerre* Abu Ali Iyad. He was a good looking young man with a neat moustache, dressed in combat fatigues.

Qalqilya stands right on the border with Israel. Its position, which is now a misfortune, used to be its fortune. During the first thirty years or so of the occupation, its people were in pole position to get jobs in Israel. At weekends, during the quieter times, Israelis would come in to do their shopping. The prices were good and it felt a little exotic. It was a couple of miles and about half a world away from the white apartment buildings of Kfar Sava, which is a prosperous Israeli town opposite Qalqilya across the green line. The mayor wanted to talk about the way that Israel was turning Qalqilya into a laboratory for what the occupation might look like if it goes into its fifth decade. Israel has built a high concrete wall along the western edge of the town that faces Kfar Sava. It has watchtowers in it, just like the East Germans used to have in Berlin, only more hi-tech, with bullet proof glass (no one used to shoot at the Vopos who manned the Berlin Wall). To build it, a strip of land 100 metres wide was confiscated from the Palestinians. Qalqilya lost thousands of acres of its best fields and nineteen wells, which provided the town with 32 per cent of its water. Road Six, the brand new Israeli highway that runs along the wall, has plenty of water. Its cuttings and embankments are planted with bushes and small trees. Irrigation pipes feed each line of plants. When they grow, there will be a fine display, even in the hottest summers. Palestinians in the West Bank often have days without running water. The wall has been built to stop infiltration into Israel by Palestinian terrorists. It is already hugely expensive. For the time being, it runs for about a mile or so, neatly hemming in Qalqilya.

The mayor talked about the Israeli planes that seemed so untouchable back in June 1967. Plenty of older people in the town still believe that King Hussein colluded with the Israelis to give up the West Bank, and that his troops were firing blanks. Although it is a bizarre story, which lacks motivation and evidence, in Qalqilya it is believed. It helps old folks to have someone to blame for a futile war that has dogged their lives and is now destroying its third generation. Maa'rouf Zahran is an efficient, go-ahead man in his mid-forties. He knew my time was short, because it was Ramadan and because the Israelis made it so hard to get in and out, so he had brought our interviewees to his office. Towards the end of the day, the Palestinians wanted to get home to break their Ramadan fast. I wanted to get back because I was not looking forward to dealing with the guards at the gate of this urban jail after dark. The mayor provided a car to take us to the edge of town. On the way out the driver showed off the memorial they had put up to the Jordanians who died fighting for them in 1967. The Russians were still on the gate, wet and tired but still yelling and bullying their way along the lines of Palestinian families.

Everyday violence between Israelis and Palestinians has been much worse since 1967 than it was before. Since the latest shooting war started in September 2000, several thousand Palestinian civilians and fighters have been killed by the IDF. Hundreds of Israeli civilians and soldiers have been killed, many of them by suicide bombers. Israel insists it is not fighting a popular uprising. It says that Palestinian gunmen and bombers were let loose by the Palestinian leader Yasser Arafat, who has returned to his real plan – to use terrorism to destroy the state of Israel.

But young Palestinians do not join armed groups to kill and maim Israeli civilians and soldiers because of blind faith in Yasser Arafat or any other Palestinian leader. Strapping on a belt containing primitive bombs packed with nails and screws, to kill yourself and as many other people as possible in a bus or restaurant or hotel packed with children and their parents, is not a decision that any human being takes lightly. They do it – and are supported by a majority of Palestinians who believe that suicide attacks are legitimate resistance – because the way that they have been forced to live has made them desperate and full of hate.

Israel had plenty of warnings about the dangers ahead. Six weeks after the end of the war the British, who had spent the previous twenty years divesting themselves of Empire, saw that Palestinian violence was already starting in the Occupied Territories and warned the Israelis that 'the longer a settlement was delayed the greater the danger of Israel falling into the quasi-colonial position which even Britain had in the end found untenable'.

An hour spent looking down on Jerusalem on a spring day from the Mount of Olives would be better spent than a year locked in the sterile exercise of debating who most deserves to live in the Holy Land. Israel has a considerable claim. So do the Palestinians. Jerusalem has been a holy city for Jews for 3000 years, to Christians for 2000 years, for Muslims for around 1300 years. The answer, of course, is that Israelis and Palestinians deserve it equally, and if they cannot accept that and learn to share it they will never live in peace.

I reject the grim view that the conflict is irredeemable, that the land cannot be split between two viable states that respect each other. It condemns generations of Israelis and Palestinians to perpetual war. Ending the occupation will cut out the cancer that is killing them. Intensive follow-up treatment will be vital to make sure it does not come back, in the shape of international guarantees and the deployment of foreign troops as peace-enforcers along the border between Israel and a Palestinian state.

Unfortunately, the chances of them doing that are not good. Throughout its history, controlling Jerusalem and the rest of the Holy Land has been a matter of power, not compromise. The last hundred years of bloodshed between Zionism and Arab nationalism have not been any different. It is all down to who has the most guns.

It would be bad enough if the misery was confined to the two nations, the overwhelming majority of whose people are decent men and women who ought to be able to live their lives in peace. But at the start of the twenty-first century, their war affects us all. It is at the centre of the new conflict between the West and the Islamic world which is escalating with alarming speed. The Holy Land, with Jerusalem at its heart, is a place where great tectonic plates of religion, culture and nationalism come together. In the last few years, the fault lines that run between them, never quiet, have opened up again. Ignoring the legacy of 1967 is not an option.

Acknowledgements

I would not have written this book without Julian Alexander, the best agent around. Thanks to all my Israeli and Palestinian friends and colleagues in Jerusalem, especially Jimmy Michel, Rubi Gat, Karen Strauss and Alon and Yonit Farago. My employers at BBC News have been extremely tolerant. Thanks especially to Richard Sambrook, Mark Damazer, Richard Porter, Jonathan Baker, Adrian Van Klaveren and Vin Ray.

Thanks also to my researchers, who found people, books and documents: James Vaughan, Mohamed Shokeir, Taghreed El-Khodary, Linda Tabar, Zeev Elron, Avi Halfon, Yoni Ben Tovim, Luba Vinogradova, Jonathan Cummings, Ranya Kadri, Sanam Vakil, Sa'eda Kaelani, Nidal Rafa and Mariam Shaheen. Thanks also to Regina Greenwell at the Johnson Library in Austin, Texas; to Moshe and Ava Yotvat, who lent me documents; to Judith Sullivan, who transcribed hours of interviews; to Christopher Mitchell, for allowing me to quote from the documentary *Dead in the Water*, which he produced and directed for the BBC; to Yoram Tamir and Hagai Mann at Givat Hatachmoshet in Jerusalem; to Mitri Raheb at the International Centre of Bethlehem; to Uri Gil; to Uri Geller; to Dilys Wilkinson who lent me her house to write in at a critical moment; and to Ibrahim Zeghari, the world's finest barman, who has been keeping me fed and watered at the American Colony in Jerusalem since 1991. Thanks to Paul McCann at UNRWA in Gaza and Susan Sneddon at Save the Children in London who let me look at material from 1967.

Thanks are also due to all the people who invited me to their homes and gave up their time to talk to me about the 1967 war. There are many disagreements in the Middle East, but on all sides there are hospitable and friendly people. The names of most of them are in the book. A few asked for their identities to be disguised.

Thank you to Andrew Gordon and everyone else at Simon & Schuster UK, who were much more relaxed about deadlines than this news reporter believed possible.

Thanks and love to my family, to my parents, who made me what I am, and most of all, to Julia and Mattie, who put up with long absences in the Middle East and even longer ones away from family life.

Notes

Abbreviations

AP	Associated Press
FCO	Foreign and Commonwealth Office (London)
IDF	Israel Defence Force Archive
ISA	Israel State Archives
LBJ	Lyndon Baines Johnson (US President)
MER	*Middle East Record*
NSC	National Security Council Histories (Middle East Crisis), LBJ Library (Austin, Texas)
NSF	National Security Files (Country File: Middle East), LBJ Library (Austin, Texas)
PRO	Public Records Office (London)
SoSFA	Secretary of State for Foreign Affairs (George Brown, UK)
SWB	Summary of World Broadcasts, BBC monitoring

Introduction

2   'The biggest Palestinian attack': Israeli government website, www.mfa.gov.il/mfa.
2   'An investigation by': Human Rights Watch report on Jenin, www.hrw.org.
3   'Lyndon Baines Johnson': Memo for the Record, 7 June 1967, NSC, Box 18.
3   'Four days after the war': Notes of NSC Special Committee meeting, 14 June 1967, NSC, Box 19.

Pre-war

6   'so bone-tired': Uzi Narkiss, *The Liberation of Jerusalem*, p. 17.
6   'from guilt that Jerusalem': ibid., p. 14.
7   'a multitude of inhabitants', 'the inhabitants of the town became panic-stricken' and 'Nobody will ever know': Morris, pp. 203–10.
7   'could not leave Lod's': David Horovitz (ed.), *Yitzhak Rabin*, p. 26.
7   'In Deir Yassin': Morris, pp. 113–15; see also Salim Tamari (ed.), *Jerusalem, 1948*.

8   'He concentrated on the rapes': interview with Hazem Nusseibeh, Amman, May 2002.

9   'A meeting was arranged': Dan Kurzman, *Soldier of Peace*, pp. 148–53.

9   For details of Abdullah's assassination, see Roland Dallas, *King Hussein*, pp. 1–3; Peter Snow, *Hussein*, pp. 33–5.

9   For secret contacts between Abdullah and the Israelis, see Avi Shlaim, *The Politics of Partition*.

10   'Despite lessons from his driver': Yitzhak Rabin, *The Rabin Memoirs*, pp. 32–3.

11   'But both sides, blaming each other': see Itamar Rabinovich, *The Road Not Taken*.

11   'From around 1952': interview with Meir Pa'il, Tel Aviv, 3 May 2002.

12   'Nasser's followers': PRO/FCO 17/456, 9 July 1968: Saunders (Baghdad) to Eastern Dept, FCO.

12   'As a young officer': interview with General Abd al-Muhsin Kamil Murtagi, Cairo, 14 December 2002.

13   'Officers regarded Amer': interview with General Salahadeen Hadidi, Cairo, 12 December 2002.

13   'Amer and his cronies': Anthony Nutting, *Nasser*, pp. 262–3.

14   'The last straw': Patrick Seale, *The Struggle for Syria*, p. 42.

14   'The Syrian officer class': Seale, *Asad of Syria*, pp. 24–40.

14   'If the same conditions': PRO/FCO 371/186923, 25 January 1966: annual report on Syrian armed forces.

14   'Colonel Rowan-Hamilton': ibid.

15   'The Syrian army': see Galia Golan, *Soviet Policies in the Middle East from World War Two to Gorbachev*.

15   'Its aggressive behaviour': Shlaim, *The Iron Wall*, p. 235.

16   'Service on this front': ibid., p. 229.

16   '"We will throw them into the sea"': PRO/FCO 371/186923, 25 January 1966: annual report on Syrian armed forces.

16   'totally inadequate': Israeli–Arab confrontation, National Military Command Center, May 1967, NSF, Box 104.

16   'the hopelessness of it all': PRO/FCO 371/186382, 15 October 1966: Evans (Damascus) to FCO.

17   because of Israeli provocations': Shlaim, p. 235.

17   'Lads, let's sing a bit': Teveth, *Tanks of Tammuz*, p. 54.

17   'How many Syrian tanks': ibid., p. 56.

18   'Using the Syrian border': ibid., p. 59; interview with Israel Tal, Tel Aviv, 6 May 2002; Patrick Wright, *Tank*, pp. 343–5.

19   'over 50 per cent': *Maariv*, 7 April 1972, quoted at www.searchforjustice.org, 4 November 2002.

19   'no amount of pseudo-legality': PRO/FCO 17/576, 5 January 1967: briefing on demilitarised zones.

19   'General Odd Bull': Bull, p. 55; John Gee, 'The Borders Between Syria and Israel', www.caabu.org.

20   'strange names like de Gaulle's nose': Van Creveld, p. 170.

20   'This is our home': *Yediot Aharonot*, 14 April 1967, quoted in Bondy, p. 337; PRO/FCO 17/473, 10 January 1967.

20   'It went this way': *Yediot Aharonot*, 27 April 1967.

20   'Along the Syrian border': Dayan quotes from Shlaim, pp. 235–6 and AP report, 11 May 1997, www.codoh.com.

21 'A small team of Palestinians': Sayigh, p. 107.
21 'Other groups appeared': Hirst, pp. 276–8.
21 'the military punch': PRO/FCO 371/186838/R109/207, 19 October 1966.
22 'He installed Ahmed Shukairy': Kerr, p. 115.
22 'large-scale operation': PRO/PREM 13/1617, 17/18 October 1966: Hadow (Tel Aviv) to FCO.
22 'early in November': Tessler, pp. 367, 378.
24 'It was bigger': Pollack, p. 295.
24 'The major and his men': PRO/FCO 371/186838, 3 November 1966: Hadow (Tel Aviv) to FCO.
24 'Nobody had died': PRO/FCO 371 186840, 21 December 1966: Dispatch No. 56 to SoSFA, George Brown.
24 'Their plan was': PRO/FCO 371/186839, 21 December 1966: Defence Attaché Amman's report on Samua and Defence Attaché Tel Aviv's report attached to PRO/FCO 371 186840, Dispatch No. 56 to SoSFA, George Brown.
25 'dazed and frightened': Bishop's account is in PRO/FCO 371/186838.
26 'He had been having secret meetings': Amman Cables 1456, 1457, 11 December 1966, NSF, Box 146.
26 'a quite extraordinary revelation': Memo from Walt Rostow to LBJ, 12 December 1966, NSF, Box 146.
27 'The King concluded': PRO/FCO 371/186839, Ambassador Adams to London.
27 'He told the diplomats': US Current Intelligence Bulletin, 15 November 1966 – filed in PRO/FCO 371/186839.
27 'he summoned all the ambassadors': PRO/FCO 371/186839, 17 November 1966.
27 'The United States was so concerned': Memo from Rostow to Johnson, 15 November 1966, NSF Country File: Israel, Box 140.
27 'The US airlifted': Memo from Robert McNamara to Johnson, 17 April 1967, NSF Country File: Israel, Box 140; Memo from Amos Jordan to Rostow, 1 December 1966, NSF, Box 146.
28 'The CIA believed': CIA Memo for the Director: 'The Jordan Regime, Its Prospects and the Consequences of Its Demise', 13 December 1966, NSF, Box 146.
28 'The people of Samua': PRO/FCO 371/186839, 15 November 1966, US Embassy Amman to SoSFA.
28 'What do they expect': *Washington Post*, 15 November 1966, quoted in Neff, p. 42.
29 'A senior security official': Amman Cable 1456, 12 December 1966.
29 'army officers': *Washington Post*, 15 November 1966, quoted in Neff, p. 42.
29 'Hussein's troubles': PRO/FCO 371/186839/272, 17 November 1966: Tesh (Cairo) to FCO.
29 'Damascus was relieved': PRO/FCO 371/186839/266, 16 November 1967: Evans (Damascus) to FCO.
30 'Even if the Syrian government': PRO/FCO 17/473, 21 January 1967: Damascus to FCO.
30 'Let the Israelis shoot at us': ibid.
30 'on 7 April': details of kibbutz in *Yediot Aharonot*, 14 April 1967, quoted in Bondy, pp. 337–42.

30   Account of battle: PRO/FCO 17/474: Report of ground/air action on Israeli/Syrian border on 7 April 1967, from Defence and Military Attaché's office, Tel Aviv, 11 April 1967; also PRO/FCO 17/473: Syria/Israel, account of incident from Eastern Department; attack on Sqoufiye reported by UNTSO; PRO/FCO 17/473, 10 April 1967.

32   'a stunned awe': PRO/FCO 17/473, 12 April 1967.

32   'Israel basked': PRO/FCO 17/473, 10 April 1967.

32   'Are you out of your minds?': Weizman, p. 197.

32   'The British government': PRO/FCO 17/498, 14 August 1967.

32   'The CIA picked up': President's Daily Brief, 13 May 1967, NSC, Box 19.

32   'contemplating an attack': text of article from *al-Ahram* read out on Cairo Radio Home Service, 0500 GMT, 13 May 1967, SWB, Vol. 2453–78.

32   'A high Israeli source': *MER*, p. 187.

33   'took the threats and warnings': ibid, p. 179.

33   'There were some': Brecher, p. 359.

33   'The message received': Riad, p. 17.

33   'the Israeli leaders had announced': Nasser speech, 22 May 1967, quoted in Brecher, p. 359.

33   'The Egyptians claimed': NSF, Paris Cable 18806, 23 May 1967, Box 104.

33   'Atassi, the head of state': Nutting, p. 397.

34   'the foster child state of bandits': Syrian propaganda from Damascus Cable 1163, 22 May 1967, NSF, Box 104.

34   'the Russians pricked the Egyptian donkey': PRO/FCO 17/498, 14 August 1967.

34   'They told me': Sadat, p. 172; Parker, *The Politics of Miscalculation in the Middle East*, p. 5; Heikal, *Sphinx*, pp. 174–5.

34   'By the evening': Gamasy, p. 21.

34   'The Soviets seem': NSF, Moscow 5078, 23 May 1967, Box 104.

34   'The Soviets wanted': interview with Amin Howedi, Cairo, 14 December 2002; Lior, p. 150; Golan, pp. 58–62; the most comprehensive discussion of the Soviet warning is in Parker, p. 3–35.

34   'A "medium level"': CIA to White House Situation Room; Soviet official's comments on Soviet policy in the Middle Eastern war, date sanitised, NSC, Box 18.

35   'I think this is difficult': comments of Gregoriy Petrovich Kapustyan, Soviet first secretary in Kuwait and KGB officer in CIA Intelligence Information Cable, 25 May 1967; Soviet intelligence officer's comment on the current Arab–Israeli crisis, NSF, Box 105.

35   'Soviet advice to the Syrians': Memo, 'Terrorist Origins of the Crisis', Saunders to Bundy, dated 'Sometime prior to June 19th 1967', NSC, Box 17.

35   'It is probable': Memo for Rostow from Nathaniel Davis, 2 June 1967, NSC, Box 20.

37   'the sad capital city': Amos Oz, *Seventh Day*, pp. 215–16.

38   'General Bull': *MER*, Vol. 3, 1967.

38   'a clear violation': President's Daily Brief, 13 May 1967, NSC, Box 19.

39   'battle order number one': document captured by Israel, quoted in *MER*, p. 185.

39   'astonished and alarmed': Gamasy, pp. 21–2.

39   'I did not': quoted in Gamasy, p. 23.

39   'Training, never a religion': interview with Hadidi.

39 'we incurred heavy losses': interview with General Abdel Moneim Khalil, Cairo, 13 December 2002.

39 'By 1967 the Egyptian High Command': Field Marshal Abdel Ghani el-Gamasy, *The October War*, pp. 37–8.

40 'Nasser is going': President's Daily Brief, 16 May 1967, NSC, Box 19.

40 'defensive-deterrent in character': PRO/Telegram No. 301, Tel Aviv to FCO, 17 May 1967.

40 'We cannot leave the south': Lior, p. 148.

41 'Outside the stadium': Michael Bar Zohar, *Embassies in Crisis*, pp. 16–18.

41 'As soon as he could': interview with General Yeshayahu Gavish, Tel Aviv, 21 November 2002.

41 'In just over a decade': Rikhye, p. 14.

42 'Egypt promised': Brian Urquart, quoted in Parker, *Six-Day War*, p. 87.

42 'To your information': Rikhye, p. 16.

42 'They were being': General Mohamed Fawzi in *Al-Ahram Weekly* online, 5–11 June 1997.

43 'war would be inevitable': Rikhye, p. 17.

43 'General, what's the occasion?': ibid., p. 21.

43 'willy-nilly be dragged in': PRO/FCO 17/479, 17 May 1967: Damascus to FCO.

43 'slogan of the unity': PRO/FCO 17/479, 19 May 1967: Damascus to FCO.

43 'On 17 May': Tel Aviv Cable 3641, 18 May 1967, NSC, Box 22.

44 'before taking any unilateral action': PRO/FCO 17/479, 16 May 1967: Tel Aviv to FCO.

44 'But other high-ranking': PRO/Tel Aviv to FCO, 19 May 1967.

44 'in the strongest terms': message to PM Eshkol, 17 May 1967, NSC, Box 17.

44 'A long-delayed': 'The President in the Middle East Crisis', 19 December 1968, NSC, Box 17.

44 'one scrofulous room': PRO/FCO 8/39, 18 November 1967: Parsons, British Political Agency, Bahrain to Balfour-Paul, British Political Residency, Bahrain.

45 'By 1959': Albert Hourani, *A History of the Arab Peoples*, p. 393; also Winston Burdett, *Encounter With the Middle East*, p. 23.

46 'The wire services': wire service reports, 22 May 1967, NSC, Box 17.

46 'if we come through': letter and draft of letter, 22 May 1967, NSC, Box 17.

47 'through sweaty, heaving, arm-flinging bodies': Rikhye, p. 64.

47 'On the evening': and other details of the Nasser–U Thant dinner, Rikhye, pp. 63–79.

47 'out to kill him': USUN 5496, 27 May 1967, NSF, Box 105.

48 'General Yariv': Bar Zohar, p. 72.

48 'decisive day': Press review, 23 May 1967, NSC, Box 17.

48 'within ninety minutes': Amos Elon, p. 7.

48 'The message passed down': interview with General Shmuel Eyal, Head of Personnel IDF, Rishon le Zion, 27 November, 2002.

49 'I was leaning': Henry (ed.), *The Seventh Day*, p. 32.

49 'One persistent 63-year-old': Elon, *A Blood-Dimmed Tide*, p. 7.

49 'refusal to panic': Bar Zohar, p. 78.

49 'rapacious animals': Ruth Bondy, Dvar Hashavua, 2 June 1967, quoted in *Mission Survival*, p. 30.

50 'You have brought this state': account of his collapse in Rabin, pp. 58–65.

50 'At about eight': Weizman, pp. 202–3.

51 'a crushing burden': Leah Rabin, p. 107.

51   'he was alone': Horovitz (ed.), pp. 40–1.

51   'Abdel Moneim Khalil': interview with General Abdel Moneim Khalil, Cairo, 13 December 2002.

51   'with the same deep chasm': Field bulletin quoted in *Mission Survival.*

52   'Fifteen years of hard work': interview with Meir Pa'il, 4 May 2002; also Martin Van Creveld, *The Sword and the Olive.*

52   'by the superior training': PRO/FCO 17/576: 'Annual Report on the Israeli Army', 27 January 1967.

52   'militarily unchallengeable': 'Israeli–Arab confrontation, May 1967', NSF, Box 104.

53   'The British estimates': PRO/CAB 158/66, 17 April 1967: 'A comparison of the Armed Forces of Israel and those of certain Arab states up to the end of 1967', JIC.

53   'in command, training, equipment': PRO/FCO 17/576, ibid.

53   'enjoys superiority': *Jewish Chronicle*, 31 March 1967, quoted in PRO/CAB 158/66, 17 April 1967.

53   'Israel's major strategic': Helms and Wheeler, NSC Meeting, 24 May 1967, NSC, Box 17.

54   'nuclear weapons': Memo from Katzenbach to LBJ, 1 May 1967, NSC, Box 17; also Rostow to LBJ, 8 May 1967, NSF, Box 145.

54   'insufficient to launch': 'Israeli–Arab confrontation, May 1967', op. cit.

55   'The generals were left fuming': Raviv, p. 93.

55   'glory of the television cameras': Rostow to LBJ, 9 June 1967, NSC, Box 18.

55   'Since 1948': Eban, *Personal Witness*, pp. 1–41.

55   'Eban arrived': ibid, p. 374; CIA Cable, 'Impact of the Arab–Israeli crisis on the French political scene', 16 June 1967, NSC, Box 18.

55   'In London': Eban, p. 378.

55   'A couple of days earlier': PRO/PREM 13/1617, 23 May 1967: note of a meeting between PM, Foreign Secretary and Defence Secretary at 10 Downing Street.

56   'Eban did a lot of thinking': Eban, p. 381.

56   'biggest crowd': Rostow account of meeting with Evron, NSC, Box 17.

56   'one of the severest shocks': Eban, p. 382.

56   'Read it': Rafael, p. 143.

56   'We have no problems on the ground': Lammfrom, pp. 535–7, documents 166 and 167; telegram from Eshkol to Eban, 25 May 1967.

57   'a hypochondriac cable': Eban, *Personal Witness*, pp. 382–3.

57   'Israel had wind': interview with Hussein al Shafei, Cairo, 15 December 2002.

57   'playing a political game': CIA Cable, UAR/Jordanian discussion, 25 May 1967, NSF, Box 105; and background on Jordan/UAR defense pact and re-examination of Jordan's position as a result of it, 4 June 1967, NSF, Box 106.

58   'During the ten-minute flight': interview with Walt Rostow, Austin, 12 September 2002.

58   'Johnston had the nasty feeling': NSC, Chronological guide, Box 17.

58   'The president would buzz': interview with Rostow.

58   'Waiting in Rostow's office': details of Israeli arguments in Dept of State Memo of interview between Secretary Rusk and Abba Eban, 25 May 1967, NSC, Box 17.

59   'not "a serious estimate"': Memo to LBJ from Rostow, 25 May 1967, NSC, Box 17.

59 'Upstairs, in the Oval Office': Johnson's furniture is at the LBJ Library in Austin, Texas.

59 'Israel was not showing': Morning Intelligence Mid-East Sitrep (as of 0700): Memo to LBJ from Rostow, 28 May 1967, NSC, Box 17.

59 'the only difference between': Oral History, Robert McNamara, LBJ Library, AC-96-10.

60 'If the Israelis attacked first': quoted in Parker, *Six-Day War*, pp. 216–17.

60 'Senior Soviet officials': Moscow Cable 5170, 27 May 1967, NSF, Box 105.

60 'The CIA's conclusions': CIA Office of National Estimates, 26 May 1967: Memo for the Director, NSF, Box 115.

60 'we are not inclined': letter to Wilson, 26 May 1967, NSC, Box 17.

61 'Eban and his team': Rostow report of meeting with Ephraim Evron, No. 2 at Israeli Embassy, 26 May 1967, NSC, Box 17; State 202587 flash telegram, 26 May 1967, NSF, Box 105.

61 'Secretary of State Dean Rusk': Memorandum of interview, Rusk–Eban, 25 May 1967, NSC, Box 17.

61 'I did not get the impression': Eban, *Personal Witness*, p. 383.

61 'Along about sundown': Meeting on the Arab–Israeli Crisis, 26 May 1967, NSC, Box 17.

61 'just a six foot four friend Texan': Raviv, p. 100.

61 'unilateral action': Winston Burdett, *Encounter With the Middle East*, p. 254.

62 'some guy out here': *New York Times*, 10 July 1967.

62 'The Israelis were finally ushered': Memo of interview, 26 May 1967, NSC, Box 17.

63 'they came loaded for bear': NSC, Chronological guide, Box 17.

63 'Eban left immediately': Rafael, p. 145.

63 'Eban and his team arrived': Raviv, p. 102; interview with Moshe Raviv, Herzliya, 6 May 2002.

64 'They feel they can finish Nasser off': description of Barbour from Hersh, pp. 159–61; Allon's comments in White House situation room Cable to LBJ, 29 May 1967; Ambassador Barbour's comments and rumours about Eban's ousting in Walt Rostow to LBJ, 28 May 1967, both NSC, Box 17; threat to Eban, also in Rafael, p. 160; Yariv's comments to Ambassador Hadow, PRO/FCO 17/498; also *MER*, p. 197.

64 'reached upper decibel range': Cairo 8072, Sitrep, Box 105, 27 May 1967; State Dept Situation report, 28 May 1967, NSC, Box 17.

65 'Physically he was': Sandy Gall, *Don't Worry About the Money Now*, p. 276.

65 'It was a confident': Text of Nasser's news conference, 28 May 1967, NSF, Box 17.

65 'sleepwalker speaking in an exalted trance of fatalism': Burdett, pp. 281–2.

65 'American diplomats': Cable, Cairo 8218 to State, 30 May 1967, NSC, Box 17.

65 'They dismissed a theory': White House Situation Room to LBJ, Arab–Israel situation report, 0430, EDT 28 May 1967, NSC, Box 17.

66 'After Nasser had finished': Ziad Rifai's account in Hussein of Jordan, pp. 38–42.

66 'New light': CIA Intelligence Information Cable, 25 May 1967, Box 105; Background on Jordan/UAR defense pact, 4 June 1967, Box 106, NSF.

66 'traditional Arab friends': Amman Cable 3775, 26 May 1967, NSC, Box 17.

67 'would result in an Israeli occupation': Samir A. Muttawi, *Jordan in the 1967 War*, pp. 106–7; Hussein quotes, p. 103: interview with Leila Sharaf, Amman, 8 June 2002.

67 'Just after dawn': account of Hussein in Cairo from Hussein of Jordan, *My War With Israel*, as told to Vick Vance and Pierre Lauer.

69 'I knew that war was inevitable': King Hussein speaking to Avi Shlaim, 3 December 1996, *New York Review of Books*, 15 July 1999.

69 'He told the officers': interview with Prince Zaid Ben Shaker, Amman, 7 June 2002.

69 'The official army minder': interview with Winston Churchill, London, 17 June 2002.

69 'The crisis was especially frightening': letters in ISA G 6301/1051; letters to Eshkol in Prime Minister's Office file.

70 'We have nothing for Israel except war': Cairo, Voice of the Arabs in Arabic, 1738 GMT, 18 May 1967, BBC SWB ME/2470/A/6.

70 'Black jokes about': interview with David Rubinger, Jerusalem, 24 November 2002.

70 'Suddenly everyone was talking about Munich': Muki Tzur from Kibbutz Ein Gev in *The Seventh Day*, p. 19.

70 'During May, more and more men': *MER*, pp. 373–4.

71 'sunny, sparsely populated': *New Yorker*, 17 June 1967; reprinted in Chace, pp. 101–11.

71 'Had there been an injury in the family?': Schliefer, p. 148.

72 'nothing had changed': Morning and Afternoon Intelligence Sitrep, 28 May 1967, NSC, Box 17.

72 'running around like mice': Bregman and el-Tahri, p. 77.

72 'We felt as if the burden was on our shoulders': Sharon, p. 184.

73 'Nobody offered Eshkol any refreshments': Narkiss, p. 67.

73 'tongue-lashing': Rabin, p. 72.

73 'the IDF's power to deter': an account of meeting from Haber, pp. 195–9; also interviews with Gavish, and with General Elad Peled, Jerusalem, 25 November 2002.

74 'My purely military': interview with Gavish.

75 'One of them': Elon, *A Blood-Dimmed Tide*, p. 9.

75 'Letters criticising': ISA G 6301/1054-II, Prime Minister's Office, correspondence.

75 'non-committal, uninspiring': Yael Dayan, p. 9.

75 'Most Israelis thought her father': Henry (ed.), *The Seventh Day*, p. 23.

75 'the leadership of the nation': Peres, *David's Sling*, p. 234.

76 'Public doubt and derision': Moshe Dayan, p. 266.

76 'He had two hobbies': interview with Lova Eliav, Tel Aviv, 2 December 2002.

76 'walked in with a heavy revolver': Moshe Dayan, p. 28.

76 'munching raw onions': ibid., p. 30.

77 'the fate of our generation': quoted in Naphtali Lau-Lavie, *Moshe Dayan*, p. 142.

77 'playing politics': Haber, p. 157.

77 'high command of the army': PRO/Tel Aviv to FCO, Ambassador Hadow reporting interview with Gen Yariv, 31 May 1967, FCO 17/487.

77 'a thundering voice': Haber, pp. 199–201.

78 'He told the cabinet': *MER*, p. 371.

78 'Nobody had told Gavish': interview with Gavish.

79 'He said "come quickly to Tel Aviv"': interview with Miriam Eshkol, Jerusalem, 9 May 2002.

79 'The British police chief': Segev, p. 475.

79 'He acted quite naturally': Haber, p. 202.

79 'It wasn't just a personal insult': interview with Gavish.

79   'The IDF has never': Haber, p. 215.
80   'Even Colonel Lior': ibid., p. 202.
80   'Arab confidence hung in the air': Abdullah Schliefer, pp. 143-45.
80   'Adnan Abu Odeh': interview with Adnan Abu Odeh, Amman, 6 June 2002.
81   'I am impressed' Lisbon cable 1517, 2 June 1967 eyes only for President and Secretary of State from Robert Anderson NSF Box 115.
81   'sport clothes' ibid.
83   'Riad told him': Riad, p. 21.
83   'not economic but purely psychological' Cairo cable 8349, 2 June 1967 NSC Box 18.
84   'a terrible bloodbath': Memo to President from Rostow, 2 June 1967, NSC, Box 18.
85   'the capability of these forces': Memo to the Secretary of Defense from Wheeler, Chairman, Joint Chiefs of Staff, 2 June 1967; NSC, Box 18.
85   'On 2 June': IDF 3/46/1980: minutes of Special Meeting of the General Staff with the cabinet defence committee, 2 June 1967.
86   'barbaric and inhuman': Brown, p. 35.
86   'He was very impressive': interview with Meir Amit, 26 November 2002.
87   'the strident Arab nationalism': PRO/FCO 17/489: Pullar (Jerusalem) to FCO, 3 June 1967.
87   'Late in the afternoon': Narkiss, pp. 87–92.
88   'If the chief of staff': interview with Mordechai Hod, Tel Aviv, 7 May 2002.
88   'He gave a terrific show': interview with Churchill.
89   'I propose to discontinue': PRO/FCO 17/489: Hadow (Tel Aviv) to FCO, 4 May 1967.
89   'At Kibbutz Nachshon': Kibbutz Nachshon bulletin.
89   'Ran Pekker': interview with Ran Pekker Ronen, Herzliya, 25 November 2002.
90   'The air force's own intelligence': interview with Air Vice Marshal Abdel-Hamid El-Dighidi, quoted in Egyptian weekly *Al-Ahali*, 29 June 1983; reprinted in *al-Ahram*, 5–11 June 1997.
91   'It is now increasingly clear': Memo from Rostow to LBJ, 4 June 1967, NSC, Box 18.
92   'The Soviet ambassador to the UN': Shevchenko, p. 133.
92   'Tomorrow it will start': interview with Miriam Eshkol, Jerusalem, 9 May 2002; also Bregman and El Tahri.
92   'War looked inescapable': Cable Amman 4040 to State, 4 June 1967, NSC, Box 23.

Day One

94   'Brigadier-General Ariel Sharon': Yael Dayan, pp. 33–4.
95   'Hod managed four hours' sleep': interview with Mordechai Hod, Tel Aviv, 7 May 2002.
95   'Battle order of the officer': AP, *Lightning Out of Israel*, p. 53.
95   'Secrecy and surprise': interview with Hod.
95   'Ran Pekker's alarm': Weizman, p. 179; Ran Ronen, 'Hawk in the Sky', *Yediot Aharonot*, 2002.
95   'The same thing': interview with Hod.
96   'King Hussein's warnings': interview with Ihsan Shurdom, Amman, 5 June 2002.
97   'Pekker . . . made sure coffee': Ronen, interview and 'Hawk in the Sky', *Yediot Aharanot*, 2002.

97   'Similar briefings': Avihu Bin-Nun's eyewitness account from Bamahane, IDF Magazine, reprinted in *Jerusalem Post*.

98   'In those days': Weizman, p. 69.

98   'By 1963': interview with Herzl Bodinger, Yad Mordechai, 1 December 2002.

98   'The pilots made models': PRO/AIR 77/581.

99   'Hod and his commanders': interview with Hod.

99   One of the pilots': interview with Uri Gil, Einhod, 6 November 2002.

99   'The next stage': interview with Bodinger.

100 'The soldiers of': Orr's eyewitness account from Bamahane, IDF Magazine, reprinted in *Jerusalem Post*.

100 'The headquarters': interview with Major-General Salahadeen Salim, Cairo, 14 December 2002.

101 'down 30 per cent': official Egyptian government figures quoted by Salim.

102 'The IAF had five': IAF summary of statistics, IDF 1983/1210/147.

102 'dinned into them': Avihu Bin-Nun, 'Bamahane', IDF magazine reprinted http://info.jpost.com/supplements .

102 'Ran Pekker thought': Ronen, *Yediot Aharonot*, 2002.

102 'Herzl Bodinger and': interview with Bodinger.

102 'The suspense was incredible': Weizman, p. 211.

103 'In 1966, he had claimed': Schiff, p. 198.

103 'The routes the aircraft': interview with Hod.

103 'Bin-Nun swung his Mystere': Avihu Bin-Nun, 'Bamahane'.

103 'Cairo was an hour': interview with Hod.

104 'In his Vautour Bodinger': interview with Bodinger.

104 'The defence minister': Weizman, p. 214.

104 'Bin-Nun and his flight': Avihu Bin-Nun, 'Bamahane'.

105 'Israel had deliberately kept': Weizman, p. 215.

105 'They had good maps': PRO/AIR 77/581.

105 'Thanks to excellent, extremely comprehensive intelligence': Black and Morris, pp. 206–35.

105 'Pilots had a target book': interview with Shurdom.

105 'Giving details of the layout': interview with Hod.

105 'Tahsen Zaki': Tahsen's story in Draz, pp. 5–20.

105 'the beating heart of Arabism': Foreign Broadcast information service daily report No. 108, 5 June 1967, NSC, Box 19.

105 'He was about to get': interview with Shafei.

106 'He could not break': Hod in *Paris Match*, quoted in *Hussein of Jordan*, p. 103.

106 'The daughters of Colonel': interview with Mordechai Bar, Jerusalem, 25 November 2002.

107 'Israeli pilots were going to dive-bomb': PRO/AIR 77/581, March 1968: altitude and operational details in PRO/FCO 17/576, 29 June 1967.

107 'Everybody started to talk': interview with Hod.

108 'We were sure that our Egyptian fighters': quote from Murtagi in El-Gamasy, p. 53.

108 'At General Salah Muhsin's': interview with Salim.

108 'It was the day of the final': interview with Kamel Sulaiman Shaheen, Deiral Balah, 30 November 2002.

109 'His job was to keep an eye': interview with General Ibrahim El Dakhakny, Cairo, 19 December 2002.

110 'Chief of Staff Rabin phoned': from IDF Southern Command publication, quoted in *Mission Survival*, p. 175.

110 'Further south': Barker, *Six-Day War*, pp. 79–80; Pollack, p. 64.

111 'Orr gave his men a last briefing': Orr, 'Bamahane', http://info.jpost.com.

111 'simple messages': IDF press release, 6 June 1967, quoted in *Mission Survival*, p. 177.

111 'In his final briefing Tal': Bar On, p. 38.

112 'King Hussein was at home with his family': Snow, p. 139.

112 'Ihsan Shurdom lay': interview with Shurdom.

112 'They asked us to give them': Hussein, *My 'War' With Israel*, pp. 60–1.

112 'When the King and the others': ibid., p. 66.

113 'before the war the Royal Jordanian Air Force': IDF 1983/1210/147.

113 'on Beni Sweif': interview with Bodinger.

113 'At Inshas base': interview with Ronen.

114 'Murtagi's command post': interview with Murtagi.

114 'Among the weaknesses': PRO/AIR 77/581, March 1968.

114 'Egypt's entire air defence': interview with Hadidi: he presided over the first court martial of the heads of the air force and the air defence system after the war.

115 'In Tel Aviv': Weizman, p. 216.

115 'Israel's air force commander': interview with Hod.

115 'Mohamed Heikal told his readers': Heikal in *al-Ahram*, 13 October 1967, quoted in *MER*, p. 214.

115 'But it was yet another bonus': Barker, p. 62.

117 'At Egypt's base at Bir Tamada': interview with Ali Mohammed, Cairo, 14 December 2002.

117 'Vice President Shafei': interview with Hussein al Shafei, Cairo, 15 December 2002.

119 'Mahmoud Riad, the foreign minister of Egypt': Riad, p. 23.

119 'Trevor Armbrister': Trevor Armbrister, 'Letter from Cairo', *Saturday Evening Post*, 29 July 1967, quoted in Chace, pp. 111–12.

119 'Winston Burdett': Burdett, p. 317.

120 'No one at the Soviet Embassy': Sergei Tarasenko, 'Blitzkrieg in Sinai', *Novoe Vremya*, No. 21, 1997, pp. 32–3.

120 'On the streets': Armbrister in Chace, pp. 111–12.

120 'At first, Cairo Radio': both quotes from Cairo Radio in War File, p. 71.

121 'I lay down': Draz, pp. 49–54.

122 'Tal's division': Van Creveld, p. 184; Barker, pp. 80–1; Dupuy, pp. 249–52.

122 'Orr, following on up the road': Orr, 'Bamahane'.

123 'Ramadan Mohammed Iraqi': interview with Ramadan Mohammad Iraqi, Cairo, 17 December 2002.

124 'UNEF troops': UN S/7930, 5 June 1967, http://domino.un.org

124 'Major El Dakhakny': interview with El Dakhakny.

124 'Fayek Abdul Mezied': interview with Fayek Abdul Mezied, Qalqilya, 29 November 2002.

125 'The bloodiest battle': Morris, pp. 413–18; Van Creveld, p. 141.

125 'On 5 June': Mutawi, p. 135.

125 'As well as the Jordanian army': interview with Tawfik Mahmud Afaneh, Qalqilya, 29 November 2002.

126 'Memdour Nufel had always wanted': interview with Memdour Nufel, Ramallah, 25 November 2002.

126 'Various estimates': Sayigh, p. 139.
127 'Dayan did a very clever thing': interview with Meir Amit, Herzliya, 26 November 2002.
127 'This morning Egypt': Tel Aviv Cable 3924 to State, 5 June 1967, NSF, Box 23.
128 'Hussein told Bull': Hussein, pp. 64–5.
128 'Bullets narrowly missed': PRO/FCO 17/489: Pullar (Jerusalem) to FCO, 5 June 1967.
128 'In a "distinctly chilly" way': PRO/FCO 17/492: Pullar (Jerusalem) to FCO, 5 June 1967.
128 'John Tleel, a Palestinian dentist': Tleel, p. 156; interview with Tleel, Jerusalem, 8 May 2002.
130 'Anwar Nusseibeh heard the news': Nusseibeh quote from Moskin, p. 104.
130 'One crackpot scheme': Schliefer, p. 168.
131 '260 Enfield rifles, 20 Sten': ibid., p. 174.
132 'In Amman the Jordanian minister': interview with Leila Sharaf, 8 June 2002.
132 'In Tel Aviv at midday': Memo for LBJ from McPherson, 11 June 1967, NSC, Box 18.
133 'At the end of June': report of Hod news conference, *Maariv*, 30 June 1967, quoted in *Mission Survival*, p. 162.
134 'By 0430 Walt Rostow': interview with Rostow.
134 'The CIA recalled that': President's Daily Brief, 5 June 1967, NSC, Box 19.
134 'Johnson, still in his bedroom': Memo for the record: Walt Rostow's Recollections of 5 June 1967, Box 18; also Memo from George Christian, 7 June 1967, NSC, Box 19.
135 'Bundy was made executive secretary': Memo for the record by Harold Saunders, 16 May–13 June, 20 December 1968, NSF.
135 'A group of foreign correspondents': Armbrister in Chace, pp. 111–12.
135 'US diplomats reported': Cairo Cable 8504 to State, NSC, 5 June 67, Box 23.
136 'Outside, the sky': Hewat (ed.), *War File*, pp. 66–7.
136 'At 1110 Bakr': Armbrister in Chace, pp. 111–12.
136 'Eric Rouleau': E. Rouleau, J. F. Held, S. Lacouture, *Israel et les Arabes: le 3me Combat*, quoted in *MER*, p. 217.
136 'The speaker of the Egyptian': Sadat, p. 174.
137 'The Jordanians gave up waiting': Mutawi, p. 127: Hussein, p. 65.
137 'In Damascus in the morning': PRO/FCO 17/489: Evans (Damascus) to FCO, 5 June 1967.
137 'At 5 a.m. Gideon Rafael': USUN Cable 5623 to State, 5 June 1967, NSC, Box 23.
138 'Within minutes': interview with General Salahadeen Hadidi, Cairo, 12 December 2002.
138 'Anwar El Sadat': Sadat, p. 175.
138 'Around 11 o'clock': Boghdady's account from Abu Zikri, pp. 295–304.
139 'The forces in the Sinai': Dupuy, p. 265.
139 'The next phone call came from Nasser': El-Gamasy, p. 57.
139 'Mohamed Hassanein Heikal': Mohamed Hassanein Heikal, *The Cairo Documents*, p. 247.
139 'Vice-President Shafei': interview with Hussein al Shafei.
141 'A reporter from the Israeli army': Yosef Bar Yosef, IDF Magazine.
142 'Somehow, six Tupolev': Riad, pp. 24–5.
142 'In Libya, the US': Cable from Benghazi to State, 5 June 1967, NSC, Box 23.

142 'Two hours later': ibid.

143 'In Yemen': Cable 750 to State, 5 June 1967, NSC, Box 23.

143 'In Basra, in southern Iraq': Baghdad Cable 2089 to State, 5 June 1967, NSC, Box 23.

143 'Aharon Yariv': IDF 1076/192/1974: Rabin and his staff meet.

143 'Saad el Shazli': interview with General Saad el Shazli, 16 December 2002.

143 'Ihsan Shurdom': interview with Ihsan Shurdom, Amman, 5 June 1967.

144 'Below them, on the runway': interview with Jordanian air force engineer, name withheld on request.

145 'The squadron commander': Hussein, p. 72.

146 'Israel bombed our airbases': ibid., p. 71.

146 'A year later': Dept of State from American Embassy, Amman, 3 June 1968; Memo of interview, 30 May 1968.

146 'It was called Operation Tariq': Muttawi, p. 125.

147 'According to Ziad Rifai': Hussein, p. 70.

147 'Pressing hard': Weizman, p. 205.

148 'Throughout the morning': IDF 1076/192/1974: discussion of war in Jerusalem.

148 'In charge was Aaron Kamera': interview with Aaron Kamera, 5 May 2002.

149 'A group of men': Kibbutz Nachshon bulletin courtesy Moshe Yotvat.

151 'Israel's 55th Paratroop Brigade': interviews with Jacov Hetz (Chaimowitz), Yokneam, 26 November 2002, and Arie Weiner, Jerusalem, 9 May 2002.

152 'Old municipal buses': interview with Hanan Porat, Kfar Etzion, 3 December 2002.

152 'He shouted': Roth, p. 212.

153 'General Rabin at GHQ': Narkiss, p. 117.

153 'The Israelis had a plan': account of Government House battle interview with Asher Dar (Drizen), Tel Aviv, 19 April 2002; Hammel, p. 297; Pollack, p. 300.

154 'An Israeli corporal': Rabinovich, pp. 116–17; Narkiss, p. 127.

154 'For the second time': Bull, p. 115.

155 'Abu Agheila was': Dupuy, pp. 257–8.

156 'General Narkiss's mobile': Narkiss, p. 123.

157 'They put the line': Ambassador Llewellyn Thompson, Memo: 'The Hot Line Exchanges', 4 November 1968, NSC, Box 19.

157 'At 0730': note from President's Appointment File, 5 June 1967, NSF, Box 67.

157 'The runway was unusable': interview with Jordanian aircraft engineer; name withheld at his request.

158 'After the capture of Government House': interview with Asher Dar (Drizen)

159 'Teddy Kollek . . . picked up Ruth Dayan': Kollek, pp. 190–3.

159 'We will dine in Tel Aviv': Schliefer, p. 174.

159 'Colonel Uri Ben Ari': interviews with Uri Ben Ari, Tel Aviv, 18 April 2002 and Hagai Mann, Jerusalem, 24 November 2002; Dupuy pp. 281, 295; Muttawi, p. 130; Pollack, pp. 303–4.

160 'An Israeli tank commander': IDF 1076/192/1974: discussion of war in Jerusalem.

160 'At about five': Kahalani, pp. 54–5.

161 'Major Ehud Elad': Teveth, pp. 190–201.

162 'At the State Department in Foggy Bottom': Memo from Joe Califano to LBJ; Press statement by Dean Rusk; Memo from Larry Levinson and Beu Wattenberg to LBJ; Memo from Walt Rostow to LBJ: all documents in NSC, Box 18.

163 'The Soviet delegation': Shevchenko, p. 133.

164 'As he was kissing': Eban, *Personal Witness*, p. 413.
164 'Millions of television': Shevchenko, p. 121.
165 'When at last instructions': ibid., p. 134.
165 'Moscow also took military': Isabella Ginor, 'The Russians Were Coming: The Soviet Military Threat in the 1967 Six-Day War', *Middle East Review of International Affairs*, Vol. 4 No. 4, December 2000.
166 'Ambassador Goldberg': Memo to Arthur Goldberg, chronology of Soviet delay on Security Council meetings, 26 June 1967, State Dept Historical project: both in NSC, Box 20; also Gideon Rafael, *Destination Peace*, pp. 153–8.
167 'But in a private meeting': Shevchenko, p. 134.
167 'President Johnson summoned his new "Special Committee"': McGeorge Bundy on the hotline meetings and the Middle East, 7 November 1968, NSC, Box 19; Rostow, Memo for the Record, 17 November 1967, NSC, Box 18.
168 'When, in late afternoon': Memo for the Record, 'Who fired the first shot', 19 December 1968; CIA analysis, 5 June 1967; Rostow, Memo for the Record, 17 November 1968: all NSF, Box 18.
168 'The State Department's own legal advice': Memo from Leonard C. Meeker, legal adviser to Secretary of State Rusk, 5 June 1967, NSC, Box 18.
169 'Abu Deeb, the *moukhtar*': Hikmat Deeb Ali's story based on oral history in *Homeland: Oral Histories of Palestine and Palestinians*, pp. 55–9.
169 'By six, Brig. Gen. Avraham Yoffe's': Churchill, p. 112; Barker, p. 87.
169 'Ori Orr': Orr, IDF Magazine.
169 'The commander of Israel's southern front': Elon, pp. 11–12.
170 'Rabin called Gavish': interview with Gavish.
170 'The Egyptians do not like': quote in Churchill, p. 118.
170 'Ariel Sharon rubbed his hands': Dayan, p. 48; account of Abu Agheila fighting from Van Creveld, pp. 186–7; Barker, *Arab-Israeli Wars*, p. 70; Pollack, pp. 67–70; Dupuy, pp. 258–63.
171 'One of their doctors': Dayan, p. 56.
171 'By eight in the morning': *War File*, pp. 74–8.
172 'At Central Command': interview with General Hadidi.
172 'The US Embassy': Cairo Cable 8539 to State, 5 June 1967, NSC, Box 23.
172 'Anwar El Sadat': Sadat, p. 176.
172 'The editors in the newsroom': Elkins quote from Moskin, p. 69.
172 'less than fifteen hours': Elkins, dispatch quoted in *War File*, p. 70.
173 'The Jordanian command': Schliefer, pp. 175–6.
173 'Tel Aviv disappeared': Cameron, p. 337.
173 'Since mid-afternoon': Memos from Rostow to LBJ, 5 June 1967, NSC, Box 18.

Day Two

174 'The Israeli paratroops': Fighting at Ammunition Hill based on interviews with Hagai Mann, Doron Mor, Jacov Hetz (Chaimowitz), Arie Weiner and Shimon Cahaner, Jerusalem, 9 May 2002; also Pollack, p. 305; Moskin, pp. 258–9; Muttawi, pp. 133–4.
174 'But General Narkiss wanted': Narkiss, pp. 156–7.
175 'At least sixty men were wounded': Diary of Central Command, 6 June 1967, quoted in *Mission Survival*, p. 225.
175 'Waiting in a jeep': interview with Yoel Herzl, Netanya, 6 May 2002.

177 'this was fighting of a sort': Gur, quoted in Churchill, p. 134.
177 'A mile away in the Old City': Schliefer, p. 179.
179 'Tank fire could have finished': Moskin, p. 272.
179 'You'd approach a house': interview with Yoseph Schwartz, Jerusalem, 9 May 1967.
180 'the noise was deafening': Rose, pp. 263–4.
180 'Before the Israeli troops': Schliefer, p. 183.
181 'Moshe Yotvat': interview with Moshe Yotvat, Tel Aviv, 7 May 2002.
181 'Among them was Yossi Ally': Kibbutz Nachshon bulletin, 6 June 1968.
182 'Hikmat Deeb Ali': Hikmat Deeb Ali's story based on oral history in Lynd (ed.) *Homeland: Oral Histories of Palestine and Palestinians*, pp. 55–9.
183 'In Beit Nuba': Dodds and Barakat, p. 39; also PRO FCO 17/217: 'Jordan's 1967 Refugees': a research report by the American University of Beirut, 31 October 1967.
183 'A Jordanian battle group': details from Pollack, pp. 308–10; Barker, *Six-Day War*, p. 113; Dupuy, pp. 309–10, interview with Elad Peled, 25 November 2002.
184 'It was like a line': Tal quote from Churchill, pp. 113–14.
184 'During the night Cairo': Pollack, p. 71.
185 'The most impressive thing': interview with Omar Khalil Omar, Gaza City, 1 December 2002.
185 'Major Ibrahim El Dakhakny': interview with El Dakhakny.
186 'Ramadan Mohammed Iraqi': interview with Iraqi.
187 'General Riad told King Hussein': Hussein, p. 81.
188 'In her villa in Amman': interview with Leila Sharaf.
188 'mostly pointed their men': Pollack, p. 463.
189 'The attack was stopped': Barker, p. 131.
189 'The attack was all that': Mayzel, pp. 137–40.
189 'An American military analysis': Israeli–Arab confrontation, National Military Command Center May 1967, NSF, Box 104.
189 'On the eve of the war': Seale, *Asad*, p. 113.
190 'In Beit Nuba, Zchiya Zaid': quoted in *Kol Ha'ir*, 31 August 1984, www.planet.edu.
190 'On the edge of the village': Dodds and Bareket.
191 'Its morning report said': Cairo Radio (Arabic), 0304 GMT, 6 June 1967.
191 'After their disturbed night': Armbrister in Chace, p. 114.
192 'In Washington the CIA': President's Daily Brief, 6 June 1967, NSF, Box 19.
192 'Inside, the staff': Cairo Cable 8572 to State, 6 June 1967, NSC, Box 24.
192 'An hour later': Cairo Cable 8583 to State, 6 June 1967, NSC, Box 24.
192 'Britain's ambassador in Kuwait': PRO/FCO 17/598: Arthur, Kuwait to FCO, 6 June 1967.
192 'Arab oil-producing countries': President's Daily Brief, 6 June 1967, NSF, Box 19.
192 'In Damascus': Damascus Cable 1248 to State, 6 June 1967, NSC, Box 24.
193 'The king was in constant': US policy and diplomacy in the Middle East Crisis, 15 May to 10 June 1967, 'Effecting the Israeli–Jordanian Ceasefire, January 1969, NSC Box 20.
193 'Reports of appalling losses': Muttawi, p. 138.
194 'Thanks to Voice of the Arabs': Muttawi, p. 158.
194 'The British military attaché': PRO FCO 17/275, Dispatch No. 2, Defence Attaché, British Embassy, Amman, 22 June 1967.
194 'We must stop the fighting': Amman Cable 4092 to State, 6 June 1967, NSC, Box 24.

195 'Narkiss was keeping': Narkiss, from Central Command war diary in *Mission Survival*, p. 226; Mordechai Gur in Churchill, p. 137; Schliefer, p. 177.

195 'Rubi Gat': interview with Rubi Gat, Jerusalem, 1 June 2000.

195 'On the Jordanian side': Schliefer, p. 178.

196 'General Riad and King Hussein': Hussein, p. 88.

196 'We agree to the retreat': ibid.

196 'Hussein and his chief of staff': Amman Cable 4128 to State, 6 June 1967, NSC, Box 24.

197 'Hussein summoned the ambassadors': Amman Cable 4095 to State, 6 June 1967, NSC, Box 24.

197 'Generals Narkiss, Dayan and Weizman': Narkiss, p. 219; interview with Doron Mor; Central Command war diary, 6 June 1967 in *Mission Survival*, p. 226.

198 'It took until the afternoon': Pollack, pp. 310–11; Barker, *Six-Day War*, p. 113; Dupuy, pp. 309–10; interview with Elad Peled, Jerusalem, 25 November 2002.

198 'Most of Jenin's': interview with Haj Arif Abdullah, Jenin, 28 November 2002.

199 'General Riad was calm': Hussein, p. 90.

200 'When he returned to Amman King Hussein': Amman Cable 4108 to State, 6 June 1967, NSC, Box 24.

201 'Their fears were based': interview with Dr Ihsan al Agha, Rafah, 30 November 1967. He is a local historian in Khan Younis who has so far documented 516 killings of civilians, using at least two sources for each. He spoke to heads of families, eyewitnesses and close relatives. He also found lists made by Egyptian authorities of families who wanted compensation. Massacre stories also corroborated by others in Gaza and interviews with refugees in Amman.

202 'Shara and the other women': interview with Shara Abu Shakra, Khan Younis, 30 November 2002.

202 'By Tuesday afternoon': El-Gamasy, pp. 67–71.

204 'Field Marshal Amer, the obvious scapegoat': Heikal, pp. 181–2.

204 'The Egyptians sent out': Paris Cable 19927 to State, 6 June 1967, NSC, Box 24.

204 'At the headquarters of the Cairo': interview with Hadidi.

205 'More than half': PRO/FCO 8/679: Graham (Kuwait) to Balfour-Paul (British Residency, Bahrain), 21 June 1967, NSC Box 20.

206 'Lieutenant Mohammed Shaiki': Bernet, p. 150.

206 'The Egyptian army': Cairo Radio, 0320 GMT, SWB, Vol. 2479–2504.

206 'By 5 p.m.': AP, *Lightning Out of Israel*, p. 99.

206 'Near the front': interview with Gavish.

207 'That would mean sending': Dupuy, p. 271.

208 'US ambassador Goldberg': Shevchenko, p. 134.

209 'There was one more twist': Ambassador Thompson on the hotline exchanges, 4 November 1968, NSC, Box 20; 6.30 timing from Lall, p. 51.

209 'The Americans had offered': Memo to Arthur Goldberg, chronology of Soviet delay on Security Council meetings, 26 June 1967, NSC Box 20.

210 'nobody expects': Memos for Rostow from Nathaniel Davis, 5 June 1967, NSC, Box 20.

210 'In Khan Younis, for the second day': interview with Abd-al Majeed al Farah, Khan Younis, 30 November 2002.

211 'As the fighting in Gaza went on': PRO/FCO 17/496: Situation in Middle East, 6 June 1967.

211 'In the mountains above Qalqilya': interview with Maa'rouf Zahran, Qalqilya, 29 November 2002.

212 'Memdour Nufel': interview with Memdour Nufel.

212 'Fayek Abdul Mezied': interview with Fayek Abdul Fattah Mezied, Qalqilya, 29 November 2002; figures from Qalqilya city archives.

213 'Red light from': interview with Khalil.

214 'One of the officers': Draz, pp. 135–46.

215 'Just outside Jerusalem': interview with Moshe Yotvat, 7 May 2002.

216 'Ben Ari said afterwards': *MER*, p. 224.

216 'In the evening, towards midnight': Narkiss, p. 242.

217 'In the 1950s, Har Zion': Elon, *The Israelis*, p. 234.

Day Three

218 'For two hours': Schliefer, including dialogue, pp. 189–90.

218 'On the Mount of Olives': Tleel, p. 161.

219 'By the third day': PRO/FCO 17/275: Dispatch No. 2 from British Military Attaché, Amman, 22 June 1967.

219 'At one in the morning': Schliefer, including dialogue, pp. 189–90.

220 'Then "a tremendous stentorian voice"': Cameron, p. 339.

220 'In Amman the minister of information': interview with Sharaf.

221 'Yahya Saad': Draz, pp. 49–54.

221 'Back in Sinai, General Gamasy': El-Gamasy, p. 64.

221 'Gamasy knew that a retreat': Ibid., p. 65.

222 'When the British defence attaché': PRO/FCO 17/496: Tel Aviv to FCO, 12 June 1967.

222 'Along the route of the retreat': Cameron, p. 343.

222 'Yoffe's tanks drove all night': report from *Yediot Aharonot*, 30 June 1967, quoted in *Mission Survival*, pp. 193–6.

223 'At dawn air strikes': interview with Uri Gil.

223 'The general staff in Cairo': Churchill, pp. 171–2; Pollack, pp. 72–3; Wright, pp. 346–9.

223 'Finally, General Narkiss': Churchill, p. 139; Narkiss, p. 245.

224 'Rubinger, a photographer': interview with Rubinger.

224 'From his garden': Schliefer, p. 193.

225 'Two hundred Palestinian doctors': AP, *Lightning Out of Israel*.

225 'Hamadi Dajani, a Palestinian trader': interview with Ahmed and Hamadi Dajani, Old City, 23 November 2002.

227 'Velni and Ronen': eyewitness testimony in Bamahane, IDF Magazine.

227 'I told my driver': Churchill, p. 140.

228 'The *Sunday Times*': McCullin, pp. 91–2.

228 'Also driving up': interview with Ava and Moshe Yotvat, Tel Aviv, 7 May 2002.

228 'McCullin followed the soldiers': McCullin, p. 92.

229 'One of them was Goren's jeep': Yossi Ronen, IDF Magazine, 'Bamahane', http://info.jpost.com/supplements.

229 'The Palestinian dentist': Tleel, pp. 165–6.

231 'Goren, said the Rabbi "did not stop"': Yossi Ronen, IDF Magazine, 'Bamahane'.

231 'For Israelis it was the emotional climax': interview with Rubinger.

232 'Major Doron Mor': interview with Doron Mor, Afula, 28 November 2002.

232 'Herzl Bodinger, the Israeli': interview with Bodinger.

232 'Then I thought': interview with Gavish.

232 'Around eleven o'clock': description of Combats by Commanders – Northern Front, IDF Spokesman's Office, quoted in *MER*, p. 226.

232 'More Israeli tanks arrived later': Dupuy, pp. 313–14.

233 'Raymonda Hawa Tawil': Tawil, pp. 91–3.

233 'It pressed home': Amman Cables 4127 and 4128 to State, 7 June 1967, NSC, Box 24.

233 'The Israeli air force': figures from IDF 947/192/1974: collection of statistics.

233 'Sharif Zaid Ben Shaker': interview with Prince Zaid Ben Shaker.

234 'The US ambassador, Findley Burns': Amman Cable 4125/4128 to State, 7 June 1967, NSC, Box 24.

234 'When the war started': interview with Badial Raheb, Bethlehem, 22 November 2002.

235 'Finally, the Soviet military': Sergei Tarasenko, 'Blitzkrieg in Sinai', *Novoe Vremya*, No. 21, 1997, pp. 32–3.

237 'Outside Amer's bunker': Cairo Cable 8641 to State, 7 June 1967, NSC, Box 24.

237 'Despair settled over the city': Armbrister in Chace, p. 114.

238 'After three days sheltering': interview with Kamel Sulaiman Shaheen.

239 'Moshe Dayan broadcast': Voice of Israel, 7 June 1967, quoted in *MER*, p. 226.

239 'A few hours after': report from AP, Hilary Appelman, 31 December 1997, quoting Narkiss' recollection of interview; www.middleeast.org.

239 'One of the paratroopers': Moshe Dayan, pp. 311–14.

239 'Later in 1967': report from AP, Hilary Appelman, 31 December 1997.

239 'Israeli soldiers went from': interview with Haifa Khalidi.

240 'At nine in the evening': *MER*, pp. 225–6.

240 'Bombing continued in and around Jericho': Dodds and Barakat, pp. 41–2; also PRO/FCO 17/217: American University of Beirut Research report on Jordan's 1967 refugees.

241 'Zaid Ben Shaker': interview with Zaid Ben Shaker, Amman, 6 June 2002.

242 'The first wave of refugees': PRO/FCO 17/214: 'The Refugee Problem in Jordan', 3 August 1967; from UNRWA Refugee affairs RE 400(7) Emergency camps, Jordan; letter by Lawrence Michelmore, UNRWA Commissioner General, 10 July 1967.

243 'Save the Children's': information on Hawkins' life from Save the Children archives.

243 'But Hawkins and the British': Save the Children Fund Jordan; Quarterly report for the quarter ending 30 June 1967; administrator's report by Lt.-Col Skelton.

243 'Thirty years before Western': PRO/FCO 26/116: Littlejohn Cook Memo, 7 June 1966.

244 'Official denials': PRO/FCO 1016/780: FCO to Bahrain, Abu Dhabi, Doha, Dubai and Muscat, 7 June 1967.

244 'In London an official': PRO/FCO 26/116: Littlejohn Cook Memo, 7 June 1966.

244 'In Saudi Arabia': PRO/FCO 17/599: Jeddah to FCO, 11 June 1967.

245 'He told the American magazine': Nutting, *Nasser*, p. 441.

245 'What was certain': PRO/PREM 13/1620: Record of phone interview, 7 June 1967.

NOTES

245 'At first, the Jordanians': Figures from Dupuy, p. 315.
246 'After the war': Lev, p. 139.
247 'The Americans were turning': 'An Approach to Political Settlement in the Near East', 7 June 1967, NSC, Box 19.
247 'President Johnson was': Memo for the Record, 7 June 1967, NSC, Box 18.

Day Four

248 'He said he had left': *New York Times*, 20 June 1967, quoted in Churchill, pp. 167–8.
249 'This was a valley of death': Sharon, quoted in Churchill, p. 171.
249 'I think the Egyptian soldiers': quoted in Pollack, pp. 78–9.
249 'Brigadier Abdel Moneim Khalil's': interview with Khalil.
250 'Another Egyptian commander determined': interview with Major-General Saad el Shazli, Cairo, 16 December 2002.
251 'Cairo had become': Cairo Telegram 8687 to State, 8 June 1967, NSF.
252 'The CIA produced': President's Daily Brief, 8 June 1967, NSC, Box 19.
252 'The English language *Egyptian Gazette*': Armbrister in Chace, p. 114.
252 'A member of the Central Committee': Heikal, *Sphinx and Commissar*, p. 173.
253 'Richard Helms, the Director': Memo for the Record, 7 June 1967, NSC, Box 24.
253 'In Moscow post-mortems': Soviet ambassador's comments on Arab–Israeli dispute; CIA intelligence information Cable, 31 May 1967, NSF, Box 106.
253 'Another Soviet official': CIA to White House Situation Room, 8 June 1967, NSF, Box 107.
253 'But most of the evidence': CIA Intelligence information Cable, 7 June 1967, NSF, Box 107.
253 'A columnist in the Cairo newspaper': CIA Sitrep, 10 June 1967, NSC, Box 21.
254 'Raymonda Hawa Tawil': Tawil, pp. 95–6.
254 'Tawfik Mahmud Afaneh': interview with Tawfik Mahmud Afaneh, Qalqilya, 29 November 2002.
255 'Eleven-year-old Maa'rouf Zahran': interview with Maa'rouf Zahran.
255 'On the first full day': interview with Samir Elias Khouri, Bethlehem, 22 November 2002.
255 'Fifteen miles to the south': Gazit, p. 37.
256 'Nazmi Al-Ju'beh': interview with Nazmi Al-Ju'beh, Jerusalem, 24 November 2002.
256 'Among the euphoric Israelis': Kollek, pp. 196–8.
257 'Tanks from Tal's division': Churchill, pp. 176–7; Dupuy, p. 278.
257 'Around twenty miles': see www.ussliberty.org.
258 'He felt "good and warm inside"': Quote from *Dead in the Water*, BBC documentary about the *Liberty*, 10 June 2002.
258 'On 8 June': Summary of Proceedings, Court of Enquiry, 28 June 1967, NSF, Box 109.
258 '*Liberty* had been redeployed': see www.ussliberty.org.
259 'At 1350': transcript in Cristol, pp. 210–23; also in Bregman, pp. 121–2.
260 'The man looking through the next': details from *Dead in the Water*.
261 'James Halman, one of the radio': James Ennes, *Assault on the Liberty*, quoted in Bamford, p. 212.
261 '*Liberty* was still trying': details from *Dead in the Water*.

395

261 'When we received word': see www.ussliberty.org.

262 'Before the torpedo attack': flag details from report by Clark Clifford, chairman of President's Foreign Intelligence Advisory Board, 18 July 1967, NSF, Box 115.

262 'Walt Rostow dictated': Memos from Rostow to President, 8 June 1967, NSC, Box 18.

262 'An hour or so later': ibid.

262 'They ordered them to': Cable from flagship COMSIXTHFLT, 8 June 1967, NSF, Box 107.

262 'The commander of the Sixth Fleet': Memo for the record, 'The USS Liberty (AGTR-5), struck by Torpedo', 8 June 1967, NSF, Box 107.

263 'Secretary of Defense': details from *Dead in the Water*.

263 'Tersely, he cabled': Cairo Cable 8705 to State 8 June 1967, NSC, Box 24.

263 'On Cairo Radio': excerpt of commentary by Ahmed Said, Cairo Radio in Arabic, SWB Vol. 2479-2504, 1–30 June 1967.

263 'In the Situation Room': Memo, 8 June 1967, NSC, Box 18.

263 'The next morning': handwritten notes of NSC Special Committee meeting, 9 June 1967, NSC, Box 19.

264 'Rusk always believed': Rusk, p. 338.

264 'Letters of apology': Letters, 8 June 1967, NSC, Box 18.

264 'Secretary of State Rusk replied': Memo, 10 June 1967, NSF, Box 107.

264 'Israel's first response': Minutes of Special Committee, 12 June 1967, NSC, Box 19.

264 'they might find it hard': President's evening reading, 16 June 1967, NSC, Box 19.

264 'Israel accepted full responsibility': details of Israel's explanations from report by Clark Clifford, 18 July 1967, NSF, Box 115.

265 'On the face of it': Report by Clark Clifford, 18 July 1967, NSF, Box 115.

265 'In his memoirs he wrote': see www.ussliberty.org.

265 'In July 1967': IDF Preliminary Enquiry File 1/67 before Sgan Aluf Y. Yerushalami, 21 July 1967, NSF, Box 143.

266 'As well as Rusk and Clifford': quotes from *Dead in the Water*.

266 'Admiral Thomas Moorer': see www.ussliberty.org.

266 'A serviceman': Udi Erel in *Dead in the Water*.

267 'For Assistant Secretary': details from *Dead in the Water*.

267 'The Amir of Kuwait': PRO/FCO 8/679: talk with Amir; Arthur (Kuwait), Telegram No. 252, 8 June 1967.

267 'The Saudi ruling family': PRO/FCO 8/756: Gore-Booth minute on talk with Saudi ambassador, 12 June 1967.

268 'Before the fighting started': PRO/FCO 8/679: Graham (Kuwait) to Weir (Arabian Dept, FCO), 12 June 1967.

268 'General David Elazar': Rabin, p. 88.

268 'A less than veiled threat': Tel Aviv Cable 4015 to State, NSC, Box 24.

269 'Rabin, on Dayan's orders': Rabin, pp. 89–90.

269 'He told Peled': interview with Elad Peled.

269 'Just before dawn': all Eshkol quotes from www.ok.org; 'The Golan in the Balance', 4 November 2002; also *Jerusalem Post*, 1 February 2000.

270 'Maybe it's a decisive time': Lammfrom, pp. 562–9, document 174.

270 'Egypt accepted': Dupuy, pp. 278–9.

Day Five

271 'Without bothering to tell': Rabin, p. 90; also Mayzel, pp. 142–3.
271 'Elazar said he could "right now"': quoted in *Jerusalem Post*, 1 February 2000.
272 'But even if the': Dayan, p. 90.
272 'Two other thrusts': Barker, *Arab–Israeli Wars*, p. 92.
272 'By Thursday evening': General David Elazar press conference, 16 June 1967; quoted in *Mission Survival*, p. 348.
273 'One Israeli paratrooper commented': Churchill, p. 184.
273 'On Friday morning': Mayzel, p. 143.
273 'The town of Suez': interview with Khalil.
274 'Cairo Radio was playing': interview with Leila Sharaf.
274 'Nasser's advisers': interview with General Gamal Haddad, 15 December 2002.
274 'Winston Churchill': interview with Churchill.
274 'Some injured men': Uri Oren, 'Prisoner of War', *Yediot Aharonot*, 14 July 1967, quoted in Bondy, pp. 214–16.
275 'But according to Israeli witnesses': quotes from AP report by Karin Laub, August 1995, www.mideastfacts.com; and from chronological review of events, 16 August 1995, http://domino.un.org.
276 'Declassified IDF documents': IDF 100/438/1969 order issued 11 June 1967 at 2310, sent to all three territorial commands, to G1 branch and some other departments of the General Staff.
276 'According to an Israeli': Bron's article in *Yediot Aharonot*, 17 August 1995; also phone interview with Gabby Bron, 22 November 2002.
278 'By all the laws of war': Pollack, p. 464; also PRO/AIR 771/581: Air Ministry office of the scientific adviser, March 1968.
278 'After the battle General Elazar': Elazar quote from press conference, 16 June 1967 in *Mission Survival*, p. 349; also Dupuy, pp. 322–4; Churchill, p. 186; Barker, *Arab–Israeli Wars*, p. 92; Pollack, pp. 463–8.
279 'The Americans wanted': Amman Cable 4181, 9 June 1967, NSC, Box 24.
279 'Hussein's biggest problem': Amman Cable 4180, 9 June 1967, NSC, Box 24.
281 'Refugees were pouring over': PRO/FCO 17/214, Amman to FCO, 13 June 1967.
281 'But Mary Hawkins': details of camp from Save the Children archives, Mary Hawkins, *Jordan Report*, 9 November 1967; and from Save the Children Fund Jordan, Quarterly Report for the quarter ending 30 June 1967.
282 'One of the best UNRWA': PRO/FCO 17/214, 'The Refugee Problem in Jordan', 3 August 1967.
282 'Any Arabs who tuned': PRO/FCO 8/679: Arthur (Kuwait) to Brenchley (FCO), 9 June 1967.
283 'Brigadier General Hod recalled': Bregman and El-Tahri, p. 94.
283 'When Israeli soldiers': FCO 17/534, AA/TEL/S.13/7, 5–10 June 1967.
283 'Before the war a small group': Pollack, p. 459.
283 'As darkness fell': Bamahane, IDF Magazine, 18 July 1967, quoted in *Mission Survival*, p. 362.
283 'By the evening Israeli': CIA Sitrep, 9 June 1967, NSC, Box 21.
284 'During the fighting': Sister Marie Therese, *War in Jerusalem*, quoted in Schliefer, p. 208.
284 'Major-General': interview with Shlomo Gazit, Tel Aviv, 5 June 2002.
284 'Various orders were issued': example of order by logistics officer of Southern Command, 8 June 1967, IDF 100/438/1969.

284 'Some of the fighting units': *The Seventh Day*, pp. 117–18.
285 'Fifty paratroopers': diary of Frieda Ward, unpublished.
    'They were "shooting the locks"': Schliefer, pp. 201–2.
286 'When Palestinian shops': PRO/FCO 17/212: Pullar (Jerusalem) to FCO, 19 June 1967.
286 'Israeli troops in Gaza': UNRWA for Palestine Refugees in the Near East; details of survey in UNRWA file LEG/480/5 (14-1).
286 'The survey documented': UNRWA File Sec/6, 1967 Emergency.
287 'The peacekeeping troops': PRO/FCO 17/214: Craig (Beirut) to Moberly (Eastern Dept, FCO), 7 July 1967.
287 'The UN had intended': PRO/FCO 17/123: report of interview with General Rikhye, commander of UNEF, New York, 7 July 1967.
287 'The parts of the Dead': Schliefer, p. 203.
287 'Dayan took his leave': Moshe Dayan, pp. 258–9.
288 'They say that his': *al-Ahram*, 5–11 June 1997, issue 328.
288 'The minister of information': interview with Mohamed Fayek, Cairo, 16 December 2002.
288 'According to Eric Rouleau': *MER*, p. 553.
288 'He told them that they had all suffered': Armbrister in Chace, p. 117.
289 'In the morning of last Monday': speech and details quoted in *War File*, p. 104.
289 'General Salahadeen Hadidi': interview with Hadidi.
290 'Amin Howedi': interview with Howedi.
290 'From all sides': Rouleau, quoted in *MER*, p. 554.
290 'The crazy Egyptians': Armbrister in Chace, p. 117.
291 'Others gathered outside': *MER*, p. 554, quoting Cairo Radio and Radio Beirut.
291 'In Port Said': *MER*, p. 554, quoting Radio Beirut, 9 June 1967; *The Egyptian Mail*, 10 June 1967, and Rouleau.
291 'Before the broadcast, Mohamed Fayek': interview with Fayek.
292 'The wife of Amin Howedi': interview with Howedi.
292 'The ruling party, the Arab Socialist': Tanjug correspondent reporting 21 June, quoted in *MER*, p. 554.
292 'Some hapless officials': *Pravda*, 31 July 1967; and Rouleau, quoted in *MER*, p. 554.
292 'Gamal Haddad': interview with Gamal Haddad, Cairo, 16 December 2002.
293 'In Damascus the government': CIA Intelligence Information Cable, 31 July 1967: conflict between the Syrian army and the Syrian government, NSF, Box 115.
293 'But during the night': Seale, *Asad*, p. 140.

Day Six

294 'Ahmad al-Mir': Seale, *Asad*, p. 141.
294 'Some reserve officers': *Jeune Afrique*, 6 August 1967, quoted in *MER*, p. 230.
294 'Later, Ba'th party': *Le Monde*, 28 June 1967, quoted in *MER*, p. 230.
295 'A senior Israeli officer grumbled': *MER*, p. 230.
295 'General Fawzi': interview with Hadidi.
296 'A week later, Michael Wall': quoted in *War File*, p. 107.
296 'In his office': interview with Howedi.
297 'In Cairo the CIA': CIA Intelligence Information Cable, 15 June 1967.
297 'Major Ibrahim El Dakahakny': interview with El Dakhakny.

299 'Once the ceasefire held': Draz, pp. 135–46.
299 'Amos Elon drove back': Elon, *A Blood-Dimmed Tide*, pp. 19–20.
299 'Ramadan Mohammed Iraqi': interview with Iraqi.
301 'What Kollek called': Kollek, p. 197.
301 'Herzog later said': Herzog, quoted in Gazit, pp. 41–2.
301 'Abd el-Latif Sayyed': interview with Abd el-Latif Sayyed, 1 December 2002.
301 'Nazmi Al Ju'beh': interview with Nazmi Al Ju'beh, 24 November 2002.
301 'Major Eitan Ben Moshe': Eitan Ben Moshe interview quoted in Tom Abowd, *The Moroccan Quarter*, Winter 2000.
302 'A middle-aged woman': ibid.
303 'It was the best thing we did': Elon, *A Blood-Dimmed Tide*, pp. 19–20.
303 'In two days it was done': Kollek, p. 197.
303 'Rabin had ordered Elazar': Rabin, p. 91.
304 'One of the commanders reported': quoted in *MER*, p. 230.
304 'When Nils-Goran Gussing': Gussing report in PRO/FCO 17/124, p. 10.
304 'From the outset': Tel Aviv Cable 4015 to State, NSC, Box 24; Bull, p. 118.
304 'Lord Caradon': PRO/FCO 17/496: Caradon (NY) to FCO, 10 June 1967.
305 'Eshkol's wife': interview with Miriam Eshkol; also Bregman and El-Tahri, p. 98.
305 'Walt Rostow': interview with Rostow.
305 'The translation of Kosygin's': hotline details and Situation Room meeting from Oral History; Helms and McNamara; Memos for the Record on hotline meetings, 7 November 1968, Llewellyn Thompson, 4 November 1968 and Richard Helms, 22 October 1968: all from NSC, Box 19.
306 'Britain's Joint Intelligence Committee': PRO/FCO 17/496: Secretary JIC to NAMILCOM, Washington, 13 June 1967.
307 'Before the offensive even began': Tel Aviv Cable 4015 to State, NSC, Box 24.
307 'Since 20 May': movements of the Sixth Fleet, (undated), NSF.
308 'General Vassily Reshetnikov': Bregman and El-Tahri, p. 95.
308 'An Israeli journalist': Isabella Ginor, *Guardian*, 10 June 2000; also 'The Russians were coming: the Soviet Military Threat in the 1967 Six-Day War', *Middle East Review of International Affairs*, Vol. 4, No. 4, December 2000.
309 'A local official': *Al Hareches* (On the Ridge), newsletter of Kibbutz Nachshon, 6 June 1968.
310 'Hikmat Deeb Ali': *Homeland*, p. 58.
310 'One of the soldiers': interview with Amos Kenan, 21 November 2002.
311 'Kenan wrote and almost': Amikam, *Israel: A Wasted Victory*, pp. 18–21.
312 'In the refugee camp': PRO/FCO 17/217: 'Jordan's 1967 Refugees', a research report by the American University of Beirut, 31 October 1967.
312 'Goldberg, the American ambassador': Rafael, pp. 164–5.
313 'They would stop': CIA Sitrep, 10 June 1967, NSC, Box 21.
313 'In June 1967': Martha Gellhorn, *The Face of War*, p. 257.
313 'But Abba Eban': Eban, *Personal Witness*, p. 416.
314 'Eshkol, Eban and the rest': ibid., p. 412.
314 'The Israeli newspapers': Elon, *A Blood-Dimmed Tide*, pp. 19–20.
314 'Ezer Weizman': Weizman from *Haaretz*, 29 March 1972; Peled from *Le Monde*, 3 June 1972; Herzog from *Maariv*, 4 April 1972.
315 'One condemned the way': Cecil Hourani in *El Nanar*, reprinted in *Encounter*, November 1967, quoted in Laquer, p. 244.
316 'Amer Ali': PRO/FCO 17/334: 'Lessons to be learned from the Arab débâcle following the Israeli aggression of June 1967', 15 July 1968.

316 'Another Arab military critic': PRO/FCO 17/334: 'The Middle East War and its Consequences', 30 May 1968.

316 'A few days after he emerged': interview with El Dakhakny.

Consequences

318 'cowards and bastards': quote by Egyptian General Riyadh to Jordanian General Khammash, in Amman 4945, NSF, Box 110.

318 'Israelis were not impressed': NSF, Box 110.

318 'By the end of July': CIA Intelligence Information Cable, 31 July 1967, NSF, Box 110.

318 'Nasser's biggest problem': interview with Howedi.

320 'On 13 September': interview with Salah Amer, Cairo, 17 December 2002.

321 'Thirty-five years on': interview with Howedi.

321 'A week before he died': copy of testimony, along with inquest report and reopened investigation report provided by Amer's son Salah.

322 'main source of danger': CIA Intelligence Information Cable, 22 September 1967.

323 'many are saying that Zion': Cameron, p. 344.

323 'reversed the policy of twenty years': NSC, 31 May 1967, Box 18.

323 'after the doubts, confusions': Memo for LBJ from Harry C. McPherson, 11 June 1967: NSC, Box 18.

324 'the time has passed': CIA Memo for J. P. Walsh, 3 August 1967, www.foia.cia.gov.

324 'it would create a revanchism': Notes of NSC Special Committee meeting, 14 June 1967, NSF.

324 'not a prescription for peace': Remarks of the president at the National Foreign Policy Conference for Educators, 19 June 1967, NSC, Box 18.

325 'We've lost something': *The Seventh Day*, p. 159.

325 'Just after the war': Arthur Hertzberg, *New York Review of Books*, 28 May 1987.

325 'not a guarantee of peace': Eban, *Personal Witness*, p. 451.

326 'an isolated realm of anxiety': ibid., p. 450.

326 'taste for flags': ibid., p. 464.

326 'Being a conqueror': *The Seventh Day*, pp. 113–14.

326 'In November 1967': David Holden, *Sunday Times*, 19 November 1967.

327 'He was stretching one hand': Yael Dayan, pp. 107–11.

327 'Hebron and Nablus': Weizman, pp. 156, 207.

328 'emptied of their Jews': Wiesel, p. 80.

328 'we've liberated Jerusalem': *The Seventh Day*, p. 139.

329 'Some suggestions emerged': CIA Sitrep, 13 June 1967, NSC, Box 21.

330 'I had the sense': interview with Hanan Porat.

330 'The IDF is total sanctity': Kook, quoted in Eban, p. 469.

330 'an astounding divine miracle': Rabbi O. Hadya, quoted in Roth, p. 220.

330 'Gershom Scholem': Amos Elon, *New York Review of Books*, 10 April 2003.

331 'The Old City of Jerusalem': Rostow to LBJ, 6 July 1967, NSF, Box 110.

331 'with all my soul': *The Seventh Day*, p. 219.

332 'Jerusalem is ours': ibid., p. 100.

332 'On 28 June': PRO/PREM 13/1622: Lewen (Jerusalem) to FCO, 29 June 1967.

332 'administrative action': PRO/PREM 13/1622: Dean (Washington) to FCO, 29 June 1967.

332 'the annexation of the Old City': PRO/PREM 13/1621: SoSFA to Tel Aviv, 16 June 1967 (sent 17 June).

333 'Israelis wanted to believe': CIA Sitrep, 13 June 1967, NSC, Box 21.

333 'as it waited for the Arabs': Gazit, p. 120.

333 'By August Gideon Rafael': PRO/PREM 13/1623: Dean (Washington) to FCO, 19 August 1967.

333 'the Arabs "seemed capable"': Hadow quotes from PRO/FCO 17/468, Israel: Annual Review for 1967, 22 January 1968.

333 'Israeli leaders are deeply divided': Saunders Memo for Rostow, 4 December 1967, NSC, Box 104.

333 'The overwhelming sentiment': *New York Times*, 6 December 1967.

334 'Moshe Dayan said': *MER*, p. 275

334 'No one at all': Dean interview with Eban, 24 July 1967, NSF, Box 110.

335 'Realising that trying': Pedatzur, pp. 40–8.

335 'When, on 18 June': ISA G6304/10, Prime Minister's Office: Yael Uzai to Eshkol, 18 June 1967.

335 'Various schemes for the future': Pedatzur, pp. 39–40.

335 'Three days later': ISA 6303/3 Prime Minister's Office: Occupied Territories, July–December 1967.

335 'The most influential plan': ISA G6304/10, Prime Minister's Office: Yigal Allon to Eshkol, 25 July 1967.

336 'if Hussein embarks': PRO/PREM 13/1623: SoSFA to Washington, 27 July 1967.

336 'an assassin's bullet': PRO/PREM 13/1623: Adams (Amman) to FCO, 8 September 1967.

337 'At the end of August': PRO/FCO 17/36, 13 September 1967; FCO 17/36, 6 September 1967.

337 'Caradon wanted it vague': PRO/PREM 13/1624: Caradon to FCO, 2 November 1967; PREM 13/1624, 22 November 1967.

338 'greatly concerned': PRO/PREM 13/1621: Caradon to FCO, 12 June 1967 (sent 13 June).

338 'The Arabs signed up': NSC, Tel Aviv Cables 4118 and 4137 to State Dept, 14/15 June 1967.

338 'A CIA source in Israel': CIA Intelligence Information Cable, 14 July 67.

338 'to blacken Hussein's image': NSF, Box 104.

339 'If the Arabs were suddenly': PRO/FCO 17/468 Israel: Annual Review for 1967, 22 January 1968.

339 'Don't allow yourself': interview with Churchill.

339 'One such person': details of Kfar Etzion from *Jewish Action*, Winter 1999; interview with Hanan Porat; PRO/FCO 17/214, Hadow (Tel Aviv) to FCO, 26 June 1967.

341 'the future of the West Bank': ISA G 6303/3, Prime Minister's Office: Occupied Territories, July–December 1967.

341 'The plans for the establishment': PRO/FCO 17/230, 26 September 1967.

341 'The Americans sent': PRO/FCO 17/214: Dean (Washington) to FCO, 30 June 1967.

341 'only temporary military': PRO/FCO 17/230: FCO to Tel Aviv, 28 September 1967.

341 'At the foreign ministry': PRO/FCO 17/230: Hadow (Tel Aviv) to FCO, 28 September 1967.

342 'great gusts of theological emotion': Eban, p. 470.

342 'The true frontier': quoted in Schiff, p. 85.

342 'By 1967 the job of settling': Gazit, p. 151.

342 'inevitable time bombs': ibid., p. 153.

343 'encouraging note of dissent': *MER*, pp. 376–7.

343 'On Israeli state radio': PRO/PREM 13/1622: SoSFA to Paris, 19 June 1967.

343 'If our dreams come true': *Wall Street Journal*, 14 July 1967.

343 'no matter what they say': *Washington Post*, 22 October 1967.

343 'fast becoming a reality': *The Times*, 10 November 1967.

344 'Successive Israeli governments': *Crimes of War*, pp. 37–8.

345 'broad and imaginative': NSC, 7 June 1967, Box 18.

345 'In his speech on 19 June': NSC, 19 June 1967.

345 'The hopes for any enduring settlement': PRO/PREM 13/1621: SoSFA to Tel Aviv, 13 June 1967.

345 'extent of the movement': PRO/FCO 17/214, Hadow (Tel Aviv) to FCO, 26 June 1967; UNRWA figures in FCO 17/217: Crawford (Amman) to Moberly (Eastern Dept), 26 June 1967.

346 'In Bethlehem': interview with Samir Elias Khouri, Bethlehem, 22 November 2002.

346 'every facility to leave': PRO/FCO 17/214, 3 August 1967.

346 'Israelis in favour of': ISA 6303/3 Prime Minister's Office: Occupied Territories July–December 1967.

346 'colossal propaganda campaign': PRO/FCO 17/214: Moberly minute of talk with Mr Anug, Israeli Minister in London.

346 'assisted emigration': PRO/FCO 17/214: draft telegram to Washington, 24 June 1967.

347 'diplomat's "houseboy"': PRO/FCO 17/212: Pullar (Jerusalem) to FCO, 19 June 1967.

347 'the process worked': *Washington Post*, 23 June 1967; Haifa Khalidi also witnessed the scene at Damascus Gate: interview, Old City, 23 November 2002.

348 'UNRWA': PRO/FCO 17/217: Crawford (Amman) to Moberly (Eastern Dept), 26 June 1967.

348 'of their own free will': ISA G6303/5 Prime Minister's Office, 22 October 1967.

349 'peasant farmers': Dodd and Barakat, p. 43; PRO/FCO 17/217, 31 October 1967.

350 'Nils-Goran Gussing': CIA Directorate of Intelligence Special Report, Arab Territories under Israeli Occupation, 6 October 1967, NSF, Box 160.

350 'young men in Gaza had no choice': PRO/FCO 17/214, 24 June 1967.

350 'Israel would like to retain Gaza': CIA, Main Issues in a Middle East Settlement, 13 July 1967, NSF, Box 104.

350 '500 new refugees were crossing': PRO/FCO: Crawford (Jerusalem) to Moberly (Eastern Dept), 16 October 1967.

350 'The news that Jews': PRO/FCO 17/216: Crawford (Amman) to Moberly (Eastern Dept), 2 October 1967.

351 'By September 1967': PRO/FCO 17/212: Lewen (Jerusalem) to Moberly (Eastern Dept), 12 September 1967.

351 'to permit continuation': ISA G6303/5 Prime Minister's Office, 30 August 1967.

352 'the British foreign secretary': PRO/CAB 129, Vol. 133, Part 1 C(67)150, 13 September 1967.

352 'half-hearted': PRO/FCO 17/215, 1 September 1967 and 19 September 1967.

352 'argument about petty details': PRO/FCO 17/216: Hadow (Tel Aviv) to FCO, 26 September 1967; also 28 September 1967; FCO 17/214: Tel Aviv to FCO, 25 July 1967.

353 'increasing evidence': PRO/FCO: Crawford (Jerusalem) to Moberly (Eastern Dept), 11 December 1967.

353 'did not want to find itself': PRO/PREM 13/1623, 30 August 1967.

353 'if I were in their place': Eban, p. 464.

354 'A typical night': IDF 100/438/1969: telegram 0900, 8 July 1967.

354 'more serious incidents': PRO/FCO 17/468, Israel: Annual Review for 1967, 22 January 1968.

355 'June 1965': PRO/FCO 17/576: McIntyre (Tel Aviv) to MoD, 21 February 1967.

355 'until the outbreak of war': *MER*, pp. 175–8.

355 'end of the war and February 1968': Moshe Dayan's figures quoted in PRO/FCO 17/577, DA/5/2/68: Rogers (Tel Aviv) to MoD, 16 February 1968.

355 'In some refugee camps': PRO/FCO 17/212: Lewen (Jerusalem) to Moberly (Eastern Dept), 16 November 1967.

355 'spokesman for Brigadier-General Narkiss': *Sunday Times*, 19 November 1967.

355 'On 20 November': PRO/FCO 17/475: Amman to FCO, 20 November 1967.

356 'Israel finally sent': Pollack, pp. 330–5.

356 'all too easy to run a truck': PRO/FCO 17B: Hadow (Tel Aviv) to Moore (Eastern Dept), 28 March 1968.

356 'A year after the 1967 war': interview with Winston Churchill.

Legacy

359 'When two rabbis from Vienna': Shlaim, p. 3.

372 'Six weeks after the end of the war': PRO/PREM 13/1623: Hadow (Tel Aviv) to FCO, 1 August 1967.

Bibliography

Abu-Odeh, Adnan, *Jordanians, Palestinians and the Hashemite Kingdom in the Middle East Peace Process* (Washington DC: United States Institute of Peace Press, 1999)

Adams, Michael, *Chaos or Rebirth: The Arab Outlook* (London: BBC, 1968)

Ajami, Fouad, *The Dream Palace of the Arabs: A Generation's Odyssey* (New York: Pantheon, 1998)

——, *The Arab Predicament: Arab Political Thought and Practice Since 1967* (Cambridge: CUP, 1981)

Aldouby, Zwy and Jerrold Ballinger, *The Shattered Silence: The Eli Cohen Affair* (New York: Coward, McCann & Geoghegan, 1971)

Allon, Yigal, *Shield of David: The Story of Israel's Armed Forces* (London: Weidenfeld & Nicolson, 1970)

Armstrong, Karen, *Jerusalem One City, Three Faiths* (New York: Knopf, 1996)

Aronson, Shlomo, *Israel's Nuclear Programme: The Six-Day War and Its Ramifications* (London: King's College, 1999)

Associated Press, *Lightning Out of Israel* (The Associated Press, 1967)

Ateek, Naim and Hilary Rantisi, *'Our Story': The Palestinians* (Jerusalem: Sabeel, 1999)

Bamford, James, *Body of Secrets* (New York: Doubleday, 2001)

Barker, A. J., *Arab-Israeli Wars* (London: Ian Allan, 1980)

——, *Six Day War* (New York: Ballantine Books, 1974)

Bar-On, Mordechai, *The Gates of Gaza: Israel's Road to Suez and Back, 1955–57* (New York: St Martin's Press, 1994)

—— (ed.), *Israeli Defence Forces: Six-Day War* (Philadelphia: Chilton Book Company, 1968)

Bar-Zohar, Michael, *Embassies in Crisis* (Englewood Cliffs, NJ: Prentice Hall, 1970)

Bashan, Raphael, *The Victory* (Chicago: Quadrangle, 1967)

Beilin, Yossi, *Israel: A Concise Political History* (New York: St Martin's Press, 1992)

Benvenisti, Meron, *The Hidden History of Jerusalem* (Berkeley, CA: University of California Press, 1996)

Bernet, Michael, *The Time of the Burning Sun* (New York: Signet, 1968)

Bettelheim, Bruno, *The Children of the Dream* (New York: Macmillan, 1969)

Black, Ian and Benny Morris, *Israel's Secret Wars* (London: Warner Books, 1992)

Brecher, Michael, *Decisions in Israel's Foreign Policy* (Oxford: OUP, 1974)

Bregman, Ahron, *A History of Israel* (London: Palgrave, 2002)

—— and Jihan el-Tahri, *The Fifty Years War* (London: Penguin/BBC Books, 1998)

Bondy, Ruth, Ohad Zmora and Raphael Bashan (eds), *Mission Survival* (New York: Sabra Books, 1968)

Brown, Arie, *Moshe Dayan and the Six-Day War* (Tel Aviv: Yediot Aharonot, 1997 [Hebrew])

Bull, Odd, *War and Peace in the Middle East* (London: Leo Cooper, 1976)

Burdett, Winston, *Encounter With the Middle East* (New York: Atheneum, 1969)

Cameron, James, *What a Way to Run the Tribe* (New York: McGraw-Hill, 1968)

Casey, Ethan and Paul Hilder (eds), *Peace Fire: Fragments from the Israel–Palestine Story* (London: Free Association Books, 2002)

Chace, James (ed.), *Conflict in the Middle East* (New York: H. W. Wilson, 1969)

Christma, Henry M. (ed.), *The State Papers of Levi Eshkol* (New York: Funk & Wagnall, 1969)

Churchill, Randolph S. and Winston S. Churchill, *The Six-Day War* (Boston, MA: Houghton Mifflin, 1967)

Cockburn, Andrew and Leslie, *Dangerous Liaison: The Inside Story of the US-Israeli Covert Relationship* (New York: HarperCollins, 1991)

Comay, Joan and Lavinia Cohn-Sherbok, *Who's Who in Jewish History* (London: Routledge, 1995)

Copeland, Miles, *The Game of Nations* (New York: Simon & Schuster, 1969)

van Creveld, Martin, *The Sword and the Olive: A Critical History of the Israeli Defence Force* (New York: Public Affairs, 1998)

Cristol, Jay, *The Liberty Incident* (Washington DC: Brassey's, 2002)

Dallas, Roland, *King Hussein: A Life on the Edge* (London: Profile Books, 1998)

Dayan, Moshe, *Story of My Life* (London: Weidenfeld & Nicolson, 1976)

Dayan, Yael, *Israel Journal: June 1967* (New York: McGraw-Hill, 1967)

Dodd, Peter and Halim Barakat, *River Without Bridges: A Study of the Exodus of the 1967 Palestinian Arab Refugees* (Beirut: The Institute for Palestinian Studies, 1969)

Donavan, Robert J., *Israel's Fight for Survival* (New York: New American Library, 1967)

Draz, Isam, *June's Officers Speak Out: How the Egyptian Soldiers Witnessed the 1967 Defeat* (Cairo: El Manar al Jadid, 1989 [Arabic])

Dupuy, Trevor N., *Elusive Victory: The Arab–Israeli Wars, 1947–74* (New York: Harper & Row, 1978)

Eban, Abba, *An Autobiography* (New York: Random House, 1977)

——, *Personal Witness* (New York: Putnam, 1992)

Egyptian Organisation for Human Rights, *Crime and Punishment* (Cairo)

El-Gamasy, Mohamed Abdel Ghani, *The October War* (Cairo: The American University in Cairo Press, 1993)

Elon, Amos, *The Israelis* (Tel Aviv: Adam Publishers, 1981)

——, *A Blood-Dimmed Tide* (London: Penguin, 2001)

El-Sadat, Anwar, *In Search of Identity* (New York: Harper & Row, 1978)

BIBLIOGRAPHY

Ezrahi, Yaron, *Rubber Bullets: Power and Conscience in Modern Israel* (Berkeley, CA: University of California Press, 1997)

Finkelstein, Norman G., *Image and Reality of the Israel–Palestine Conflict* (London: Verso, 1997)

Gall, Sandy, *Don't Worry About the Money Now* (London: New English Library, 1985)

Gazit, Shlomo, *The Carrot and the Stick: Israel's Policy in Judea and Samaria, 1967–68* (Washington DC: B'nai B'rith Books, 1995)

Gellhorn, Martha, *The Face of War* (London: Virago, 1986)

Ginor, Isabella, 'The Russians Were Coming: The Soviet Military Threat in the 1967 Six-Day War', *Middle East Review of International Affairs*, Vol. 4, No. 4, December 2000

Glueck, Nelson, *Dateline: Jerusalem* (Tel Aviv: Hebrew Union College Press, 1968)

Golan, Aviezer, *The Commanders* (Tel Aviv: Mozes, 1967)

Golan, Galia, *Soviet Policies in the Middle East: From World War Two to Gorbachev* (Cambridge: CUP, 1990)

Goldberg, David J., *To the Promised Land: A History of Zionist Thought* (London: Penguin, 1996)

Gordon, Haim (ed.), *Looking Back at the June 1967 War* (Westport: Praeger, 1999)

Gruber, Ruth, *Israel on the Seventh Day* (New York: Hill & Wang, 1968)

Gutman, Roy and David Rieff (eds), *Crimes of War: What the Public Should Know* (New York: W.W. Norton, 1999)

Haber, Eitan, *'Today War Will Break Out': Reminiscences of Brigadier General Israel Lior, Aide-de-Camp to Prime Ministers Levi Eshkol and Golda Meir* (Tel Aviv: Edanim, 1987 [Hebrew])

Hadawi, Sami, *Bitter Harvest: A Modern History of Palestine* (New York: Olive Branch Press, 1991)

Hammel, Eric, *Six Days in June: How Israel Won the 1967 Arab-Israeli War* (New York: Scribner, 1992)

Heikal, Mohamed, *The Cairo Documents* (New York: Doubleday, 1973)

——, *Sphinx and Commissar* (London: Collins, 1978)

Hersh, Seymour M., *The Samson Option: Israel's Nuclear Arsenal and American Foreign Policy* (New York: Random House, 1991)

Herzog, Chaim, *The Arab–Israeli Wars* (New York: Random House, 1982)

——, *Living History* (London: Phoenix, 1997)

Hewat, Tim, *War File* (London: Panther Record, 1967)

Hirst, David, *The Gun and the Olive: The Roots of Violence in the Middle East* (London: Faber & Faber, 1984)

Horovitz, David (ed.), *Yitzhak Rabin: Soldier of Peace* (London: Peter Halban, 1996)

Hourani, Albert, *A History of the Arab Peoples* (London: Faber & Faber, 1991)

Hussein, King of Jordan, as told to Vick Vance and Pierre Lauer, *My 'War' With Israel* (New York: William Morrow, 1969)

Hutchison, E. H., *Violent Truce* (London: John Calder, 1956)

Irving, Clifford, *The Battle of Jerusalem* (London: Macmillan, 1970)

Israel's Foreign Relations, Selected Documents, 1947–1974, Ministry for Foreign Affairs, Jerusalem, 1976

Johnson, Lyndon Baines, *The Vantage Point: Perspectives on the Presidency, 1963–69* (New York: Holt, Rinehart & Winston, 1971)

Kahalani, Avigdor, *The Heights of Courage* (Tel Aviv: Steimatzky, 1997)
Kerr, Malcolm H., *The Arab Cold War* (New York: OUP, 1971)
Khan, Zafarul-Islam, *Palestine Documents* (New Delhi: Pharos, 1998)
Kollek, Teddy, *For Jerusalem* (New York: Random House, 1978)
Kovner, Abba (ed.), *Childhood Under Fire* (Tel Aviv: Sifriat Poalim, 1968)
Kurzman, Dan, *Soldier of Peace: The Life of Yitzhak Rabin* (New York: HarperCollins, 1998)

Lall, Arthur, *The UN and the Middle East Crisis, 1967* (New York and London: Columbia University Press, 1968)
Lammfrom, Arnon and Hagai Tzoref (eds.), *Levi Eshkol: The Third Prime Minister, Selected Documents (1985–1969)* (Jerusalem: Israel State Archives, 2002 [Hebrew])
Laqueur, Walter (ed.), *The Israel/Arab Reader, A Documentary History of the Middle East Conflict* (New York: The Citadel Press, 1969)
——, *The Road to War: The Origins and the Aftermath of the Arab–Israeli Conflict, 1967–68* (London: Weidenfeld & Nicolson, 1969)
Larteguy, Jean, *The Walls of Israel* (New York: Evans, 1969)
Lau-Lavie, Naphtali, *Moshe Dayan: A Biography* (Hartford, CN: Hartmore House, 1968)
Lev, Igal, *Jordan Patrol* (New York: Doubleday, 1970)
Levine, Harry, *Jerusalem Embattled* (London: Cassell, 1997)
Lynd, Staughton, Sam Bahour and Alice Lynd (eds.), *Homeland: Oral Histories of Palestine and Palestinians* (New York: Olive Branch Press, 1994)

MacLeish, Roderick, *The Sun Stood Still* (New York: Atheneum, 1967)
Marshall, S. L .A., *Swift Sword: The Historical Record of Israel's Victory, June 1967* (New York: American Heritage Publishing, 1967)
Masalha, Nur, *Expulsion of the Palestinians: The Concept of 'Transfer' in Zionist Political Thought, 1882–1948* (Washington DC: Institute of Palestine Studies, 1999)
——, *Imperial Israel and the Palestinians: The Politics of Expansion* (London: Pluto, 2002)
Mayhew, Christopher and Michael Adams, *Publish it not . . .: The Middle East Cover-Up* (London: Longman, 1975)
Mayzel, Matitiahu, *The Golan Heights Campaign* (Tel Aviv: Ma'arachot, 2001 [Hebrew])
McCullin, Don, *Unreasonable Behaviour* (London: Jonathan Cape, 1990)
Melman, Yossi and Dan Raviv, *Behind the Uprising* (New York: Greenwood Press, 1989)
Middle East Record (Jerusalem: Israel Universities Press, 1971)
Morris, Benny, *The Birth of the Palestinian Refugee Problem, 1947–49* (Cambridge: CUP, 1989)
——, *Israel's Border Wars, 1949–56* (Oxford: Clarendon Press, 1997)
Moskin, Robert, *Among Lions* (New York: Arbor House, 1982)
Muttawi, Samir A., *Jordan in the 1967 War* (Cambridge: CUP, 1987)

Narkiss, Uzi, *The Liberation of Jerusalem* (London: Valentine Mitchell, 1992)
Near, Henry (ed.), *The Seventh Day: Soldiers Talk About the Six-Day War* (London: André Deutsch, 1970)

BIBLIOGRAPHY

Neff, Donald, *Warriors for Jerusalem* (New York: Linden Press/Simon & Schuster, 1984)
Noor, Queen, *Leap of Faith: Memoirs of an Unexpected Life* (London: Weidenfeld & Nicolson, 2003)
Nutting, Anthony, *Nasser* (New York: Dutton, 1972)

Oren, Michael, *Six Days of War* (New York: OUP, 2002)

Parker, Richard, *The Politics of Miscalculation in the Middle East* (Bloomington and Indianapolis: Indiana University Press, 1993)
Parker, Richard (ed.), *The Six-Day War: A Retrospective* (Gainesville, FL: University Press of Florida, 1996)
Pedatzur, Reuven, *The Triumph of Embarrassment: Israel and the Territories After the Six-Day War* (Tel Aviv: Yad Tabenkin & Bitan, 1996 [Hebrew])
Peres, Shimon, *David's Sling* (New York: Random House, 1970)
Pollack, Kenneth M., *Arabs at War: Military Effectiveness, 1948–91* (Lincoln, NE: University of Nebraska Press, 2002)
Pryce-Jones, David, *The Face of Defeat: Palestinian Refugees and Guerrillas* (New York: Holt Rinehart Winston, 1972)

Quandt, William B., *Peace Process: American Diplomacy and the Arab–Israeli Conflict Since 1967* (Washington DC: Brookings Institution Press, 2001)

Rabin, Leah, *Our Life, His Legacy* (New York: Putnam, 1997)
Rabin, Yitzhak, *The Rabin Memoirs* (London: Weidenfeld & Nicolson, 1979)
Rabinovich, Abraham, *The Battle for Jerusalem* (Philadelphia: The Jewish Publication Society, 1987)
Rabinovich, Itamar, *The Road Not Taken: Early Arab–Israeli Negotiations* (New York: OUP, 1991)
Rafael, Gideon, *Destination Peace* (New York: Stein & Day, 1981)
Rapaport, Era, *Letters from Tel Mond Prison: An Israeli Settler Defends His Act of Terror* (New York: The Free Press, 1996)
Raviv, Moshe, *Israel at Fifty* (London: Weidenfeld & Nicolson, 1997)
Rose, John H., *Armenians of Jerusalem* (London: Radcliffe Press, 1993)
Roth, Stephen J. (ed.), *The Impact of the Six-Day War* (New York: St Martin's Press, 1988)
Riad, Mahmoud, *The Struggle for Peace in the Middle East* (London: Quartet Books, 1981)
Rikhye, Indar Jit, *The Sinai Blunder* (London: Frank Cass, 1980)
Ronen, Ran, *Hawk in the Sky* (Tel Aviv: Yediot Aharanot, 2002 [Hebrew])
Rusk, Dean and Richard Rusk, *As I Saw It* (New York: W. W. Norton, 1990)

Safran, Nadav, *From War to War: The Arab–Israeli Confrontation, 1948–1967* (New York: Pegasus, 1969)
Sayigh, Yezid, *Armed Struggle and the Search for State* (Oxford: OUP, 1997)
Schiff, Ze'ev, *A History of the Israeli Army* (San Francisco: Straight Arrow Books, 1974)
Schliefer, Abdullah, *The Fall of Jerusalem* (New York and London: Monthly Review Press, 1972)
Seale, Patrick, *The Struggle for Syria* (London: I. B. Tauris, 1986)

——, *Asad: The Struggle for the Middle East* (Berkeley, CA: University of California Press, 1988)

—— (ed.), *The Shaping of An Arab Statesman: Abd al-Hamid Sharaf and the Modern Arab World* (London: Quartet, 1983)

Segev, Tom, *One Palestine, Complete* (London: Little, Brown, 2001)

Sharon, Ariel, *Warrior* (New York: Simon & Schuster, 1989)

Shevchenko, Arkady N., *Breaking With Moscow* (London: Jonathan Cape, 1985)

Shlaim, Avi, *The Politics of Partition* (Oxford: OUP, 1998)

——, *The Iron Wall* (New York: W. W. Norton, 2000)

Snow, Peter, *Hussein: A Biography* (London: Barrie & Jenkins, 1972)

Sternhell, Zeev, *The Founding Myths of Israel* (Princeton: Princeton University Press, 1998)

Stetler, Russell (ed.), *Palestine* (San Francisco: Ramparts Press, 1972)

Stevenson, William, *Strike Zion!* (New York: Bantam, 1967)

Tawil, Raymonda Hawa, *My Home, My Prison* (New York: Holt, Rinehart & Winston, 1979)

Tessler, Mark, *A History of the Israeli–Palestinian Conflict* (Bloomington and Indianapolis, Indiana University Press, 1994)

Teveth, Shabtai, *The Tanks of Tammuz* (London: Weidenfeld & Nicolson, 1968)

Tleel, John N., *I am Jerusalem, Old City* (Jerusalem: Private Publication, 2000)

Turki, Fawaz, *The Disinherited: Journal of a Palestinian Exile* (New York and London: Monthly Review Press, 1972)

Weizman, Ezer, *On Eagles' Wings* (New York: Macmillan, 1976)

Wiesel, Elie, *A Beggar in Jerusalem* (London: Sphere Books, 1971)

Wright, Patrick, *Tank: The Progress of a Monstrous War Machine* (London: Faber & Faber, 2000)

Zikri, Wagih Abu, *The Massacre of the Innocents on 5 June* (Cairo: Modern Egyptian Bookshop, 1988 [Arabic])

Index

Arabic surnames prefixed by al- or el- ('the') are listed under the following element, eg Asad, Hafez al-. Arabic surnames beginning with Abu, and Jewish surnames beginning with Bar, Ben or Bin, ('son of') are listed under those elements, eg Ben-Gurion, David.

411